American Years

AMERICAN YEARS

by Harold Sinclair

Foreword by Ward Sinclair

Introduction by Robert Bray

University of Illinois Press

Urbana and Chicago

Library of Congress Cataloging-in-Publication Data

Sinclair, Harold, 1907–1966.
    American years / by Harold Sinclair; foreword by Ward Sinclair;
introduction by Robert Bray.
        p.   cm.—(Prairie State books)
    ISBN 0-252-06037-7 (pbk.: alk. paper)
    1. United States—History—1815–1861—Fiction.   I. Title.
II. Series.
PS3537.I84437A85   1988   88-17424
813'.52—dc19   CIP

For my sons,
WARD and MICHAEL.

AUTHOR'S NOTE

THIS BOOK was conceived as a novel, a work of fiction, and for the most part it is fiction. But very obviously some of the characters portrayed are not fictitious. This is especially true in that portion of the book which concerns Abraham Lincoln and the men who knew him best, who helped make him President. To attempt to make these men appear as "fictitious" characters, in order to maintain the theory of the work being a novel, seemed to me not only impossible but pointless. Some of these names have long since become a part of American history; others are perhaps not so well known but are nevertheless "historical." I have tried to make them appear as men, moved by the common motives and emotions of men. Peace to their ashes!

"And you America,
  Cast you the real reckoning for your present?
  The lights and shadows of your future, good or evil?"

—WALT WHITMAN

CONTENTS

FOREWORD

Had Harold Sinclair ever submitted to the standardized aptitude or intelligence tests—and there is no evidence that he did or would have—the results would have confounded the experts. He was a man of baffling complexity, a rough-hewn genius whose mind and motivation were never fully understood by those closest to him. He revered the written word and he was above all else a writer, a high school dropout who achieved considerable note in American literary circles. But he also was a musician and dance-band leader, a self-taught Civil War scholar, a heavy machine operator, a hardware man, a mechanic and inventor, an accomplished horticulturalist and a telegrapher, among other things. He was a political iconoclast who nonetheless adored his nation's political history and was on more than casual terms with the likes of former governor Adlai E. Stevenson II, an occasional visitor in his Bloomington home, and Paul Douglas, the Illinois senator. He disdained academicians—held most of them in contempt, actually—and yet he reveled when they sought him out. He was a certified bohemian, always seeming out of place in staid central Illinois, yet unable to tear himself away for more than brief periods.

By the time he died of cancer in 1966, at the age of fifty-nine, weakened by chronic alcoholism, he was dispirited and disillusioned. He had published eight novels, some to wide acclaim; a history of the port of New Orleans; and a stack of short stories, articles, and book reviews—an accumulation of no little accomplishment. His biggest commercial success, *The Horse Soldiers* (1956), went from the *New York Times* best-seller list to the cinema as a John Ford–directed film starring John Wayne and William Holden. *American Years,* his second novel, was a Literary Guild selection that earned him a Guggenheim fellowship in creative writing.

And yet for all this, he seemed somehow unfulfilled, driven somehow by the notion that he never lived up to the early promise. A nationally published review of his first novel, the autobiographical *Journey Home* (1936), predicted that of two new authors on the literary scene, Harold Sinclair seemed certain to rise to higher renown than John Steinbeck. Events turned out otherwise, of course, and decades later Sinclair listed Steinbeck, Faulkner, Wolfe, and Sandburg as the great American writers.

Although Sinclair in 1960 told an interviewer—facetiously one must assume—that he became a writer for the money, he in fact earned very little. He never owned property, only once and briefly held a mortgage, and usually had not enough income to keep a wife and children above what is today called the poverty line. In the later years, the occasional royalty checks and book advances went more often than not for alcohol or personal acquisitions—a sports car and phonograph records here, a new stereo or a musical instrument there.

Sinclair was born in Chicago on May 8, 1907. His father, a railroad man, abandoned the family about 1910. Sinclair and his infant sister were sent to live with their mother's relatives in Bloomington, while she worked as a waitress. Sinclair delivered newspapers and did odd jobs as a boy, and he learned to play the trumpet. In pique and defiance, he dropped out of Bloomington High School as an eleventh grader after he was accused of stealing a musical instrument. He always insisted he was wrongly accused.

FOREWORD

He worked as a Western Union messenger and eventually climbed to the exalted post of telegrapher before moving to Chicago in the 1920s, where he got into the hardware trade. He wrote poetry, none of which remains, and insinuated himself into the literary crowd that hung out at the old Dill Pickle Club, a boîte on the near North Side. His first published piece was a poem, sent to a small, now-forgotten Chicago newspaper by Gregg Rice, a novelist friend. "It was a proud day for me," he later was quoted. He returned to Bloomington and in 1933 married Ethel Moran, a country schoolteacher and tower of strength who believed abidingly in his potential as a writer. He went to work in the hardware department of the local Sears, Roebuck and wrote at night.

Journey Home appeared in 1936 and then came a productive rush—*American Years* (1938), *Years of Growth* (1940), *Westward the Tide* (1940), *Years of Illusion* (1941), and *The Port of New Orleans* (1942). World War II brought a break in the writing. With six young children and no academic degree, he was rebuffed in his efforts to enlist in the military, which caused him lasting regret. He spent the war years as a machine operator in a Bloomington defense plant, usually riding a bicycle the five miles between the plant and his rented farmhouse west of town. Those were difficult years economically, made survivable only by a huge vegetable garden and the penuriousness of Ethel Sinclair. She canned the produce, kept a small flock of chickens, pigs, and goats, and distilled begging, borrowing, and scrimping to a fine art.

After the war, with her children growing and money scarce, Ethel Sinclair became the family's breadwinner. She was hired as a librarian at the *Daily Pantagraph,* the local newspaper, and produced the income that after 1948 subsidized Harold's full-time writing. *Music out of Dixie,* his favorite novel, was the first result, published in 1952. It was a paean of sorts to New Orleans, his preferred city, and Dixieland jazz, his preferred musical form. He interspersed the writing—a block longhand that raced across narrow-lined notebook pages—with his own idea of appropriate atmosphere: liberal doses of spirits and jazz recordings, played always at night and always at top volume. Those hijinks brought complaints from neighbors and occasional visits from a gentle and tolerant Bloomington gendarmerie.

In most senses of the phrase, Sinclair didn't give a damn about public opinion. His standard mode of transport was bicycle—in an era, remember, when the sight of an adult male on a bike usually evoked laughter in Bloomington. In the warm months his usual dress, causing more veiled derision, was sandals and Bermuda shorts. His most common destination was the Withers Public Library, where his name and regular patronage opened special access and privilege. On occasion, the bicycle would detour to such nearby redoubts as the Twenty Grand taproom or some other downtown blue-collar dram shop. The bicycle, presumed lost, was usually retrieved the next day by a Sinclair child dispatched after a sympathetic barkeep's telephone call.

Sinclair's few friends gave him a wide berth when he was in his cups, accepting his caustic or abusive outspokenness as the way of artistic genius. When he was not drinking, he was a graceful raconteur. He is remembered by his children as dour and taciturn, yet his sense of humor ran deep and his laugh was loud and explosive. The grace showed in unexpected ways. A stained note found in Ethel Sinclair's papers reads this way:

> I tried to mix the butter and then I saw why nobody wanted to or really could mix it with this goddam no good wart on the sternum of progress. I think we should either get a new dingfad at the dime store or a piece of tire iron from the junk yard—you know old automobile springs are shaped just right for patting oleomargarine into a shape like butter.
>
> Very truly yours,
> Harold Sinclair.
>
> P.S. Have I told you lately how I love you? No? Well, whaddya want—Christmas Eve every day?

FOREWORD

When Sinclair was in one of his productive writing bursts, the atmosphere around the home was tense. The children, who rarely understood why, usually were herded out of doors to prevent interruptions. When weather permitted, Sinclair, a sun worshipper, would don his shorts and work in the backyard chaise lounge, where he scribbled into his loose-leaf binder. Manuscript first drafts rarely contained erasures or strikeovers. Sinclair wrote fluidly and often for hours on end, yet he maintained in interviews that he worked as little as possible because he was lazy.

Publication of *The Horse Soldiers* in 1956 provided a new moment in the public eye that long had eluded him. The book was a commercial success, buttressed by its sale to Hollywood for a mere $50,000 and additional income for Sinclair as a technical advisor to director Ford. After spending time on location in Louisiana, the author, who had heretofore regarded John Wayne as the antithesis of art, became suddenly ebullient about his "good friend, Duke." He kept a photo of himself and Wayne near the treasured photo of himself and musician Duke Ellington, whom he idolized.

The writer's life after *The Horse Soldiers* took a downward turn. His last novel, *The Cavalryman,* appeared to only lukewarm praise in 1958. The criticism—most said it simply didn't meet *The Horse Soldiers'* standard—seemed to bother Sinclair inordinately. He continued writing, but bouts with the bottle became more intense. The writing became more disjointed, the story teller's precision somehow dulled. Kenneth Littauer, his longtime New York agent, reacted to each new manuscript with gentle criticism or rejection, warmly cajoling and urging that Sinclair get to the point. Sinclair's letters reveal that he was in pain ("I feel like Hell most of the time," he told Littauer in 1959) but indicated that he would continue trying.

But the despondency and melancholy were unrelenting. At one point, Sinclair stacked manuscripts of his rejected novels on a backyard pile and set fire to them. Ethel Sinclair, stricken, retrieved some of the works but never could make a full account-

FOREWORD

ing of the losses. A number of short pieces and perhaps half a dozen manuscripts of unpublished novels were among the survivors. The literary agent's critiques indicate that none of the works came near the level of quality that he expected from Harold Sinclair.

The great sleigh ride ended on May 24, 1966. Just as he had feared, he did not awaken from surgery that would have removed a cancerous lung. Doctors said the disease had spread through his body; survival would have entailed more intense pain. His family, friends, and admirers said farewell at a Unitarian funeral service that included jazz music, Bach, and readings from Walt Whitman and *Journey Home*.

Harold Sinclair then was returned to the deep black prairie soil that was a source of his inspiration, a source of the powerful story he told in *American Years*. He left an estate of less than $5,000, a checking account of $238.76, and a battered 1957 Karmann-Ghia coupe. He probably still smiles about that.

WARD SINCLAIR

INTRODUCTION

"For the past four months I have been buried under a stack of Americana, dealing with the period in Illinois history from 1830 to the close of the Civil War. So far I have written and thrown away probably 50,000 words, and at the moment have got on paper about 2,000 words that I am reasonably well satisfied with. My work is improving rapidly. I know that, and I'm sure that I'll eventually make the grade. Maybe not soon, but eventually."[1] So wrote Harold Sinclair on February 7, 1936, describing the genesis of what would become, more than two years later, his second published novel, *American Years*. In the first stages of composition, he was turning up a lot more sand than ore—keeping but one word out of twenty-five—and the work must have seemed painfully slow for a new novelist trying to get on with an ambitious manuscript. But what Sinclair was really demonstrating was his writer's discipline. He was answering a query from Burton Rascoe, an influential New York editor and literary critic who had been "enchanted" by Sinclair's first book, *Journey Home*, and was naturally curious about this young writer from Bloomington, Illinois, who had seemed to come out of nowhere with what Rascoe called "one of the best sustained examples of vicarious wish-fulfillment I have encountered in a long time."[2] *Journey Home* was a "depression picaresque" tale of male wanderlust, told very much in the first person (hence the "wish-fulfillment" Rascoe found so attractive). In other words, it was the autobiographical exercise many beginning male writers have to get out of the way before moving on to more serious work. Callow or not, however, *Journey Home* caught Burton Rascoe's attention; it was his advocacy with Doubleday, Doran and Company that led them to sign Sinclair to a four-book contract. "Your literary future is one I would bank on," he wrote Sinclair late in February, 1936, and to show their agreement the publishers advanced $1,000 to Sinclair after reading the early chapters of *American Years*.[3]

"My work is improving rapidly. I know that. . . ." *American Years* was indeed the book that made Harold Sinclair a writer. But it did not quite make him *as* a writer, which was a sharp disappointment both to Doubleday and to their new young author. On the eve of publication (June, 1938) mutual expectations for *American Years* were very high—unreasonably high, we can say in retrospect. While Sinclair was aware of the book's unconventional nature (no plot, no protagonist, no love-interest—formal features discussed below), he nonetheless believed that his long regimen of patient research, hard writing, and careful revision had resulted in a potentially fine novel with broad appeal. He was confident that Doubleday, Doran (and the Literary Guild) could and would market the book effectively. For their part, the publishers, though mindful of the risk ("Frankly, there are some sales problems here. . . ."[4]), were talking about another Kenneth Roberts, another *Northwest Passage*, another blockbuster that would keep them near the top of the best-seller list (where Roberts's novel had put them in 1937).[5] To this end, advance advertising and dust-jacket prose proclaimed *American Years* "an extraordinary departure from the field of historical fiction," which it certainly was, as both readers and critics would soon discover. Yet despite almost uniformly positive national reviews, *American Years* proved a modest sales success, nothing more.[6] Why didn't the book take off as anticipated? This is ultimately an imponderable question—best-sellers are remarkably hard to predict, and even the savviest of publishers, including Doubleday, Doran, are often wrong about the potential of their books—yet at least part of the answer must lie in Harold Sinclair's central artistic decision for the novel: to reject conventional historical romance in favor of "an extraordinary departure."

Even before he began writing seriously, Sinclair was an omnivorous reader; he also had in abundance the confident empiricism of a self-taught critic. Thus the idea for *American Years* grew from his own wide reading of historical novels, which he saw as falling into two general types: those with fictional characters superimposed on a background of actual persons, places, and events; or those that featured a generational family saga with historical props. There were, of course, plenty of good and bad novels of both types; but all of them had plots, and most of the plots had love-interests of a romantic sort: the course of true love not running smooth, sudden or gradual impediments which are suddenly or gradually removed, and the whole business turning out to be much ado about nothing—as witness the winding up of the action in marriage or plans for marriage. Sinclair remembered puzzling over this time-honored form and asking himself: "Why should an historical novel be written in either of these ways? Perhaps there is another way. So I hit upon the idea of writing a novel in which an American town would be the chief character, with the human beings (which are the bones and sinews of any novel) as the background. . . . But, then, what is a town or a city except a number, large or small as the case may be, of human beings? Without them a town is no town but only a ghost, an empty receptacle. So if I told the story of an American town the only way I could do it was to write about the people who were the town, who gave it human validity."[7]

Such an approach would necessarily be heavy on documentation. Sinclair would draw his sources from the material and literary culture of a community or region as well as its biographical record, great and small citizens alike. Moreover, he would need an intimate knowledge of folkways and local his-

INTRODUCTION

tory, with the amorphous whole given structure through a kind of intensely foreshortened perspective: wilderness, pioneering, town-building, the beginnings of community and empire—all compressed into the first thirty years of a town's existence: the American Years (consummation and decline and fall were other matters coming after the Civil War and therefore reserved for the latter two volumes of the trilogy, if ever he got that far on the project).

For his anytown that could be everytown, Sinclair chose the place he knew best, the place where he lived and worked, and the place he could find out the most about—Bloomington: "I naturally put Everton, my American town, in the prairie country of Illinois. It was modeled . . . upon a very real town; but it *could* have been any one of a thousand similar places in Ohio or Indiana or Iowa. Even the Lincoln incidents included could have actually occurred in a half dozen other Illinois towns. . . ."[8]

Could have, to be sure, but didn't. For Sinclair was generally scrupulous in fictionalizing History with a capital "H." Everton's "people who were the town, who gave it human validity," were fashioned individually from the democratic mass, including a number of history's heroes but a much more numerous procession of forgotten figures from Bloomington's past. Lincoln was a command performance, of course, though in *American Years* he would be neither debunked nor glorified—just there, in all his inexplicable singularity. Lincoln's cohorts among Bloomington's "founding fathers" also loomed large in the narrative, particularly David Davis and Jesse Fell. But it was lower-case history that charged *American Years* with democratic energy and made it different from what Sinclair called the "mine-run stuff" of historical fiction. He noted that anyone might easily find out who the mayor of a town was, even a long time ago, but what about "the brave soul who first installed one of those fearsome engines, an indoor bath with running water?" And he added: "To me the latter character was, from a fictional standpoint, vastly more interesting." Nineteenth-century Bloomington and McLean County were blessed with "characters" and worthy books about them. One of the most important was Etzard Duis's *Good Old Times in McLean County* (1874), from whose "two-hundred and sixty-one sketches of Old Settlers"—a kind of honor roll of local democracy—Sinclair drew many of his portraits.[9] Not quite historical fiction "from the bottom up," but as close as he could come. *American Years* is populated by characters who seem stranger than fiction because they probably were. Sinclair might freely adapt their inchoate stories, but rarely would he need to embellish or invent.

This, then, was the subject of the novel whose composition preoccupied Harold Sinclair for more than two years, from late 1935 through June, 1938. Yet the real beginnings of *American Years* went back even further than the publication of *Journey Home* and Sinclair's correspondence with Burton Rascoe early in 1936. The literary germ of *American Years* (in fact of the entire Everton trilogy) came from Sinclair's life experience in Bloomington, first as a boy and later when he settled there for good. He initially came to live in Bloomington back in 1916, at the age of nine, when he was sent to stay with an aunt and uncle to escape a homelife that was "disruptive and chaotic." Several years previously, his father had abandoned the family in Chicago, and his mother, "a woman of no professional training," had tried, through a series of temporary menial jobs, to keep them together. She failed, so down to Bloomington went Harold and his sister Elizabeth (two years younger).[10] It was to be a pattern for many years: something like family, something like nurture, but never any real sense of economic security.

In Bloomington Sinclair worked from a very early age, delivering newspapers and then clerking at the telegraph office. He quit high school during his junior year to work full-time for Western Union, where he trained to be a key operator. This was followed by four years in a hardware store, where he learned a business specialty that would in later years support his family when writing couldn't.[11] In 1926—still shy of his twentieth birthday—Sinclair went out on his own for the first time, to Ocala, Florida, where he sold hardware by day and played jazz at night. Music, especially jazz, was always his avocation, some-times much more. He played trumpet, doubled on sax, and could sit down at the piano when need be. Evidently his Florida band was doing well, making money, when the whole dream drowned in the disastrous hurricane of 1926, which sent him back north again, this time to Chicago, the city of his birth.[12] He returned once more to the hardware business, this time in building and construction rather than retail. "Quite a conven-tional job," he recalled, "but all the people I met weren't so conventional."[13]

In fact Sinclair "went bohemian" for a spell, at least to the extent possible with an eight-to-five job. Much of this story is recounted, scantily clothed as fiction, in the Chicago section of *Journey Home*. Sinclair lived in Hyde Park, worked in the Loop, and partied on the North Side, becoming "an habitué of Arthur Masha's [place] on Clybourne Avenue."[14] The emphasis now was on liberal politics and modern literature rather than jazz. In his Chicago thousand-and-one nights he met Carl Sandburg, Max Bodenheim, and Ben Hecht, among others, which must have been exhilarating for a young man who later claimed he'd wanted to write ever since he could read.[15] But his literary ac-quaintances never became more than that, never deepened into friendships, and Sinclair himself was apparently not yet writ-ing—or at any rate he did not mention anything literary happen-ing. What did happen, and strikingly, was Life. But even as he lived the bohemian human comedy, Sinclair behaved more like a self-conscious Jamesian observer than a participant. He was al-ready confirming the personal aloofness—not alienation, really, but a kind of ironic detachment—that would soon be second na-ture if it wasn't already ("I am not a very social person and have very few close friends," he would say in 1936).[16] Still, it was a good deal more than going through the motions: days moving hardware, nights at the Dill Pickle, talking, boozing, dallying, and talking some more. And when the book talk failed, it was time for an insouciant "Any good murders in town tonight?" Or a late night walk on the wild side and listening to someone's new phonograph until dawn.[17]

A few years later Sinclair would recall his sojourn in bohemia in two different but related voices. First, that of James Hall, narrator and protagonist of *Journey Home,* describing the group that included his lover: "The people at the Studio I came to know better. I felt that they lived on a queer sort of plane which was not mine and never could be, much as, in a sense, I envied them. Sondra belonged, for, after all, Bohemia is more than any thing else a state of mind. I liked them and I think they liked me. They accepted me, at any rate, as one worth toleration, and I was satisfied with that."[18] If James Hall was on the outside looking in, yearning to belong but not expecting to, the same might be said for his creator, who spiced his autobiographical recollection with just the right amount of self-satire: "Some years ago, before I was old enough to vote, I knew something of the near north side Bohemia in Chicago (You remember—the Literary Capital of America?). Ah me! Gorgeous memory. How we sat around and read poetry by candlelight and discussed Sherwood Anderson and read Joyce in the Paris editions and listened ecstatically to Honegger and Prokofieff on a thin-voiced phonograph. Shades of Henri Murger! It was beautiful; we talked about Life and were bitter about Sacco and Vanzetti. But nobody wrote anything worth a tinker's hoot."[19]

It is clear from this that the Chicago years were not Sinclair's literary apprenticeship, nor did the city's literary modernism seem to have "taken." The late 1920s were, after all, the very end of the Chicago Renaissance, whose freshest and best literary impulses were long over. To Sinclair a decade later, the whole show and his young and mainly vicarious part in it must have seemed mannered and hyperbolic: "You remember, the Literary Capital of America?" Nobody he knew well was writing anything decent; *he* certainly wasn't and wasn't likely to. He may also have grown weary of bohemianism. So when he lost his job early in 1929, what on earth was there to keep him in Chicago?

INTRODUCTION

Hearing of an opening in a large building-hardware firm in Ft. Worth, Texas, Sinclair applied for the position, got it, and made the move, continuing there until the Depression brought construction to a dead halt near the end of 1931. Broke and jobless, he returned to Bloomington in the first months of 1932 and resumed living with his relatives and his sister Elizabeth. As far as work was concerned, it was catch as catch could—day labor and work on NRA projects like the new post office—but the periods of unemployment did leave plenty of time for his first sustained attempts at writing and for courtship. He soon met Ethel Moran, a schoolteacher from Cropsey, Illinois, who occasionally spent weekends in Bloomington with her good friend, Elizabeth Sinclair. Ethel Moran Sinclair later recalled the situation that led to manuscripts and marriage: "Harold was blue and out of a job."[20] When she would come in from dates around midnight, he would be waiting up; they would talk away his blues, sometimes until nearly morning. Presumably prominent among the topics were books and writing—his writing, no doubt, but, alas, someone else's books. Sinclair and Ethel Moran were married on ten dollars and no prospects other than his dreams of writing. Soon after their marriage, however, Sinclair did find a decent job—hardware once again, but this time managing the retail department at the local Sears outlet. With a semblance of economic stability, the Sinclairs could prepare for a family, and Harold could spend his late evenings writing without worrying too much about eventual publication and sales.[21]

So at last he was writing, regularly and with commitment. But writing what? Not long after arriving in Bloomington, he had begun a column on books for the *Bloomington Journal,* a weekly paper published by the Gummerman printing firm. The column, appearing intermittently for several years, reflected Sinclair's wide reading (then and later he haunted the public library), a slight critical chip on his shoulder, and, surprisingly, an interest and expertise in book collecting. These essays and notices, the first words Sinclair ever published apart from one "very bad poem in an obscure magazine," are important because they help establish the literary context out of which *American Years* grew—or against which it reacted.[22] The column and its reviews also demonstrated the traditional heart and mind beneath the outspoken and iconoclastic persona (whether the two were at war is a biographical crux too deep to explore here).

What were his likes and dislikes? In his very first column Sinclair wrote warmly about William McFee, an adventure novelist whose tales of the sea are as forgotten today as Sinclair's own books. He proclaimed, time and again, the immense greatness of Thomas Wolfe; *Look Homeward, Angel* was for him perhaps the chief masterwork of twentieth-century literature. On the other hand, the same James Joyce he and his Chicago friends had read "in the Paris editions" was now deemed "unintelligible," and American technical modernists—especially Faulkner, who was at his most creative during these years—were conspicuously absent from the column. As for nineteenth-century American literature, the only writer to receive serious attention was Mark Twain, whose *Huckleberry Finn* Sinclair recognized as a vernacular classic: "There are single paragraphs which surpass in truth and effectiveness whole belabored chapters of such moderns as Sinclair Lewis, Zona Gale, Sherwood Anderson, and Willa Cather. . . . I know of no description in American writing which equals that of Mark Twain's storm in *Huckleberry Finn*."[23]

Both the grass-roots subject and the laconic, idiomatic style of *American Years* owe something to Twain's masterpiece, though it would be hard to claim a similar influence for the swollen prose of Sinclair's other favorite, Thomas Wolfe. It may be that Wolfe's novels provided a model for the autobiography of *Journey Home*: the rock of individuality against the snares of the social web; accommodation with community versus critical distance. Yet when Sinclair spoke out publically in his "Books" column, it was with an exaggerated and satirical voice ultimately derived from Twain. The targets of his scorn were both popular reviewers and academicians. "The truth is," he wrote on September 8, 1933, "there aren't a half dozen pieces of literary composition per year in the United States that are worth criticizing as literature. On the other hand, there probably aren't half a dozen critics in the United States who would recognize a piece of literature if it came up and bit them."[24] The inference is right there for the making; this poor, unknown, unschooled, unpublished young man from Bloomington, Illinois, is one of fewer than six real writers and critics in America, though America hasn't yet got the word.

Not that Sinclair wasn't trying. Sometime in 1932 or 1933 he finished a novel manuscript called "Concerto in American," which he tried unsuccessfully to peddle in Chicago, working through an old friend, Ben Abramson, proprietor of the Argus Book Shop and a well-connected person in Chicago and New York publishing circles (it was Abramson who later brought *Journey Home* to the attention of Burton Rascoe). "Concerto in American," as its title implies, seems to have been about a Gershwinesque composer who wrote classical music in a jazz idiom, though no one knows for sure. The manuscript was never published in Sinclair's lifetime and has since been lost or destroyed.[25] In the same letter that announced *American Years,* Sinclair mentioned to Rascoe that he had for quite some time kept the manuscript of "Concerto in American" on his writing-room shelf as a memento of "past sins" (presumably literary), while working diligently on new material—lots of it, including *Journey Home* (which would be his publishing breakthrough), and, after *Journey,* a promising new piece entitled "The Texture of Life," which Sinclair described to Rascoe as "dealing with a newspaperman in a small Illinois village."[26]

A few tantalizing references in correspondence comprise all that is known of "The Texture of Life," for like "Concerto in American" it was never published and the manuscript subsequently disappeared. But even Sinclair's passing reference is suggestive. After writing in many different directions, he had come home, settling into a local, regional, midwestern subject and setting, where he would stay put for the next four books—the entire Everton trilogy, beginning with *American Years,* and the historical novel about George Rogers Clark in Illinois, *West-*

ward the Tide (1940). The five years between 1936 and 1941 were to be Sinclair's most intense and productive, resulting in nearly half of his published output. Of this work, *American Years* would prove the most original fiction to come out of his "Illinois immersion."

The research for *American Years* was enormously time-consuming and exhausting—particularly for someone who was now selling hardware all day and being a father mornings, evenings, and weekends. But once he started on the actual writing, Sinclair made steady progress on the manuscript. He remembered setting himself a punishing regimen and sticking with it until the book was finished: "three thousand words at a stretch, working Sundays, holidays, and from eight every evening to one in the morning." Even when the thing he most needed "in the world was sleep . . . sleep for days," Sinclair kept writing.[27] The contract for *American Years* had been signed late in January of 1937, and by October Sinclair had mailed four hundred and fifty pages of typed manuscript—more than half the novel—to Doubleday, Doran for consideration by his editor, Harry Maule. More pages followed in December, and by January, 1938, the whole manuscript was in Maule's hands. Maule wrote back that he was "tremendously impressed" with it, despite marketing anxieties about a novel with a *town* for a protagonist instead of a person and notions of democratic community rather than romance.[28]

The editorial correspondence between Sinclair and Harry Maule reveals the editor as assiduous but overly timid and sales-minded, the author as deferential and obliging—not generally to the novel's benefit. Where *American Years* used historical personages, Maule worried about libel (even though all the actual models for the characters were long dead) and urged Sinclair to change a few of the names, which he readily did. Sinclair was also concerned about potential lawsuits, and he wanted to continue living peaceably in Bloomington. Thus Isaac Funk, landowner, cattleman, and Republican stalwart, became Isaac Frink, landgrubber, tightwad, hog farmer, and Jacksonian Democrat.

INTRODUCTION

More striking was the change in Asahel Gridley, "Bloomington's first millionaire," in whom Sinclair discerned a plutocratic rascal perfect for the role of villain in *American Years*. Gridley became "Abel Green," still a bad lot but no longer nominally connected to the Gridley family. When *American Years* was published, this thin device fooled no one in Bloomington. Most local readers knew whose pretentious Italianate mansion stood over on Grove Street, and they knew it wasn't anyone named "Abel Green" that Jesse Fell warned about wildcat banking one lovely autumn evening in 1852, even as David Davis lectured him on democratic civic responsibility: "'I'll try to make myself clearer,' Davis said into the moonlight. "'Railroads are a business proposition and therefore to a certain extent a gamble. What a man does with his own money is largely his own business, Abel, but you can't gamble with tax money. For your benefit I'll go further than that. So long as I'm judge of this circuit I'll rule in favor of any citizen who brings suit against his town or county owning stock in any railroad project.'"[29]

Sinclair had worried about naming names long before his editor brought the matter up. But he was probably caught off guard when Maule criticized "the overplus of profanity in the book," pointing up the example of *Northwest Passage*: "Roberts has been brilliantly successful in giving a feel of the talk of rough men without using very much profanity. As you know, NORTHWEST PASSAGE was the most successful book of 1937, and is still selling at the rate of a thousand a week. The fact that it can be recommended for schools, can be sold to young people, and that it does not offend the sensibilities of that vast silent audience of readers which ignores the Hemingways, the Caldwells and the Faulkners is part of it." Maule continued in a manner that patronized both Sinclair and those writers he wasn't supposed to emulate: "I don't think that your book is in the field of the experimental boys, nor of the deliberately shocking young fellers." And he concluded by hinting that he thought there was just a chance for a "blockbuster," providing that Sinclair joined the right party: "I think the decision rests in whether you want to be, in this book, one of the school of shockers, which, in spite of great publicity, do not have the wide potential sale, or whether you want to aim for the big-time Roberts market."[30]

Put this way, Sinclair really had no choice. He set about toning down the objectionable language (this was largely a matter of culling the "Jesus Christs" and "God-damns," leaving a few oblique references to parentage and the dullish repetition of "hell" as the novel's only cussing) and quickly wrote his editor that he was not, had never been, nor could ever be a member of the modernists.[31] *American Years* was as far from Faulkner as he could make it, though that didn't automatically put it close to Roberts or his audience. This should have been obvious to anyone involved with the book. But not even Sinclair himself seems to have perceived the fundamental narrative difference between *American Years* and *Northwest Passage*. As in all of his best books, Roberts wrote in the first-person, his protagonist telling the tale in a voice with just the right blend of the heroic and the everyday. But however believable and appealing, Roberts's narrators were, necessarily, characters before they were historical figures; they acted out events, or so Roberts insisted, but the "I" invariably got in the way of the historical "big picture." *American Years* transposed the equation. Not only did it lack a hero, but among the panoply of voices, many fascinating and all having their say, none was privileged. Risky artistry, but it worked; readers could welcome a major character like Dr. John Flournoy Henry into the midst of the narrative, identify with him, and then wave goodbye as he moved on to Iowa—sad to see him go, but not apprehending his departure as a loose end. In this Sinclair may have been more original than he knew, much closer to the narrative and documentary montage of John Dos Passos's *U.S.A. Trilogy* than to Kenneth Roberts. His artistry pushed point of view beyond third-person onmiscient; at its best *American Years* sounded like history talking.

With the final revisions done late in February, 1938, Sinclair got some good news from Doubleday, Doran on March 2. Their affiliated book club, the Literary Guild, had selected *American*

Years as its main selection for June, which meant an outright cash payment of three thousand dollars, plus the prospect of several thousand more sales for the book and enhanced prestige for the author. Sinclair was happy and relieved. "I can't tell you how I feel about this Literary Guild business," he wrote Maule, intimating the high price he had paid for pushing *American Years* to completion: "I'm not sure whether you know it or not, but AMERICAN YEARS was written largely at night after I had already done a day's work. . . . The advance which you paid me was a very, very great help; but it didn't come anywhere near paying the annual expenses of a growing family. I had to keep on working anyway. Just now I'm tired as hell, a sort of accumulated tiredness that a weekend or occasional holiday doesn't help much. Now I feel as though I had been let out of jail." [32]

The next three months were a time of euphoria, yet increasingly tempered by the anxiety of waiting for publication. Finally, late in May, the first advance reviews appeared, beginning with Burton Rascoe's in *Newsweek* (more a notice than a full-scale review). Always the publicist, Rascoe played up the Lincoln aspect of *American Years* and simply didn't mention that the book was plotless, heroless. But he did attest to its strong "illusion" of history-in-process: "Here is a story full of dignity, honesty, and beauty, a historical novel which evokes our pioneer past in the Middle West with such a fine effect of illusion that I felt . . . I was there." [33]

Writing in the *Saturday Review of Literature,* James Gray, himself a popular historian of Illinois and the Midwest, faulted *American Years* for its missing protagonist, but (somewhat inconsistently) was impressed by the sheer human range of the book, comparing it favorably to Edgar Lee Masters's *Spoon River Anthology:* "The people are all vividly alive. They do not speak in the lugubrious tone of Masters's prairie folk; nor do they express his defeatist philosophy." Gray was determined not to see any strain of the "village virus" in *American Years,* even if that meant ignoring Sinclair's telling social criticism. For him, the saga of town-building that began in the 1830s was "a high-

spirited conflict" from which emerged "a hardy set of values"—
democracy in practice, helping create the optimistic, progressive
national character that was now, a century later, being redis-
covered as the "usable past" of Roosevelt's America.[34]

The reviews in the *Nation* and *New York Times Book Review*
were much more perceptive, noticing the long dark shadows on
the prairie landscape that the author had decidedly put there.
Writing in the *Nation* for June 11, 1938, Dorothy Van Doren
praised Sinclair's "admirable fictionalized history," thus dis-
tinguishing *American Years* from ordinary historical novels
in a way other reviewers hadn't. She further noted that *American Years* was "not a happy story": in and around Everton, as
elsewhere on the frontier, the division between rich and poor,
haves and have-nots, was already wide enough—barely two decades beyond the wilderness incursions of the first pioneers—
"to drive a team through." And it only got worse as the Civil
War approached.[35]

Stanley Young's piece in the *Times* (June 5, 1938) was as serious, probing, and detailed a review as any author could wish
for. He proclaimed *American Years* to be historical fiction "at
its realistic best," with the "smell and feel and accent of the land
on it." In addition, there was an important social point to the
book, which in Young's view "brilliantly foreshadows the problems of the present that have risen out of rugged, and sometimes
pretty ragged and rotten, individualism." Instead of arguing the
point like a "political thesis," Sinclair dramatized and let human
action carry the intellectual weight: "One of the finest things in
this writing is the deftness and trueness with which historical figures are woven into the pattern of pioneer life without distorting
the scene." Given the lame cameo appearances of the great in
most historical novels, this was a rare virtue indeed. And, alone
among the reviewers, Young recognized Sinclair had developed a
very serviceable style to realize his elaborate drama of pioneering: "Truly it is a fine book; its humor is sly and right and collo-
quial as the words which carry it."[36]

As the national reviews came in—many strongly favorable,

none harsh—Sinclair was greatly encouraged about the critical fate of *American Years* and at least hopeful concerning sales. But he naturally worried about the local reception of the book. Would Bloomington appreciate being immortalized as "Everton," potholes and all? He waited for the *Pantagraph*'s review, which would be a key measure of town opinion. But he waited in vain. No genuine review of *American Years* appeared in the paper, then or later. Instead, the *Pantagraph* on May 29 ran what the editors explicitly denied was a review (it was a "news story," they insisted). The piece prominently mentioned Burton Rascoe's high opinion of both *American Years* and its author and advised local readers to rely on Rascoe, should "their judgment be thrown off by being too close to the story." The *Pantagraph* itself wasn't prepared to have a viewpoint: "Because the book is about our own town, it is difficult to evaluate," and, "we are spared the task of describing Mr. Sinclair as either the hope or despair of American letters." The facetious tone continued right to the end of the article: "We might as well warn Mr. Sinclair that the curry combers of history will be after his book for errors. We hope Mr. Sinclair will be spared the banality of explaining that "American Years" is a story and not a time table." [37]

What Sinclair thought of this peculiar non-review isn't known. He might have been amused or outraged, depending on what he thought was going on behind the scenes at the *Pantagraph*. Judging by the headline and leader of the article ("Author Portrays Difficult Period in 'American Years' and "Harold Sinclair's Book Readable, Dignified"), someone at the paper was trying to be friendly in the face of embarrassment—critical gossip about the book, perhaps, or a private difficulty in the editorial office. Still, a standard review of *American Years* certainly should have appeared. Since the publication in 1936 of *Journey Home*— which the paper greeted warmly—Sinclair had been well known in Bloomington, and *American Years* was unquestionably the biggest literary event in the town's history. It was, moreover, an event that Harold Sinclair would have helped orchestrate, making sure that the newspaper received a review copy and possibly having a say about the reviewing assignment. So what went wrong? We can speculate. The *Pantagraph* did in fact receive a review copy and sent the book to Harry Pratt, a Lincoln specialist in Springfield who knew Bloomington and Illinois history well. Pratt's doctoral dissertation had been on David Davis, and he had recently taught history at Illinois Wesleyan University. Pratt must have seemed like a good choice. But he did not like the book and said so rather vehemently in his review, citing a number of historical inaccuracies, implying plagiarism, complaining of Sinclair's iconoclasm, and, yes, deprecating the novel's profanity. When Pratt's manuscript came in (we're still speculating here), someone at the newspaper showed it to Sinclair, who was naturally angry and demanded that it not be published on the grounds that Pratt was being grossly unfair to the novel. Whether the editors agreed with Sinclair (the sarcastic reference to "the curry combers of history" in the article makes this probable) or simply bowed to his wishes, the review was killed, and *American Years* never got its local notice, unkind or otherwise.[38]

Sinclair had worried about what academic specialists might make of *American Years*. He was interested in the forest, and they didn't seem to do much more than count and classify trees. But Harry Pratt was much more than a pedant; he was a guardian of tradition and the temple, one of the high priests and hagiographers of Lincoln and his times. He was predisposed to dislike even Sinclair's mildly revisionist portraits of Lincoln and one of Lincoln's towns. In *American Years* Lincoln is politically ambitious, homely in countenance, often distant or furtive in his social relations. Sinclair humanized him realistically (Lincoln is seen visiting the outdoor "rear premises" of an acquaintance in Everton) and generally dressed him in anything but mythic clothing. All this was unforgivable. "Too much of the book is set in taverns," Pratt sniffed, "and Lincoln will scarcely be recognized in Sinclair's characterization."[39] No matter that the Lincoln of *American Years* had a dignity and even a mystery

INTRODUCTION

about him that only realistic portraiture could provide; no matter that episodes like the famous "Lost Speech" of 1856, given at Major's Hall in Bloomington as the highlight of the first Republican state convention, were as carefully grounded in both fact and oral tradition as Sinclair (or anyone else) could make them.[40]

Because Pratt's review went unpublished, Sinclair avoided the task of responding to his criticisms; yet he did have a copy of the manuscript and should have been troubled by some of the problems Pratt raised. While the characterizations and alleged "iconoclasm" of *American Years* were matters of historical interpretation and therefore debatable, the other charges deserved the author's immediate attention. For there *were* errors of fact and consistency in *American Years,* from minor mistakes that should have been caught in copyediting to more serious inaccuracies that would have been corrected, ironically, if Pratt had been given the manuscript to read instead of the finished book. A typical lapse, for example, was making Peter Cartwright a bishop, when anyone really familiar with Cartwright's career would have known that his personality barred him from methodism's highest office. But of course Sinclair read only *parts* of Cartwright's *Autobiography*—the best parts, stories of militant preaching and camp-meeting adventures, far from the boring institutionalism of church politics.

Much more serious, however, was Pratt's imputation of plagiarism. To use the root meaning of the word, Sinclair silently "plundered" his sources (and there were hundreds of them). He declined to provide a bibliography or a prefatory note on what he had found most useful. This was common practice in historical fiction (and a perennial annoyance to academic and specialist critics who wanted "full disclosure"). Pratt pointed out Sinclair's free adaptation of an exciting pioneering story from Rebecca Burlend's *A True Picture of Emigration* (1848). When her husband severely cut his leg with a scythe, she undertook the entire harvesting of their field of overripe wheat—it was a case of cut it or lose it—with children in tow, daylight to dusk during the hottest days of summer. Then she fought a prairie fire that threatened to consume all the sheaves she had struggled to bring in. Then she sat down and thanked God for what was saved and for sending the Burlends to Pike County, Illinois.

Sinclair moved the family northeast, changed the year, and renamed them. He smoothed out and elaborated upon the narrative (which occurs in the 1830 section). This was all in accordance with his fictional license to handle documents. But he went further; he took as his own a source that was not oral but published, not purely documentary history but personal recollection and autobiography. In other words, *A True Picture of Emigration* was already someone else's *literature,* and Sinclair should have acknowledged it. Another instance, which Pratt does not mention, is even more glaring. *American Years* has a camp-meeting scene at the "Willow Bend Tabernacle" in 1835, with Peter Cartwright presiding. It is an impressive piece of writing but mostly not Sinclair's. He borrowed the scene, the structure, the incidents, and many of the narrative details from Francis Grierson's marvelous camp-meeting climax to *The Valley of Shadows* (1909). It was as if Sinclair recognized he couldn't match Grierson's imagination, so he appropriated it wholesale. To reveal this before publication, or even afterwards despite the embarrassment, would have been the honest thing to do and the best way of paying tribute to the Illinois past he was representing to the world as archetypally American.

As it turned out, however, Sinclair didn't need to protect the long-term reputation of *American Years.* There wasn't to be any. After selling steadily for a few months (probably some six thousand copies in all), the book dropped from sight, to be revived briefly by the Doubleday Dollar Book Club, but until now never reprinted. Sinclair soon went on to other—and very different—books. With the aid of a Guggenheim fellowship, he was able to complete the Everton Trilogy (*Years of Growth,* 1940, and *Years of Illusion,* 1941), but in these books he abandoned "history talking" in favor of more conventional plotting and fictional characterization. He also relied less on idiom and slang, which may have left too little color in the "jogging common-placeness" of his style.[41] Perhaps as a result, neither *Years of Growth* nor *Years of Illusion* was as fresh and original as the first volume (and they didn't sell nearly as well), though it is only fair to note that Sinclair himself did not think *American Years* his finest work.[42] Just before publication he confided to Harry Maule: "I think I will write as good a book as N.[orthwest] P.[assage]; but this isn't it."[43] What he had in mind was a rous-ing, adventurous first-person novel about George Rogers Clark (though not told by him), which he proceeded to write even before finishing "Everton." *Westward the Tide* became the his-torical novel Sinclair was proudest of, both for its well-made Robertsian shape and because the specialists pronounced it "the soundest historically" of all the fictional accounts of Clark's revolutionary exploits in Illinois.[44] Much later there would be a novel about the jazz world with a black protagonist (*Music out of Dixie*, 1952), Sinclair's personal favorite, and *The Horse Sol-diers* (1956), a Civil War adventure story based on Grierson's Raid and his only novel to be made into a movie.[45]

Harold Sinclair had a respectable though not spectacularly successful career as a writer, with nine books appearing over a span of twenty-three years. Yet if he must be remembered and read through one book, it ought to be *American Years*. Nothing else he wrote so effectively embodies the language, the critical vision, and most of all, the people of midwestern America. There is something definitive in being able to walk through Harold Sin-clair's Bloomington and conduct a dialectic of yes and no with him about Everton. In the yard behind Asahel Gridley's mansion on Grove Street still stand the two old oaks that give the house its name. We can think of them—perhaps Sinclair did too—as Fell and Davis, still guarding Everton from the social and eco-nomic depredations of Abel Green. The oak called Fell is thin and desiccated, rough bark split as if the skin were too tight for the energy within; Fell leans slightly north toward Normal, the town he founded, but his branches are drawn in, away from politics. The Davis oak has twice Fell's girth. His trunk is smooth and round, branches reaching outward gracefully to balance great weight. He looks beyond Fell and Everton to Chicago and Washington. Their communication is silent and complete. As Sinclair put it: "They didn't need close contact with each other. A word, a sentence . . . usually sufficed for whatever business was in hand. They probably understood each other as well as two men ever can."[46] Not accurate historical portraits? In some details Sinclair no doubt got his subjects wrong. But he made them live, as Jesse Fell and David Davis haven't lived before in history or biography. Near the end of the book, for example, Sinclair described the heavy depression of a heavy man: a defeated Davis on his return from Lincoln's first inaugural. The authority of such characterization goes far toward obviating the objections of the "curry combers of history," then and now.

So rich and varied were Sinclair's Bloomington and Illinois human resources that, among the democratic dozens of folks in the pages of *American Years,* only one important personage was entirely fictionalized. The rest lived lives that they would surely recognize, even with their names changed. Which character wasn't "real"? Well, as *American Years* is now republished after half a century and for a new age of readers, perhaps that will be a good test of Harold Sinclair's central premise about town and community in our nation. Can we distinguish, in essentials, the difference between fiction and history?

NOTES

1. Harold Sinclair to Burton Rascoe, 7 Feb. 1936, Harold Sinclair Papers, Illinois State University Milner Library, Normal, Illinois. Unless otherwise noted, all letters and manuscript citations are from this collection.

2. Rascoe to Ben Abramson, 30 Jan. 1936. Rascoe had read *Journey Home* in pages already printed, but unbound, from another publisher, Hartley, which had gone bankrupt before the book could be issued. At Rascoe's urging, Doubleday, Doran picked *Journey Home* up and brought it out later in 1936. It was thus Sinclair's first published book, though the second novel he had written (see note 26).

INTRODUCTION

3. Rascoe to Sinclair, 28 Feb. 1936; Rascoe to Sinclair, 14 Jan. 1937.
4. Harry Maule to Sinclair, 14 Dec. 1937. Here is Maule's complete comment: "I am tremendously impressed by the first part of the manuscript, which is a beautifully done picture of the development of a town. Frankly, there are some sales problems here in its lack of one central figure or succession of figures on whom to fasten the interest and focus the sales appeal. Nevertheless, the book has great value and we will study the challenge of the sales problem with just that much greater interest."
5. Alice Payne Hackett, *Seventy Years of Best Sellers, 1895–1965* (New York: R. R. Bowker, 1967), 155; also Maule to Sinclair, 4 Feb. 1938.
6. No authoritative sales figures exist at Doubleday, but Sinclair estimated some 6,000 copies sold in the original hardback editions and another 12,000 through the Doubleday Dollar Book Club ("Sales of Previous Books by Harold Sinclair," MS, Harold Sinclair Papers).
7. Harold Sinclair, "A New Type of Historical Novel," *Wings,* June 1938: 4.
8. Ibid., 4–5.
9. Ibid., 5–6; Sinclair to Rascoe, 7 Feb. 1936.
10. Eleanor Ann Browns, "Harold Sinclair and the Technique of the Historical Novel (master's thesis, University of Illinois, 1947), 8.
11. Ibid., 8–9.
12. Ibid., 9–10.
13. Ibid., 10.
14. Ibid.
15. Harold Sinclair, "Harold Sinclair," *Wings,* June 1938: 9.
16. Harold Sinclair, autobiographical sketch, *Sears News-Graphic,* 15 Sept. 1936: 15.
17. Harold Sinclair, *Journey Home* (Garden City, N.Y.: Doubleday, Doran, 1936), 154.
18. Ibid., 153.
19. Harold Sinclair, autobiographical manuscript, manuscript book: 677.
20. Browns, 12.
21. Ibid., 13.
22. Sinclair, *Sears News-Graphic,* 15.
23. Harold Sinclair, "Books," *Bloomington Journal,* 27 Jan. 1933.
24. Ibid., 8 Sept. 1933.
25. Browns, 14; Sinclair to Rascoe, 7 Feb. 1936; interview with Bernard

INTRODUCTION

Gummerman 19 Jan. 1988. Gummerman did not remember the excursion to Chicago that he and Sinclair were said to have made, nor did he know what had happened to the manuscript of "Concerto in American."

26. Sinclair to Rascoe, 7 Feb. 1936. Rascoe eventually read the manuscript of "Texture of Life" and got Doubleday, Doran to accept it as part of Sinclair's four-book contract. The novel was scheduled for publication in 1937 but withdrawn, probably for two reasons: the publishers had another "small-town newspaperman" story recently in print; and the developing *American Years* looked like a much better bet (Rascoe to Sinclair, 13 Oct. 1936, 4 Jan. 1937, 11 Jan. 1937, and 14 Jan. 1937).

27. Browns, 14–15; Sinclair to John Beecroft, 7 Mar. 1938.

28. Maule to Sinclair, 14 Dec. 1937.

29. Harold Sinclair, *American Years* (Garden City, N.Y.: Doubleday, Doran, 1938), 303; Maule to Sinclair, 28 Jan. 1938; Sinclair to Maule, 31 Jan. 1938.

30. Maule to Sinclair, 4 Feb. 1938.

31. Sinclair to Maule, 7 Feb. 1938; Sinclair, "Check-list of Profanity Deletions," MS, Harold Sinclair Papers.

32. Sinclair to Maule, 7 Mar. 1938.

33. Burton Rascoe, "Book Week," *Newsweek*, 23 May 1938: 28.

34. James Gray, "Building America," *Saturday Review of Literature*, 4 June 1938: 5.

35. Dorothy Van Doren, "American Heroes and Rascals," *Nation*, 11 June 1938: 677.

36. Stanley Young, *New York Times Book Review*, 5 June 1938: 2.

37. *Bloomington Pantagraph*, 29 May 1938: 8.

38. The evidence supporting this speculation is indirect: a full, copy-edited typescript of the review (unsigned) exists in the Harold Sinclair Papers at Illinois State University's Milner Library; there is also another draft, apparently a typed copy of the edited manuscript, with the heading "Copy of Pratt's Review of *American Years*." Finally, there is the following suggestive postscript to Maule's 9 June 1938 letter to Sinclair, responding to a point Sinclair made in a letter to Maule (no copy in the Sinclair Papers) dated 7 June: "I . . . do not blame you for being sore at Mr. Pratt's review. I know exactly what you mean by the state of mind these specialists get themselves into. I don't think I need to see a transcript of his review and personally, I am glad that it is not going to be published." The assumptions made here are that "Mr. Pratt" is indeed Harry Pratt and that the review he

wrote was intended for publication in the *Pantagraph*. Unfortunately, no information was obtainable from the *Pantagraph* to corroborate the scenario as outlined in the text.

39. Pratt MS, 4.

40. Evidently a number of readers wanted to know what sources Sinclair used for the "Lost Speech," especially for Lincoln's climactic avowal, "We won't go out of the Union, and you shall not!" Sinclair explained his approach in a detailed letter to the *Saturday Review of Literature*, 25 June 1938: 13.

41. The phrase occurs in an unsigned review of *Years of Growth*, *Saturday Review of Literature*, 24 Feb. 1940: 10.

42. About 3,000 for *Years of Growth* and some 2,500 for *Years of Illusion* (Sinclair, "Sales of Previous Books by Harold Sinclair").

43. Sinclair to Maule, 7 Feb. 1938.

44. Sinclair, "Sales of Previous Books by Harold Sinclair."

45. *The Horse Soldiers* (1959), directed by John Ford and starring John Wayne.

46. Sinclair, *American Years*, 248.

American Years

CHAPTER ONE

1830

J AMES ALLIN SAT ON A STUMP in the chip-strewn dooryard
of the cabin, polishing industriously at the rust spots on a saw
and letting his rheumatic shoulder joints soak up the warmth of
the sun. He was a small man, slender and wiry, with steady gray
eyes and a high forehead that lost itself in the shiny baldness of
his pate. Now in his early forties, he had wandered by devious
and sundry ways over a dozen states and territories, finally
ending here in Illinois, a goodly piece from the Rhode Island
where he had been born. Three or four times he had figured he
had found the place to end his wanderings, but always the grass
had seemed a little greener somewhere else. Now he was sure
that this lush Illinois prairie was the greenest spot a man of his
age would be likely to find. He had come here from Vandalia
the previous October, with a stock of general merchandise and
part of his household belongings, and spent the winter with the
Goodheart family, east of the Grove. His wife and five children
he had left in Vandalia, and shortly he would be going after
them. Everything was ready now, and there wouldn't be much
business until after the spring planting was done.

For two years before he came to Maple Grove he had worked
in Vandalia, that hard-cased seat of government in one of the

[1]

Union's youngest states. He had been a clerk at the Prairie House, and as such had received a thorough grounding in the principles and practices of the democratic method. Full many a senator, his brow heavy with cares of state and his innards heavier with Monongahela whisky, Allin had piloted to bed, and many a matter of critical state importance he had seen or heard settled at the Prairie House bar. Naturally, a man in his position made a good many friends, and for favors done he had been offered several sinecures at the State House. But he had always refused them, for he had other plans. Not the plans of an empire builder, perhaps, but plans of a definite and practical nature nonetheless. He had heard tales about the richness of the north central part of the state. That section was growing; it must grow; the flood of newcomers must go somewhere. And this place, so the tales had it, was the fairest in a fair state. Now that he had seen it, he knew the tales were true. There would be new counties formed, roads built, new towns springing up. There would be more and more people to sell goods to—and Allin was a trader by nature.

Now, on this bright blue-and-gold morning in April, he looked upon his world and found it, not perfect, but so far satisfactory.

The cabin had been begun in early March, as soon as the snow was gone. It was a saddlebag affair: two cabins built facing each other, with a covered runway between them. One room boasted a fireplace and served as living quarters; the other was fitted with a rude counter and a set of rough shelving along one wall. On the side of the cabin nearest the road there hung a sign made from a walnut slab, smoothed down by hand and the letters burned in with a hot iron. The sign bore the legend:

JAMES ALLIN, ESQ.,
GEN'L MDSE OF ALL KINDS
I DON'T SELL WHISKY.

The stock on the shelves was small but well assorted, and at the moment was the only one of its kind nearer Maple Grove than Pekin, thirty-five miles away on the Illinois River. There were salt, sugar, candle cotton, beeswax, millsaw files, bar iron, thread, pit- and hand-saw files, sieves and riddles, grindstones, axes, shovels, smoothing irons, cutlery, lead, powder, penholders and paper, shot, plug tobacco, looking glasses, flannels, muslins and combs. It was frontier merchandise—the kind of goods which could not easily be made at home, but which a man could scarcely get along without.

From his vantage point on the stump Allin could look southward to the bluish line where the rolling ocean of prairie ended at the horizon. The grass was already tall as a tall man's head, the turf underneath more than a foot thick and as tough as the bed bolts of hell. It ought to be; it had been growing and settling for ten thousand years, since about the time the last glacier went south. The rolling monotony was broken by occasional clumps of stalwart oaks or walnuts or maples, sometimes three or four together, hardly ever more than a dozen.

Maple Grove was a different matter. Its towering green walls extended for three miles east and west in an almost straight line, and northward it extended more than half as far. The muddy wagon track which skirted the southern side of the timber was the main, in fact the only, road to Vandalia, and it turned abruptly to the left at the far corner of the timber. The Allin store was just between the Grove and the road, where no passing traveler could possibly miss it.

The man on the stump glanced up from his polishing and eyed a beetle maneuvering among the chips at his feet. Without moving his head he shot an unerring stream of tobacco juice at the laboring beetle, then chuckled silently as it struggled madly under the sudden deluge. Somewhere out in the moving waves of grass a meadow lark sang like a mad fool, and above Allin's head, in a tall elm, two squirrels scolded each other happily. Then a sudden shift in the direction of the breeze brought the man the faint musical tinkle of an ox bell. He listened for a moment, then stood up and stretched, and as he did so a startled doe that had been loitering at the timber darted back into the green security

[3]

and vanished. Allin went in and put the saw away, then came back and stood waiting in his doorway.

The road wasn't quite as much of a mud haul as it had been a week or so before, but it was still a long way from being a boulevard. The wagon hove into sight a minute later, loaded to the roof and making heavy weather of it. A man and a woman were on the seat, and a pair of towheaded, freckle-faced boys, as alike as two peas, rode on the tail gate and dangled their bare feet behind. The outfit was patched in a hundred places and had seen many a long, hard mile, but in these parts that was no novelty. Most outfits had seen hard use or they wouldn't have been here in the first place. But it was the appearance of the couple on the wagon box that held Allin's attention. They looked as if they'd seen harder use than the wagon, and that within the last few hours, something like a minor war, maybe. The oxen settled back comfortably in their tracks and hung their heads to blow.

"Howdy," said Allin. "Fine day."

"Howdy," said the driver, and spat over a wheel into the mud. "Sure is."

Allin continued to stare. The man was carrying one arm in a sling made from a dirty rag, and his shirt hung in shreds about his chest and shoulders. His face and the upper part of his body looked as though he'd gone through a grist mill backwards. The woman was battered and skinned about as badly, except that all her legs and arms seemed to be intact.

Allin wondered if they treated each other that way.

"You got anything that 'd help these scratches any?" the man asked then.

"I reckon," Allin answered. "I got some salve that's good for saddle an' collar galls. That oughta be good."

"We'll try it," the man said, and got down over the wheel and introduced himself.

He said his name was Yancy, originally from South Carolina, more recently from Slemmons Prairie, forty miles east of Vandalia. They were moving up country and the night before had stopped at a grove six or seven miles to the southwest.

"What happened?" Allin asked. "Did you try to bed down with a wolf pack?"

Yancy thoughtfully touched a deep gash and sighed. He looked off at the horizon as though reluctant to speak of the regretted past.

"Well," he began finally, "we came up to that grove like I told you, an' decided to stay the night there. We found a cabin that didn't have no door nor no fireplace to it, and it looked like nobody had lived there fer quite a spell. Maybe never had. After we got settled I seen signs of some hogs that 'd been in the place, but I jest figgered they'd belonged to some drover that 'd passed that way. We built a fire in the hole where the fireplace should of been, brushed up the place a little, and turned in early. We was all pretty well tuckered."

He paused, to let Allin get the setting clear in his mind.

"Well, sir," he continued, "I woke up about midnight, a-hearin' the damnedest gruntin' and yowlin' a man ever put ear to. The fire had died down, but there was still a middlin' bed of coals, an' behind them coals was a dozen o' the biggest, mean-lookin', damn long-snouted hogs you ever laid eyes on. Then I lept up, an' there was three or four more climbin' over my feet an' a dozen more headin' in through the door. I yelled at the woman an' boys an' then threw an armload o' wood onto the fire, where it blazed up bright, an' I could see what in tarnation was comin' off. Well, sir, when the blaze flared up I could see one solid mass o' hogs clear to the edge of the clearin' an' on into the timber. There in the light you could see some o' them hogs had tushes anyway two inches long, and they was nearly as big as calves. I boosted the young uns up to the crosspoles an' yelled to the woman to git a billet o' wood an' watch the fire hole while I took over the doorway. I took a couple o' good clouts at them already inside, an' they was so surprised they headed easy. But them in the back kept pushin' up, an' from then on she was sure enough a battle. I smashed an' battered at them hogs till

[5]

I thought my arms would drop plumb off. They kept chargin' the door, and sometimes they was piled three an' four deep there in the doorway. The woman had it a little easier 'cause she had the fire betwixt her an' them. But twice or three times I went down, an' then she had to come an' fight 'em off me an' then them on her side would gain on her. Once I knocked the snout clean off one rarin' old boar, an' he went tearin' off through the rest of 'em, makin' fer the woods and a-yowlin' fit to curdle a man's blood. We musta fought 'em at least a full two hours. Finally, when we was both jest about to cave in, a couple of old boars broke for the timber, an' in five minutes there wasn't a hog in sight."

"Them was Isaac Frink's hogs," observed Allin.

"Un-hunh. Well, we was too shook up to do any more sleepin', so we jest sat up till sunup an' then got loaded ready to pull out. Jest as we was fixin' to leave, up come a whisky barrel of a man with a face like a flint rock. His two boys was with him an' all of 'em carryin' rifle guns like they meant big business. Right off he began cussin' an' layin' us out proper, wantin' to know what in the consarned hell we meant, abusin' an' maulin' his hogs an' half killin' I don't know how many."

"He thinks more o' them hogs than he does his own kinfolks," Allin observed.

"I reckon," Yancy agreed. "Well, he wasn't no madder 'n I was. But I couldn't reach my gun, an' there was three of 'em. Pretty soon, though, he calmed down, an' he seen how beat out we was. Then we talked it over an' interduced ourselves, an' he invited us to come over to his place an' rest up if we wanted to, but we jest said much obliged an' come on."

"That's Isaac Frink, all right. They say he knows every hog he's got by sight, an' he's got more hogs than any six men in the county. He's a hard man, but fair an' honest accordin' to his lights."

"Un-hunh. There was some nice-lookin' land down that way, an' I kinda thought o' stoppin' off. But we come on. A man don't want them hogs always worryin' him baldheaded."

"There's plenty of good land," Allin told him. "On to the northeast edge o' the Grove and beyond. Up north of the Goodheart place. All the land a man could ever ask for, with plenty o' timber an' water."

"You been here long?" Yancy asked.

"Only since last fall. But it's a good country, an' more people comin' in all the time."

"It's a long ways to a town," Yancy said. "Me, I don't like to git too far away from things."

"It's a long ways to a town now," agreed Allin. "Pekin, the county seat over on the river. But it won't always be that far."

"How do you figger that?"

"Because I'm goin' to start me a town within a mile o' here."

"Un-hunh. When?"

"This fall—jest as soon as the legislature meets and we can get a new county fixed up."

"Well, I sure do like the looks of this country around here myself. But it's a little late to get a crop in this year."

"Not if you git right at it. Get your corn in by the middle o' May, that's soon enough. You got a month yet."

The Yancys stayed until after noon, made a few minor purchases, then went on.

"You stop and see Goodheart," Allin shouted after them as a final reminder. "He'll tell you anything you need to know about that country up around there."

The battered wagon pulled out of sight, and Allin went back to his saw polishing. He hadn't done much business, but one more settler had come, probably to stay. He went on with his polishing, thinking about his plans for a town. As he had told Yancy, fall would be soon enough. Then the legislature would meet, and he and the others in the Maple Grove region would get the authority they needed. He, Allin, had the Vandalia end all fixed; that would be easy. Now, in the meantime, he could plan other things. How, for instance, he could do himself the most good in this future town he was planning.

[7]

AMERICAN YEARS

II

The meager track of road wandered eastward for three miles, to the edge of Maple Grove, then turned northward again, finally to vanish altogether at the bank of the Mackinaw. And between Allin's store and the Mackinaw perhaps ten families were more or less settled, most of them in sight of the thin road track, as though clinging to something familiar.

And how should they be called: Adventurers? Farmers? Pioneers? Riffraff who couldn't make a success in the more settled East, or the strongest blood and sinew in America, scornful of the East's easy ways and unmindful of frontier hardships? Well, they were all of these and still not completely any of them. A frontier is almost always like that. Certainly they were as motley a crew of individualists as might be found in North America, yet they had certain common characteristics. Most of them were as tough as the wolves they fought in winter, hard workers, free men who took physical hardship and political freedom—such as it was—as a matter of course. Most of them were of the second generation after the Revolutionary War—their grandfathers had fought *that* war—but many of them, especially the older men, had seen service in the War of 1812. And most of them were of the second wave of settlers, those who really put something into the land, or tried to; those who, consciously or otherwise, wanted to build something permanent, something a man could look at and say, "This is mine, and shall be my children's." Some of them would succeed; others would give up and move on to a place that looked easier but wasn't; others would build something good for those who came after them to steal legally.

Generally speaking, they all held the same superstitions, the same distrust of the few Indians left hereabouts, and the same superb belief in their own capabilities. One and all they settled close to the big timber. For didn't it stand to reason that ground which would grow trees like these could grow crops accordingly?

[8]

1830

It did. And the grass-grown prairie—the grass had grown and died and matted there for ten thousand years, and the sod was tougher than the back pastures of hell. You might graze a cow on it, but no man alive could plow as much as a bean patch without at least a four-ox team. It wasn't worth the effort. Furthermore, in places the prairie was as marshy and boggy as Ireland. Still, it was the fairest land between the Mississippi and the Alleghenies. These settlers knew, for most of them had seen for themselves.

First beyond Allin's store lived the Widow Moore and her four boys. The widow was the head of the family, and a good one. Dan Moore had been drowned when the family crossed an Ohio river in a spring freshet. Lizzie Moore buried him, said a prayer, hitched up the horses and drove on to Illinois. Nowadays she would be pointed out as a stirring example of the pioneer spirit, but nobody around Maple Grove thought so then. For what else was there for her to do? She took hardship as a matter of course, and life in Illinois wouldn't be any harder than it was in North Carolina. In Illinois she could take up land; in the Carolinas there wasn't much that was worth anything that hadn't already been taken. So here she was, with the four boys who were getting big enough to make good hands, in a cabin that the neighbors had helped with and on land that she and the boys had cleared. Her worst worry was the wolves that continually bothered the sheep.

Next beyond the widow lived Josiah Wick, an Englishman who had come to America to join Newman Flower's settlement at Albion, in the southern part of the state. Wick had been bitten by the bug of independence shortly after he arrived in Albion. Flower, not a freeholder in England, had emigrated to be free. But after he founded Albion he had been accused, probably with reason, of trying to set up the same kind of social structure which he himself had fled in England. As a result, Josiah Wick and a good many of his compatriots had struck out for themselves. Why not, when land, good land, could obviously be had for little more than the taking?

[9]

AMERICAN YEARS

And on beyond the Wick place lived William Goodheart, his wife and the five offspring. Perhaps this Goodheart, of all the settlers around the Grove, was the man of most copious parts. As such he deserves special mention. He had been born in 1790, near Glasgow, in Scotland, and when William was twelve his father took the family brood to Holland, where William was apprenticed to a plasterer and stonemason. William stayed six months—just long enough to learn the fundamentals of the trades—then deserted and joined the crew of a Dutch merchantman in Rotterdam. Six days out, the ship was captured by an English privateersman, and a bare week later both were taken into camp by a French man-o'-war. So William joined the French navy. There wasn't much choice; it was join or walk the plank. But he must have been adaptable, for a few months later he was a chief petty officer, and a year from then he was a noncom with Napoleon's cavalry in Italy. Or perhaps it was because he was Scotch by birth, and as such beyond the precepts of mere chauvinistic patriotism. He has said that during the Italian campaign he carried his pay in gold in a money belt about his waist, and that its very weight galled him. It is not recorded that he unburdened himself by spending any of the money. He followed the eagles of the Little Corporal on through the years, made the trip to Moscow, saw it burned and the monstrous retreat begun. Further, and much more to the point, he saw it ended. At least he himself came back, and to England, of all places. But there were still new worlds to be seen, and he was a man of considerable experience. He joined the British navy and a few months later found himself a gun captain on a man-o'-war in Lake Erie, where one of Perry's crack shots promptly shot the moorings completely out from under Goodheart's gun. The Scotsman swam ashore during the resultant excitement and was taken prisoner by Harrison's infantry. That night he escaped and headed, so he thought, for the raw interior wilderness. But he was a novice in the timber, and the next morning he was right back where he started, at the American camp. So once more he made a deal: he fought the rest of the war as an infantryman under Harrison. When the war ended he moved on to Ohio, got married, entered a claim, and promptly left his bride, to make a flatboat trip to New Orleans to earn money to pay for the claim. In the bayou country fever came nearer to laying him low than anything else had ever done. But he was Scotch, and a hard man to kill. He came back to Ohio, after being gone nearly a year, and found himself father of a son. He paid for the claim as agreed, sold it almost at once, and started for Illinois.

He was then twenty-six years old.

Impossible? Well, he did it, and the end is not yet. In Illinois he met Peter Cartwright, the Lord's helper in the wilderness, who immediately turned this whipcord-and-wire Scotsman into a Methodist. William rarely spoke of his past adventures, but he was fond of saying that the two great heroes of his life had been Napoleon and William Henry Harrison, but that now he loved Jesus Christ better than either one of the others.

At the time the Yancys came up the road from Allin's store, Goodheart was fooling with the experiment which proved to be his best contribution to the progress of Maple Grove. On his pasture ground east of the Grove he had discovered a patch of clay which brought back memories of his apprentice days in Holland. Already he had rigged up a crude kiln, and in another six months the chimneys and foundations of Maple Grove would be built of good honest brick in place of the usual "cat-and-clay." Almost anyone can soldier; it took a man of serious application to produce bricks from little more than a patch of stiff prairie clay and fire. The Little Corporal would probably have considered the whole business nothing less than sheer treason.

Two miles beyond the Goodheart place lived Henry Green and his wife, good solid Presbyterians from Vermont, and on the far side of them lived Laban Smith, a bachelor from nobody knew just where.

So they went, a motley crew of individualists, independent as a hog on ice, every last one of them, but good neighbors all, ready at a moment's notice to lend an axe, or a horse, or a day's labor. The very necessities of life were scarce at best, and a man never knew when he himself might have to borrow. Few of them had more than a smattering of academic education, though many, probably the majority, could read and write. But they all had a large fund of experience and common sense. A man had to profit by his experience in order to stay even on the frontier. He couldn't afford to make the same mistake more than once. These people knew what they knew, but a knowledge of Shakespeare or the quantum theory would have been just so much mental deadwood. Their needs were few and simple; their desires, relatively so.

While at the moment the population of the country around Maple Grove was four or five adults per square mile, there was already a community feeling. The county in which the Grove was located was just a little smaller than New Jersey, and a good many of the settlers resented the fact that Pekin, the county seat, was thirty-five miles away. Not that they had much legal business or needed the protection of the law. They didn't. It was just the idea of being a sort of orphan district. James Allin had been actively agitating since the previous fall. They could have their own county if they wanted it, build their own county seat right here at the Grove. Most of those whom he approached agreed with him; those who were not positively in favor of the idea had nothing much against it. If other people wanted it, there was no particular reason to object. Change was in the air. Just what it would be or what direction it would take, none of them knew. But it could hardly be anything but for the better. They had little more than a wilderness on their hands now.

III

Down East, what passed for civilization moved apace. The Baltimore & Ohio Railroad was an actuality; the Erie Canal had been operating for some five years, and steamboats on inland waters were a commonplace. In Washington, John Quincy

Adams was still serving his country as representative from Massachusetts, while Jackson as President was giving that same country a taste of real homespun democracy. Nicholas Biddle and his Bank of the United States, backed by the federal treasury, was doing a flourishing business, with Biddle keeping a wary weather eye on Jackson, avowed arch-enemy of the Bank. The final eruption which laid the country financially prostrate was still seven years away. Here and there, especially in the West, people were talking of a National Railway, to be built and operated by the federal government.

In Illinois, Abraham Lincoln was barely old enough to vote; in Ohio, a small boy named Grant was still learning to read and write and cipher. Down on the Kickapoo, south of Maple Grove, Captain Buler (War of 1812) took time off from fighting the wilderness and delivered himself as follows:

> Great western waste of bottom-land,   181-2
>   Flat as a pancake, rich as grease;
> Where mosquitos are as big as toads,
>   And toads are full as big as geese.
>
> Beautiful prairie, rich with grass,
>   Where buffaloes and snakes prevail;
> The first with hellish-looking face,
>   The last with hellish-sounding tail.
>
> I'd rather live on a camel's rump,
>   And be a Yankee Doodle beggar,
> Than where they never see a stump,
>   And shake to death with fever *ager*.

The captain was clearly no anticipator of Keats or Shelley, but he was fairly honest.

So, in part, was the world on that April morning when James Allin stood in front of his store and listened to Ed Yancy's account of the battle with Isaac Frink's hogs.

AMERICAN YEARS

About five miles from Allin's store, at the northwest corner of the Grove, near Sugar Creek, was the eighty acres owned by John Gorman, a Yorkshireman who had arrived in the neighborhood about the same time as Allin. Gorman, his wife, and ten-year-old son had come from England by way of New Orleans and St Louis, fixing upon this spot in Illinois because of the glowing accounts of it written by another Englishman who had since moved on.

Partly because he was a Yorkshireman and partly through ignorance of frontier business methods, Gorman had at once bought the pre-emption rights to a farm already located by a man named Willis. This pre-emption right was merely a certificate which signified that the holder intended eventually to buy the land. He could live on and improve the land as he wished, and at the end of that time acquire title by paying the government price of a dollar and a quarter per acre. If he did not buy he could still continue to live on the land until some other purchaser came along. The newcomer could then force the original settler to move immediately, without regard to any improvements the latter might have made, though as a rule some kind of an agreement covering the improvements would be made. Willis' pre-emption still had two years to run, and Gorman would not have had to pay for the land until the end of that time. But he did pay for it. He had come to America to become a landowner and so became one in the quickest possible way. In fact he even rented a horse from William Goodheart in order to ride to Kaskaskia and pay his hundred dollars in at the land office. It gave him a feeling of satisfaction which squatting never could have done. Further, it tied him rather definitely to one spot before he got a chance to become dissatisfied.

At that the sixty dollars he paid Willis for his rights was a fair enough bargain. In addition to the purchase right he got a fairly good cabin, a log stable, a dug well and a few tools. There were about four hundred sugar maples on the place—something which Gorman had never heard of until Willis explained—and Willis threw in his crude sugar-making utensils. Further, twelve acres had been broken and crops raised on them. Three acres were already sown with winter wheat when Gorman purchased. He could have gone farther and done much worse. He had as good an eighty acres as there was around the Grove, though by the time he had purchased a cow and three pigs his capital was reduced to less than four English pounds.

The family got through that first winter fairly well, though it was even harder than they had expected. Gorman spent about half his time cutting and carrying firewood, and then only partly kept the cabin warm. But when spring came they all felt better and were sure things would go well. It started well enough— Julia Gorman was delivered of twins, and they very nearly lost the second one at birth. But the twins survived, and Gorman got on with the corn planting. Children, after all, were a commonplace. The frontier seemed to have more children than anything else.

Toward the end of June the wheat began to ripen, and Gorman saw it would be ready to cut in a day or two. "What do you think, Julia," he said as they sat at the noon table, "can we afford to buy sickles?"

"I don't know," she answered, a little troubled. "How much would they cost, do you think?"

"A dollar apiece at Allin's."

"We have less than two pounds left now."

Gorman sighed. "Best let be for a little. We can borrow from Mr Oakes. But I'd better get them at once. See here—maybe you'd like to leave the boy with the babies and walk over there with me. Maybe the air would do you good."

"Perhaps so. I do need a little change," she said wistfully.

"Sure, Mother," piped George. "You go on. We'll be all right."

So after dinner was finished they started for the Oakes place.

It was two miles away, through the timber—little more than a half-hour's walk. They spent an hour in talk with the Oakes family, and by three had started for home. Then, as they crossed a little swale, engrossed in quiet talk, Gorman stumbled suddenly and fell headlong over a half-hidden log.

"John! You've hurt yourself!"

"No," he said, gasping. "I don't think so. It's nothing."

But he *had* hurt himself, much worse than even he thought. He had fallen directly on the sickle and cut a great gash in his right leg just above the knee.

"You shouldn't walk on that leg," Julia said, a little illogically.

"I *have* to walk on it, and that soon. We'd best get on before this leg begins to stiffen. It 'll be stiff enough the morrow."

They went on home without a great deal of trouble, and Julia cleaned and dressed the jagged wound.

John expected it to be stiff the next morning, but he wasn't prepared for the searing pain which flamed through the whole side of his body when he awakened a little before daybreak. He couldn't move from the bed, and Julia did the chores before she got breakfast. At noon the pain was still worse, and by evening he was far gone in delirium. That was a bad night, and Julia got almost no sleep.

The next day was worse. The fever had increased a little, but for some strange reason the injured leg suddenly turned cold. Julia did the chores, looked after the children, dosed the injured man with everything she had at hand and, in between rushes, prayed.

George didn't require much attention, but the twins did. They still had to be nursed and dried every few hours, with small attentions in between. Nervous and worried almost to the point of distraction, Julia tried to decide what to do. Should she go for help and leave the children, or should she look after John and have him get so bad no one could help him? Harried and tired as she was, she couldn't seem to make up her mind, though she mulled over the problem continually.

At sundown of the third day the cow came to the cabin and

lowed reproachfully. Julia recalled that she had forgotten to milk that morning. She leaned her head wearily against the cow's flank as she milked, and then with a sudden start she noticed the ripening wheat a few rods away. In the rush of other things she had forgotten that, too. Now a little breeze stirred the wheat ears, and she was further startled as she saw a few tiny grains drop from one of the nearest stalks. Could it be possible? It was. The grain had been ready to cut when they had gone to borrow the sickles. Now, with the dry, ninety-five-degree temperature of the past few days the grain was reaching a crisis. Because of the very nature of the harvesting process, it was disastrous to let the grain get too ripe. The ears would harden and dry out, and when the stalks were struck by the sickle the grain would be scattered and lost in the straw and on the ground.

She stood there in the scorching sundown, the foaming pail of milk in her hand, looking at the waving yellow field. Tears welled unwillingly from her eyes and mingled with the sweat on her flushed cheeks. She *must* do something about the wheat, for the wheat was life. The corn crop might not be so good—it had been planted a little late—but here was a wheat crop asking to be taken before it went to waste.

For three days now John had eaten nothing, only drunk a few cups of coffee brewed from their precious store. But on the morning of the fourth day the fever was broken, and in a few hours the swelling began to go down. The patient sat up and decided he could eat a couple of soft-boiled eggs. Julia fixed the eggs, brewed some fresh coffee, then sat down and allowed herself to weep distractedly. After that they talked about the wheat. Julia insisted she could manage the harvest with the help of the boy, and John remonstrated, but in the end he gave over. There wasn't a great deal to be said; both of them knew how important that wheat crop was. So it was decided that Julia and George would work in the field, and when the twins needed looking after John could call her.

The next morning John felt able to sit up on a three-legged

stool and lean against the wall with a pillow behind his back. By a great effort he could brace himself against the wall and hop around to the water pail or the twins' crib or the open door. Julia and the boy, with the chores done, were in the field by six. By eight the sun was blistering at ninety in the shade, and the two toilers were dripping sweat at every pore. Julia, like most women on the frontier, wore an outer dress of linsey-woolsey, with but a single cotton undergarment, and before ten the clothing stuck to her back and hips like wet plasters. A cloth tied around her forehead kept the moisture out of her eyes, but she could feel the sweat running down her legs into her shoes. The sickle was soon dulled, and she found that the makeshift flint whetrock which John used was little more than an aggravation. England seemed a long way off, yet that morning she remembered the cool, overcast skies of Yorkshire in vivid retrospect.

Julia wielded the sickle, and George trailed behind, raking the cut grain into loose sheaves. The twins had left their mark on Julia, and before noon the shooting pains in her back became almost unbearable. She felt that she must rest, so she sent the boy to the cabin for a gourdful of water and, not wanting to leave the field, half lay, half sat upon a piled heap of the grain. When she was resting, the pain seemed much easier. Well, they had at least gotten at it in time. They should lose very little of the crop if they could only manage to keep on.

In a moment the boy came back with the cool gourd. She smiled at his weary face. "Did you have some, son?" she asked gently, wanting to say something else but not able to find the words.

"Yes," he said simply. "I'm hungry, Mother. Are we going to eat dinner pretty soon?"

"In about an hour," she told him, shading her eyes as she looked toward the sun. Then, as she turned her face back to the boy's, she saw his cheeks go chalky white and his eyes widen in terror. His mouth opened, and she was so close she could see his numbed tongue cleave to the roof of his mouth. "Son, son! What is it?" but the boy was so stricken he could not speak, and she turned to follow his staring eyes. Then she felt her own nerves snap taut like a suddenly tightened fiddlestring. From under the grain heap, where she sat, a six-foot timber rattler lurched lazily out into the hot stubble, its body a dirty gray against the yellow of the wheat. For an instant she sat quiet as a stone. Please, God, what? Then, without a moment's hesitation, she grasped the sickle which lay under her hand and in the same motion struck the rattler one blow about a foot behind the flat head. It was sheer luck. The blow struck just as the tail whirred and began the whiplash curl to a striking position. The snake's body was severed completely.

Julia dropped on her knees in the wheat, holding the sobbing boy tightly against her own shaking body. The dismembered body of the rattler jerked spasmodically, and the murky blood stained the stubble a dark maroon. Julia smoothed the boy's tousled hair and crooned to him softly. "There, there, it's nothing, nothing. Come on," she said, and managed to laugh a little, "let's go to the cabin now. After all, it *is* practically time for dinner."

So went the first day.

After a little they became inured to the killing labor, and in a week the two of them had cut and sheaved the three acres of wheat. After that they had to carry all the sheaves to the smooth, hard patch of ground in back of the stable, where the wheat would be winnowed by hand in the wind. Julia devised a means of carrying the grain. They would lay two eight-foot poles on the ground, after the manner of a stretcher, and then pile the sheaves crosswise on the poles. Most of the weight was piled back of the center, and then Julia would take that end, thus bearing the bulk of the load. Together that way they could carry more, and do it much more easily, than they could by working alone. Gorman could now get about on a makeshift crutch and give them instructions in stacking properly.

Only one other mishap occurred. Like most settlers, the Gormans were continually working at clearing more land. The method was simple: a tree at the edge of a clearing was girdled, then, when it was dead, set afire. Through the hard labor of the harvest Julia had managed to keep several trees burning at the edge of the wheat field. It was a foolish thing to do, but she couldn't have thought of everything. They were working on the opposite side of the field and didn't see the flames eating out toward the end of a rotting branch which hung directly over the stubble. They weren't aware of anything wrong until John came back from a trip to the cabin and instantly began shouting wildly and pointing at the darting flames in the dry stubble. It took two hours of gasping, lung-searing labor before the last leaping tongue of flame was stamped out.

The fire destroyed about one quarter of the crop, so from the harvest they emerged with about sixty bushels of grain. Of this, ten bushels were lost because of the "cheat," a weed which looked almost exactly like the wheat and which had to be removed before marketing. Ten bushels more had to be saved for seed, thus leaving about forty bushels that could be sold. James Allin offered fifty cents per bushel in cash, or fifty-five cents in trade. So for the summer wheat crop the Gormans got a pair of shoes each, a cheap plow, two tin milk bowls, eight pounds of coffee, two bushels of meal, and five dollars in paper money—this last of dubious value in Illinois.

They had no animals to draw the plow, but bought it because they hoped to have some in time for spring plowing the following year.

They weren't too poorly satisfied with the wheat crop. It could have been worse, and they still had eight acres in corn. The corn didn't look especially good, but it was bound to bring something. In the spring there would be a little something from the sugar maples—they would have the hang of sugar making down better next year. And last, or perhaps first, there was hope. It must be true that there is always hope. If that were not true, then the frontier would never have been beaten.

1830

V

In the heavy, stuffy darkness of the cabin, old man Leary yawned, stretched and turned over. He pushed Ma Leary's knees out of the small of his back and pulled irritably at the dirty bedcoverings. Why in the tarnation hell, he mused sleepily, didn't the womenfolk make them coverlids long enough to cover a man's neck and feet at the same time? Out near the lean-to stable the three dogs howled long and loud. Leary cussed them silently. Damn-fool dogs, always yawpin' and roarin' at nothing but their own shadows. He found a comfortable place on the shuck mattress and settled down blissfully. These November nights were hellish cold, but they were great for sleeping. He wished Ma wouldn't snore quite so much, though after twenty-five years he was pretty well used to it. In a moment he was asleep again.

But five minutes later he was wide awake, nerves taut, ears strained. The dogs were going great guns now, and the hogs were grunting and squealing nervously. Something *was* wrong. In an instant he was out of bed and on his feet. The fire was covered with ashes for the night, but in a moment Leary had the door open. The sight which met his startled eyes stopped him dead at the threshold. He stood there, his eyes popping and his tobacco-stained jaw agape, the cold north wind whipping his shirt about his bare, knobby legs. Automatically he reached for a chew, then remembered he'd left his plug in his pants.

Northward, across the dry, dead fall growth of the prairie, the world seemed afire. The flames were now perhaps two miles north of the Leary place and extended across the rolling ground like a curving, five-mile-long scimitar of fire. The smoke rolled skyward in great surging billows, the red reflections of the flames lighting them brilliantly, and from the cabin door Leary could see myriads of animals silhouetted against this backdrop. Deer, rabbits, foxes, ground squirrels, hogs, someone's cows, a few sheep—running madly before the demon. Already he could hear the snapping crackle of the flames, and his own dooryard was so light he could have read a newspaper—or he could if he'd had one and known how to read. He stood there in the doorway for perhaps two minutes, his ordinary faculties paralyzed by the catastrophic beauty of the burning night. He made another futile grab for his eating tobacco, then came to with a start. He turned to the sleepers in the cabin and began yelling.

"Ma! Pete! Sarey! Eb! Cal! Come out o' there. Hell's loose an' bearin' down on us!"

Another moment and the pandemonium of the Leary family arising was in full swing. Pa found his buckskin pants where he had left them by the fire and was breaking in a chew as he pulled his boots on.

Outside, he was snapping cuss words and orders at the three boys and the two women.

"Ma, you an' Sarey fill up every vessel you kin lay hand to and git 'em out there by the stable. Cal, pen that stock up so it cain't git loose—we might's well have 'em burned as scattered all over hell an' half of Indianny. Pete, you an' Eb grab every hoe an' shovel an' axe you kin find an' start throwin' dirt out there at the edge of the clearin'. The rest of us 'll be out there to help yuh soon's we kin."

They snapped to it. This was no time to dawdle, and they knew it. If they could keep the fire away from the buildings they had a chance; if it once got past them they'd have nothing but a pile of ashes by sunup. The curving arm of fire was much nearer now. Already the smoke was smarting in their nostrils, and the wind had risen a little. The eastern end of the fire was now, for some reason, advancing a little faster than the other.

Along the eastern edge of the Leary clearing, and extending a little way around toward the north side, there was a small creek. That should protect the clearing along that front, and if it didn't, then there was nothing the Learys could do about it. Along the rest of the north side and curving slightly toward the south, they were digging a shallow trench and throwing the loose earth up on the fire side. That too might not work or might not be done in time. The top crust of earth was frozen a little, and the digging was devilish hard. All they could do was throw dirt and hope they'd get enough done to protect themselves. Except for backfires there was no other way of fighting these prairie blazers, and the wind was too high to take a chance.

Old man Leary straightened up and wiped his dripping forehead. "Look!" he shouted, and pointed eastward toward the Wick place.

Wick had cut his corn and shocked it that fall instead of shucking in the usual way, and now the flames were in the shocks. Farmer's luck. If the field had been even a hundred yards farther east the fire would have missed it altogether. As it was now the Wick cornfield was the eastern end of the blaze. The Learys could see Josiah Wick beating at the burning roof of his hog pen with a blanket.

"Too bad," old man Leary said. He discovered that his throat was dry as sand. "Cal, you go an' fetch out that jug. A little dram 'll do us all a heap o' good."

The sixteen-year-old came back in a moment, and they passed the jug around, starting with old man Leary and ending up again with Cal, who got his along with the rest of them.

Then the advance guard of the fire was upon them, and they hardly had time to draw breath. The creek was what saved them, for it gave them a chance to concentrate all their efforts on the north and west sides of the clearing. The roof of the lean-to stable caught fire, but Ma and Sarey killed that with the water and wet comforters. The old man and the boys fought along the trench, watching every tongue of flame that leaped the barrier, stamping hot earth until their legs ached and their feet were blistered through their stiff boots.

But they whipped it. The fire threw itself against the barrier of Maple Grove, like a wave against a granite cliff, and in the end died out completely. Toward morning the wind fell, and by the time the flames reached the Grove their real fury was gone. They burned into the timber as much as a hundred yards in a few places, then gave up. Why? No one knew.

AMERICAN YEARS

Old man Leary sat down wearily upon a chunk of wood near the door of the cabin. He was dog-tired, had a nice set of blisters on his hands and feet, and had burned off his eyelashes, his eyebrows and part of his greasy, wind-tangled whiskers. "Cal," he said, "hand me that jug if there's anything left in it to drink." He took a good long turn at the jug and helped himself to a fresh chew. Northward and westward, as far as he could see, the prairie was a black, charred desert, with here and there a gaunt tree trunk standing alone like a grim sentinel. It seemed impossible that the earth would ever be green there again. But somehow it would be. Old man Leary knew that it would. He spat reflectively and sighed a little. "Yuh know," he said mildly and to no one in particular, "I git mighty blame' tired o' these fires sometimes."

VI

The two men sat stiffly on the straight chairs and waited, speaking now and then in low tones, as though afraid of making any unwarranted noise. The room was on the second floor of the capitol of the sovereign state of Illinois, but no one would have guessed that from its appearance. It was a bare, uncarpeted cubbyhole with one window which looked out upon an unlovely mud haul which passed for a street. There were four straight chairs along one wall, a small plain table stood against another, and a capacious spittoon was located in the center of the floor. There were two framed engravings on the walls: one of George Washington and one of Thomas Jefferson. Abraham Lincoln's likeness had not yet become a necessary part of a politician's office furniture.

A pleasant-appearing young fellow came out of the inner room, smiled vaguely, and said Mr Caldwell would see them now. The two men rose awkwardly and entered the office of the Honorable J. P. Caldwell, Speaker of the Illinois House of Representatives. He was a soft-spoken man, hailing from the Cairo district, and greeted his visitors affably. "You gentlemen wished to see me?" and without waiting for an answer he asked, "Which of you is Mr Latta and which Mr Rhodes?"

"I'm Latta," said the chunky man with the square-cut beard. "This is Mr Rhodes."

"Just so," smiled Caldwell. "Best to get these things straight at the beginning. I believe my clerk said you had a petition of some sort which required my attention."

"That's right," said Latta. He was a preacher of sorts, and so had apparently been delegated to do the talking. "We also have a letter for you personally from Mr James Allin. He said you'd probably remember the name."

"Allin?" the Speaker murmured aloud. "It's not an uncommon name. I don't recall knowing the gentleman at the moment, though no doubt I should. Well, since it's of a personal nature, let's have the letter first."

Latta handed over the letter, and Caldwell, after muttering an apology, opened and read it. He read it again, coughed a little, and said, "Er—do you gentlemen by any chance know the contents of this letter?"

"No, sir," Latta answered. "Mr Allin just said it was a personal letter to you. He said you were an old acquaintance of his, and that when you remembered him you'd no doubt do all you could to speed our case."

"Just so, just so," Caldwell said, in a relieved tone. "And now let's see the petition. We'll see what can be done."

Of course he didn't see fit to explain the contents of the letter from Allin. In fact he had already put that missile in the inner pocket of his coat. He didn't want it around his desk where the clerk might run across it, either. Not, really, that anyone but the Speaker could have made much of the letter. It reminded Caldwell of the time he had been living at the Prairie House and a certain comely mulatto wench had fallen asleep and forgotten to leave his room before daylight. Of course he hadn't been Speaker then. James Allin, who was the clerk on duty, had seen his duty and done it. Not that he approved of Mr Caldwell's morals, you understand; far from it. But he was working for the Prairie House, and it had a reputation of sorts to maintain. The letter gently called upon the Speaker to remember the little incident, though not, of course, in just so many words, for Allin wasn't quite that kind of fool. Mr Caldwell, however, knew exactly what Allin was driving at.

The Speaker glanced but briefly at the petition; it seemed quite in order.

"Well," he said heartily, "I don't see any good reason why your request shouldn't be complied with."

"You mean it'll go through right away?" Latta asked eagerly.

"Well, now, sir," the Speaker said in a deprecatory tone, "I can't promise definitely. You gentlemen know how these things are. I have *some* influence, of course, but there's the rest of the House and the Senate to be considered. However, I'd advise you not to worry very much. What can be done, will be."

They thanked him profusely and rose to go, when Caldwell stopped them. "Why, er—one thing I intended to ask you. Does Mr Allin own property in your community, by any chance?"

"Why, yes," Latta said. "He owns a nice quarter-section near the middle of Maple Grove. But Mr Rhodes here and myself are property owners, too——"

"Of course, of course. Naturally, I understand that. But is Mr Allin interested, say, in locating the county seat?"

Latta and Rhodes looked at each other. What was the right answer? But Latta, after all, was a man of God, so he told the truth. "Well," he said, "Mr Allin is a very public-spirited man, and I suppose he is interested in the location. I've heard it said that he had offered to donate the land necessary for the county property. Though of course," he added a bit hastily, "that would be a matter for your honorable body to decide."

"To be sure, to be sure," agreed the Speaker. "But you gentlemen know how it is. It's always best to hear all sides of these matters. By the way, I suppose there are a good many Democratic voters in your community?"

"Oh yes," Latta said. "A large majority of the voters, I should say." Which again was not only diplomatic but true.

"Thank you very much," Caldwell said courteously. "Will you be in Vandalia for a few days yet?"

"Well, we thought we'd stay a day or two to see if there 'd be any news to take home with us."

"Good. Then suppose you come here to my office about five tomorrow afternoon. I'll probably have something to tell you by that time."

So they thanked him and went away.

As Mr Caldwell had said, he was not without influence. The next morning the Clerk of the House duly read the petition of the residents of Maple Grove, asking that a new county—to be called Dane—be set up in the eastern portion of what at that time was Tasman County. The petition was signed by that long list of names which were to become part of the warp and woof of Dane County—the names which through the years would appear on title deeds, tax receipts, marriage and death certificates, and on the flyleaves of plush-covered family Bibles; and the names which would appear on the lists of killed and wounded at San Jacinto, Gettysburg, Shiloh, the Wilderness and Vicksburg, at the Little Big Horn, at San Juan Hill, at Château Thierry, Belleau Wood and the Argonne: Hendrix, Rhodes, Goodheart, Wick, Gorman, Scott, McNulta, Davis, Cox, Brokaw, Allin, Major, Temple, Magoun, Hogg, Baker, Guthrie, Trumbull, Harbord, Hovey, Cusey, Schmitt, Havens, Coon, Hodge, Hall, Hay, Warlow, Fletcher, Kitchen, Latta and a host of others.

The House passed the enabling bill that morning, without a record vote. In the afternoon the Senate did likewise. Dane County became a fact.

At five that afternoon Caldwell imparted the news to Latta and Rhodes. He told them that two commissioners would shortly visit the district and locate a county seat. Then, as a sort of afterthought, he bade them take his regards to Mr Allin, and turned to other and more important business.

Rhodes and Latta, jubilant over the early success of their venture, prepared to begin the hundred-mile ride home the next morning.

That night the prairie fire which ousted old man Leary from his bed burned Rhodes' log stable, four hogs and six sheep. Things just naturally seemed to happen that way.

CHAPTER TWO

1831

Nᴏᴛ ʙᴇꜰᴏʀᴇ ᴏʀ sɪɴᴄᴇ has such a snow as that one been recorded in Dane County. Up until that time—the 29th of December, 1830—the winter had been milder than usual. Clear, cold but not too cold days, the ground frozen just hard enough to keep it from mudding easily, an occasional very light skim of snow. But on the 29th of December, in the afternoon, snow began to fall in real earnest. Gently at first, with almost no wind, the snow fell almost straight down, but as the afternoon wore on, the flakes became larger and the fall heavier. It was like a heavy white curtain, completely shutting off the view at less than a hundred yards. By sunrise of the 30th there was more than a foot of snow on level ground; by morning of the 31st, more than three feet, and by night the fall had in many places reached four feet.

On New Year's morning the temperature—it had been only slightly below freezing until then—fell to ten degrees above zero. The day was bright and sunshiny, and Dane County was a solid, glistening block of snow. Men tried to feed stock and couldn't reach the log stables and pens. The womenfolk, accustomed to emergencies and as a rule not worried by them, began to eye their larders with sober looks.

Nothing could move. The crust which was forming on the snow would only hold up a man's weight in a few places, and nowhere would it bear horses or oxen. The deer tried to forage, broke through the crust and floundered madly, panic-stricken. Many of them broke legs and, when their plunging panic had subsided, stumbled into gulleys or sloughs and died where they lay, food for the famished wolves which hunted them unceasingly, either dead or alive. So was it with all the abundance of game which thronged the Grove. Only the squirrels got along without much suffering.

The Reverend Sylvester Peasley was a great believer in the efficacy of prayer, though, judging from the outward appearance of himself, his wife and five children, the cabin and lean-to stable, his belief had never done him much practical good. But Sylvester would be the first to agree that outward appearances didn't mean anything in the eyes of the Lord. Cassy, his wife, didn't always think so. She sometimes imagined that there must be a better world somewhere, though in her own experience she hadn't seen much that really looked better, and after ten years of wedlock with Sylvester she was pretty well convinced that the vineyards of the Hereafter were the only changes for the better that she could look forward to.

The Peasleys had forty acres of the best ground in the Grove vicinity, and got less from it than any other family in the neighborhood. The trouble was that Sylvester's preaching interfered mightily with the work around the place. He had no regular charge and took whatever preaching jobs came to hand. This Sunday it might be here at the Grove; next Sunday it would be at some rabbit-run settlement thirty miles away. Then, in order to get there on time, he'd have to start about Friday, and sometimes, if there was a wedding or a christening to be taken care of, he wouldn't get home until Wednesday or Thursday. So the weeds in the corn prospered exceedingly, the hogs— when he had any—ran the place to suit themselves, and the woodpile was always either in bad shape or worse, depending on the weather. Cassy was a good Baptist, but at times she found the Lord's ways, and Sylvester's, mighty hard to fathom.

Just now the woodpile was down to about a half-cord, and the bacon, which had come from the last job of preaching, had been finished on Christmas. There was about a half-peck of meal in the cabin, a few pounds of lard and perhaps a handful of salt. In a corner of the cabin's one room there stood a covered vessel which did duty as a slop jar, and the cover had long since ceased being any help in holding down the smell. It had been impossible to get the baby's pants dry and clean, and they added their bit to the atmosphere. Be it said, though, that the Peasleys didn't mind that a great deal; they were used to the cabin's winter odors. After all, they weren't odors which were peculiar to the Peasley domicile. But the shortage of food was another matter entirely. The cow in the stable was dry, so there was no milk. They could eat the cow, of course, but it was their most valuable possession and could be turned into beef only as a very last resort. Or the two shabby shoats could be turned into pork. But it was bread they needed. The smaller children, aged two, four and five, couldn't live on pork and stay well—or as well as they ever were. Cassy's own milk was getting thin. She was sure that the baby's fretfulness was caused by its never-appeased hunger.

On New Year's morning Sylvester went hunting for anything that looked like game. But everything had gone to cover, and he wasn't a very good shot anyway, so after wasting the morning and some valuable ammunition he came back to the cabin with a brace of rabbits which the family made off with at noon. The bread problem was still unsolved.

"I'll have to use most of the meal for supper pone," Cassy said dispiritedly. "That might last through breakfast in the mornin'. After that there won't be nothin' left."

She wasn't necessarily accusing Sylvester. It was just a plain statement of fact.

"Well," Sylvester said, "the Lord's always pervided, an' I'm not goin' to lose my faith in Him now."

AMERICAN YEARS

"I reckon He'll pervide all right," she answered heatedly, "but that ain't no sign you won't have to go git whatever He's goin' to pervide. It ain't likely to fall on the roof."

"Now that sounds more 'n a little like plain blasphemy," Sylvester said solemnly. "I'd say it was shore if it 'd come from anybody but my wife."

"Call it whatever you like, Sylvester Peasley, but it's the dead open-an'-shut truth, an' you know it. If you don't stir yer lazy carcass out 'n here an' git down to Allin's store, I will—though I don't see how you're goin' to feed the young un if I do have to go."

But it was all talk. He knew it and she knew it, and in the end he went, as he'd known from the first he would. But then something *might* have turned up. You couldn't never tell. . . . The Lord had worked miracles before, and there was no more faithful Baptist in the world than Sylvester Peasley.

At two that afternoon the preacher was on his way. He had put on all the clothing he could find, but even that was hardly enough to hold off the near-zero temperature. He got as far as the stable without much trouble, for already he had beaten a sort of path to that nearest outpost. But beyond that the going was terrible. All trace of the trail had long since disappeared, and even familiar landmarks looked queer and seemed to be in the wrong places. Sometimes he could negotiate thirty or forty feet of the slippery crust without trouble. Then the crust would give way and plunge him more than waist deep in the powdery snow beneath. He would struggle sometimes for as long as ten minutes before getting back on the crust at a point where it would bear his weight. Frequently he would have to lie down full length, like a man climbing out through a hole in river ice, before the capricious crust would hold him safely. Snowshoes would have helped. But Peasley was a Southern man. He'd never heard of snowshoes and, if he had, probably wouldn't have known how to use them.

That struggle through the snow was the hardest work he'd ever done in his life, and he'd done some fairly hard work in

[32]

spite of his frequent derelictions. Time after time, panting and exhausted, ready to collapse, he thought that he must rest for just a little. But he was a stubborn cuss; he had set out for Allin's store, and get there he would and must. After the first hour his hands and feet were numb with cold and, beat them as he would, he couldn't seem to help them much. That was one reason why he was afraid to stop and rest, even for a few minutes. If he stopped he might not be able to get started again.

It was dark long before he reached Allin's. It was a bit over five miles from the Peasley cabin, and he reached it a little past seven. He caught a glimpse of the candlelight in the store a half-hour before he reached it, and managed to thank God with what little breath he could spare for the purpose.

They put his hands and feet into fresh snow and thawed him out. Allin stood there in the firelight, watching the grime on Sylvester's feet darken the clean snow.

"You look mighty tuckered, Brother Peasley."

"Well, yes, I reckon I am. But the Lord looks after His own, Brother Allin, don't you fergit that. It was a hard fight, but He seen me through." He pondered for a moment. "You know, though," he said thoughtfully, "there was a time or two I wasn't shore I'd make it. But I jest threw out my heel corks an' settled back in the breechin', an' here I am."

"Did you hear that they'd made us a new county hereabouts, Brother Peasley?"

"Shore enough? I did hear some talk o' the like, but I didn't know it was a settled fact. Well, now, sir, that's fine. That shore is fine now."

The Allins pressed him to stay the night, pointing out that it was getting colder and that it would be foolhardy to make—or try to make—the trip back that night. But he was adamant. "I made it here. I reckon the Lord 'll see to it that I make it back all right—an' Cassy's outta meal. A man cain't let his young uns holler fer food when he's still able to carry it to 'em."

So at nine he started on the return trip. The brilliant moon had risen, and he hadn't the least trouble in seeing. Further, he

[33]

had his own path—such as it was—to follow, so there was no danger of losing his way in the night.

But now it was colder, almost zero, and he had fifty pounds of shelled corn in the sack which bowed him down. He hadn't figured on that, but now was no time to worry about it.

He had only one bad setback. Hunting for a harder patch of crust, he had come down a little slope. His numbed faculties told him that it was the channel of a familiar creek, but he thought nothing of it. It didn't occur to him that there could be any ice around that wouldn't bear his weight. But there was. The snow had formed such a thick, warm blanket over the thin ice of the creek that, in spite of the cold, the ice had remained thin. Once more the crust broke under his weight and he went through three feet of snow, an inch of ice, and on into eight inches of water. That was a bad ten minutes, but with herculean efforts he finally made the other bank.

In a few moments his boots and leggings were solid chunks of ice. And it was then that fury rose in his breast like an engulfing tide. He stood there in the cold moonlight and let the sack rest in the snow. He was panting again, and his breath rasped his throat.

"Lord!" he shouted, and his voice reverberated in the green-and-white winter stillness. "Lord! You jest fergit fer about three minutes that I'm a preacher!" And for three minutes he cursed the whole universe in language that would have made the toughest frontier bullwhacker stare in slack-jawed envy, and he never repeated himself once. Then: "Lord," he said contritely, "I'm sorry. But this would make make even You mad as hell." And with that he picked up the corn sack and started on his way again.

It was four in the morning when he got home. Both feet were frozen, as well as his ears, and they had to pry his fingers loose from the neck of the sack.

"You shoulda waited till mornin'," Cassy said.

"Well, it wouldn'ta been no warmer this mornin'," he said

doggedly. "I figgered the Lord 'd see me through if'n He aimed fer me to git through."

And so He had. Or maybe it was the Reverend Sylvester Peasley's naturally inborn guts and stubbornness. At any rate, he had made the ten-mile round trip in sixteen hours, frozen both feet, both ears and part of one hand. In return he got a bushel of corn—the hearts would make meal and the hulls hominy—worth forty cents, and the satisfaction of knowing that his family wouldn't starve—at least not for a few days yet.

I I

Take them any way you please, five hundred head of hogs add up to a lot of pork. Consider that hogs are dumber than cattle, but that it takes a smarter man to handle them; that from Isaac Frink's home stand to the Galena lead mines was a matter of one hundred and twenty-five miles; that Frink had only himself and his two boys to handle the hogs—and you have a problem in transportation that is formidable, to say the least. One thing was certain: Galena was the most thriving industrial town in the state, and wherever men draw reasonably good wages and work hard for them there is a market for meat. So Isaac Frink and his hogs were frequent visitors to Galena. He could always get a higher price there than at St Louis or Chicago, the latter only a cluster of shanties on a marshy spot near Lake Michigan.

Some people thought Isaac Frink was a fool, and others knew he was, but one and all they agreed that he knew more about hogs and did more downright, back-breaking work than any other man around Maple Grove. People were divided on the question of whether Ike worked that way because he liked to or because that was the only way he knew of making more money than anybody else in the community. For already he owned five times as much land as any other man in Dane County.

Ike and the two boys, Absalom and Eugene, started the five hundred half-wild porkers on the road to Galena on the morning of the 29th of December. They aimed to get as far as the Mackinaw by night and cross the river the first thing in the morning. It began to snow in the afternoon, a slow, gentle fall, and they thought nothing of it. It was natural to expect snow this time of year, and a light fall wouldn't hurt anything, anyway. But by morning the snow was a foot deep and making them plenty of trouble—not insurmountable trouble, but still trouble. They didn't worry much; surely it would stop before long. They crossed the river all right and only lost three or four hogs in the process. Ike cussed and stormed for a half-hour and then forgot it. After all, you had to figure on losing a few head on a drive like that.

By noon things were looking different. The hogs were strung out for nearly a quarter of a mile, and it was practically impossible to keep them together. The snow was still falling, hiding even the hogs at a distance of a hundred yards. All signs of the meager trail had long since been obliterated, and Ike, who was up front, kept on in the right direction largely by instinct. At intervals they would yell at each other to make sure they were still together. Ike would cup his hands to his mouth and bellow to Ab, who was sixteen and worked the center of the herd, and he in turn would yell back at Eugene, seventeen, who was entrusted with the rear guard. It was slow going. A mile an hour was good, extremely good.

Ike stumped along, a stout figure in a greatcoat so old it had long since faded to a nondescript greenish color, a wool muffler wound about his thick neck and a fur cap on his head. He alternately cussed and urged the drooping hogs in a sort of grunt-and-cluck language which they seemed to understand, occasionally kicking an obstinate shoat back into line with a manure-spotted boot. He didn't mind the hard going so much, but he was losing hogs, careful as he and the boys were. Every mile or so a hog would grunt and lie down, and when that happened there was just no getting it up again. And, watch as they would, groups of two or four or five would stray and vanish into the white wilderness of snow. Losing those hogs was what worried Ike the most, for hogs were money, and it took money to buy land.

A man and two boys, five hundred head of half-wild hogs, eighteen inches of snow at noon of the second day out and no road that you could find. The going was just plain, old-fashioned, undecorated hell.

Where is the figure of the typical frontiersman, the romantic hero of the great Western saga? Ike Frink, a lard barrel of a man in a faded greatcoat and hog-manured boots, driving a thousand dollars' worth of pork to market and cussing hell out of the weather? It must have been, for Ike was there. Twenty years later he owned more black, rich farmland than any other one man in the United States, without exception, and every foot of it was paid for.

But they literally outwalked the storm. Six days later they drove the hogs into Galena. The going was plenty bad all the way, but it had gotten better. Most of the snow had fallen in Dane County, and at the mines there was less than six inches. They lost a few over two hundred head of hogs and walked most of the meat off the rest, but they got them there. Out of years of driving hogs to market that was, with one exception, the biggest loss they would ever have.

Ike bought each of the boys a new pair of boots and gave them a dollar apiece, with instructions not to spend the money in hell raising.

III

At Simon Hawley's tavern in Springfield the price of supper, lodging and breakfast was three bits. If you wanted dinner at noon that was one bit extra. The two men who became Hawley's semipermanent guests on the 30th of December tried to talk him out of a flat weekly rate, but Simon wouldn't talk. For the visitors, Jonathan Hawk and Carl Mizner, had early let it be known that they were on official business for the state of Illinois—to establish their social standing, as it were—and Simon saw no reason why he shouldn't make his next year's taxes off them. After all, the state was paying the bill, and it had more money than he did, hard up as it was claimed to be.

Of course when the two visitors landed from the Galena-bound stage, they hadn't expected to stay more than a couple of days, or at most until the staging got better. The stage driver was either dead game or a fool, and drove on. He got fifteen miles farther, pulled in at a settler's cabin and stayed there two weeks. It took him three days more to get the outfit back to Springfield. And at that the snow wasn't as bad there as it was on up in Dane County.

There was practically nothing to do except drink Hawley's whisky and play euchre, so they'd get started right after breakfast and work steadily until about eight at night, with time out for dinner and supper, and by that time they'd all be too drunk to see the cards, so they'd call it a day and go to bed. Of course it took several days before they got really settled in the routine. For a couple of days the travelers took turns telling stories and trying to interest Hawley's fat eighteen-year-old daughter in themselves. But they didn't have any luck with her, and neither one of them cared much about the game, anyway. So after three days they got to know all of each other's best lies by heart and settled down to the liquor and euchre in earnest.

Two weeks later another stage got in from St Louis, but could go no farther. It was another two weeks before a driver would tackle the trip on farther north. There was no passenger traffic to speak of, and if the mail didn't go, well, it just didn't. Hawk and Mizner didn't leave until the 16th of February. Before long they discovered that by ganging on Hawley at the euchre table they could easily win enough to pay their whisky bill without arousing Hawley's suspicions, and since the state was paying their board, they hadn't a care. They'd both seen better taverns than Hawley's by far, but they also remembered that they'd seen worse ones. Since they couldn't go any place else anyway, they made the best of what they had. And besides, they argued, how could they pick a county seat when there was still so much snow on the ground that you couldn't tell whether

[38]

what looked like a pasture was really a swamp or a young mountain? There was more than a little truth in that point of view, enough anyway to keep them at the whisky and euchre.

But they finally got started and rode up to Allin's in the stage with a serious-faced young man who said his name was Abel Green. It was bitterly cold on that seventy-mile ride, and Hawk and Mizner hospitably offered young Green the jug. But he steadfastly declined.

"Well," Hawk told him genially, "this is a free country, young man, and a man can do or don't as he pleases, but it's a damned sight better to take a drink than freeze to death."

Green still declined with thanks. "I just don't drink," he said, "though I surely have no objection to anybody doing it that wants to."

"Well, now," Mizner drawled, "that's shore nice of you. Where you from, young feller?"

"Cazenovia, New York."

"Never heard of it," said Hawk promptly, "but then that don't prove it ain't there. What you aimin' to do in this neck o' the woods? You don't look much like a farmer."

"No," Green agreed, "I'm not a farmer. I've got a stock of goods coming from Warburton and King in St Louis as soon as the weather breaks."

"Un-hunh," dubiously. "I dunno, though. This part o' the state's gettin' a little more civilized than it was—might amount to somethin' someday. Damned powerful lot o' timber hereabouts, though—take a long time to clear it all, and you can't grow anything on this blasted prairie. The Devil himself couldn't plow it with a ten-horse team."

"Oh, I expect it will take a good while to get located right," Green said.

"I understand this feller Allin's got all the store business hereabouts," Hawk told him.

"So I understand. But then you gentlemen are going to locate a new county seat. That ought to help business, hadn't it?"

"Ye-ess. Ought to be room for a couple stores, I reckon. At least when these people get some kind of a town organized."

"I figure to go easy for a year or two," Green said. "By that time a man ought to be able to see a little of what's what."

"I reckon," Hawk said, losing interest in the talk. "Hand me that jug, Carl."

On the second day from Springfield they stopped at James Allin's, and that worthy managed to find places for all of them to eat and sleep. The two commissioners conferred privately with Allin, made a somewhat perfunctory examination of the countryside, and three days later decided that the county seat should be located on the quarter-section owned by James Allin near the center of Maple Grove. The exact report was as follows:

February 24th, 1831.

We the commissioners appointed to locate a county seat in the County of Dane on the second Monday of January or within five days thereafter, owing to the severity of the weather and the great depth of the snow it was impossible for us to proceed to locate the same at the time specified by law; but as soon thereafter as practicable we proceeded to examine the situation of the county, and have located the same on the land of James Allin, near the center of Maple Grove, for which we have his obligation for a donation of twenty-two acres and a half of land, to be used for county purposes. It has further been decided that the name of the county seat be called Everton, until such time as the residents may wish to change it by legal vote.

Jonathan Hawk
Carl Mizner, comms.

Under their authority they also appointed Thomas Orendorff (a friend of Allin's) temporary assessor, though that was not set forth in their report. Since the citizens of Maple Grove now had a county and town of their own, it was no more than fair that they should pay taxes. Thus the first officer appointed in the fledgling county was the tax assessor.

Orendorff was also charged with the duty of posting election notices, so shortly at Allin's store, at Stevens' grist mill and at Granger's mill there appeared written notices to the effect that on the 6th of March an election would be held at James Allin's store. They were to elect a board of three commissioners and a sheriff. The commissioners in turn would appoint their own clerk and the county treasurer.

On election day the roads were practically impassable, but the business of government went on inexorably, and forty-two citizens showed up to vote. It was an informal affair, held in the yard at Allin's. Of course Allin was by now recognized as one of the big men of the community, and he was nominated as a commissioner but refused the honor. In the end they elected Jesse Havens, John Cheney and Timothy Hoblit commissioners, and Greenberry Larison sheriff. The board held a short caucus and appointed Isaac Baker, who was known to write a pretty fair hand, as clerk, and Thomas Orendorff as treasurer. It will be remembered that Orendorff had had some small experience in office already.

Thus the governmental machinery of Dane County became an actuality. It was a sober occasion—to begin with. But when the serious business of the day was completed, the jugs passed freely and the American custom of election day was seriously attended to. There was only one fight, but by four o'clock everybody was ready to go home and call it a big day. It *had* been a big day.

IV

On the 16th of May the commissioners met for the first time—met formally, that is. The most important business was the decision to hold an auction sale on the Fourth of July and sell, or try to sell, the land which was Allin's gift to the county. They hoped to take some cash into the treasury and perhaps raise enough money to build a courthouse. For who ever heard of a proper county seat without a courthouse?

Between the 1st of January and the 1st of March much of

the gigantic snow disappeared. But even so, when the spring thaws set in there was still an enormous amount of snow on the ground. The real thaw began on the 10th of March, and within two days Dane County took on the appearance of a minor ocean. Every ditch was a river and every creek a roaring torrent. Much of the county was middling low ground, with no man-made aids to drainage, and pasture and prairie became lakes that refused to drain away or dry up. Once more neither man nor beast could travel far except by strenuous effort and under pressure of dire necessity.

Nevertheless, certain human activities went on regardless.

Nat Britten, who was justice of the peace, looked up from his wood chopping and waited for the boy to come up to the block. While waiting Nat took a fresh chew and sat down on a chunk, grateful for almost any interruption. "Howdy, Bob," he greeted the visitor.

Bob Rutledge, a fresh-faced, well-made country boy of eighteen or nineteen, looked worried. He was muddy from head to foot and evidently had had a hard trip. He worked for his father, whose farm was four miles north of Sugar Creek, eight miles from Everton. "Howdy, Nat," he said. "I come down to see you on business."

Nat spat copiously and looked interested. "Mighty power-ful kind o' business to make a man travel in this weather," he observed.

"Well, you might say this is powerful business. I wanna get married, Nat."

"Great Lord!" Nat exploded. "You 'n her must have it bad. Cain't you hold off a spell—anyway, till it dries up a little?"

"Yeah, I reckon *we* could—but you know ol' John Weed-man."

"Sure, but you ain't marryin' him."

"No-o-o, not exactly. But he's Charity's old man, and he 'lows that if we ain't married by the twentieth o' this month he'll fill me so full o' lead I cain't marry nobody."

1831

"I thought you said you *wanted* to git married," Nat said dryly.

"Well, that's right. We been aimin' to do it right along, but what with the big snow an' one thing an' another we just didn't git to it. There ain't nobody mad except old man Weedman."

"Un-hunh." Nat nodded understandingly. "Sometimes he ain't got a lick o' sense, Bob. How long you been courtin'?"

"Since last July, when we was all over to the Little Prairie camp meetin'."

"Un-hunh. Well, it's been kind of a dull winter, at that. I guess John figgers he ought to have somethin' to bellyache about. Course, I know how it is," he added hastily.

"Do you reckon you could come up to our place on the eighteenth? That's when we figgered to have the weddin', an' all her folks 'll be there."

"I reckon I'll have to help y'all out," Nat said. "After all, I'm a public official, you might say, an' I got my duty to do. I'll be there, come hell or high water."

It wasn't so much of a duty as Nat might have intimated. For, as he had said, it had been a dull winter, and he himself welcomed anything that would vary the monotony.

On the morning of the 18th, when Nat started for the Rutledge place, he had plenty of both hell and high water. He rode Nig up past Gorman's, past Wick's place, and on to the bank of Sugar Creek. Or rather he came to where Sugar Creek had been. Now the ground was covered with water, from six inches to two feet deep, as far away as a quarter of a mile from the bed of the creek proper. The creek itself had vanished, and in its place was a slashing torrent, ten times as wide as normal. It had been raining again for two days, and the water was higher than it had been all spring, which was saying considerable.

But Nig was a good horse, and Nat had promised to officiate at the wedding. He urged Nig into the creek, and the horse tried gamely. The torrent was heavy with logs and dead limbs

[43]

and all sorts of debris, and they weren't forty feet out when a speeding six-inch log caught Nig squarely in the side of the neck. It got his wind and panicked him badly. He struggled, went under once, and Nat wisely headed him back where they'd started from. Once more they tried it, and this time Nig's legs got entangled in some submerged willows and again they had to backtrack. Altogether they tried it six times, but it was just no go. They worked their way to a little higher piece of ground where Nat could cuss, Nig could blow, and they could both rest.

Nat hated to give up. He'd promised to be there, of course, but it wasn't the promise so much as it was that he just naturally didn't like to be whipped by any two-by-four creek temporarily on a rampage. He was starting to figure new ways and means when he caught sight of someone in the timber on the other bank. It was Bob Rutledge, and he waved for Nat to come downstream a ways, where the creek was narrowest.

"Cain't yuh make it?" Bob yelled.

"I ain't yet," Nat said doggedly, "but that don't prove I cain't. I was just studyin' on it."

So for a while they studied together, but in the end they got nowhere. It appeared that Sugar Creek just wasn't being crossed that day.

"Cain't yuh put it off fer a day or two?" Nat suggested hopefully.

"No, Nat, I cain't," Bob said desperately. "Ol' John Weedman's up to the house with Charity and his rifle gun."

And it was then that Nat had an inspiration. "I tell you what," he said happily. "The law says I got to marry you in person, but that's all it says. I reckon you'd call it in person long's I was near enough to see an' hear you. How about you bringin' 'em all right down here to the crick?"

"By golly! That's the ticket. I'll be back in less 'n an hour." And with that the pushed but willing bridegroom was off through the flooded timber at a dogtrot.

He was as good as his word. In an hour the combined Weedman and Rutledge families showed up at the creek bank, the womenfolk filling a rickety buckboard and the men and boys on foot. They backed the buckboard into the creek as far as possible, and the bride and groom stood up on the tailboard, facing Nat on the south bank.

Barring the intruding waters, it was a nice setting for a wedding. The sylvan background was unmarred by the hand of man, the young couple equally uninhibited by social custom. The bride was considerably more rotund in some portions than would be considered good form, either then or now, but that was beside the point. After all, and as the prospective bridegroom had said, the snow had been deep and the water high.

So Nat began. He hoped his voice would hold out. It did, and a few minutes later he yelled in stentorian tones: "I hereby pernounce you man and wife!"

"I'll pay you soon's I kin git to town," Bob yelled.

All in all, the wedding was a conspicuous success—at least, everybody concerned seemed to think so. And who or what else mattered? It was too, incidentally, the first marriage performed in Dane County. Not the first in the vicinity of Maple Grove, but the first in Dane County as such.

v

The auction of the land which Allin had deeded to the county was scheduled to take place on the Fourth of July. Allin and a number of others, of course, had been planning for the event since the announcement of the date. Not that the actual auction date made a great deal of difference; those most directly interested had been planning long before that. In fact Allin had sold his first claim early in the fall of 1830 and then acquired the quarter-section from which he later donated the county lands. Knowing, of course, that the county land was to be sold as town lots, he had gratuitously laid off the land into lots and streets, almost but not quite exactly in the center of his quarter-section. No one objected, and the commissioners were glad to have the job done for nothing. They themselves had no funds to finance a surveying job. After all, hadn't Allin donated the land, and should he not have some say about what was to be done with it? Naturally. And as a result Allin owned, and had divided into town lots, every foot of ground surrounding the county plot. It was his land; if he wanted to fool around with it that way, it was his own business. Nobody had to buy lots, and in the opinion of the cynics about the Grove nobody would. For where would you get enough people to build a town which was big enough to cover a whole quarter-section? Why, Vandalia itself wasn't much bigger than that.

Allin persisted nevertheless. It was his land; it was practically covered with timber; it wasn't good for anything but a town unless a prodigious amount of labor were expended in clearing it; and he didn't have anything to lose except his time and the few hundred dollars he had put into the timbered quarter-section. Early in the spring he had built himself a new house and store, larger and much more pretentious than his first home, and located just beyond the county acreage. Several more houses had been built in the vicinity, but most of those who planned to live in the new town were waiting for the disposal of the county land, for obviously that plot would be the center of whatever town eventually grew.

The morning of the Fourth dawned dry and hot, and the crowd began to arrive early. The land sale had been widely advertised, and there was a general feeling in the community that this should be made a gala occasion.

As usual the crowd came afoot, ahorse, and in every known kind of vehicle. The babes in arms, the aged and decrepit, the courting couples—they were all there. Old man Leary was an early arrival and, with the aid of Pete and Cal, had set up a bar under a shade tree close to the improvised auction platform. The bar was a hand-hewn slab supported at each end by a whisky barrel. Leary dispensed the provender at the bar and took in the money, and the two boys stood watch over the spare jugs. Of course a lot of people brought their own liquor, but at that old man Leary did better than he had expected.

Allin was circulating among the different visiting groups, wearing his Sunday beaver and looking important. Cheney, Havens, Hoblit and the other county officers were holding serious parley with settlers from the farther ends of the county. Larison, the sheriff, was displaying his pistol with some prominence and occasionally admonishing a youth who appeared a little too boisterous—just to keep his hand in, as it were. Green was conspicuous in his store clothes and was moving around, getting acquainted with people he hadn't seen before. There were even a few land dealers present from Pekin and Kaskaskia, and a party of miners on their way to Galena. Men greeted neighbors they hadn't seen in months and compared notes on the big snow. Stout-thewed county boys threw up dust in impromptu wrestling matches, and by ten o'clock there had been two first-rate knockdown fights.

It started out to be a successful day, with all the get-together fervor of a camp meeting with the depressing influence of frontier religion left out.

A little after one, John Cheney mounted the auction platform and bellowed for silence. John was no orator, but he was blunt and to the point and got his thoughts off his mind without any undue delay. Now he stood there on the platform, wiping sweat from his red country face, shuffling his booted feet uncertainly, waiting for the crowd to quiet down.

"Folks," he began, "I reckon you-all are well acquainted with the reason for this get-together, and there ain't no use in me goin' into it except to say one or two things which are on my mind. Dane County is pretty young, and we're startin' from scratch, as you might say. This here sale is for the purpose of raisin' money which the county needs bad. You-all know that there ain't a single cent in the treasury, because you-all know that you ain't paid a cent in county taxes yet. Now we ain't askin' you to donate anything. We're askin' you to buy these lots as a business proposition. Everton an' Dane County is here to stay, an' whatever you pay for a lot will be cheap. Tom Orendorff will do the auctioneerin', an' Baker here will keep the record of each sale. That's all I got to say."

The crowd whooped and yelled and applauded, and Orendorff got up on the platform and prepared to do business. The crowd yelled ribald advice, shuffled expectantly and waited for Tom to get under way. He cleared his throat.

"Ladies and gents, folks, neighbors and strangers, we are offerin' here today what are prob'ly the greatest bargains in the Union's greatest state!" Much applause. "You're bein' offered an opportunity that cain't come but once, because from this day on Everton will cease to be jest a wide place in the road an' start to become one of the nation's great cities. These lots will be cheap at any price you can name. If you traded the best farm in the county for the poorest lot we offer here, your children would rise up and bless you, for their inheritance would be that much greater."

Tom was just beginning to warm up. Out at the edge of the crowd Ike Frink spat and said sneeringly: "You couldn't raise a hog on a dozen o' them grave-sized lots o' his." But Ike was to get his; he couldn't ever resist land in any form. Old man Leary scratched absent-mindedly and said: "Well, by hell, where do you reckon Tom got all that eddication?"

". . . We offer now, folks, lot number one, plot number one, of the future metropolis of the Golden West, Everton, Illinois. Come one, come all. Who'll have the honor of settin' a top price on this, the first golden egg in the overflowing basket?"

One of the speculators from Kaskaskia hooked his thumbs in his vest and grinned. "Two dollars," he said.

"Two dollars!" Tom roared. "Well, by God! Do you-all hear that? Stranger, you say those words in jest. Come, come, will you have this stranger shame you?"

"Three dollars," Ike Frink yelled.

"Four," said Allin from the edge of the platform.

So it began. Slow at first, naturally, until the crowd and Tom warmed up together. Ten minutes later lot number one went to Jesse Havens for twelve dollars. It wasn't a bad start. Tom worked like a trooper, and gradually the crowd got into the spirit of the thing.

Twelve dollars was actually the lowest price brought by any lot. All the county officers bought, and Ike Frink and Allin bought two each. Even old man Leary, carried away by the spirit of the occasion, plus other more potent spirits, acquired a piece of city property. The newcomer, Green, paid the highest price—fifty-one dollars—given for any lot. He secured a corner on the south side of the block-square plot which had been reserved for an eventual courthouse.

Long before sundown the last lot had been knocked down and the crowd had begun to drift away through the timber. By dark only Allin, Havens, Larison, Nat Britten, Green, and a few others were left at the trampled, dusty clearing.

"It went even better than I had expected," Allin said. He was pleased, and his voice showed his pleasure. "Even better than I had expected. What do you aim to do with that high-priced piece o' ground you bought, Green?"

The young New Yorker had been boarding with the Allins, and James had found him pleasant enough. Not that he *liked* him, exactly. It was just that in Green he recognized certain qualities which he respected but which he himself did not possess. Green, for example, was better educated. Further, he had an ambitious drive and a certain business sharpness which Allin lacked. Green had put off opening his store until after the auction, having had his goods held up indefinitely by the St Louis wholesalers. Allin knew that, when Green eventually opened his store, he, Allin, would be driven out of business. But Allin didn't care. Green could have it and welcome. Allin's mind was on the real-estate business.

"Well," Green said, "I had in mind building on that lot. I did pay a good price for it, but it was cheap in some ways, and it's the best location in town. Don't you think so?"

"Yes, I do," Allin admitted. "Maybe it won't always be the

best, but you've certainly got a good stand now. When do you aim to start?"

"Right away, I think. I'd like to be opened up for business by fall."

"Un-hunh. Well, that suits me fine. I reckon there's room for both of us, but I don't aim to do a lot with the store now."

"You don't mean you're going out of the mercantile business?" Green's surprise was genuine, and he couldn't keep it out of his voice.

Allin chuckled silently. This youngster was a smart one, but he didn't know everything. "I reckon I'll stick to land," Allin said. "In fact I reckon I'm in the land business whether I like it or not. I'll leave the store business to you young fellers. Never cared much about it, anyhow."

The sale had been a very real success, better in fact than the most optimistic ones had hoped for. The folk had had a gala Fourth, there had been a great sight of postponed visiting done, nobody had been more than slightly wounded, and Dane County had taken in a little over eight hundred dollars. Everton was certainly rejoicing on its way.

V I

The village grew.

The original land sale was no more than over when Allin announced that he was laying off a new subdivision. Green had built his store at the southeast corner of the empty square, as he had promised, and by September was doing the bulk of the town's mercantile business. Dr Stipp had finished a new house not far from Allin's, and on the west side of the square a man named Paist had opened a tavern where the east- and west-bound stages made more or less regular stops. A mile east of town William Goodheart was making bricks and in between times doing a few jobs of plastering in what new buildings were going up. North of the square, across the big slough, Abe Brokaw was operating a blacksmith shop, and near him

William Brewer had erected a tannery—as the town was well aware whenever the breeze was in the north.

September was a big month. The summer weather about over, most of the people who had been dropping with fever ague began to perk up and feel better. The Methodists held a successful camp meeting south of town near Randolph Grove, the Reverend Latta and the Reverend Cartwright (not yet the reverend bishop) officiating during a riotous week of preaching and general soul saving. Certain of those who loafed about Paist's tavern had lately put on a couple of horse races to while away the time, and the Reverend Latta took occasion to remark that "there is a class of people who cannot go to hell fast enough on foot, so they must get on their poor mean ponies and go to the horse race. Even professors of religion are not guiltless in this respect, but go under the pretext that they want to see such or such a man, when they know in their hearts that they want to see the race." (It was said that Sheriff Larison was a horse enthusiast.) The Reverend Cartwright had lately been smarting a little under the criticisms of certain elders in the Eastern halls of Methodism, and he informed one audience that "they represent this country as a vast waste, and the people very ignorant; but if I was going to shoot a fool, I wouldn't take aim at a Western man, but go down by the seashore and cock my fusee at the imps who live on oysters." He may have been right or wrong, but it is certain that most of Dane County's citizenry agreed with him.

In town, the county commissioners held a meeting and talked about building a courthouse. Outside of garden-variety cabins, none of them knew much about construction, and they were a little at a loss to know just how to proceed about such an important matter as a courthouse. Once more it was Green who seized opportunity's forelock. He explained to Cheney and Havens how down East it was customary to let the contracts for public buildings to someone who would do the job for a lump sum. Havens and Cheney were skeptical. They didn't think they could get anybody around Everton to do it that way. "I will," Green said, and to his surprise they took him up. Privately he admitted that he knew practically nothing about the building business. But he was sharper with figures than anyone else in town, and he knew it. He did some figuring and decided that the job couldn't possibly cost him more than two hundred dollars. So he put in a bid of $339 and they gave him a contract for "a building one story high, eighteen feet by thirty, to be finished as a comfortable dwelling house," and he had the job done by Christmas. Of course he was lucky as usual. For a week after he got the contract a carpenter and builder named Bill Dimmit wandered into town. He heard of Green's contract, and in less than five minutes' conversation he knew just how little Green knew about building. Further, he let Green know that he knew, and Green promptly hired him at considerably more than the prevailing wage rate. However, it was Green who held the contract, made the lion's share of the profit, and got credit for being an up-and-coming citizen. It was even then an old American custom. Green, in less than a year, was doing very well for himself in Everton.

CHAPTER THREE

1832

S PRING THAT YEAR wasn't as wet as the one before, though the roads—what few there were of them—were the same old mud sinks.

Dane County grew, and Everton grew with it. There were now thirteen buildings of one kind and another in the village proper, and the Methodists were talking of building themselves a church. Green had taken on a partner, his brother-in-law Robert Danly, who had come from the East during the winter. The firm was now known as Green & Danly and was doing most of the county's store business. Allin still kept store but left the running of it to his oldest boy John, while he himself fooled around with real estate. Here and there other new-comers set up in business, adding slowly to the town and making it more interesting to the farming settlers out in the county. The county itself was beginning to fill up. Not that there wasn't still plenty of room, but each week saw one or two new families settled at one or another of the groves which dotted the prairies—the prairies which most people let severely alone.

That is, they had let it alone until Joe Dawson and his three boys started throwing a rail fence around a hundred acres of bald prairie ground east of Maple Grove. Then the old-timers began to hoot and jeer. Who ever heard of working the prairie? It just naturally couldn't be done. Even if a man had all the working stock he could want—and few of them had—there wasn't a plow made which would scour under that black, heavy muck from which the prairie grass grew.

John Cheney, Wick, Ike Frink and a few others happened to corner Joe in Green's store one Saturday and promptly opened fire.

"You aimin' to raise diamond bushes on that fenced-in piece o' yours, Joe?"

Dawson was a lanky, good-natured fellow who hailed originally from Pennsylvania, and he took the jeering in good part, as though he halfway thought he had it coming. "Well, I kinda thought I might, at that," he said. "Might be a good money crop."

They grinned at each other.

"Why, great God, Joe," Ab Folsom said, "if'n you an' them boys had put all that rail-splittin' work into plain honest timber clearin' you'da had the best an' biggest place in all these parts."

"Yes," Cheney added, "how come you-all seem to prefer rail splittin' to honest clearin'? Looks mighty fishy to me."

But Dawson wouldn't be baited too far. "Oh, I dunno. It was just an idee o' mine. I been in the deep South in my day, an' I seen the crops they raise on muck land down there. Don't see why a man can't do it up here, if he could jest git her plowed once."

Cheney spat. "Ain't a plow on earth 'll work in that stuff," he observed.

"No," Dawson admitted, "I reckon there ain't, John. But that ain't no sign there won't *ever* be."

They scoffed.

"You wait an' see," Dawson insisted. "Some smart Yankee 'll come along with a plow that 'll do it, an' when that day comes I'll raise me the biggest damn corn crop in this or any other state."

1832

He was right. Except that they didn't have to wait for a smart Yankee.

Again they laughed and passed more or less ribald remarks. All but Ike Frink. Ike leaned against a salt barrel and took a fresh chew. He wondered. If Dawson should happen to be right, what a crop a man could grow on that land! He made a mental note in the filing cabinet which served him as a brain.

The talk drifted to other channels.

"Powerful lot o' talk about Black Hawk an' them pesky Injins o' his," someone said. "Maybe he aims to git himself into a real mess o' trouble."

"If he does start trouble he'll shore git the livin' hell kicked out'n him," Folsom bragged. "Why, he'd be a bigger fool 'n anybody thinks he is to start a warpath in this state."

"I'm not so sure," Cheney said soberly. He'd heard more correct rumors, perhaps, than most of them had. "There's them that think he aims to start a sure-'nough war. And not that he ain't got cause. Course," he added hastily, "we've all got to stick together an' protect our own natural rights."

"It's a long ways to the Rock River," Dawson said. "Not much chance of any fightin' gettin' done hereabouts."

"That's so. But don't you fergit there's still a couple hundred Kickapoos up around the north end of the county. They're peaceful enough now; but let real trouble start, an' see whose side they're on."

"Old man Bartholomew from up Money Creek way was over an' talked to Little Bear the other day," Dawson put in, "an' Little Bear told him they didn't want no trouble."

"Yuh cain't trust an Injin no farther 'n you kin throw a bull by the tail," Folsom said.

"Maybe not. But Bartholomew said that he thought Little Bear was honest enough in his intentions. An' he ought to know more 'n most—he's fit Injins ever since he was big enough to tote a rifle gun."

And again the talk drifted to other things.

As for the Indian talk, all of them were partly right and partly wrong. For a year now Black Hawk had been more or less at odds with the whites, and with all the cause in the world. He and his people had been bilked, cheated, lied to and generally trampled on by the whites, from the White Father in Washington to the meanest squatter who had invaded the Rock River Valley, and Black Hawk, for all that he was a forbearing and intelligent savage, had about reached the end of diplomacy. Not that the average Illinoisan cared about these things. He didn't. He regarded the rights of the Indians in a little less than the way a Georgia planter viewed the rights of his slaves. That is, in the last analysis these "rights" didn't exist. The average Illinoisan could not possibly see that the Indians had any title whatever to the lands which had been home to the tribes for countless years. It is true that the whites occasionally "bought" land from the Indians, but it was done simply as the easiest way to avoid trouble and always as a lordly concession on the part of the invaders. Further, there is no record of a white man ever getting the short end of a land deal with an Indian.

In this particular case it was true that Black Hawk's people broke a treaty. But it was also a treaty which had been forced upon them at the point of a gun by a power which they couldn't possibly overcome or even hope to resist for long. So when the Sacs recrossed the Mississippi to the east for the last time, it was the final gesture of a people trying to take back the land that was their own. Black Hawk probably knew that it was a lost cause. But he also knew that if he stayed immediately west of the river, as the treaty stipulated, it would be only a question of time until the whites thrust a new treaty at him and forced him to move westward again.

The backward trek of the Sacs and Foxes began early in April 1832. Between six and seven hundred warriors, accompanied by their families and goods, proceeded up the Rock River as far as the Kishwaukee River junction, and there they made a temporary camp, perhaps waiting to see just what would happen when the white authority discovered they were there.

They had not committed a single overt act. The march had been as peaceful and quiet as it could possibly have been. In fact they even marred the countryside far less than the same number of whites would have done.

They didn't have long to wait.

Black Hawk had no more than crossed the Mississippi when the news was rushed to Governor Reynolds, who acted at once. He called for fifteen hundred volunteers to the state militia and demanded aid from General Atkinson, who commanded the nearest detachment of U. S. Army regulars. Atkinson was willing but in no hurry. Possibly experience had taught him the value of caution. At any rate, by the 27th of April eighteen hundred volunteers, under the personal command of Governor Reynolds, and a detachment of regulars were moving slowly toward the Rock River and Black Hawk.

II

The crowd of men and boys milled about restlessly in the dusty courthouse yard. The day was warm for April, and the jugs which passed freely added to the warmth of the occasion. The freer spirits in the crowd yelled hilariously and generally damned all no-account Indians. There were a few scuffling matches going on and much ribald laughter, but at the open door of the log courthouse a little knot of men conferred earnestly. Then John Cheney stood up and spoke to the crowd. Standing next to Cheney was a stranger, an aide from the adjutant general's office. "Shut up!" someone shouted from the edge of the mob. "Let's hear what John's got to say."

Cheney cleared his throat. "We finally got the vote counted," he announced, "an' here it is."

"Who's captain?" shouted a country youth.

"Jest hold your horses," John said calmly. "I'm givin' it to you fast as I can. First, Merrit Covel is elected captain."

They cheered wildly. Covel, a well-set-up young fellow of thirty or so, grinned a little self-consciously as men shouted in his ears and slammed him on the back. He had lived in the county only about a year and hadn't really expected the captaincy, especially with Green and several others wanting it. He let the mob yell itself out and then said: "Be quiet, all of you. Let John finish readin' the rest of the names!"

Again they listened, and Cheney read from the paper in his hand: "First Lieutenant, Abel Green!" More cheers, with Green looking pleased enough. "Second Lieutenant, Moses Baldwin. Sergeants, Bailey Coffee, Charley Gates, David Simmons, Ike Murphy. Corporals, Charley Vezay, Henry Miller, Reuben Dodson, Jim Durley. That's all, except for Captain Haley here. I reckon you all know who he is. He'll give the oath whenever he's ready."

Haley conferred for a moment with Covel, then formed the embryo soldiers into two wavy lines across the yard, called the roll of the company, and administered the oath.

A moment later the mob of country boys and farmers were officially members of the armed forces of the state of Illinois and the United States.

Covel addressed them briefly and a bit nervously: "I've got my orders from Captain Haley here. We're to join the command of Major Stillman, which is leaving Peoria tomorrow, same as we leave here. We'll meet his troop somewhere north of the Mackinaw late tomorrow and be under his orders from there on out. We march from here at six in the morning. Be on hand with your equipment promptly at five-thirty." He hesitated. Then, a little awkwardly: "Company, dismissed!" He thought that was the correct command. At any rate it got results.

It was late afternoon. The company whooped and scattered, to say good-by to families, to rustle equipment, and to make the most of this last evening before starting on what looked like a fine lark.

Green shortly had Captains Haley and Covel in serious discussion. It appeared that Haley had the authority to order needed supplies, and soon afterward the supply wagon pulled up in front of the Green & Danly establishment, where it loaded all the ammunition, bacon, coffee and whisky that the firm had in stock. Eight hundred dollars' worth of supplies—60 per cent profit. Green had collected his pay in advance.

It was a scraggly-looking crew that answered roll call that first morning. Dressed in buckskin, blue jeans cloth, linsey-woolsey, wearing everything in headgear from coonskin caps to wool hats and a few scattered beavers and shakos. They were armed with pistols, rifles, buffalo guns, squirrel guns, shotguns, dirks, and even a couple of rusty sabers left as souvenirs of the War of 1812. Three stalwarts hadn't been able to lay hands on any firearms, and the horseflesh was as weird an assortment as ever got together in one place in the West.

But they were willing, and promptly at six the ragged lines formed some semblance of a cavalry troop and moved out of town at a trot. (For some of the plow horses present a trot was a real effort.) It was a beautifully cool and still spring morning, and before long most of the whisky heads wore off.

Joe Draper leaned over and spoke to young George Wiley: "I hope it ain't all over 'fore we git up there."

"I reckon it won't be," Wiley said. "They say the governor's waitin' for all the troops to git there to once before they start any of the real fightin'."

That's the way most of them felt—they hoped it wouldn't be over before they got there.

They joined Major Stillman's somewhat larger command in midafternoon and camped for the night, joy once more reigning unconfined about the fires.

In the morning the column, its ranks more ragged and amateurish-looking than ever, moved on towards Dixon, where they were to wait for the main body of volunteers under Governor Reynolds and General Whiteside. At Dixon all was serenely peaceful, with no signs of either Indians or soldiery. But the column had its orders: it was to wait at Dixon.

That was on the 2nd of May.

They waited three impatient days before the first companies from the main army began to trickle slowly into Dixon's Ferry.

The boys from Peoria and Dane counties cheered. Surely there would be some action now. If they didn't hurry, the Indians would be back across the Mississippi and out of their reach. But by the time the bulk of the troops were encamped, there were a hundred rumors rampant. They were to stay indefinitely at Dixon. They were not to move against the Indians until Atkinson's regulars put in an appearance. They were not going to fight at all. A peaceful settlement was to be made.

The camp was torn by dissension. There was little or no discipline; whisky was a regular ration, and almost continual fighting and bickering was the order of the day. The junior officers were young and, what was worse, had almost no control over their men. As how should they have? The men had elected them officers, to begin with, largely because they happened to be popular or prominent citizens. Having made these particular men officers, the troops considered that honor enough and saw no reason why they should obey every petty order. And the officers, from General Whiteside down, for the most part felt the same way. The men were their friends and neighbors, among whom they lived and did business. They were content to leave well enough alone, for when this was over they would all have to go back to the old routine at home, and the situation wasn't grave enough to provoke wholesale antagonism.

Ten days went by and the situation appeared to get no better. It was now known of course that they were actually waiting for Atkinson's troops. Governor Reynolds had firmly decided that no fighting whatever would be done without the strong, seasoned backing of the regulars.

As a matter of sober fact, no one at Dixon knew exactly where Black Hawk's forces were. Again there were all sorts of rumors, but not a man could say with certainty that there was any given number of Indians at any particular spot.

1832

III

At noon on the 13th a group of officers stood under the big shade tree outside Governor Reynolds' headquarters and argued earnestly. In the group were the governor, General Whiteside, a couple of their junior aides, Majors Bailey and Stillman, Captain Eades of the Peoria contingent, Captain Covel, and Lieutenant Green.

The governor glowered at his cigar and spat angrily. "They're your own men, Major Stillman!" he snapped. "You're in command. It's your business to control them."

"I know," Stillman said apologetically. "But you know the general situation here in camp as well as I do. The men are restless. They either want to fight or go home. Isn't that true, Captain Covel?"

"Yes, sir," Covel answered unhappily. "It seems to me that they've about reached the point where there's nothing much we can do."

"This is supposed to be a military camp," the governor barked.

"I realize that," Stillman said, "but, begging your pardon, it's not been run that way so far, and it's too late to start now."

Reynolds glared at Whiteside, who looked off into the forested distance and said nothing.

"Your troops, Major Stillman, have been more unruly than any other contingent in camp," Reynolds observed, perhaps a little beside the point. No one knew that better than Stillman.

"They've been in camp longer than any other group," Stillman said angrily. "You must remember that. Another thing. I think I'm right in saying that every officer here sympathizes with your point of view." He looked around, and all of them nodded. "But," he went on, "we're here now because we want to do something before it's too late. You realize that if one group pulls out it will be only a matter of time before the rest follow."

Reynolds chewed his cigar and said nothing. He knew.

"Well, if these men desert, or start to desert, are we to arrest them? Or try to arrest them?" Stillman waited a moment before he went on: "I said attempt, for that's what it would amount to. If desertion once started there'd be absolutely nothing we could do about it. I think you all know that."

The governor sighed. "And you think action of some kind would stop this?"

"I do. They are either going to fight or go home. We must make our choice now if we expect to keep any sort of control."

"Very well, then," Reynolds said, as though having come to a decision. "It is reported this morning that there are Indians in force near the head of Old Man's Creek. You are familiar with the place, Major?"

"In general, yes."

"All right. Then suppose you take your two battalions up there on a scouting expedition. Will that do?"

"Yes, sir. Anything will do that looks like action."

"Whiteside," the governor said, "you write Major Stillman an order covering that and I'll sign it."

A few moments later the governor handed Stillman an order which directed him to proceed to the vicinity of Old Man's Creek and "coerce into submission" any or all hostile Indians he might find there.

"I'm doing this thing strictly against my better judgment, Stillman," the governor said. "Your troops are green. So are all of them, and that's why I've wanted to wait. You understand that when I hand you this signed order, the responsibility for what may happen becomes altogether mine. I can't avoid it. But that's by the by. I accept the responsibility; I can't do otherwise. However, I do feel that if you and your officers had had your men properly in hand this wouldn't have happened. Do you understand that?"

"Yes, sir, I do," Stillman said unhappily. Eades' lip curled in a silent sneer at the governor's foolish qualms. Bailey, Covel and the rest said nothing. There was nothing more to be said.

An hour later the two battalions whooped their way jubilantly out of camp, hooting at the rest of the troops who watched them go. "We're goin' after some real Injins," they jeered. "You'll get calluses on your tails if you stay here an' wait for Reynolds to make up his mind an' them beef-chawin' reg'lars to come crawlin' up here on their bellies from Prophetstown."

The stay-at-homes had little to say. But they all felt a little better. Of course none of them knew what had taken place at that noon conference, but obviously *some* of them were at last going into action. Any kind of action would be better than this loafing. Maybe their turn would come next.

The Dane County boys moved out at the rear of the column. Two of Covel's men dropped back to let their horses drink, and the rest of the troop splashed on across the river. While they waited they passed remarks with a pair of fishermen who were taking their ease on the bank.

"Where you boys from?"

"Springfield," said one of the fishermen laconically. "An' where do you-all think you're goin'?"

"To Canady—to see if there's really any Injins left in the country."

"Oh, all right. I was jest askin'. But all you fire-eaters 'll wish you'd stayed here where grub an' liquor's free."

"Maybe so," said the Dane County boy. "Say, is your captain that long, tall bird with a neck like a turkey?"

"Shore—an' what about it?"

"Oh, nuthin'. We was jest wonderin'. Some of the boys was sayin' awhile back that he was shorely the ugliest man in this army. What's his name?"

"Name of Abe Lincoln. One of the finest in all Sangamon County."

"Oh, shore. Well, so long."

"So long, Napoleon. Bring us a mess o' scalps fer breakfast if you're back in time."

The two battalions camped ten miles out that night and were on the march again at dawn. Noon found them not far from the head of Old Man's Creek, where Indians were alleged to have been seen. Stillman had out an advance guard of five men —five men who were supposed to recognize Indians if they saw them.

The column had just finished its noon meal when one of the scouts came tearing back, his horse in a lather and himself yelling at the top of his lungs: "Injins! Injins! Hundreds of 'em! Where in hell's Stillman?"

"Here, man," the major called. "Here, calm down. Talk some sense so we can understand. Now, where are these Indians and how many of them are there?"

"Me and Simmons were together on the other side of the crick, about two miles up. We saw three Injins together, walkin' towards us, an' jest as we reined up Simmons seen two more lookin' out of some brush about a hundred feet to one side of them three——"

Already the column was in tangled confusion. Men had dashed for their horses at the scout's first yell of "Injins!" The yell had been the spark in the powder barrel of inexperience. Men shouted at each other and tried to control horses frightened at the sudden excitement. Officers tried vainly to restore some kind of order. They might just as well have commanded the wind. A moment later another scout rode in and reported to Stillman. This man too had seen five Indians. Whether they were the same five, he couldn't say.

But only one fact was obvious: there *were* Indians near at hand. And surely the five who had been seen were not just out for a lark; they must be scouts for a larger body, perhaps even for Black Hawk's entire force. Who knew?

Almost to a man the two battalions had felt that scalp-tingling threat of lurking, unknown danger, and now the greenness was beginning to show.

In ten minutes or so the officers got over the idea that the column was to form and advance toward the place where the

Indians were last seen. Instantly loose equipment was cast aside. Some fool suggested that the supply wagons would only be in the way now, and there was a concentrated rush for the wagons. Ammunition was grabbed by the handful and in another moment the whisky barrels were broken in. Men threw away water and filled their canteens with liquor. Even coffee pots and powder horns were filled with whisky, and men raced up and down the lines offering each other drinks. It was an opéra-bouffe scene, outlandish, a travesty upon Indian warfare and all military tactics.

The column, if it could be called such, advanced. It moved on at a walk, a trot and an occasional gallop, spread out over an area fifty yards wide and two hundred long, and now altogether without an advance guard.

Then the three Indians were sighted, not far from where they had been last reported, on the same side of the Creek as the militia. They were armed, of course, and one of them carried a bit of what looked like white rag. On the opposite side of the Creek there were five more Indians, in plain sight but moving cautiously. Stillman threw up his hand and tried to halt the column. But it was a useless gesture.

The three Indians stood stock still, huddled together, mingled looks of fear and apprehension on their faces. In a moment they were surrounded by horsemen. One of the Indians was trying to make himself heard above the infernal din around him.

"Stand back, you blasted fools!" Stillman yelled angrily. "Let me handle this!"

Again he might as well have shouted at the wind.

Then a drunken trooper spurred his horse into the close-packed mob, and the savage with the white rag was knocked to the ground. The white rag was instantly trampled into nothing by a dozen hooves, and someone yelled, "Get those guns!" The weapons were snatched from the hands of the two Indians still on their feet. Stillman cursed like a demon and tried to make himself heard. Then from somewhere in the rear a rifle cracked sharply, and on the other side of the Creek an Indian slumped slowly to the ground. Instantly the other four vanished.

Stillman groaned and talked hurriedly to what few officers he could reach. It was reported that Black Hawk had six hundred warriors. He, Stillman, had a matter of 275 men in his two tangled and confused battalions. This might mean annihilation. Well, they'd wanted action, Stillman thought grimly. Now they were going to get it.

In some mad manner they got most of the men across the stream and started them advancing on the rising ground beyond. There the ground rose sharply for perhaps a hundred feet and then rolled away in grassy meadow for a half-mile to the timber beyond.

Ten minutes later the first Indians rode out of that timber, and Stillman ordered the men to fire at will and hold their ground. There was a sudden ragged volley from the advancing Indians, and Stillman could almost feel the line wilt on either side of him. He set his teeth. Spasmodic firing broke out to his right and left, and a lone Indian slipped from his horse and lay quietly in the high grass.

They came on steadily at first, then with a rush. Stillman and Covel crouched together, watching a little bewilderedly. They looked at each other. "What do you make of it?" the major asked in a low voice.

"Forty to fifty at the most," Covel answered.

"So do I. There's something awful damned wrong here." Then, shouting: "Hold your ground, men! We've got 'em outnumbered five to one!"

He could have been right or wrong, but he was too late. The panic was on, and it swept the ragged ranks like wildfire. A couple of men broke for the Creek, and in an instant ten more followed. A moment later the whole force was retreating in a hysterical, yelling mob. Stillman, Eades, Covel and a few others cursed and tried frantically to rally them, but it was no use.

Eades shouted an order to form up at the Creek bank, and Covel, confused momentarily, shouted another order to cross and form on the other side. A few hardy souls obeyed Eades, a few Covel, and the balance rode in every direction except toward the advancing savages.

Now the Indians had spread out, and a few had already crossed the Creek above and below the retreating militiamen, flanking them on both sides. And still at no time were there more than fifty Indians in sight.

The three prisoners, tied to a tree and forgotten until now, began yelling, and their comrades' fire became heavier, though not much more damaging. Considering the fine targets Stillman's mob had presented, the Indians had been remarkably poor shots —almost as bad as the militia—and so far had killed only six men and wounded ten more.

Stillman saw that the jig was up, that there was nothing more to be done with this thoroughly scared, hysterical mob of farmers, so, just to keep the record straight, he gave a final order to retreat.

Doughty militiamen dashed madly through the now darkening timber, three fourths of them panic-stricken and running, supposedly, for their very lives, and the balance running because alone they were not enough to fight successfully. It was every man strictly for himself, and leading the van was Lieutenant Green of the First Company, Dane County.

Until the first shot was fired at Stillman's Run, not a single overt act had been committed by either side. In a few short hours an armed force of militia had ignored and trampled a flag of truce, started a war that could and should have been avoided, and been overwhelmingly defeated by a force of Indians one seventh their number. So reads the record of that afternoon.

Black Hawk's scouts had reported the arrival of Stillman's force directly to Black Hawk, who had about forty men with him on what was merely a scouting trip. And Black Hawk, knowing what he was up against—not with Stillman especially but with the entire force of the state opposing him—had already decided to capitulate and take his people back across the Missis-

sippi. Stillman's was the first force he had encountered, and he
had accordingly sent forward a flag of truce with a request for
a parley. He wished to open negotiations for a truce and be
assured by Governor Reynolds that there would be no difficulty
in recrossing the Mississippi. The five other braves he had sent
forward to observe the reception of the flag bearers. They saw,
and four of them returned to tell the tale to Black Hawk. In an
instant Black Hawk was in a towering rage—as why should
he not be?—and the Black Hawk War was begun.

On the morning of the 15th, ten men from the First Company,
Dane County, reported themselves present at Camp Dixon.
Among them were Captain Covel, Corporal Dodson, and Privates
Brown, Dimmit, McCullough, Davenport and Oatman. Two
other privates, Draper and Isham, had been left dead at Stillman's Run. The rest never did report for duty as members of
the First Company, either at Dixon or elsewhere. They were
scattered all the way from Stillman's Run to Everton, and, to
the last man, they were heading south. On the muster roll at
Camp Dixon they were put down as "absent without leave," but
only temporarily. For the militia, then as ever, was officered by
men who were politicians first and officers last, and eventually,
casually, and without explanatory remarks, the A.W.O.L. was
changed to "absent *with* leave."

The ragged remnants of Stillman's two battalions having
returned with their tale of disaster, and Atkinson's regulars
having finally arrived that morning, the governor paraded the
entire force of Camp Dixon that afternoon. Reynolds chose the
occasion to deliver some choicely bitter words concerning the defeat of Stillman in particular and of the whole Black Hawk War
in general.

It was a strange assembly of military. Probably not even
General Washington, at any given time during the Revolution,
could have found upon his muster rolls as many names that were
to become bywords in American history. On the one side the
unkempt, straggling settler-soldiers of Whiteside's militia, awk-

ward, unruly, altogether independent, not much caring what Reynolds might have to say to them or of them; on the other side, Atkinson's regulars, slouchy but alert, casual, hard-bitten, efficient, most of them with actual campaign experience of some kind.

At the moment, lost in the wavy ranks of the militia, these: Captain Abraham Lincoln, an empty place in the world's hall of fame already awaiting him; Private Edward Baker, later senator from Oregon, to be killed at Balls Bluff, wearing the uniform of a Union colonel; John Stuart, private and great Illinoisan, in whose office Lincoln studied Blackstone and the revised statutes; Private William McCullough, to be famed as the one-armed lieutenant colonel of the Fourth Illinois Cavalry; and many another of lesser renown.

Among the regular ranks, these: Lieutenant Albert Sidney Johnston, whose name will be known as long as Shiloh is remembered; Colonel Zachary Taylor, second in command, to be President as the result of the Mexican War; Captain Harney, whom that same Mexican War made a general; Lieutenant Robert Anderson, later Major Anderson and national hero, commandant and defender of Fort Sumter; and, finally, Lieutenant Jefferson Davis, whose destiny the high gods were perhaps already pondering.

The rolling years awaiting them, they stood there in the hot afternoon sun and listened to Governor Reynolds' bitter words about Stillman's Run and the war which was now a reality. The night before, as an aftermath of Stillman's Run, eight whites, living at isolated and widely separated points, had been dragged from their beds and massacred. Tomorrow at dawn Camp Dixon was to be deserted and the real advance upon Black Hawk begun.

The battle of Stillman's Run ended with the mad retreat which started in late afternoon. At sundown on the following day Lieutenant Green rode up to the house of his brother-in-law in Everton. Green was the first man home, though all the fleeing members of the First Company, their speed depending upon the physical condition of their horseflesh, were not many miles behind him.

Green dismounted and sat down weakly upon the doorstep, handing the reins of the drooping horse to the thunderstruck Danly. "My God, man!" Danly was gasping. "What's happened? The others——?"

And Green—he *was* exhausted by the ride and his terror—told the story of Stillman's Run. Or rather, he told *his* story, now, with a little recovered horse sense, not forgetting a great many phrases such as "So it seemed to me" and "As near as I could tell"—the gist of the tale being that Stillman's command had been defeated, after a heroic stand, by a force of Indians numbering not less than two thousand, and that, so far as he knew, he was the lone survivor from Dane County. Of course he had already told the best parts of that story at various settlers' cabins which he had passed in the north end of the county, and as a result wild rumor was already speeding abroad: Black Hawk was racing southward with two or three thousand blood-mad warriors; the few run-down Kickapoos living north of the Mackinaw were also on the warpath and even now were planning a raid on defenseless Everton; Governor Reynolds and General Atkinson had both been killed. These were the worst imaginings; and there were a hundred more.

By midnight, of course, a few more retreating stragglers had begun to drift into Everton. Their stories differed from Green's in detail, but the general tenor was the same. Maybe that was because they had a chance to hear some of Green's harrowing account before they began telling their own. At any rate, their tales only added to the growing terror. Older men and women remembered other days and other places, when and where the Indian menace was a grim reality, and by morning whole families, especially those from the northern end of the county, came into the village. Everton took on the appearance of an armed camp.

That was the 17th of May.

Now if the accounts of the returning soldiery had been true—

and at the moment Everton had no reason to suppose they were not—there would have been reason for the strongest kind of apprehension. For on May 4th, less than a week after the First Company departed for the front, the Second Company had been raised in Everton. They moved northward at a leisurely pace and arrived at Camp Dixon just in time to hear the first accounts of Stillman's Run and then move on to bury the dead on that disgraced field. As a result, therefore, almost all the able-bodied young men of Dane County, with the exception of those from the First Company who were daily straggling into town, were in the northern part of the state. How many had been killed by the alleged southward sweep of Black Hawk, no man could say. True, no one had any facts whatever in his possession, but that made no difference.

Consternation generally prevailed. Those settlers who did not move into Everton built a blockhouse at Money Creek, near the north end of the county, and old Captain Bartholomew, far-famed as an Indian fighter, took charge. Nothing happened, of course, but men talked, worried and quit work to look to the state of their ammunition. They mounted guard, wore out the new spring turf in the timber with scouting expeditions and consumed unbelievable quantities of liquor and food.

And the situation remained the same : nothing happened. Presently the fear died down. Here and there families quietly packed up and went back where they belonged. They began to realize that the corn was past due in the ground and something had to be done about that. By the 29th of May only the most timid or the laziest refugee families were left in Everton or the Money Creek blockhouse. It may have been too that some of the returned heroes, their memories having begun to function a bit more accurately, were beginning to wonder what really had happened to those of the First Company who hadn't yet shown up. They were also beginning to wonder what *would* happen when the First and Second companies did turn up. Perhaps they quietly decided, each man for himself, that enough was enough and that there was such a thing as running it into the ground. . . .

Abe Brokaw, whose blacksmith shop stood north of the slough, the northernmost building in Everton, stepped to the door for a breath of air. He swallowed a gourdful of water and wiped sweat from his dripping face. It was hot for a May afternoon, even late May.

Then Abe looked off down the dusty track of road, and his jaw dropped. "Charley!" he yelled at his helper. "Good God Almighty, Charley, c'mere an' see what's comin' down the road!"

Charley came, and together they watched what remained of the First Company of Dane County Volunteers, followed by the Second Company, come home from the war. Their services no longer required, the two companies had been mustered out of service on the 27th of May.

The surprise of Abe and Charley had been really genuine. When some thirty-odd of the First Company had been reported seen or heard in and about Everton, it had become obvious that the carnage at Stillman's Run hadn't been quite as bad as first reported. However, Covel, Dodson, McCullough, Dimmit, and the others who returned to Camp Dixon had not put in an appearance at Everton. Their absence at least gave some credence to the report that they had been massacred. But now Abe and Charley stood in the shop door and watched them ride by in the flesh.

"Howdy, Covel. Howdy, Dimmit."

"Hi, Abe. Hi, Charley."

The cavalcade, dusty and tired-looking, splashed on across the slough and up Main Street toward the courthouse square. Whether it was altogether prearranged or not is immaterial. Captain Covel, heading the two troops as senior officer, marched the dusty column up to the store of Green & Danly and gave the order to halt. The men sat their horses silently, waiting. Just what had happened to the rest of the First Company, none of them knew exactly. But they too had heard rumors, and two things they did know: that the remainder had not reported for duty and that only two of them had been killed at the Run. They could guess the rest.

[72]

1832

It was an odd scene. A still, hot afternoon in late May. Fifty-six dusty, silent militiamen waiting for—they didn't know exactly what. It had all been left up to Covel. Tom Orendorff came out of the courthouse and started toward Green's. Then Danly came out on the low porch of the store and spoke to Covel. "Why, hello, Covel. Say! By God, I'm glad to see you boys. Why——"

"Howdy, Danly," Covel said evenly. "Is Green here?"

"Why, er—yes. He's busy right now——"

Ominous mutters from behind Covel.

"—but of course I'll call him."

Then Green came out and faced them. If he was in the least nervous he didn't show it. He was on his home grounds now and, to their disadvantage, so were most of the men before him. Most of them owed him money; he knew all about them. He said, "Howdy, Covel. Something maybe you wanted to say to me?"

"Just a word or two, *Lieutenant* Green," said Covel, with all the hatred in his voice that he could ever manage to get there. He touched a saddlebag. "We stopped off here to tell *you*, because you were a *lieutenant*, and all the other yaller skunks that showed their tails at Stillman's Run, jest how low-down yaller these men know you-all are."

Green's lips set, and he went a little white, a very little. "Is that all?" he asked.

"No, not quite," Covel said. "Here in this bag I've got the official discharge of the First Company. And if it's any comfort to you, you-all got an honorable discharge, the same as these men here that *weren't* yaller skunks an' rattlesnakes. I'll see that the notice is pasted up on the courthouse, so all of you can see how skunks, if they're good Democrats, git served the same as good men!" He turned to the silent, waiting troopers. His voice snapped in the quiet: "Company, dismissed!"

So—almost—ended the Black Hawk War for Dane County.

Practically everyone in Everton knew Agnes Dooley. Practically everyone knew all the Dooley family as well—all thirteen of them. They were all a little queer, but Agnes, who was twenty-two and the eldest of the brood, was the queerest of them all. It seemed that when God had come to Agnes He had apparently forgotten that a human being should have at least *some* brains, and concentrated on the rest of her. She had the face of an Irish angel and a body that was as near perfection as human flesh ever is. Males of all ages, newly come to Everton, would take one startled first look at her and then wonder if their eyes were deceiving them. Then, when they got close enough to see her eyes, the bottom would fall suddenly out of their normal desires. For Agnes' eyes were blank as a stone wall, and her talk seldom got beyond a childish babble. More than one youth had looked upon Agnes with hot eyes and itching hands, wondering what it would be like, but she was still virginally immaculate. Something, something none of them could understand exactly, had always held the boys back at the last moment.

On this May day Agnes had been sent on an errand by her mother. She was to go five miles out on the Money Creek road and get a piece of linsey-woolsey Mrs Wick had promised Mrs Dooley. She got to the Wick place all right, stayed for dinner, and started back toward town about two in the afternoon. She had come about halfway back when, at a sudden whim, she left the road and wandered aimlessly off into the timber. In a little while she had gathered a handful of wildflowers, and soon her hand was so full that she dropped more than she saved each time she bent to pick more. That didn't bother Agnes in the least. She'd keep picking them until some vague wisp of thought moved her off on another tack.

It was there that Agnes' virginal luck quit her; her particular benevolent Providence momentarily turned its back.

Ed Garvey, late private in the Dane County Volunteers, took a short cut home from the brief mustering-out ceremonies at the Everton courthouse. (Ed was a short, red-faced chunk of a man. His front teeth were missing as the result of some forgotten frontier brawl, and when he opened his mouth it looked

1832

like the yawning entrance to some tobacco-flooded cavern. Ed was forty and had had eight children by his slatternly, worn-out wife, who weighed ninety-six pounds and still did the work of two men around the Garvey place. Ed really hadn't had much fun at home for quite a spell.) He came out of the timber into a little glade and saw Agnes bent over there in the lush grass, her back toward him. She hadn't heard him coming, and he sat there on his mule for a moment, watching her and suddenly wondering if she were really alone so far from the road. He was conscious of the greasy feel of the bridle reins in his hands and of the sudden excited chattering of a gray squirrel. He got off the mule and walked toward the stooping girl.

Not until then was she aware of him. She stood up and turned to face him, grinning that vacant grin that she used on all occasions and babbling at him incoherently.

Ed ran his tongue over his dry lips and looked at her. God, she was sure a pippin! If only she wasn't so completely crazy . . . But he brushed that thought aside. It was lucky, for him, that she was.

"Hello there, Agnes," he said, and tethered the mule to a handy bush.

She grinned again and held up the flowers, showing them with the air of a triumphant child. She babbled gleefully.

"Shore, they're purty," Ed said, stroking her arm and thinking of anything but the bedraggled flowers. . . .

It was even easier than he had thought it would be. For Agnes a man, like this, was altogether a new experience, and if Ed was short on looks he certainly made up for it in energy and enthusiasm. And if Agnes' brain was only about 20 per cent normal there was nothing whatever wrong with her from the neck down. As a result they both enjoyed themselves thoroughly and were completely unworried by thoughts of the spiritual and esthetic nuances of the sexual act. Certainly they were hardly what would be called an ideal couple, and they were no compliment to the sylvan setting. But then, when is life ever ideal?

Presently he led her back to the road, looked carefully to see

[75]

if anyone was about, then gave her an awkward pat on the shoulder and headed her toward Everton. "It's gittin' late," he said. "You'd better git on home."

She went off down the road obediently, and he watched her for a moment before he headed the mule back into the timber. Shore be funny, he thought, if it took. He grinned covertly at the thought.

IV

By and large, a town probably deserves the kind of citizenry it gets—and breeds. In the most infant years of its existence, Everton was no exception to the average town of its place and time. If most of its citizens were not saints in morals or manners, then neither were they criminals defying the laws of God and man. Because the town was in the second phase of its frontier state, its people were inclined to be industrious and were law-abiding because there were few laws to break and they hadn't much time for those. But there were no geniuses among them. The town had nothing to attract any such from the outside world, and obviously hadn't had time to bear any of its own.

But the year 1832 brought Everton its first real luck in that respect: Jesse Fell.

Fell was born of Quaker parents in Chester County, Pennsylvania, in 1808. He got what education was available in the boarding schools of the neighborhood, mostly, be it said, through his own efforts, for his father felt unable to pay the boy's way. In 1828, when he was just turned twenty, he set out for the West. At Pittsburgh he fell in with one Reese, who set him up as a traveling book agent, peddling Malte Brun's *Geography*, Rollin's *Ancient History* and the works of Josephus. With this means of (so he thought) defraying expenses, he boarded a steamer for Wheeling. On board he met a certain Mr Howell, who published a vagrant liberal sheet called the *Eclectic Observer*, a journal of protest against slavery, capital punishment, and any other worldly ills that might come to the editor's attention. Howell took a liking to the earnest young Quaker, and in

Wheeling, a few days later, his enthusiasm knew no bounds when Fell turned out a ringing piece titled "The Abolition of Imprisonment for Debt." But Fell declined even the lure of an assistant editorship. His eyes were on the West.

A few weeks later found him on the National Road, in central Ohio. But even Fell's natural eloquence failed to put over Rollin and Josephus with people engaged in defeating a wilderness. An illness took his small savings and, discouraged for the first time in his life, he turned back to Wheeling and spent the winter in Howell's office, learning the rudiments of the literary trade and the printing business.

Spring found him peddling his books in Ohio again, and this time doing a bit better.

He was learning something of the world now, and he saw that book-agenting would get him nowhere. He felt that he must learn a profession if he was to get what he wanted from the world. And luck rode with him. In Steubenville he approached a chap of about his own age, hoping to make a sale. In the course of the talk it came out that the young man was far too poor to buy books, but that he could and would introduce Fell to the firm where he was studying the law.

Fell was delighted; and there was a place for one more student with Stokely & Marsh.

Two years later, in October 1832, Jesse Fell was admitted to the Ohio bar, and two days later again set out for Illinois. On the day he entered the state, Henry Clay, for whom Fell had campaigned with Stokely and a young Steubenville friend named Edward M. Stanton, was defeated by Jackson. Armed with letters from Stokely, Fell visited the legal lights of Danville, Decatur and Springfield, asking their advice concerning a likely place to settle and build a practice.

Near sunset of a warm day in late November, a youth carrying a carpetbag and a stout stick, trudged up a dusty street in Springfield. It was the supper hour, and almost no one was about. The first person Fell saw was a friendly-appearing man of early middle age, sitting quietly upon the front step of his house. The younger man stopped, and the sitter grinned at him. "Anything I can do for you, son?" he asked affably.

"Yes, sir. Could you direct me to John Stuart's house?"

The other stood up and stretched.

"I," he said, "am John Todd Stuart, and how can I be of service to you?"

Stuart confirmed Fell's hearsay about the infant village of Everton. And, yes, it seemed to be a likely enough place, and so far as Stuart knew there was as yet no lawyer there.

Fell stayed the night with the Stuarts and the next day went on to New Salem, where he was regaled with stories of the now finished Black Hawk War. And it was there that he first heard the name, Abraham Lincoln.

Farther up the road, near Delavan, he stopped at the home of one William Brown, who was the big man of the community, and some of whose family Fell had known in Pennsylvania. Once more he was welcomed cordially. Brown offered him a job teaching a sort of semiprivate school for the winter. The students would be the Brown children and those of a few favored neighbors. Fell agreed. But first he must acquaint himself with Everton and Everton with him. Winter was closing down; there would be little activity until spring; but he wanted to get himself known.

He stayed two days in Everton, talked with Allin, Green, Dimmit and others. One and all they liked him and urged him to stay on. This he would not do, but promised to return with the coming of spring.

When Fell made a promise he kept it. And so was Everton in luck when Fell promised to come back to stay.

v

Dr Robert Baxter sat before his fire, his head dropped a little forward upon his breast, his eyes half closed, watching the flames. It was hot so near the fire, but when he moved far enough away to be momentarily comfortable he was soon cold.

Even so, since he had had Dimmit plaster the cabin it was a little more comfortable than it had been the year before. Nowadays, he reflected, he got cold more easily than he once did. Well, why not? At sixty-five what else could he expect? In Philadelphia today there would be many pleasant festivities. . . . But no matter; best not to think too much of that. Philadelphia was a long way off—farther, perhaps, than he would ever go again.

He listened for a moment to the sound of Emma's activities in the other room. She was finishing the dinner things, and again in memory he tasted the pig Jim Allin had given them for the Christmas dinner. It had been good pig. He looked thoughtfully at the bottle standing on the mantel, shrugged, and put two inches of the whisky into his pewter mug. Accustomed to it as he was, the liquor burned his throat and made him blink. He stood in the doorway for a moment, getting a breath of fresh air and looking out into the white stillness. Allin's house, Green's store, the little courthouse—he could see them all from where he stood. Again he sighed.

Very carefully he prepared a fresh quill and sat down at the table to make the regular weekly entry in his journal. Usually he did that on Sundays. But today he felt in the proper mood to do it, and Sunday was but a day off anyway. Perhaps he wouldn't have time to do it then. Slowly but steadily, in his neat, very legible script, he began to write:

"December 25th, 1832. A fine, quiet day, snow on the ground but weather not too cold. For dinner a fine young pig given me and Emma by James Allin, our good neighbor. No calls today, thank God, though the day is not over yet. How strangely quiet it is this day. It always is, of course, but today the stillness seems almost oppressive. Not even the occasional beat of a horse's hoof or the clang of Brokaw's hammers.

"This year almost finished. Only another week. Almost four years for Emma and me here in Illinois—two of those years here in Everton. Not bad years on the whole, about what could be expected in a raw near-wilderness as this country is—and will be for a long time yet, I'm afraid. Sometimes I wish I had stayed on in Philadelphia and faced the possibility of disgrace—even though I was not guilty of the crime of which I was accused. But on the whole I have no regrets except the regret of man's inhumanity to man, which is a pointless one at best. These years have been a little hard on Emma, I'm afraid, but if she regrets the course we chose, no word of complaint have I ever heard from her lips. Could ever a man ask for a better wife?"

He dipped fresh ink, but before he could begin writing again there were hoofbeats outside, and in a moment someone was banging on the door. The doctor cursed under his breath and went to let the rider in. It was Albert Hardy, a settler who lived twelve miles southwest of Everton.

"It was like this, Doc," Hardy was saying. "Me an' John was droppin' this tree, an' he was on the off side. She started to go, an' I yelled for him to git out of the way. He whirled, an' started to run, but his foot slipped in the snow an' he fell. One of the big lower branches caught him square in the chest."

"All right. I'll be ready to go in a minute. You might saddle Kate for me if you want to help hurry things along."

Hardy left, and Baxter put away his journal and gathered up his bag. In an outside pocket of his greatcoat he slipped a quart flask of whisky. He told Emma good-by and as usual reminded her that there was no telling when he'd get home.

The wind seemed fresher as they mounted and rode off. Hardy turned his face into the wind and sniffed. It was blowing from the north, against their backs as they started.

"Getting colder?" Baxter suggested.

"Sure is," Hardy answered. "Plenty colder. Must have dropped ten points anyway since I left home a couple hours ago."

And indeed it did turn colder. On top of that, snow began driving out of the north—thick, blinding snow that hid the landscape at fifty yards. It slowed them a great deal, and it was nearly dark when they finally reached the Hardy cabin.

1832

Baxter saw at a glance that there was nothing to be done for the injured man. He was already a good part of the way to Kingdom Come. The jagged branch had caught him squarely in the chest, as Hardy had said. It had missed his heart, but that didn't matter; it had smashed one lung almost completely, and already he had practically bled to death. Baxter shook his head. "A matter of an hour or so at most," he told them.

He ate supper with the Hardys and waited patiently for the man to die. It wasn't such a long wait: until about eight o'clock. The family pressed the doctor to stay the night, but he would have none of it.

"It's a hellish night out, Doc," Albert Hardy said. "Can't hardly see your hand in front of your face for the snow, and it must be 'way below zero now. You're a fool to face a night like this, if you ask me."

"No," Baxter said. "It's Christmas, and I intend to stay the night at home. Besides, somebody else might need me before the night's out."

The first mile wasn't as bad as he had expected. But Hardy had been right. It was below zero now—eighteen degrees, to be exact. The snow, however, had eased a bit. The doctor took a good long pull at the flask at about what he judged to be every quarter-mile. His innards felt pleasantly warm now. He recalled vaguely that he'd seen worse weather, though now he couldn't remember exactly where or when. At the end of four or five miles he was intolerably sleepy. He kept telling himself that he must stay awake if he expected to get home. He even tried holding to the bridle and walking beside the horse, but the snow was altogether too much for him. He got sleepier and sleepier and occasionally had to bring his head up with a jerk. Presently he realized that he could barely move his legs. But he didn't mind; he couldn't remember ever having felt more completely contented.

In the crackling, frost-glittering daybreak Emma Baxter went to the shed to feed and milk the cow. The doctor wasn't home yet, but she assumed he had stayed the night at the Hardys'. The snow squeaked under her feet, and she held her shawl tightly across her mouth. She felt her stomach muscles tighten as she caught sight of the horse's lower legs there in the stall. Then she saw the doctor. At first she thought he was merely drunk. His feet still in the stirrups, the upper half of his body had fallen forward across the saddle, his mute face laid almost caressingly against the coarse hair of the horse's mane. His right hand hung stiffly at his side, mittened fingers clutched around the neck of the empty flask. Emma reached up to disengage those fingers, and then she knew what had happened. The arm and fingers were like iron. For some reason she struggled until she got the flask away from the hard fingers. She dropped the flask in the manger hay and then, suddenly, sat down on a pile of straw and wept silently, the tears warming her thin, cold cheeks. Presently Kate whinnied nervously. Emma roused herself, wiped her eyes on her apron, and went to fetch Jim Allin.

So ended the year 1832.

CHAPTER FOUR

1835

T HE TREMONT HOUSE IN PEKIN was no great shakes of a
hotel. But it was the best the town had to offer, and because
Pekin was an important river port the hotel was a sort of
general business and social exchange. It was here that Jesse Fell
first met David Davis. Fell, on a business trip to Pekin, had
been introduced to Davis by a mutual lawyer acquaintance.

"How do you find business, Davis?" Fell asked.

"Nothing to write home about—except maybe to get a loan,"
Davis answered, and shrugged his shoulders. When Davis
shrugged, the movement meant something. Even now, as a
young man of only twenty, he was big. It wasn't just that he
was fat; he was naturally big. "But I didn't expect to make my
fortune in my first year out here. Then too, as Mason told you,
I've been sick. This town is full of fever and ague. I'm just out
of bed a week or so."

Fell looked him over again. If illness had ravaged Davis, he
certainly didn't show it. He might look a little peaked, but sickness certainly hadn't touched the huge frame or the fullness of
the flesh thereon. Fell didn't miss many details when he was
really curious.

"I've been in Everton a couple of years now," Fell was saying. "Maybe I've been lucky, but I've done pretty well so far. Of course, up until a few months ago I was the only lawyer there. That helped, naturally."

"I haven't done so well," Davis confessed. "Oh, I've won a case or two. But I've found out, too, how much I don't know. I had a chancery case in which John Stuart was attorney for the plaintiff. You know Stuart—from Springfield? Well, he helped me make up my brief. I went to him and told him frankly that I had been engaged to defend and didn't know how to write my plea. He helped me all he could. But I lost."

Fell laughed aloud. "I know Stuart," he said, "and he's one of the best. But I've been thinking of something, Davis. You're a young fellow; so am I. Everton's at least a healthier place than this, and I've got the beginnings of a business started there. I've been thinking I could use a partner."

"Probably not enough business to support both of us," Davis observed.

"Not just now, to be sure. But there will be. And I'm not sure I want to stay in the law, anyway. I've been thinking about the whole matter a great deal of late, and I think I'd like to try my hand at something else, at least for a while. You could come into my office at once as partner. As fast as I can I'll turn my business over to you, and you can work up your own business as you see fit. At least you'll have *some* business, and you can't be any worse off than you are here. And Everton's certainly a healthier place to live."

Davis considered for only a moment. "I'll do it," he said decisively. "As you say, I can't be worse off than I am here, and I have a feeling that things will be a good deal better. How long are you staying in town?"

"I have to see a man around ten in the morning. I'll be ready to go as soon as I finish with him. Can you be ready by then?"

"Easily," Davis said. "About all I have to do is pack my clothes and a few books. Suppose I meet you here at the Tremont lobby about ten-thirty?"

"Good," Fell agreed. "I've got my own rig, and we ought to

be in Everton for supper unless we bog down somewhere on the road. That isn't impossible—or improbable, either."

Before eleven the next morning the two were eastbound for Everton in Fell's rig, and Davis had said his few farewells to the mudholes and shanties of Pekin. He wasn't sorry to leave the place. Business was no good, anyway, and he had an active dislike for the roistering waterfront life which made up more than half the town. But he liked Fell, had liked him instantly. He thought Fell felt the same way about him. They would get along.

Totally unlike in many ways, both then and later in their lives, in many other ways they were very much alike. Undemonstrative, serious-minded, their real emotions were deep-rooted. They both had an almost unerring faculty of appraising men, seeing their real value and using them—or asking to be used, as the case might be—accordingly. At the moment, driving through the everlasting mud of an Illinois April, they had no deep feeling of friendship for each other. But each sensed in the other some essential bedrock of character. Each thought: "Here is a man I can depend on."

They were both right.

II

"Don't foller so close to me, boy," Joe Dawson said. "You keep trampin' right on my heels an' throwin' me outta my stride. It's enough to try to steady this God-blasted contraption without havin' to keep you off me."

Obediently the small boy fell back a pace or two. He was silent for a moment; then he said: "Pop."

"Well, what is it now?" Joe asked absent-mindedly. He heaved at the "God-blasted contraption" that the oxen were dragging through the prairie turf and spat at a beetle.

"Pop, when will you tell me some more about Charley Indian an' his flyin' mule?"

Joe suddenly laughed explosively and yelled "Whoa" at the

oxen. The animals stopped dead in their tracks and began to blow contentedly. Joe sat down on the crude beam of the plow and raked sweat from his brow with a calloused forefinger. "Lordy me," he said, and touched the boy's shoulder awkwardly, "I done fergot all about Charley Indian. I reckon I did promise to finish that yarn. Yessir, I done fergot all about it. What in hell did you do with that jug, son?"

"I left it settin' under that pin oak there by the fence, Pop."

"Reckon you could git it right quick?"

"Yessir." The boy skipped lightly across the rough furrows and in a couple of minutes was back with the jug.

Joe drank deeply from the drop-beaded jug. "Ah," he said, "that's the stuff to take the wrinkles outta your hide."

"What about Charley Indian, Pop?"

"Well, now, I'll tell you—you help me clean the moldboard again, an' when we go to the house fer dinner at noon I'll finish the yarn. How's that?"

"All right, Pop," Willy said obediently. But he looked disappointed.

Joe took two hand-whittled paddles from his hip pocket and handed one to the boy. They fell upon the mud-encrusted plow and in a few minutes had it fairly clean again. Joe wrestled the plow back into the furrow again and hollered, "Giddap, you lazy bastards!" The first jerk almost tossed him over the plow handles, but he dug his boot heels into the turf and held on mightily. In a moment the share point was finding its way again and they were plowing ground.

It was a queer tableau. In front, the two husky, patient oxen, dragging behind them the caricature of a plow—the crazy plow which was jointly the product of Joe's years of back-breaking experiment and Abe Brokaw's blacksmithing ability. Behind the plow, Joe Dawson, a man with one consuming ambition: to plow the prairie sod or break his back trying. And behind Joe, Willy Dawson, four years old and Joe's youngest boy, now carrying the water jug and wishing for dinnertime and the finish of the tale of Charley Indian and the famous flying mule.

[86]

1835

For three years now Joe had been trying to plow the prairie. He was convinced—and rightly—that the sod-grown prairie would be a paradise for crops if he could only get it plowed. Three years before, he and his three older boys had fenced off a hundred acres of bald prairie, and he'd been trying to work it ever since. He'd tried everything—or at least everything he knew of. Wooden plows, cast-iron shares, wrought-iron shares, none of them would work. They would all plow, but one and all they would not scour, and scouring is two thirds of plowing. He had enlisted Abe Brokaw in the campaign, and this spring they were taking one more shot at it. And this time it was with a plow of Abe's design: a walking plow of conventional design but with the share and moldboard made from two wide strips of *steel,* the remains of a discarded pitsaw. It was crude, and the fact that it had to be pieced was quite a drawback.

And on this particular morning Joe was making an epochal discovery: the steel would scour. This particular plow wasn't scouring as it should, as witness the necessity for cleaning it, but that wasn't the fault of the design. Rather the saw steel was too light for such heavy work and had buckled a little. Also, she was a little out of balance, causing a lot of side draft and keeping Joe wrestling with it to hold it in the furrow. But those were minor matters. It was scouring, that was the thing.

For this experiment Joe had selected one corner of his fenced-in hundred acres. Early that morning he had started to work on a square perhaps ten rods on a side, plowing from the outside and constantly paring down the size of the island in the center. The sod was a good six inches thick, and the dried and broken grass and weed stems two and three feet high even after the winter snow had lain on the growth for months. The newly plowed ground would have to be worked for a year or two before it would handle as it should, but that was a minor matter now. Joe knew he had it whipped. Next year he would have a hundred-acre cornfield.

"Pop," Willy said.

"Well, what is it now?"

AMERICAN YEARS

"Couldn't you finish up the story while we're plowin' here now?"

"No," Joe said shortly, "I cain't. I got to keep my mind on my business here. Don't be botherin' me."

Willy sighed. "All right, Pop," he said resignedly.

The square of unplowed ground was growing smaller now, and Joe was more concerned with its size than with what was in it. He was wrong, and he should have known better; but his mind was on the plow. He had forgotten for the moment that the Illinois prairie had been home to its animal and reptile life for years beyond man's count of time, and his plowed-up piece was no exception. Now, with the little unplowed island reduced to a plot some ten feet square, it was literally crawling with life. Rabbits, ground squirrels, moles, weasels, field mice—and snakes. But Joe had forgotten. He stopped the oxen for a moment. "Look!" he said exultantly to the uncomprehending boy, and pointed toward the sun, "ten or fifteen minutes more an' we'll have her whipped to a standstill."

"Then will you finish the story?"

"Shore. Hand me the jug again, boy."

He tipped the jug back over his arm, and out of the corner of his eye he could see the boy watching him proudly. Then his ear heard the whirred warning, but he was too slow in reacting. His mind on the plow, his hearing dulled by the pleasant swallowing, his instinct failed him. He tossed the jug aside, but at the same time a brownish-gray streak shot from the rank growth and sank its fangs into Willy's bare leg. In a split second it drew back to strike again, but this time Joe was alert, his nerves like stretched wire. His heavy boot struck the rattler's head unerringly, knocking the snake spinning, and in another instant the other boot ground the head to bloody pulp.

The strike had caught Willy off balance and sent him sprawling into the fresh earth of the furrow. Now he was tremendously frightened, and his sobs shook his small body. "There, son, don't cry," Joe was saying tenderly. "We'll make it all right. I'll take care o' you."

[88]

He was working feverishly now. He ripped Willy's lone suspender strap out by the roots and wrapped it loosely about the leg above the wound, then thrust one of the wood paddles through the strap and twisted until the boy cried out in pain. He gathered the small body into his arms and looked down at the freckled, tear-stained face. "All right, now, son?" he asked.

"My leg hurts me, Pop."

"I know. But Annie's home. Her teeth are good, an' she can suck that leg an' fix it right up fer you. We'll be home in a jiffy."

"Will you tell me the story then, Pop?"

"Shore, son. Ready? Here we go."

He managed to reach a pocket and dig out a plug of tobacco. He stuffed the chew into his mouth, got a fresh hold on the boy and started running clumsily across the rough ground. At a hundred yards he stopped, gasped for breath and smacked the freshly chewed cud against the red spots on Willy's leg.

Then he set his teeth, held the cud against the wound with one open palm and began to run in earnest. At the edge of the grove a half-mile away he could see noon smoke curling from the cabin chimney. Annie's teeth were good; half of his were decayed. He didn't dare take a chance. He prayed a little and began to feel stabs of pain through his lungs. He thought Willy was whiter now. He tried to run faster. . . .

I I I

The Willow Bend campground had been in use for a little more than three years, and each year the faithful had built the tabernacle a bit larger. Originally it had been about fifteen feet high in the center, sloping off to perhaps nine or ten feet at the outer edges of the roof. The building was really nothing more than a slab roof supported at somewhat irregular intervals by posts varying from three to six inches in diameter, and was open all the way around. The floor was sawdust; the benches were hand-hewn planks set on legs and without backs. Of course the roof leaked. But since the tabernacle was rarely used except in late summer or early fall, the leaks didn't matter much. The roof at least kept off the broiling sun, and if it happened to rain during meeting all but a small part of the congregation was kept reasonably dry. At one end of the building was the preachers' dais, a platform with a puncheon floor laid on a massive trestle-work of logs.

It was crude. But its name was the clue to its spiritual value: tabernacle. Were not the meeting places of the Old Testament folk called tabernacles? Of course Dane County and Everton had churches. But the tabernacle was something altogether different. For one thing, ten times as many worshipers could get under the Willow Bend tabernacle roof at one time. Where more worshipers could assemble, there too would be more of the best preachers. More, for that matter, of everything which went to make up the social life of the community. And so the Willow Bend campground was fast becoming an established institution.

The Calverts were headed for the meeting in the same wagon that had hauled them from Vermont to Illinois. The canvas cover and its supporting hoops had been permanently removed, but otherwise it was the same wagon, still good for years of service. John Calvert and Cora were on the front seat; Robert, Hepzibah, Luke and John's wife, Mary, in the back with the baskets of food and the bedding. As they drew near the campground the traffic became heavier. Here a husband and wife doubling on horseback, there a family on foot, carrying their necessaries over their shoulders in grain sacks. Here were surreys and buggies and all manner of conveyance, all drawn by the lodestone of Willow Bend.

John Calvert heard a wild yelling on the road behind him. He glanced over a shoulder and then took a firmer grip on the reins. His face hardened. "It's them Carpenters—Zack an' Henry an' the old lady."

"I'd hoped," Mary said acidly, "that we Christians'd be

1835

spared their hellishness this year, but I guess not. You'd better pull over a little an' give them hellions plenty o' room, John."

But Calvert was already pulling the wagon over as far as the road would allow. In another moment the Carpenter buckboard passed them in a cloud of dust. Zack was driving, with Henry on the seat beside him, both of them with their legs braced against the dashboard and Zack pouring the whip to the frightened horses. The old lady, mother of the two hellions, sat on a roll of blankets in the back, arms and legs braced against anything available, her lips set in a hard, straight line, eyes looking neither to right nor left. As the speeding vehicle passed the Calvert wagon Henry let out a couple of special yells and thumbed his nose at John Calvert.

"Varmints," Calvert said half to himself.

The buckboard careened madly on, took a bend in the road on two wheels and disappeared.

"They're sure primed fer trouble, looks like," Mary said.

"Un-hunh," John said. "An' they'll probably git it," he added grimly.

A few minutes later they emerged from the timber and stopped at the brow of the hill. Spread out below them lay the parklike meeting ground, the tabernacle in the center and the brown river, beyond, curving in a wide loop about the whole. Already the campground was dotted with people and vehicles, and smoke rose from some of the flimsy cabins. They watched the Carpenter buckboard tear on across the grounds, Zack driving standing up now and both boys yelling as if they were possessed. Here and there mothers hastily drew children out of the Carpenters' path, and tethered animals shied nervously.

"Giddap, Nancy, giddap, Joe," Calvert said. The wagon started slowly down the hill, and the Calvert children looked on in wide-eyed silence and wonder.

Old Mrs James sat on a stump, talking to Mary Calvert. She had long since lost her last tooth and now and again had to pause

[91]

in her knitting long enough to adjust her pipestem. It kept slipping when she talked, and once a hot coal fell into her lap and she cursed roundly when she saw the little burned spot. Mrs James was seventy-six and fully expected to outlive Ike James, who was only sixty-five and her third husband. She had seen her first husband killed and scalped by the Hurons, and her second had died from a knife stab incurred in a tavern brawl. She had borne sixteen children, and of the ten who had passed on only two had died natural deaths. If experience is worth anything, Eliza James should have been the wisest woman in Dane County. But she was old enough to know that she wasn't.

"It jest ain't natural," Mary said. "She lets them two young hellions carry on any which way, an' she don't care in the least."

"Well," Mrs James observed, "what do you expect her to do —turn 'em across her knee?"

"No-o-o, of course not. But she don't even seem to *care* what them two do. An' she's a godless woman herself to boot. She don't even confess her own sins. I don't know what in the world she comes here for. The preachin' an' religion don't mean nothing to her."

"Oh, I don't know, Mary. You know how the story goes, I s'pose. They say she set a great store by that man o' hers 'fore he got killed. Some women air that way. I never was myself, but I've seen plenty that was. I reckon she jest naturally sees the man in them two boys, an' even if they air hellions she's bound to put up with it."

"She might come into the church herself."

"Shorely she might. But maybe that wouldn't set so well with the boys—sort o' turnin' again 'em, you might say. An' she probably worries more about what they think o' her than what the neighbors thinks."

Mary changed the subject: "The meetin' don't seem to have much spirit to it, does it?"

"No, it don't, an' that's a fact. But I've seen a many a camp meetin', Mary Calvert, an' I know how they air. Some of 'em

jest naturally seems to roll along o' their own accord; others is
slow in gittin' started. The fear o' God is slow in reachin' down
into some sinners' hearts. We only been here three days. Sometimes it takes a heap longer 'n that to git the spirit workin'
proper."

"John said that with Peter Cartwright himself here they hoped
to do better 'n this. This is Sunday, too," she added a little
wistfully. "This ought to be a good day."

"Peter Cartwright is a godly man," said the old lady dryly,
"but I never see a Methodist preacher yet that could do miracles.
If the Lord ain't ready to start the sinners to repentin', why,
then He jest ain't ready, Cartwright er no Cartwright."

"Here comes John," Mary said, "an' he looks in a powerful
hurry."

Calvert was in a hurry. "You'd better git over to the wagon
with the young ones," he said. "There's trouble startin' over
near the river. A bunch o' them young hellions are plannin' to
throw all the preachers in the river, an' Peter Cartwright is
plenty mad. He says it's all right to turn the other cheek as the
Book says, but if that don't do no good, then a man has to stand
up fer his rights."

"You be careful, John," Mary warned.

"Don't spill no more blood than ye have to," said Mrs James,
and calmly continued her knitting.

It was a hot, muggy Sunday afternoon, and the unregenerate
were spoiling for trouble. From the look of things they were
going to get it. The righteous were hurrying to the river bank,
most of them carrying good stout clubs, and in a moment the
fight was on. A gang of toughs had propelled the Reverend
Cartwright to the very brink of the river, and he had offered no
resistance. But as they loosened up to get a fresh grip and toss
him in, he broke loose and turned on them like a wounded and
enraged bear. He was scattering his assailants as chaff before
the wind when more help arrived. The hellions were getting a
first-rate beating when someone yelled: "Look out, here comes
the Carpenters!" The fighting mob looked up long enough to see

a speeding buggy heading straight for its center. Zack and Henry were between the shafts, a half-dozen more brigands in the back pushing. And that was what the two Carpenters apparently didn't know. The mob parted abruptly, the buggy shot through the opening and on over into the river with a mighty splash. The Carpenters went over with the buggy, and the fighting began again, now with the toughs getting very much the worst of it. A wet, bedraggled figure climbed up over the river bank and pitched into the yelling mob.

Calvert showed up at the wagon at suppertime.

"You hurt any, John?" Mary asked anxiously.

"Only a few scratches an' bruises," Calvert said grimly, "but there's others got more 'n that. I reckon we learned 'em a lesson. There won't be any more disturbances while this meetin' lasts, anyhow."

Again at seven o'clock the tabernacle was filled to overflowing. But there was no fire in the meeting. The mourners' benches were conspicuously empty. A lanky, long-haired farmer was leading the congregation through an endless series of hymns, all sung with noticeable lack of enthusiasm. The preachers and exhorters were holding a conference in the rear of the tabernacle, delaying the main meeting in the hope of finding some way to kindle the spiritual fire.

The night was hot and sticky, as had been the day. There were no stars, and heat lightning played about on the horizon. The candles flickered fitfully, as though gasping for air to burn properly. A feeling of ominous unrest hung over the whole assemblage.

The singing went on.

Someone slipped up beside Calvert and whispered excitedly. In a moment John turned to his wife. "It's Zack Carpenter," he said softly. "They just found his body in the river." And with that he was gone into the darkness.

Mary shivered. Was this God's sign?

In a few minutes the preachers filed in and took their places on the platform. Almost in the same instant there was a sudden stir at the opposite end of the building. Something was happening. The close-packed crowd murmured like a restless sea.

The storm struck with almost hurricane force. Rain fell in blinding masses, and a few roof slabs were carried away on the furious wind. Then, like the hammer of God, the jagged chain of lightning struck a stalwart elm standing a bare hundred feet from the huddled throng. Like a flaming sword it clove the huge trunk to the very grass, and even as the thunder rolled behind the lightning bolt, they saw the trunk part, hesitate momentarily, then fall faster and faster toward the ground, ending at last in two mighty crashes.

Then with another lightning flash they saw Calvert and five others, like pallbearers, carrying Zack Carpenter's sheeted, dripping body up the aisle and on up the steps of the platform, where they laid it at the feet of the bearded, hard-faced preachers.

A vast sigh escaped the audience.

And with the next blue flash Cartwright was on his feet, hands upraised, his face aglow with holy zeal. The faces of the other preachers stood out momentarily like carved stone.

"The gates of hell stand ajar for the unwary!"

His voice rolled like that of some super-Moses, and the crowd was stilled. Then again:

"You are being weighed in the balance! Thy God is a just God, but an avenging one! Come, ye sorry sinners!"

"Amen! Amen! Amen!"

Outside, the storm had passed as quickly as it had come. The night was deathly still. Then again from the rear of the crowd there was a wild scream. Mrs Carpenter made her way through the packed aisle, and people drew aside to let her pass. Gone now was the hard, relentless face. She was suddenly older, and her mouth worked as though in pain. Now she knelt by the damp body, sobbing, sobbing.

Cartwright touched her shoulder. "Take your place on the mourners' bench, Sister Carpenter," he said harshly, "repent of your sins to the Lord." And then again his prophet's voice echoed and re-echoed against the walls of the hushed timber.

"The Lord giveth and the Lord taketh away! Praise ye the name of the Lord!"

"Yea, Lord!"

"Amen!"

Then the shouting and the tumult. The mourners' benches began to fill up, to spill over with the repentant. There was a great crying out and weeping. Beside the platform, almost at Cartwright's feet, a young couple lay clasped in each other's arms, their faces white with ecstasy. This was the night of nights, and Cartwright knew it. His voice rolled on, endlessly, swaying them like wheat in the wind.

All night the revival went on, and the next day and night, and the next.

I V

Three of the horses stood quietly at the starting line, but the fourth, a long-legged bay named Gun Fannon, wheeled and reared nervously.

Aleck Dale, who rode a black called Tiger, laughed at Bill Foley, riding the bay. "They may teach them Kaintucky horses to run, but they shore don't teach 'em to behave, eh, Bill?"

Foley got the bay back into line again, patting his neck and speaking gently to him. "Don't put your hand on him, Greenberry," he said to the sheriff, who was acting as starter. "It makes him jumpy. Let him get his bearin's a minute." Then, to Aleck: "Well, I only got ten dollars left in my poke—do you want to cover that?"

"Taken!" Aleck snapped. "I've got fifty more here I'll bet on the Tiger's nose. Anybody want it?"

Up to now the Tiger had consistently been the fastest horse in Dane County. When he was beaten, it was usually by a stranger or because the black was off form.

Greenberry Larison looked again at the broad chest and slim legs of Gun Fannon. He'd seen Kentucky horses run before, and this one looked like the real thing. "I'll take half of it, Aleck," he said quietly.

"Anybody else?" Dale called.

There had been a little murmur in the crowd of men and boys watching the line-up. Now they came forward with a rush.

"Ten here, Aleck."

"And five more."

"Ten here," yelled John Cheney. "Want any more, Aleck?"

"No," Dale said shortly. "That's my pile, an' if this black devil don't come home in front I won't dast go home neither. Not that I'm worried any."

"Get ready," Larison said. "We been foolin' long enough. All bets down?"

"All down," somebody answered.

"All set, then. Ready."

The four riders tightened bridle reins and leaned forward expectantly. Tiger pawed the ground with one front foot. The crowd watched tensely. It was very quiet there in the October sunshine. Larison's pistol cracked sharply, and the four were away together perfectly. Then the crowd broke loose in a mad conglomerate of yelled encouragement and imprecation.

The course was on a dry, flat piece of ground a few miles east of Everton and belonged to John Cheney. The ground had been burned over, and the track itself was a measured three quarters of a mile, laid off in a long oval. It was no Epsom Downs, but it served as well. There was nothing to show that it was a racecourse except the track itself. The crowd sat its own horses, in its own vehicles, or squatted or stood on the ground. Each man gambled as he felt he could afford, and whisky was cheap and plentiful. There were no womenfolk present. But it was a race track for all that, a contribution to man's passion for order. You worshiped in a church, held court in a court-house, begat children in a house and held horse races on a race track. Drinking was something else; a man could drink anywhere.

Gun Fannon had got away to a slow start, probably because

of his nervousness, but he was well out in front now. They were coming around the last turn now, and the Kentucky strain was showing. Dale was pouring the whip to the Tiger, but it was no use. The bay was running free and easy, and the black was simply outclassed. Gun Fannon came across the finish line, in a shower of cheers and curses, a good four lengths ahead, the Tiger a poor second.

Bill Foley wiped the bay down and tossed a blanket over him. "Good work, boy," he said fondly; then, to the crowd around them: "He wasn't even runnin' hard, an' you can take my word for it." He started collecting his bets.

Dale paid. He didn't like it, but he paid. "You got a good horse, Bill," he said grudgingly. "I don't want no more o' him myself. He'll carry my money from now on if anybody hereabouts is fool enough to ride agin him."

Bets paid and the jugs handed around again, some of the crowd left and others congregated in little groups and yarned. The sun was only pleasantly warm, but they sat in the shade out of habit. Bill Foley, old man Leary, Larison, Cheney and Pete Crumbaugh sat on the ground in the shadow of Leary's wagon. Greenberry, Foley and Leary were in high spirits, and the Leary jug passed freely.

"You up to the Methodist camp meetin', Greenberry?" Leary asked, and wiped his bearded lips on the back of his hand.

"Yeah, I got around that way," the sheriff said. "That young Zack Carpenter got hisself drownded, you know. I had to look into it. But it was jest one o' them things that seem bound to happen. It was his own fault."

"Shore," Leary said. "I hear they had some high ol' ructions when they got warmed up."

"I reckon so. Pete Cartwright was at his best fightin' weight, an' I guess he give 'em hell-an'-brimstone to a fare-you-well."

"Don't he always, though?"

"I mind when I was down Kentucky way after Gun Fannon," Foley put in. "I heard a good one on Cartwright. He was holdin' a whoppin' big revival somewhere down in that country, and right in the middle o' one o' his sermons ol' Andy Jackson hisself come in an' sat down. Somebody whispered to Pete an' told him who had come in. But Pete wasn't fazed fer a minute. He jest hollered out in that Bull-o'-Bashan voice o' his: 'Andy Jackson, who's he? If he's a sinner let him git hisself up here on the mourners' bench with the rest o' the repentant!' They say ol' Andy's face got red as a beet, but he never said a word an' set out the rest o' Pete's sermon."

They grinned in appreciation, passed the jug again and settled more comfortably.

"You got anybody in the jail, Greenberry?" Crumbaugh wanted to know.

"Only one—that crazy Jack Sharp. He stole some harness an' a saddle from old man Brady an' then was fool enough to try an' sell it all back to him. Claimed he found it somewheres. Brady is a forgivin' sort o' cuss, an' if it 'd been anybody else but Jack he'd probably said nothin' about it. But he's a roarin' Baptist hisself, an' he's hated Jack's guts ever since Jack got that piebald horse an' named it John the Baptist. So I had to throw him in the jail. He's the only one, though. Things is a mite quiet."

"I don't know why exactly," Leary said, "but that harness an' saddle reminds me about an uncle o' mine. This was back in the old days, and it was forty mile from his place to the nearest town. Not that that made much difference. This feller was tighter 'n a bull's bung in fly time an' wouldn't spend a nickel he didn't have to. Well, durin' the winter he made him up a set o' harness, an' he made it out'n green leather. Spring that year was turrible wet, an' the whole country was jest one big swamp. He went to the timber with the new harness one day, an' he got along all right until along toward evenin'. He started fer home with a heavy load o' rails an' got about a quarter-mile from the house when the front wheels hit a sinkhole an' he bogged down proper. Hand me that jug, John."

He took a long drink and spat reminiscently.

"Well?" Bill said impatiently.

"As I was sayin'," Leary went on, "he bogged down proper. But he had a good team. In fact it was the best team in the whole state. But he didn't figger on that green harness. He got down off the wagon to ease the load an' then began pourin' the whip to 'em. Well, sir, that team pulled an' that green harness began to stretch. It stretched an' stretched, but my uncle never noticed. The first thing he knew he'd drove that team plumb into the barn lot but hadn't moved the wagon an inch."

"What 'd he do then?" Cheney asked.

"Well, he was naturally surprised fer a minute, but he wasn't put out. He hooked the collars over a post an' stabled the team jest like nothin' had happened. An' he knew his business all right. Sure enough, the next mornin' the sun come out hot, an' that harness began to dry out an' shrink up. In less 'n an hour after breakfast there that load o' rails was, standin' there in the barn lot slicker 'n a gut. Pass me the jug, John."

Intent on the story, they hadn't seen the horse and rider that now came flogging up in a cloud of dust. It was Allin's boy, Dave. He slipped panting to the ground before the little group and gasped out his tale between breaths.

"It's that crazy Jack Sharp, Greenberry," he piped. "Pop says fer you to hurry."

"What happened, boy?"

"Pop says that crazy Agnes Dooley came by, an' Jack yelled through a crack fer her to come an' open the door, an' she did. Now Jack's drunk an' ridin' up an' down Main Street, shootin' off his pistol an' cussin' an' vowin' he's gonna kill old man Brady soon's he can git around to it. Pop says fer you to hurry."

"Well, I'll be teetotally doggoned," Greenberry ejaculated. "Who'da thought that crazy loon had enough sense to do that!"

"Do what, Greenberry?" Leary grinned. "Kill old man Brady?"

"I dunno," the sheriff said. "Either one. See you later, boys."

They rode off together.

"You want to go to town, John?" Leary asked.

"Naw," Cheney said. "Greenberry'll have him back in jail by the time we'd git there now."

"All right. Pass me the jug, John."

v

Without fanfare or bustle the three of them—Fell, Green and Allin—had made themselves the presiding elders of Everton. They did not outwardly admit it—that is, they made no public point of it, and they didn't talk of it, even among themselves. In fact they probably did not consider the matter objectively as such even in their private thoughts. Such is almost always true of the guiding spirits in any democracy—at least in their most youthful periods. They were unable now, after assuming it, to gauge their own strength, and they had no desire to do so. But quietly, noiselessly, they had set themselves in the seats of power. They were the seemingly natural anachronisms of a democracy, though they had probably never heard of the phrase, and didn't intend to let themselves become anything else.

Thus when Fell conceived the idea of establishing a newspaper he naturally tried to enlist the aid of Allin and Green. They talked the matter over in Green's store one early autumn evening, and Allin and Green were thoroughly in accord with Fell. For Allin, however, there was one drawback: he was woefully short of cash. True, he had sold a great deal of real estate, but he had been obliged to accept notes in payment for a major portion of it, and he had had little capital to begin with. He agreed that the idea was a good one, but he absolutely refused to strain himself in its favor. Perhaps he lacked the natural reverence for the printed word which came easily to the others because of their earlier education.

Finally it was agreed that Fell and Green would put up the money—providing the total needed did not run to more than $500—and Allin would lend the project his moral support. Green was leaving shortly on his fall buying trip to Philadelphia. He was to engage a man capable of editing and printing a newspaper, an assistant if necessary, and, with the aid of the editor thus engaged, buy the needed mechanical equipment.

It was like them to decide between themselves to house the embryo paper in a vacant room in the courthouse. Of course the courthouse properly belonged to the populace of Dane County; but were they not conferring a favor upon the county? They hoped to make a profit out of the thing themselves, of course, but that was beside the point. They would therefore, having decided upon the feasibility of the project, use the county's property for its own good whether the county liked it or not. They were, perhaps, the natural ancestors of the generations of businessmen who were to follow them. Everton was emerging from the frontier stage.

Green returned to Everton in mid-November, reporting to Fell that in Philadelphia he had made a deal with one William Hill, a printer-editor, and Hill had hired an assistant named Dan Brigham. The printing equipment (luckily found secondhand) had cost in the neighborhood of $300. The remaining $200 he had advanced to Hill and his assistant as traveling expenses and salary. Green had as usual made the trip home overland by stage. Hill, Brigham and the machinery would follow as quickly as possible by the less expensive route, the Ohio, Mississippi and Illinois rivers to Pekin.

And from Philadelphia Green also brought news of another sort: Everton's first knowledge of the financial foreboding which was becoming prevalent in the East. He was too young and too inexperienced in matters of intricate finance to know what all the talk meant. But he didn't fail to absorb the knowledge which would do him the most good financially. That was the time-honored process of reducing your own obligations, driving your debtors unmercifully and putting all possible assets into their most negotiable form. Green was never slow to learn.

Nowadays Green was titled "General," and quite soberly too, unless perhaps by the little coterie of stalwarts who survived Stillman's Run with some honor. A year after that painful fiasco a standing company of militia had been organized in Dane County. Actually it was little more than a fraternal organization with some political leanings, and Green, because of his business standing in the community, had been elected provost marshal. That was the highest office in the affair. Sometime after that, by means of devious and sundry wire-pulling, the state adjutant's office had made him technically a general. There were a great many such generals, but it was nevertheless a sop to Green's pride and a public proof that his courage could not be questioned. Green had learned how very easily people forget things. Now he was actually a general, with a gilt commission to prove it; he *had* been in the Black Hawk War. Strangers put two and two together, assumed the obvious, and Green was satisfied.

CHAPTER FIVE

1836

THE STREETS ON THE south and east sides of the courthouse yard were visible from the office windows of the Dane County *Advocate and Intelligencer:* Main Street on the east, Washington on the south. There was little to choose between them. The mud was as deep and the livestock as numerous in one as in the other, with hogs perhaps dominating in Main Street and chickens in Washington. Hill looked dejectedly out the south window and watched Andy High pilot a load of rails toward the street intersection. The process was not without a sort of impersonal interest to Mr Hill. He knew that High hadn't been to town for a month, and he knew that the particular sinkhole for which the wagon was heading had gotten deeper day by day since the first thaw. High couldn't know how bad the hole was, and in the ruts the wagon was now following he couldn't possibly miss it. The soupy mud which stood level with the top of the hole was beautifully deceptive. Hill put his unshaven chin on one hand and gazed out the window, fascinated.

The printer sat on a high stool before the type case, smoking a corncob and singing excerpts from Watts' *Hymnal* dolefully from one corner of his mouth. The singing was simply a habit, Hill insisted, and it got on his nerves badly at times.

"Dan," Hill said dreamily, "c'mere and look at Andy High. He's headin' straight for that bottomless pit out there an' don't know it. You know," he went on admiringly, "I've been watching that hole for three weeks now, an' she's a bitch. Give her three more weeks an' you can drop a wagon through it plumb to China."

The boy came over and looked out the open window at the spectacle. They could have yelled and stopped the incautious driver; it didn't occur to either of them to do so.

"Bet you a drink he can't get out without another team," Hill said suddenly.

"I'll take you."

In the street outside there was a sudden sucking *plop,* and the wagon's front wheels went in six inches over the hubs. The ox gear creaked and groaned for a minute or so, then the animals stopped suddenly and waited expectantly for High to do something. He did. He got down off the rails, sank past his boot tops when he tried to kick a recumbent hog, and cursed steadily and sulphurously. In the end, after several fits and starts, he went off in search of another team he could borrow.

"You lose," Hill said. "I'll take the drink now."

Dan got the jug from under the hand press and came back to the editor's desk, the composing stick still in his hand. He looked at the editor accusingly. "You was drunk again last night," he said.

Hill looked up at the youth in extravagant surprise. "The hell you say! Seems like I do remember something like that happening, come to think about it. Well, it sure beats hell. But I'll probably be drunk again tonight. You haven't heard of anyone seriously objecting, have you?"

"Well, not exactly. Mister Fell don't like it much, though."

"Un-hunh. But Mister Fell ain't running this benighted paper. He only owns it. And what does our esteemed Brother Green think about it, may I ask?"

"Oh, he don't give a damn. He don't give a damn what anybody does as long as he can make something off them."

"Well said, my young and learned friend, well said indeed. Brother Green doesn't give a damn. I'm surprised at the powers of observation displayed by one so young. It was Brother Green who talked us into this damned emigration in the first place."

"*You* talked *me* into it," Dan said.

"Even so, Green was the prime mover. If it hadn't been for him I wouldn't have hired you. But you wanted to see what the Great West was like. What the hell you kicking about?"

"Oh, I dunno. But I've seen damned near all I want to see of it."

"Well, live and learn, my boy," Hill said with mock gravity. "But don't worry, you'll run into some shapely corn-fed country gal before long, and then you'll like the country all right. Why, imagine, someday this will be a great city, a center of culture and gentility, the hub of a mighty empire——"

"For God's sake," Dan said bitterly. "We got to get out a paper. Do you know how to spell Steve Douglas's last name?"

"Well, don't *he* know how to spell it? He wrote that notice himself, didn't he? Can't you read it?"

"I can read all right, but he can't write—or he couldn't the last time he was in here. He could hardly hit the ink with the pen, let alone write. Is there one 's' in it or two?"

"Let me see it," Hill said. He inspected the scrawl on the sheet of paper a couple of times, adjusted his spectacles and tried it again, then handed it back. "I'll be damned if I can read those hen tracks. Put two 's's on it, and then he can't claim he didn't get all he had coming even if it is wrong."

"All right," Dan said. "Where 'll I put this advertisement o' Godey's?"

"Put it on the back page," Hill ordered. He looked out the window again. High was putting a team of horses ahead of the oxen. . . . Godey, Philadelphia . . . he knew how the boy felt. But he'd get over his homesickness. They all had to have it sooner or later. Best just to let it wear off. That was the surest cure in the long run. For that matter he too missed Philadelphia. This wilderness had damned little to recommend it—except to people like Fell and Green, who already owned half of it and would, given time, own all of it.

He looked out the window again and saw Davis picking his way gingerly along the solid turf at the edge of the courthouse yard. Probably heading for Killip's Tavern, Hill thought. He looked at his watch, saw that it was noon, and decided to follow Davis to the tavern. Again he thought fleetingly of Philadelphia. There would at least be no multitude of flies on the dinner tables of that city. At Killip's, even in April, it was sometimes hard to tell the flies from the food. One of the younger Killips would do his best with the fan, but it would only serve to keep the damned insects excited. Hill could hardly be called a fastidious man—but even so . . . He decided to have another good stiff drink before tackling the tavern food. Then presently he called Dan, and together they followed Davis' path across the spongy turf toward the tavern.

Meanwhile, Everton was the possessor of almost five hundred inhabitants, one newspaper, seven stores, a post office, two saloons, two taverns, two steam sawmills and several blacksmith shops and harness establishments. Not much of a town, on the whole, but a far cry from the lonely store set up at the edge of Maple Grove six years before.

The news and editorial content of the Dane County *Advocate and Intelligencer* left much to be desired, but when was that not true of almost any newspaper? By and large it was as good a mirror of its locale as could reasonably be expected. On April 8, 1836, thusly:

The editor complained, in his leading and only editorial, about the continued irregularity in mail-stage arrivals. The front page contained most of the pure reading matter in the sheet, all clipped from other papers and periodicals: an article about the astuteness of Talleyrand, a piece about Dean Swift and his Gulliver, and an excerpt from the works of that popular humorist of the day, Sam Slick, otherwise known as S. C. Hammet. There was also a brief notice on the doings of Congress, mostly with references to some of Mr Clay's remarks about abolitionists.

Walter Brown, lawyer and postmaster, had to pay for his law notice, but his publication, alphabetically, of a list of some 150 undelivered letters lying in the post office, was carried free. Mr Killip, tavernkeeper, stated that he would pay cash for 1,000 bushels of oats and corn, also for any and all other produce. Allen Withers too offered cash for a quantity of small grain. Green advertised that he would pay cash for 20,000 rails delivered to one of his farms. E. Boggs said that he had a complete stock of harness and saddlery and that he needed the services of a journeyman.

Under the heading of professional services were the notices of George F. Markley & Stephen A. Douglass, Fell & Davis, and Walter Brown, lawyers; and W. C. Hobbs, dentist. J. F. Fraley stated that he could and would make anything reasonable, including stoves, from his stock of sheet iron.

Under the head of general merchandise came the ads of Green & Danly, S. Baker & Co. (newly moved to the building south of Killip's Tavern), James Allin & Son, Haines & Son, and Ortogruel Covel, who also offered himself as agent for the Protection Fire Insurance Company of Hartford, Conn.

Persons who had bought land from Allin, Green & Prickett were publicly notified that if their accounts with that firm were not settled by July 1st they would be handed over to the courts for collection. Green, as agent for the owner, one John Griggs of Philadelphia, listed for sale a great quantity of town lots. (Allin, Green & Prickett having sold the absentee owner the lots in the first place, Green was now collecting commission for reselling them.)

Editor Hill announced that the *Advocate* did all manner of printing, including (a little wistfully) wedding announcements, and business was urgently solicited.

From distant parts, these advertisements: Conner & Cooke of New York City, advertising printing types and ornaments, the statement being made in the body of the ad that any paper or periodical publishing the ad three times could collect its pay in type. Last, and the biggest splurge of all, was the space occupied by Mr Godey of Philadelphia, extolling the merits of his magazine. He also urgently recommended the novels of Bulwer and Marryatt and made a liberal agents' offer. Anyone selling $30 worth of subscriptions—and remitting the cash—for *Godey's Magazine* would receive *all* the novels of the great English man of letters, Sir Walter Scott. For $15 worth of subscriptions, one half of Sir Walter's novels. Thus was literature offered the frontier, and, for better or worse, not a little of it was taken.

Editor Hill's rates were modest and perhaps a true indication of what he thought his space was worth: ads not exceeding twelve lines, one dollar for three insertions, larger ads accordingly. Certainly he had no illusions of advertising grandeur. He operated the *Advocate* as well as he saw fit, and the paper's original instigators—Fell, Allin and Green—left him almost altogether to his own devices. They had brought the printed word to Everton, and that in itself was a sure sign of progress. If thereafter the paper managed to stand on its own bottom, that was sufficient for them. Their private affairs kept them busy elsewhere.

II

On the north side of the square Dr John Flournoy Henry owned five lots. On them he had erected a two-roomed building, which he used as an office, and a modest house. The house was small but was probably the best-appointed in Everton. For Dr Henry had come to Everton from the "dark and bloody ground" of Kentucky, not so much to make his fortune as to live. He had been, variously, a surgeon's mate under General Harrison at the Battle of the Thames in the War of 1812, congressman from Kentucky for one term, after which he refused to stand for re-election, and professor of obstetrics at the Medical College in Cincinnati. Further, he had served through a cholera epidemic in that city, and the result had been a monograph titled *Cholera: Its Cause and Cure,* which for years remained a standard work on the subject.

Dr Henry was, in a word, the most literate man in Everton. But he had leanings toward the aristocratic manner, and that Everton vaguely resented. The surrey in which he drove his family to Everton long remained the most elegant vehicle in Dane County, and the surrey, incidentally, had been driven northward by two Negro slaves who had been given their freedom at the end of the journey. Dr Henry did not smoke or drink or chew, and no one had ever heard him use an oath. Even when he became angered, his voice, contrary to custom and human nature in general, became softer instead of louder. All of which Everton would have held more or less against him. But to cap the whole situation he never allowed himself to be seen in public without being cleanly shaven, his boots polished, clothes pressed, and wearing a starched white shirt, a necktie and a high hat. To Everton it just didn't seem natural.

But he found his place in Everton easily enough. Men like Davis, Fell, Allen Withers and James Miller recognized Henry for what he was, and they respected him mightily. Anyone who consulted him professionally soon discovered, if they were at all literate, that here was a man who knew all there was to know of medical science in the 1830s. In short, Dr Henry had not only education and brains but a background of culture that was a new and strange thing to Everton. Minerva, his wife, was a gracious soul and kindly, a true example of what Kentucky womenfolk were alleged to be but rarely were.

On this particular bright June morning Dr Henry sat in his office, reading and enjoying himself. Professionally he was not very busy, but that didn't worry him. His private means were considerable and his needs for the most part simple.

There was a knock at the door, and he looked up from his book. The visitor was a stranger, but Henry suddenly remembered seeing him as the driver of a travel-stained wagon which had rolled past the square earlier in the morning.

"Are you Dr Henry?"

"Yes, sir, I am. What can I do for you?"

"My name is Crow, Doctor—John Crow. I'm traveling toward Pike County with my wife and two daughters. We just drove into town this morning." His voice had a worried tone. "Well, we're a little low on cash right now, and I . . ." His voice trailed off.

"Well," Henry said a little shortly, "how can I be of help to you, Mr Crow?"

"It's my youngest girl, Martha," Crow said. "She's taken pretty bad. I was wondering if you'd——"

"Come, come, man," Henry said brusquely. "Who asked to see your purse? Where is the child?" He reached for his hat and bag.

"We're at the Nichols House," Crow explained as they walked toward the tavern. "I'm from Ohio—Putnam County —and we're on our way to Pike County. I've got a brother out there who's doin' pretty well."

They found the woman and the two girls in the cheapest room in the tavern. The child was badly ill, and it took Dr Henry just about two minutes to diagnose the case. He looked around at the others. "How long has she been like this?" he asked.

"Well," Crow said, "she's been feelin' bad four days, but she's been bad like this just yesterday an' the day before."

"I see," Henry nodded. "Have any of you others," he asked casually, "ever had smallpox?"

The man and woman looked at each other, startled, fright glowing suddenly in their eyes.

"Good God!" Crow blurted. "Is that it? Why, none of us has had it, I guess."

"That is it," Henry said, with a reproving frown at the oath. "Of course you had no way of knowing exactly what it was, but you might have guessed. All of you have been ex- posed—very much so, in fact. I'm taking complete charge of you now. I'm thinking not only of you but of my responsibility to the town. The child here I will take to my office and look after personally. The rest of you will stay here in this room and not stir from it except at my specific orders. Is that clear?"

The man protested. "I can't afford to stay here, Doctor. Besides, if the landlord finds out what's wrong——"

"I'll take all that responsibility," Henry said, and from the set of his jaw Crow realized that he would do just that.

A few minutes later Bob Nichols looked up from his account book in the main room of the tavern, astonishment upon his face as he saw the tall figure of Dr Henry carrying the blanket-wrapped body of the child. He got up and started across the room.

"Don't come any closer, Nichols," Henry warned. "I'm taking the child to my office to look after her. I'll talk to you later about the others. I've ordered them not to stir outside the room. See that they don't." He started off.

"Here, Dr Henry," Nichols said, trying to get his faculties working. "What the hell's coming off here, anyway? What's the matter with the kid?"

"Smallpox—I think," Henry said calmly. "And if you know what's good for you and for all of us you'll do exactly as I say. I'll be back shortly and talk to you."

"Hey, wait a minute!" Nichols was shouting at the doctor's retreating back. "You can't do this! I tell you I won't stand for it."

"I'll be back," Dr Henry said imperturbably.

And he did come back, after putting the child to bed in the back room of his office. He gave Nichols explicit orders that the Crows were not to be allowed out of their room, that they were to be fed, and that he would pay the bill if Crow could not.

Nichols argued and cursed Dr John Henry, the Crow family and all plagues. "By God," he finished, breathless, "I won't stand for it!"

"You will unless you're a complete fool, Nichols," Henry said, and went back to his office. But on his way he stopped and talked with Greenberry Larison.

"I don't like it, either," the sheriff said. "I don't much blame Nichols for raising hell. It's his hotel."

"All right," Henry said patiently. "But don't you see that Nichols, several people at the tavern, and no one knows how many others, have already been exposed? Running the Crows away will only spread the thing farther, and if it's going to take hold here, then the damage has already been done. If they follow my orders we have every chance of stopping it here and now."

"Maybe you're right," Larison agreed dubiously. "But you know how people are, an' smallpox is a damned good thing to be scared of. This is liable to make big trouble."

"Let it, then. I'll stand my part of it if you will."

So there they let the matter rest. But that afternoon Larison started for Pekin, pleading mysterious but important business.

Dr Henry watched the child through the rest of the day. He saw almost no possible chance to save her life, but he was bound to do what he could.

Of course the news spread like wildfire through the village. Women hurriedly gathered their children home, and here and there men eyed Henry's office and the Nichols House and muttered.

The early night was hot and still and very dark. The moon would not rise until nearly ten o'clock. Dr Henry sat by the candles in his outer office and tried to interest himself in his book. Occasionally he went in to look at the tossing child, returning to his chair with a frown and a slight shake of his head. A matter of perhaps twenty-four hours now, he thought. Not more than that.

He looked at his watch, saw that it was near nine o'clock, and as he returned the timepiece to his pocket he heard them coming. He hadn't been quite unprepared. Now he shoved the loaded pistol into the waistband of his trousers and waited calmly. Then he heard his name called sharply, and he got up

and went to the open door, his tall, spare figure sharply silhouetted against the candlelight.

"Well?" he said.

There were perhaps fifteen or twenty of them there on the
grass in front of the office. It was too dark for him to see their
faces, and anyway they stood well away from the path of light
from the open door. But he recognized several familiar voices.

"You know why we're here," a voice said. "There's no use
wastin' words, Doc. We're goin' to run that smallpox outfit out
of town, an' we want the kid in there to go with the rest of 'em.
We don't want no trouble with you, Doc, so if you know what's
good for you you'd better git busy."

The crowd shuffled, and other voices shouted, some whiskily
abusive. The tall man in the doorway waited until they quieted
down again.

"Now, gentlemen," he said, and his voice was soft and calm,
but it carried perfectly into the still darkness, "you're a pack
of fools and don't know when you're well off. But I won't
waste words, either, so we'll pass all that. The child is near
death and cannot be moved under any circumstances—nor will
she be. Not one of you dare touch her, anyway—you're all too
yellow, every last mother's son of you. As for the rest of them
at the tavern, I'll not have them moved. Is that clear? I can
see and hear the tavern from this spot. The moon will be up in
less than an hour, and I will be here all night. I give you my
sacred promise here and now to shoot down the first man that
makes a cross move within my sight or hearing."

They muttered. The doctor waited a moment and then went
on.

"You're fifteen to one," he said, and there was cold contempt in his voice now. "Speak up, any or all of you, or *get off
my property!*"

They were deathly quiet, and the doctor could feel his skin
prickling. Either he had them whipped now or in an instant
they would be on him like a pack of wolves.

1836

Then a voice laughed shortly, nervously, and said aloud: "Oh, hell. *I'm* goin'."

Two minutes later they were all gone.

The doctor stood in the doorway until the last man had vanished. He breathed deeply and relaxed as he saw a bulky figure materialize out of the darkness of the courthouse yard across the street. It was Davis.

"Hello, Doctor," he said. "Is there anything wrong? Allin and I heard there was some trouble up here."

"Good evening, David. Oh, a little disturbance—some of the citizenry questioning my right to handle this smallpox situation as I see fit."

"Did you have any trouble?" Davis's voice was anxious.

"No. Not particularly, that is."

"All right. How is the child?"

"Bad. She can't live until another sundown."

"Un-hunh. Too bad. Anything I can help you with, Doctor?"

"No, nothing. Thanks."

"Well, all right. Good night."

"Good night, David."

True to his word, Henry spent the night in his office chair, at intervals taking a turn about the moonlit square and then down past the Nichols House. There were no disturbances except the owls and the occasional howl of a restless dog. At sunup he yawned, put the carefully oiled pistol back in a desk drawer and went across the yard to the house. For some minutes he had been aware that Minerva was stirring about and making breakfast sounds.

Both Allen Withers and James Miller lived to see stranger things in far places; but neither of them ever forgot that bright afternoon when, after making the plank coffin for him, they helped Dr Henry load it into the back seat of the surrey and take it to a pleasant knoll on the doctor's land near White Oak Hill. Dr Henry and his wife rode in the front seat, with the coffin on the floor in back, and the two boys rode their own horses behind the surrey.

At the burial place the doctor got down and started to take off his coat. "Never mind, Doctor," Withers said in rather an abashed tone. "Jim an' me 'll do it."

So Dr and Mrs Henry waited there in the rank grass while the younger men dug the grave. Afterward they stood uncovered while the doctor prayed. And the younger men were never to forget the scene: Dr Henry in his black frock coat and his starched shirt, standing knee deep in the grass at the open grave, his hat in one hand and his Bible, unopened, in the other. The breeze ruffled his graying hair as he prayed quietly, earnestly, without cant or declamation, ending, "And so we command her immortal soul to the merciful God, Master and Creator of the children of earth. Amen."

Neither Withers nor Miller ever spoke to each other about that afternoon, but when the doctor said simply, "Thank you both, gentlemen," and drove away, they both knew, somehow, that they had received an indelible lesson in human character and the dignity of man.

In Everton Dr Henry, gentleman, scholar, physician, went on in the even tenor of his way. He had earned Everton's profound and lasting respect in one of the few ways the town could understand, but it made little difference to him. He was content to let it go at that and go on healing the sick and minding his own business.

III

Ike Frink never lived in Everton. His home farm was some eight miles southwest of the town, but he was a part of Everton for all that.

He was one of the earlier settlers of Dane County and came to Maple Grove—or its vicinity—in 1825 with his wife Cassandra and two boys. Absalom was then ten years old and his brother Eugene eleven.

In the beginning Ike, like almost all settlers, built a one-roomed cabin, but two years later it burned to the ground and he had to build another. This too was a one-roomed affair but larger and with a lean-to. And Ike, who was a practical man and had had considerable experience in trying to keep a cabin warm in winter, built this one with two doors—one in each of the walls which stood at right angles to the great fireplace. Then, when the fire needed a real replenishing, he and the boys would roll a ten-foot log up to one of the doors, open the opposite door and snake the log into the living room with a length of chain and one of the oxen. Then all they had to do was get the meager furniture out of the way and roll the fresh log into the fireplace. It saved time, kept the cabin warmer than most, and a good big backlog would last a week even in cold weather.

There were two ruling passions in Ike's life: hogs and land; and for these two things he had what seemed to be a natural genius. For example, the matter of the hogs. To Ike it was the simplest thing in the world. Wherever there were men there would be a need for meat, and they would buy meat before they would bread. Furthermore, you had to haul grain, haul it laboriously and at great cost, to market, but hogs could walk. The answer was clear as spring water. A lot of settlers couldn't see it, but Ike couldn't see anything else.

Ike eventually knew more about hogs than he did about his children.

His second love was land. Shortly after his first land was paid for he started to buy more, and as long as he lived he never stopped buying. When he died he owned more *good* land than any other man in the United States. There were larger acreage owners, by far, but every acre of Ike Frink's land was rich, black Illinois prairie, most of it in Dane County, destined eventually to be one of the richest farming counties in the world. In good times and in bad—especially in bad, for then prices were lowest—Ike Frink bought land. In 1825 he bought his first quarter-section, 160 acres; in 1829, 1,040 acres; in 1830, 400 acres; in 1832, 400 acres; in 1834, 560 acres; in 1836, 760 acres. Thus by the end of 1836 he owned, free of debt, 3,320 acres of land. There may have been other men in Illinois who held as much, but it is doubtful. Certainly no other man in Dane County owned one quarter as much. And in Illinois land was power.

Year by year children were born to Ike and Cassandra, and most of them were born with Ike's passion for land, though without his genius for acquiring and paying for it. For many years the Frinks were more nearly a clan than a family, and Everton and Dane County would have been much the poorer without them. They were born like this: Eugene, Absalom, Adam (the only one of the clan to die young—at twenty), Jacob, Francis Marion, Sarah, Isaac Jr, Duncan McArthur, and the departure from the commonplace, at least in names, Marquis de Lafayette.

Even in the matter of the timber Ike was canny. Once Maple Grove had been the geographical center of Dane County, and because the groves in general were so numerous it was the only one to which much attention was paid. Gradually, and for any number of reasons, the groves were cut down, thinned out, and disappeared, making room for corn and oats. But not Ike Frink's grove. His original homestead had been located almost at the center of the grove, and eventually he owned it all. But that timber was never cleared. It was cut and thinned out and used, yes, but never cleared. In the beginning the timber did very well for the hog-raising business, and later, when Ike was a farmer on a huge scale, he could afford not to use the old grove. In the course of the century after Ike's settlement more than a million dollars' worth of timber produce was taken out of it. A century later it was to be the largest single tract of timber in many a flat mile of corn country. In the spring now, as then, the violets grow in wild profusion, the sweet williams, the jacks-in-the-pulpit, the dutchmen's breeches, cover the old brown earth. The wild plum and crabapple shower the ground with blossoms, and the wild grapes entwine the trees in endless clinging strands. There, too, Ike Frink lies buried, his tombstone still the largest in a small forest of stones all somewhere labeled "Frink," as though those who in later days came to erect headstones purposely avoided overshadowing that of Isaac the elder. . . .

Meanwhile, in 1836, Ike bred hogs, bought more land, begat the beginnings of a cornland dynasty and met his financial obligations on the dot.

IV

In his blacksmith shop just north of where the slough crossed Main Street, Abe Brokaw shoed horses, made and repaired tools of all kinds, mended iron kettles and skillets and wagons. Also he was now building plows with steel shares, plows that were to conquer the prairie and make agricultural history.

It was a slow process. Every finished plow was a triumph of trial and error, and more often than not the brave customer who bought a plow would have to haul it back to Abe's shop for adjustment a half-dozen times. Frequently it would require a complete rebuilding before it would function reasonably well. Steel was expensive and hard to come by at any price. True, it was being made in Kentucky now, but communication was slow and freight deliveries even slower. And when it was finally delivered it was sometimes almost impossible to use. There was no sheet-rolling process available, and sheets were almost always uneven in thickness and texture. Lighter or heavier shares caused a plow to balance differently and the side draft to vary, hence Abe's necessary trial-and-error method of manufacture.

But they were making plows, that was the important thing. In '35, the year Joe Dawson discovered that the prairie could be turned, Abe built and sold three plows. The next year he made and sold seven and had orders for ten more to be delivered by spring of 1837. Thus by the end of 1837 there would be available an even twenty plows to work Dane County's some thousand square miles of tillable prairie—which is something like trying to empty a lake that size with twenty ordinary buckets. But it was a start for all that, a start toward making Dane County one of the richest farming regions in the world.

AMERICAN YEARS

Abe Brokaw and Joe Dawson were not the first men to make the epochal discovery that steel would plow the prairie turf. Up near the Rock River an American immortal named John Deere had learned the same thing at about the same time. And here and there across Indiana and Illinois and Missouri other men were making the same discovery. It was something like the evolution of another famous American product, the long rifle—men everywhere bringing their common experience and ability to bear upon a common problem. Some merely succeeded better than the others.

The tools, crude but altogether practical, were at hand. Now it was only a question of time until the prairie frontier moved westward and made way for a civilization—for better or worse.

V

He called himself "Doctor" Hobbs at first, and advertised in the *Advocate* as a practising dentist, but that didn't last long. There was no law to keep him from calling himself "Doctor," but also, after a little experience with him as dentist, there was nothing to make patients expose themselves to his fierce energy. He knew practically nothing about dentistry, at least no more than could be learned in, say, a half-hour. If you had a tooth-ache he cured it by the simple method of *twisting* out the bad tooth by main strength and awkwardness. It wasn't such an unusual method of treatment at the time and place, but Hobbs was even rougher and more awkward than the average practitioner. At first he got a few customers, driven to him by searing toothaches and a willingness to try anything once. But with Hobbs once was enough for even the bravest sufferer; they preferred the pain to Hobbs's cure for it. So shortly, being effectively advertised by past patients who had tried him and lost, Hobbs's standing as a dentist gradually diminished.

Hobbs was a loquacious man and pleasant enough. He would talk at great length on any subject and at any time or place, but it was years before anyone discovered that in all the talking he did he said very little about himself. There were all sorts of rumors. It was known that he had come originally from Maryland. It was *said* that he had once been wealthy and occupied a social station of importance, but had been cruelly jilted by his one true love. It was hinted that he had dissipated his fortune in an attempt to drown his sorrow, and that having spent his substance and failed in the drowning process, he had come West to start over again. These and vaguer rumors persisted for years, but Hobbs himself said little or nothing about them. People as a whole took him as he was, as they did most others, and didn't bother about his past. He was a teetotaler, used a little snuff but no tobacco, and was quite a ladies' man. But not in the usual meaning of the phrase. By a certain kind of attention to all women he kept away from any one woman in particular. He would rather talk to a woman than a man any day, but he was equally gallant and expansive whether the woman was eighteen or eighty. Having apparently only the most honorable of motives, their age mattered little to him. So after the menfolk got used to his ways he didn't worry them, and at social gatherings they found him handy to have around. They could, if they wished, ignore their women without the women being able to claim that they were altogether neglected; Hobbs was always ready to step into the social breach with pleasant gallantries which flattered the women and which they couldn't have gotten from their own men anyway.

Dentistry languishing, Hobbs opened a "loud" school, and because he stood well with the matrons of the town the school prospered somewhat. He was a better educated man than most of his neighbors, but he was in no sense learned as, say, Dr Henry. Probably he couldn't have tied himself to the petty business of primary schoolmastering if he had been. But he did well enough with reading, writing, simple arithmetic, geography and spelling. In addition he gave his pupils instruction in a subject which was more than a little strange to Everton: manners. His ideas on etiquette were stilted and stagy, it is true, but to children who came from homes with earthen or puncheon floors, where Father likely as not spat on the floor at will, almost anything was an improvement over what they had.

The school did very well, and before long Hobbs was a logical part of the town. Gradually the assumed title of "Doctor" was lost and he again became just plain Mister Hobbs. His name was William Cullom Hobbs; but no one was ever heard to call him Bill or William or Will or even Hobbs. He was always Mister Hobbs.

The school was established in an abandoned cabin a half-mile south of the little courthouse, and on Sundays the Baptists used the cabin for a church. Just beyond the courthouse Main Street sloped downhill for a quarter of a mile, to a little brook, and there, to all intents and purposes, the street ended. But a thread of road went on up the other wall of the little valley, and the schoolhouse stood in the timber at the top of the hill. With Hobbs school was strictly a business proposition, so he operated six days a week the year round. There were no terms in the sense of beginning or ending, and children came or not as their parents were willing to pay the small tuition and send them.

For some of the youth school was irksome, as it has been from time immemorial, and this was especially true when the sap began to run in the spring. None of them, perhaps, was actually aware of the endless pageant that passed before their eyes. But the virgin, lovely land was there, to be seen by any who would look.

A fourteen-year-old, not too intent upon the pigtails of a Minerva Haines or a Julia Allin, walked through a magic forest on his way to Hobbs's school: a forest of burr, white, red, black and chinkapin swamp oak; of linn, honey locust, hackberry, coffee nut, sassafras, ironwood, black cherry, choke cherry, white elm and slippery elm, black and white walnut, shellbark hickory, pignut hickory, sugar maple, white maple, blue and white ash, sycamore, cottonwood, aspen, mulberry, box elder, buckeye, red bud, red haw, black haw, willow, service berry, sumach, prickly ash, bluebeech, pawpaw, crabapple, wild plum, elder, wahoo, cedar and, occasionally, persimmon. Underfoot the violets, sweet williams, jacks-in-the-pulpit, may apples, and dogwood ran riot. A horse, seeking an open path through the thick timber, would have his four legs crimson to the knees with the juices of the wild strawberries which he had trodden. And on the sun-swept slopes of little ravines and on open hillsides wild roses grew in mad profusion.

And for the unseeing eye of this hypothetical fourteen-year-old, at the varying time of year, this life of timber and stream and marsh and sky: black bear, Virginia deer, opossum, raccoon, otter, red and gray squirrels, prairie wolves, foxes, rabbits and an occasional elk; wild turkey, prairie chicken, partridge, quail, sandhill cranes, snow geese, Canadian geese, mallards, pintails, wood duck, butterball duck, teal grebe, mud hens, Virginia rails, water rails, golden, ringed and Kildeer plovers, woodcock, curlews, snipe and pigeons and turtledoves.

Almost all these were food. There were others which added nothing but beauty to the pageant, but in this year of growth these were unnoted by listing naturalists. A man with eyes and hands and hunger could hardly starve except by insistence. Nature herself provided almost everything for the fools and the naturally improvident. Almost. For instance, nature invented the cash crop but not the cash to pay for it. And the settler, whoever he might be, came not so much to buy the wilderness as to possess it in order to sell it—sell it to almost anyone. So the pageant went by largely unseen except by those who had occasion to curse its necessary cruelties. Man was here. Already the end was in sight.

CHAPTER SIX

1837

THE SIMPLE REASON USUALLY GIVEN for the panic of the year 1837 is this: President Jackson withdrew the funds of the United States from the privately owned United States Bank and deposited them in what have since been known as the federal reserve banks. Thus the simple fact of cause. It was perfectly legal—except in the minds of those to whom constitutionality meant their own personal pocketbooks; it was inevitable; and it was part of the American pattern that the rabble-rousing Jackson should be the man to do it.

But its repercussions rolled far and wide, and the results were also inevitable. That they had asked for it didn't make the citizenry take it any easier. For how, they asked, did they know what they did want?

The Bank, faced with sudden ruin, was forced to call loans to Eastern business. (It was not Sudden Ruin, actually, but it was part of financial method to put up a calamitous front, and the practical results were the same.) Business was forced to demand payment, immediate payment, from debtors who heretofore had taken six months' credit or a year's credit as a matter of course. Indeed, with communication and transportation what they were, six months was no more than a week was to be a century later. From Everton, in Illinois, a Green or a Haines journeyed to Philadelphia in early fall and bought merchandise to be delivered the following spring. As a matter of course they paid for it in the fall following spring delivery, when crops were sold and accounts settled for the season. It was, for them, the logical way. But now Jackson had carried out a mandate from the folk—or so he said. Things were suddenly different. Complacent storekeepers in what had a few years before been the Northwest Territory got peremptory demands for payment from Eastern jobbers who heretofore had—so they thought— been their friends.

There is a psychology of Panic and Depression, and historical juxtaposition seems not to matter in the very least. It is always the same.

The pompous financier of American fact and fiction was still uncelebrated in print, but he existed nonetheless. In Chestnut Street, Philadelphia, and in Wall Street, New York, he was a fact, regardless of what the West might imagine. He might be, and probably was, thin rather than paunchy, and he didn't wear diamond buttons on his vest, as the caricatures were later to insist. But he was there. And the West could hardly imagine it. Experience, cast in the frontier mold, could produce fantasy in the vein of Charley Indian or Mike Fink, but it could not conceive heroes like Nick Biddle or the Josephs brothers.

But fact was fact, and the panic of the seaboard was communicated to the West in a hundred ways: by the price of hogs and corn, the inability to collect any Eastern debt, no matter how small, the whispered tales, the doleful letters from relatives and friends, the madly exaggerated accounts (not all of them exaggerated) of travelers, weird word-of-mouth advertisings. All of these contributed to a gelatinous state of mind in the West.

Everton was no exception, even if she should have known better.

AMERICAN YEARS

I I

It was late for Everton—nearly nine o'clock.

Jesse Fell came up the steps to the second-floor office which he still shared with Davis and Davis's newly acquired law partner, Wells Colton. He saw light under the rough door, and when he entered the little front room he found his younger brother bent over a book beside the candles on the table. Kersey Fell was twenty-two and had come out to Everton a few months before at Jesse's express instigation. Jesse had seen little of the youth in the previous six or seven years, yet he was more than a little fond of him. He was glad that Kersey was here in Everton now. With some of his own blood near at hand he felt somehow more at home, that Everton *was* more nearly home. For Jesse had been here four years now, and he knew that Everton was the place he belonged in. He could not have explained his reasons in so many words, but he knew just the same.

"Good evening, Kersey," he said quietly, and took off his heavy coat.

"Oh, hello, Jesse." Kersey smiled across the candles at his elder brother. "I was so interested here I guess I didn't hear you on the steps."

"Interested?" Jesse said. "In what?" He walked across to the table and glanced down at the calfbound volume of Chitty's *Pleadings* which the boy had open before him. "Chitty, eh? I daresay, even as dry and dull as he is, he isn't as bad as the account books at Haines'. How about it?"

"Well, yes," Kersey said, a little abashed. "Not that I mind Haines, Jesse. I didn't mean that at all. I like it well enough there, in a way. But I don't know—it doesn't seem to amount to much, clerking in a country store. I guess you know what I mean."

"Yes, I guess I do." The older man sat down and leaned his chair back against the wall and closed his eyes tiredly. "Of course, boy. But everyone has to get started somewhere, you know. Haines isn't so bad to work for, is he?"

"Oh, no," Kersey said quickly. "I didn't mean that. But I just came back this afternoon———"

"Back? From where, boy?"

"Well, of course you wouldn't know. Let's see—you've been gone six days. Mr Haines had some business with Mr Stuart in Springfield, and he let me go down and take care of it for him. I spent a whole day loafing around Mr Stuart's office."

"John Stuart, eh? So that's it. Well, I met John Stuart the first night I walked into Springfield, and he's been a good friend to me ever since. But has he been giving you ideas?"

"No-o-o, not exactly. He didn't say a whole lot to me. But I met a fellow there who's reading law in his office, a fine fellow, Jess, and he made me think a lot."

"Oh, John always has a student or two on the string. Do I know this one?"

"I don't know." Kersey paused a moment, remembering his student friend. "He was a funny kind of a fellow—and I guess the most ungainly-looking critter you ever saw. He told me he'd done a lot of things. You know—kept store, done some flat-boating, split and hauled rails, farmed—everything. And he didn't have any education to speak of. I told him that I didn't, either, and he said he didn't think that would matter if I wanted to study the law bad enough."

"What was his name?" Jesse asked idly. "Maybe I know him."

"His name is Abraham Lincoln. He's no child, Jesse. He's been around quite a lot, and Mr Stuart seems to think a good deal of him."

"Lincoln? Lincoln? Oh, sure, I remember hearing the name around Salem. Wasn't he in the Black Hawk War?"

"I guess he did say he was. He didn't talk much about it, though."

"So? Well, 'twas nothing for anybody to be very proud of. Not that that was young Lincoln's fault. He did himself well in that, so I recall hearing. And so he's reading law in John Stuart's office. I heard of him a few years ago, when I first came to Illinois. He was just over being a captain in the Salem Volunteers then. I remember I passed through the town at the time, and they seemed to think a lot of the lad thereabouts. If Stuart thinks that too, then he must be all right. And has this Lincoln been giving you ideas about the law?"

"Well, you might put it that way, Jesse. *He* likes it. And he said that if I wanted to do it he didn't see that my education had much to do with it. I haven't had much, but it's more than he had."

"Un-hunh. I see. Well, once I thought the law was a fine thing. I suppose I still do. But it didn't suit me as well as other things. What do you want to do about it, boy?"

"Well, I talked to Davis———"

"Oh, you did, eh?" Jesse grinned at him. "Making up your mind fast. And what did David say?"

"He said I should talk to you; that if you thought it was all right I could come in here an' study with him and Colton for a while and we'd see how I made out."

Jesse was thoughtful for a moment. "I don't see any harm in that. You're old enough to know what you want to do— or you ought to be. Just take a few days to think it over, to be sure. Anything exciting happen while I was gone?"

"No, not much of anything, I guess. But I've been gone for several days too, you know. I see Mr Guthrie has the new courthouse nearly done. It's going to look better than I thought it would when he started. Trade is pretty slow at the store. Everywhere else too, I guess. Everybody says things are getting worse in the East."

"I know. Things 're bad in Chicago too; very bad."

"I guess that means you didn't bring off what you went up there for."

"I'm not sure, but probably you're right. There's no money to be had at any rate of interest—anywhere. I hate to lose that bit of Chicago property. It's not worth a lot now—less than a lot of other things I have a finger in—but I had high hopes for it. That town certainly is growing. Oh well, a man gains or loses, that's the way it goes."

"They say it's all that crazy Andy Jackson's fault," Kersey said hotly.

"Pooh, now," Jesse said. "You'll make a poor lawyer if you jump to conclusions like that, boy."

"Well, why isn't it his fault?"

"Your question is wrong: it should be, why *is* it his fault— if it is. I never voted for Jackson, but the people elected him. If they choose to go mad after getting him, is that his fault? Of course not. But people are like sheep—they flock first in one direction, then another. This panic will pass, Kersey, though just how soon only God knows. Maybe He isn't altogether sure."

"Are you really hit bad, Jesse?"

"So far not so bad. But I have no money at hand and no prospect of getting any. If this would pass soon I'd be all right. But I'm afraid it won't. People are slower to be optimistic than they are downcast."

"Your credit is the best. Everybody says so," Kersey said loyally.

"Of course, boy. And what good is that?"

"You can borrow, surely. Enough to see you over the hump. From Mr Frink, or Green, or maybe even Davis."

Jesse smiled kindly and shook his head a little. "No, I can't. They're all in the same boat. I came by Green's store on my way up here. He was there, working on his books. And he's about ready to give up. Every cent he has in the world is either in goods which are worth less every day, or in his accounts receivable. Today he can't collect a cent of cash in Dane County. He won't last four months the way his Eastern creditors are pushing him, and he knows it. He's worried—badly."

"And Davis?"

"Davis is my very good friend—this is more than confidential, boy—but what money he has now really belongs to his wife. Of course it's his, but then . . . Why should he lend to me at

[129]

interest, even very high interest, when with a few thousand dollars he can buy a future fortune? You might as well learn this now—don't expect too much of people, even your good friends!"

"Well, Frink is the richest man in the county. What about him? You've done him some good turns."

"So I have. And what about it? Ike Frink is the biggest land-holder in Dane County. He'll probably continue to be just that, and he got that way by buying cheap and never selling. This panic will be a godsend to him. His one passion is land, and he'll never again be able to buy it as cheap as he will now and for the next year or so. Ike knows it, too, and he'll want every cent of his own that he can lay hands on."

"What will you do, Jesse?"

The older man shrugged. "Nothing, I suppose. That's what most people do. Just hang onto all I can for as long as I can and see how it ends. That's about all I can do. Oh, by the way, did I tell you that I'd sold the *Advocate* machinery?"

"No. Who to?"

"Fellow in Peoria. He's going to come and haul the stuff himself. Coming over after it in a few days. I didn't get much for it, but what I did get was cash."

"Un-hunh. It seems a shame—losing the paper, I mean. Sort of a backward step for Everton. You've always said that a paper was a fine thing for a town."

"Of course it is. But I guess Everton just wasn't ready for it. At least it wasn't ready to pay for it. The first three months that Hill was here we broke just about even. Since he left and I've been editing the thing we've gone steadily downgrade. Even figuring my time as worth nothing, we were still losing money. None of us can afford that, so I guess it's best that we got rid of it. Allin and Green have been after me to sell the machinery, so I'm glad it's done. Perhaps someday we can try it again."

Kersey yawned widely, and Jesse looked at his watch.

"Lordy, we've been chewing the fat here for over an hour.

Time for us to be in bed, boy. Hester will be wondering what's become of us."

"But about the law, Jesse. You do think it's all right for me to try it?"

Jesse clapped him fondly on the shoulder. "Why, of course, Kersey. If you've made up your mind that's what you want, then do it. Davis and Colton are good men. They'll do their best for you if they agree to take you in." He laughed in the darkness as they went down the steps. "Might be a good idea to have at least *one* working lawyer in the family."

III

In time Dr Henry came to know more about the physical and mental ills of Everton than any other man. He knew more and said less—less, that is, to people who were not concerned. To those who were concerned he gave his best advice. Of course it wasn't always appreciated, but Henry didn't mind that in the least.

He was one of the very finest physicians in the West, and for that very reason some of his colleagues were apt to consider some of his opinions unorthodox, which is a mild word for what they said. Further, he was a scholar, and probably his strongest passion was his dislike of fools. He might sometimes listen respectfully while Ike Frink talked about some aspect of hog raising, but if Ike ventured some opinion about national affairs, for instance, Henry would tell him bluntly that he was a jackass and stalk away.

Most of his neighbors never thought much about Dr Henry's kindheartedness, or lack of it; yet he was a physician first of all. He was more than generous with his time and money and medical knowledge, but he was never known to gush sympathetically or sentimentally over anyone. He never tried to hide his ignorance, which, colossal as he himself knew it was, was still 90 per cent less than that of most of his frontier colleagues. More often he told his patient flatly that he didn't know what the trouble was, or perhaps that he did know but couldn't do much about it. He hated all sham and hypocrisy and unnecessary ignorance, and he never bothered to conceal his hatred. To him that would have been just so much more sham on his part.

In most things he had a very good memory, but in the case of Brady Dale he remembered the boy's first visit to him in connection with something else.

As was usual with him he was this night sitting in his office, reading and waiting for any chance patient that might come in. On this particular evening he had opened two newly received copies of the *Southern Literary Messenger*. They were for consecutive months, but, the mails being what they were, he had received them only a few days apart. And in them he had found the first and second installments of *The Narrative of Arthur Gordon Pym*. The author he had never before heard of. But he had read only a few thousand words when he knew that Edgar Allan Poe was something altogether new in American literature. Dr Henry was scholar enough to know. He went back and started the tale over again, reading now with closer attention, getting the full flavor of the tale.

Then Brady Dale came in and at Henry's invitation sat down very gingerly on the edge of a chair. He sat there silently, twisting his hat in his hands, embarrassed beyond words.

Dr Henry looked him over critically, then grinned, trying to put the boy at ease. He guessed his age at twenty-two, though of course in this country you could never be sure. Youngsters matured quickly on the edge of the frontier.

"You don't look as though you need the services of a doctor," Henry said pleasantly. "And, by the way, I've seen you around, but I don't believe I know you. What do you do?"

"I work for Mr Kelvin—you know, the linseed-oil mill, and I haven't been here long. I came here from near Danville. Things were slow on the farm place, an' I got this job through my father —he knows Mr Kelvin real well. We've only been here in Everton about two weeks."

"We?" said Dr Henry. "Who is 'we'?"

"My wife an' me," and he blushed at the unaccustomed phrase, "my wife."

"Hmmm. I see. And what can I do for you?"

"Well, er, that is, it ain't *me*," Dale said hesitantly. "It's my wife."

"Oh? And did you bring her with you, or is she too ill, or what?"

"No, sir. You see, she wouldn't come with me. I guess she ain't too sick. At least she's able to be about an' do the housework. But she wouldn't come, said there wasn't nothin' wrong with her to be runnin' to a doctor about."

"Well, women are sometimes that way." He somehow sensed that there was more to the boy's story than he had so far told. "How old is she, boy?"

"Seventeen."

"I see. And how long have you been married?"

"A little more 'n two weeks—just before we come here." Again the embarrassed blush.

The doctor pursed his lips and frowned a little. "Listen to me," he said then. "I know you want help of some kind or you wouldn't have come to me, and if I can help you I will. But I'm no magician, and there's a very great deal about human beings that I don't know—that no mere doctor knows. Remember that, and then tell me exactly what's on your mind."

So lamely, hesitantly, Dale told him. Of course they had slept together the first night they were married. She had bled terribly. They had both known that she would, of course—some. But not like that. Not those terrible, seemingly endless streams. The boy shuddered a little at the memory.

"Well, boy," Dr Henry said, "that's not so terribly uncommon. A slight hemorrhage, perhaps. That would account for it. So what then?"

"She felt kind of puny like for a few days, and I—I mean we—didn't do nothing. Then when we did it was worse than the first time. God! Dr Henry, you wouldn't think any human could bleed like that an' live."

"And what has happened since?"

"Nothing." The youth sat with eyes miserably downcast. "Just nothing. She's scared to death—and I guess I am, too."

"Hmmm," Dr Henry said dryly. "I imagine so. An odd case, in a way, though it may have some reasonable explanation. But of course you know that I couldn't tell you very much until I examine her."

"I know," Dale said. "But I thought I'd best talk to you about it. Around town they say you know more about doctorin' than any man in the state."

"Well, that's a moot question. I do what I can. You might say that my strength lies in my knowledge of my own limitations. Have her come in and see me. Will you do that?"

"I will if I can. But I don't know. She wouldn't come tonight. I tried to get her, but she wouldn't."

"Ah, well, she's young. Naturally she's a little embarrassed. Most of them are like that at first. After she's had a couple of husky children she won't feel that way. Bring her down in the next day or two if you can, and we'll see what we can do."

"Yes, sir," Dale said. "I'll do it if I can. But I don't think she'll come."

When he had gone, Henry sat for a few moments, pondering the boy's tale. Not an uncommon thing, in a way. Yet he had a hunch that the case was an uncommon one. Not from the meager symptoms the boy had described, of course. Yet he had that feeling. And so many times he *was* brought face to face with the startling fact of how little he did know. As a professional that hurt his inner pride. Yet he didn't know anything he could do about it.

He turned back to his marked place in the *Literary Messenger*, and in a moment he was lost with Arthur Pym in another world.

The girl never came around. And though Everton was still but a small village, Dr Henry did not see the boy often. Dale of course worked long hours, as did every laborer, and Henry seldom found himself with business in the vicinity of Kelvin's mill.

The next visit came after midnight more than a month later, when Dale roused Dr Henry from a sound sleep. "It's Brady Dale, Doctor," he said, and his voice was full of fear. "My wife —she's pretty bad."

It was midsummer now, and the streets were deep with dust. Their feet made tiny padding sounds as they walked. It was dark and very still, and the only visible light was in the front window of Killip's Tavern.

"She felt bad last night," Dale was saying, "and I wanted to fetch you, but she wouldn't have it. She said it was nothing much. This morning she seemed to feel a little better. Then when I came home tonight she was in bed and feelin' mighty bad. Said she was mighty sick to her stumick—maybe something she'd et. I dunno." He sighed a little. "I'm scared it's somethin' worse than that."

In the little cabin Henry got down to business. He took off his coat and ordered Dale to bring more light—"a half-dozen candles," he said, "or a dozen if you've got them. Maybe God can perform miracles in the dark, but I can't."

She was a nice, ordinary-looking girl, or normally would have been. Her great mop of hair was blue-black, even in the candlelight, and her face a pleasant oval punctuated by full lips and long, sweeping lashes. Her skin was deathly white, and now she was wildly delirious. Her eyes were wide open, but she recognized neither of them, only talked and ranted incoherently. Her pulse was like a racing trip hammer, and when Henry touched her forehead he winced involuntarily. Never in his experience had he known flesh as hot.

"Hmmm," Henry said. "Shut that door and then lift her shoulders and help me pull that nightgown off. It's a filthy mess, anyway."

It *was* a mess, a terrible, inhuman mess. It was as though bowels and bladder had conspired to compose some hellish travesty of human excrement. Now she was vomiting again, and that too was like nothing human. John Flournoy Henry had seen as much disease, including cholera rampant, as any man alive, and yet, he told himself, he had never seen anything like this. Never, he thought, had he seen a human being as terribly, unbelievably ill as this one.

"Can you help her, you think?" Dale asked him, and his face was pale and strained.

Dr Henry looked at him quietly. "Son," he said, "I don't think so, but I don't know. I doubt that any mere doctor can help this."

"But what is it?"

"I don't know—yet. I'm trying to find out. Better open that door again. This air is pretty bad."

Of course the cabin was badly ventilated, and the stench was indescribable. Henry saw the boy shiver and swallow, hard. "Go on out and sit on the steps for a while, boy," he said kindly. "It 'll do you good, and if I need anything I'll call you."

It was dawn when Dr Henry finally left. And he knew little more than when he had come five hours before. She was a little quieter now, but he thought that was merely a symptom of growing weakness. He wasn't sure. He wasn't sure of anything except that he had never before seen anything quite like this.

"I'll be back about nine," he told Dale wearily. "Don't hope too much. She's very, very bad. More than that I can't tell you. I wish I could."

He walked slowly toward home, trying to make his brain function in orderly fashion. It was one of the few times in his life that he had come upon a case which was an absolute blank wall. Quite often he had been puzzled, not sure of himself; but almost always he had had an inkling, a hint, of something. This he could not even attempt to diagnose. It might be any one of a hundred things, but one by one, during the night, he had rejected every theory he had so far touched upon. Again, in his weariness, he felt the appalling weight of what he knew was his own ignorance, and he silently damned the mountain he could not move.

Would anyone, he wondered, ever invent something with which a doctor, not gifted with a godlike eye, could see what went on inside a human body? My God, what a marvel that would be! Then he dismissed the thought, laughing a little at his fancy. He guessed he was tired.

Alice Dale had an advanced case of intestinal tuberculosis, and now it was simply rending her very vitals. An otherwise healthy virgin, the disease had lain more or less dormant for years. Occasionally she had had pain and been a little sick, but that was no uncommon thing, even among the healthiest of women. Now, after her marriage, the disease had suddenly come into its own and was working its terrible havoc. If she had been born a hundred years later there still wouldn't have been much anyone could do for her. Doctors would have known very well what was wrong with her, but only the condescension of God could have cured her.

But Dr Henry never knew what was wrong with her. He only knew that he did not know and that no other physician in the world would have known, either.

He guessed now that she would not live through another night. But he was wrong about that, too. She was to live for three more terrible years, and Dr Henry was to learn from Alice and Brady Dale a number of things, none of which was concerned with mere medicine.

IV

Bert Killip surveyed the taproom contentedly from his vantage point behind the hand-hewn walnut slabs of the bar. There might be a panic on, but this was a pretty good night, even for a Saturday. Men will buy liquor, Bert reflected vaguely, when they can't buy anything else. He'd heard a great deal of talk about Green and Allin and Haines and other merchants being broke, or the next thing to it. Well, that's what you could expect of those credit businesses. It wasn't that way with liquor. You bought for cash and sold the same way. If you made money it was yours, and you had it in your poke instead of in a ledger.

There were slow hoofbeats outside, and then Albert Hardy came in through the tavern door, his eyes blinking in the light. He nodded and spoke to a half-dozen of those present, then leaned against the bar and took a fresh chew, replacing the one he had just spat into the sawdust on the floor.

"Howdy, Al," Bert said genially. "What's yours?"

"Rye," Hardy said, "and don't be as damned stingy with it as usual."

"We aims to please. A little water, Al?"

"No," said Hardy. "Tonight I ain't aimin' to build me a fire jest to practise puttin' it out. Have one, Ned?"

"Don't mind if I do," Ned Bostwick said. He was a near neighbor of Hardy's. "Make mine the same, Bert."

"Sure." Killip put four fingers of rye into each of two tumblers and slid them down the polished walnut. "You look a little weary, Al," he said. "Where you in from?"

"Jest this minute pulled in from Chicago," Hardy said, addressing the others in the tavern as much as Ned and Killip. "And by God, I tell you, gents, I'm disgusted—jest plumb disgusted."

"I hear it ain't much of a town," someone said.

"Well, it ain't that which gets me down so much, though it's probably true enough," Hardy said. "But to tell the truth, it ain't such a slouch of a town, at that. I heard they got a whorehouse there already, an' a good one, though mind you, I didn't see it. But no, it ain't that. It's jest that I been wonderin', all the way back to Everton, what the sweet hell this country's comin' to."

"Oh, it ain't so bad, Al," Killip said. "Times is hard, sure. But that 'll pass. We've seen hard times before. Jackson was a good man, but eight years of him was enough. We got a new man in there now, an' this Van Buren 'll make them Eastern bastards come to time."

"Van Buren!" The name was more like an oath than a statement. The speaker was a tall, gaunt man with a huge beak of a nose. He was sitting at a table with a short, fat man and a pimply-faced youth who was obviously the latter's son. Again he repeated the name. "Van Buren! That errand boy for Andy Jackson! What the hell do you think *he'll* do for you?"

"This is Mr Connors and Mr Allman," Killip said to Hardy, indicating the tall man and the short one in that order. "They're for Ioway," he explained.

Hardy shook hands. "Ioway, hunh?" he said. "I've heard it's good country. Where you from—if that's a fair question?"

"New York State," Connors told him.

"New York, eh? It's a long way from there to Ioway, stranger. There's lots o' land this side the river—if land's what you're lookin' for."

"We are lookin' for land," Connors said, "but land that we can afford. Ioway's still Wisconsin Territory—a man can farm there without money, or at least without very much. And it's farther from them maggots an' rattlesnakes in Washington that calls themselves the federal government. To some of us nowadays that's worth a lot of trouble."

"By cripes!" Hardy said. "Maybe you're right. I never thought about it that way, I guess. Will you have a drink?"

"Don't mind if I do."

"I was jest sayin'," Hardy went on when the drinks were poured, "that I don't know what the hell this country's comin' to. Now take my case, for instance. Here I break my back raisin' them hogs an' feedin' 'em the whole year. Then I haul the six of 'em to Chicago in the wagon—six hogs that 'll average more 'n two-fifty apiece. I hauled 'em to keep from workin' the fat off 'em that walkin' would do. And how much do I get for 'em? A stinkin' twenty dollars an' sixteen cents! A year's work; a trip of a hunderd an' thirty miles each way. Twenty dollars an' sixteen cents. Why, man, it's an insult, that's what it is."

"Nobody made you sell your hogs," said a slow voice from a back table.

"No," Hardy said. "Nobody made me sell 'em. But what the hell do you think I raise hogs for? What does anybody raise hogs for? Because I like the stink of hog manure? Or because I like their sweet an' lovin' dispositions?"

"Now, gentlemen," Killip said placatingly, "we all have our little disagreements, but let's don't get personal. The drinks are on the house. Will you name 'em?"

They did, and for a few minutes the bar was busy and the talk impersonal.

Connors had gotten up from his table, and now he leaned against the bar, his freshly empty glass in his hand. "I tell you, gentlemen," he said, and his speech was slightly more academic as the liquor took hold, "man and boy I've lived in New York State for forty-five years. I was at Niagara in 1812, and I saw the bastard British burn Washington city. They left their mark on me, too, or rather their stinking Iroquois did. But damned if I know now. Maybe it would have been a good idea to let the bastard English have the country back." He laughed bitterly, as a man will who has endured great trials and lived to see them in perspective as farce. "Jackson," he went on, "and his bootblack, Van Buren! I'm no great believer in the theory that God intervenes in matters of democratic government. But if He does, then He's a miserable failure."

"Sir," again announced the same slow voice from the rear table, "you're insulting the name of Jackson, so far, next to Washington, the most able President this country has ever had, and his able successor, Van Buren, who has so far done no wrong against you or any other decent citizen." It was Mason, the millwright, speaking, a Democrat with minor political leanings, as yet unsatisfied, and his voice sounded like a stump speech.

"I didn't catch your name," Connors said softly.

"Robert Mason, sir. A good Democrat and damned proud of it."

"Then my regards, Mr Mason," said Connors, and flung his empty glass.

The heavy tumbler caught Mason squarely between the eyes as he sat upright in his chair. The glass broke into a dozen pieces, and a thin trickle of blood appeared on the man's forehead.

Instantly there was confusion. Allman, Connors' traveling

companion, had the big man by one arm, and Hardy was holding him on the other side. Killip and a couple of others were clumsily wiping Mason's forehead and trying to keep him from falling out of the chair.

"For God's sake, Mr Connors," Killip was mumbling, "this is no place for a brawl." Then, to one of the other local boys: "I guess he's not hurt any to speak of, but there's quite a gash there on his forehead. Maybe a couple of you better take him over to Doc Henry an' have him looked at, just in case."

"I'm sorry, landlord," Connors said. "My apologies to your house. But"—and his voice was icy again—"answering a liar and a fool is hardly brawling."

"No, no, of course not. Call it whatever you want to," Killip said hurriedly. "It's just that I don't like trouble in my place. After all, you're the stranger and he's the local man. If there was any real trouble, you're the one who would eventually get the worst of it."

"I can take care of myself, thanks," snapped Connors.

"Of course, of course," Killip soothed. "This one is on the house. What 'll it be, gentlemen?"

Again the bar was lined, and they drank.

A slim little man, really not much more than a youth, came up to Connors. "My name is Robinson," he said, and extended his hand. "I understood you to say you were from New York State. So 'm I. I wondered if you know the country around Robertsville?"

"Glad to know you. No, I don't know it well. I've been through there a couple of times, that's about all. You from there?"

"My family has lived there since long before '76."

"Un-hunh. Nice country thereabouts, as I recall. What are *you* doing out here?"

Robinson shrugged a little. "What everybody else is doing— trying to make a living."

"Doing it?"

"Just about. I came here about six months ago. I'm working in Haines' store right now. I've got a little stake put away.

When times are better I aim to set up for myself. I'll be well enough acquainted by then to chance it."

"Tame kind o' business for a likely-lookin' feller like you. By God, if I was your age do you know what I'd do?"

Robinson confessed that he couldn't say.

"I'd git to hell out of this ague country and join up with Sam Houston down in Texas. There's a country that'll amount to something someday, you mark my word."

"Maybe." Robinson smiled faintly. "But if I wanted to be a road agent I wouldn't have to go to Texas to do it. As far as I can see, Sam Houston's generaling a gang of highwaymen. No, I'm stickin' here till times get better and then set up for myself."

"Times 'll get better when every rotten Democrat is run out of Washington an' they let us operate the country ourselves like it ought to be. But I'm not startin' any more political arguments around here tonight. One is enough. Like this part of the state?"

"Yes. It's good country. And this is a good town. Good people here, for the most part. Steady, not fly-by-nights like you find in so much of this country these days."

"How long's this territory been settled up?" Connors asked curiously.

"Since '25," Hardy put in. He had returned from Henry's, reporting that beyond two stitches and a headache Mason was all right but no longer in a mood to debate the superiority of the Democratic party. "I was one of the first ones in this county. I was so damn sick of venison I never want to see another buck as long as I live." He laughed a little, then became serious again: "Then there was the time the government put the public land up for sale. Public land! Godalmighty! Land that we'd worked our guts out for, tryin' to make something out of it. Well, it didn't stay public long. Everybody from this neighborhood went downstate when they held the auction at the land office, an' they went with their rifles over their arms. There was a bunch of speculators there from the East, but I didn't hear any of 'em biddin'." He laughed again at the memory. "You're goin' to Ioway, Connors, you'll see the same thing there."

1837

"If we do we'll know how to handle 'em," Connors said.

"Everton's been a town now for more 'n seven years," Robinson told him.

"Too civilized for me," said Connors. "Me and Allman here are going just as goddam far as we can. We aim to find a place with elbow room, a place not already cluttered up and stinking with politicians. I s'pose we got to have the bastards, but if we do we'll raise our own batch."

"Maybe that'd be a good idea," Robinson said seriously. "I know how you feel."

One by one they drifted out of the bar or away from the tavern. Somebody helped Al Hardy climb over the wagon wheel and untied the horses for him after he'd started to drive home without untying them.

It was a little after nine when Killip locked the front door and called the boy in from the kitchen to help him clean up. Bert considered. All in all, not a bad evening. Many a Saturday night was worse; only one casualty tonight, and that one not bad. They *would* argue politics, and that almost always led to hard words. But arguments over politics were more intelligent than arguments over nothing at all, so Bert thought at least. He grinned to himself. That Connors—he was sure a dead shot with a bar glass. He hoped, for the sake of business, that Mason wouldn't stay mad.

v

There *was* a panic, of course.

But in Everton, as in every other American town, the panic left no scars which were not erased easily by time, and that shortly. There was a shortage of ready money, though that certainly was nothing new for most frontier dwellers, and prices were unbelievably low. But of what special moment was that? For most of Dane County's population cash was not an absolute necessity anyhow.

If a man needed an axe he could trade corn or hogs or chickens to a Green or a Haines for the needed tool. The market for the produce was at absolute bottom, of course, but so was the price of axes, so in the long run it balanced up.

If a man needed new boots he could do business with Frank Walker, the shoemaker, who had to eat like everybody else, and trade a shoat for a pair of first-rate boots. Or he could drive a steer into Jake Waldo's tannery and swap it for three already cured hides. He could then take the leather to Frank, who would use one hide to make the boots and the other two to pay for his labor. Waldo in turn would have beef to eat and another hide to trade to someone else who needed leather. It was a cumbersome system; but it worked. And nobody starved or even had much less to eat than usual.

The panic did, however, put a thorough stop to the mad speculation in land which had been the order of the day. Land was still bought and sold, but more often at a price somewhere near what it was worth. Speculators in Boston and New York and Philadelphia no longer bought and sold handfuls of lots and farms without knowing exactly whether the property was in Everton or Canada or Texas. A man with a few saved dollars could now buy a lot upon which to build a house or a farm and not feel that he had paid a price for gold-bearing property.

And everywhere, Everton and Dane County included, those of little faith sold wildly and cheaply to those with faith and a little cash. Ike Frink bought improved farm land—improved, that is, as much as any—for two dollars an acre and almost wept because he didn't have a gold mine at his disposal. If he had he would probably have owned the biggest part of Illinois, though he did very well as it was.

In Everton, progress assumed visible form. The new courthouse, contracted for and begun in 1836, was finished. It was forty-five feet square and two stories high, built of good red brick and hand-sawed oak and walnut and cherry—probably the most imposing building north of Springfield, and even Springfield didn't have much to compare with it. It had cost almost $8,000, which looked like a lot of money to men who had preempted their land at $1.25 an acre and raised their own cabins by hand, and not a few complained loudly. Nevertheless it was an imposing structure in a land of log cabins and one-storied frame buildings, and it seemed to lend credence to the theory upon which the county had been settled in the first place.

And even in the bad years Everton grew, for the depression in the East was one of the greatest reasons for settling the Middle West. Everton was on the East-West stage road, and all through the depression years there was greater traveling activity than the town had so far known. Travelers were for Ioway, for Missouri, for Wisconsin and all points west. Some of them stopped in the town, most of them because they liked its looks, a few because they were just too discouraged to go any farther.

The newcomers were, by and large, those who for one reason and another had found life a failure in the East. But failure assumes a myriad of forms, and they were not necessarily riffraff and rabble. And they added to the wealth, physical and spiritual, of Illinois. A great many of them didn't have much left from the ruin of the East, but what little they did have left they brought with them, in their heads and hearts, in their purses and saddlebags and in their lumbering wagons.

And mostly they were Americans. They were emigrants only in the sense that they were moving from one part of their own country to another, moving in an attempt to escape a world which seemed composed of Biddles, Jacksons, Van Burens, Josephs and Democrats, a world in which the inexorable interest rate was the first law of existence. Their abiding failure was that they couldn't escape themselves, but then that, after all, is like saying that they couldn't help the fact that they were human beings.

In the meantime, Everton did well enough. It grew in spite of the specie shortage and the seemingly necessary evil of a federal government.

CHAPTER SEVEN

1840

D AVIS WAS ONLY TWENTY-FIVE years old, but already he had practically given up riding horseback; he was too big, and the available horses were too small. As a result he was doing his campaign traveling in a top buggy, a buggy which so far could easily enough be drawn by one horse. With the years Davis was to acquire still more bulk, and the buggy, in spite of improved roads, two horses.

The law business being what it was, his time was of no great value just now. It was still three weeks until election, and he had already stumped the biggest part of the district. He very much fancied a seat in the legislature. True, it was not the best political job in the state, but it was a step toward it. And he was young yet.

This wasn't quite his first foray into politics. His friends had the year before put him up as Whig nominee for state's attorney in the eighth judicial district. He had lost, although the vote in the legislature was close. Dave Campbell, lawyer, Democrat, and one of the best fiddlers in the state, was elected, 61 to 58. But it had given Davis an idea of the possibilities. It might be the other way next time.

Though the law was in itself no great way of making money,

it was nevertheless a good thing to be in. It was first of all a stepping stone to politics, and it gave a man connections which he could hardly have had otherwise. Davis & Colton had done about as well as any other law firm during the bad years—the bad years which were not all over yet—and Davis himself had had one real stroke of luck, just how much luck he didn't realize until years later. Fell was deeply involved in land operations of one kind and another. In '38 he had about reached bottom and either had to have *some* cash or lose his grip on almost everything he had. Davis had some money, but Fell approached him only as a last resort, a man grasping at straws. He was almost bowled over with surprise when Davis readily agreed to let him have the money—on a short-term mortgage on eighty acres of land lying partly in the town of Chicago. Davis really thought he was doing Fell a favor, and he was, for Fell probably would have lost that land and everything else to boot without the cash which he got from Davis. Eventually Fell told him that he couldn't raise the money, to go ahead and foreclose. Business, after all, was business. As a result Davis owned eighty acres in what was even then the fastest-growing town—nay, city already—in the country.

On this bright October morning the air was just brisk enough to make a man feel good. The timber was heavy with its autumn glory, and the roads were more than usually passable. Davis was in one of those moods when a man assumes naturally that he can whip the world with one hand tied behind him.

Specifically, he drove into Waynesville—which bore the name of a town but was actually a wide place in the road with four cabins clustered about it—about eleven in the morning. It was just a casual trip, for Waynesville was only twelve miles from Everton and he had driven down since breakfast.

But as he drove into the clearing who should he behold but John Moore, burly, red-faced, politically experienced Democrat, his personal opponent for a seat in the legislature. Davis tethered his horse and turned to shake hands as Moore got up from where he had been sitting in the center of a group of men.

"Good morning, John," Davis said. "I'm not a little surprised to find you here. How come? I heard you were over in the eastern counties."

Moore shrugged lightly. "Ah," he said, "I was. But a good general moves his army fast, Dave, and we Democrats travel the same way. I could hardly let Dane County be without the truth concerning the Democratic party."

"I'll bet it's heard plenty already," Davis said dryly, "depending on just how long you've been here."

"Sure now, what else could a man expect from a Whig?" Moore waved an expansive hand at the group of slack-jawed natives which had gathered around them. "This, gentlemen, is my honorable young opponent, Mister Davis. He's young, yes, but what he lacks in age he makes up for in size. Seen Lincoln lately?" he asked Davis.

"No," the other said, "not for several months. I guess his own affairs keep him busy down Springfield way."

"I reckon. I don't know why, but I always liked that long, tall satchel-britches, even if he is a Whig. Takes as long a pull out of a jug as a good Democrat. But look here, Davis, your comin' in here like this has interrupted a matter of importance to this fair community. Early last night my good friend Dan— Dan——" He looked inquiringly at one of the loafers.

That worthy spat a long, brown stream and said: "Dan Shortwell."

"Dan Shortwell, to be sure," Moore went on. "My old friend Dan Shortwell last night passed to his heavenly reward. I came in here this morning to make a brief address and find there ain't a single soul hereabouts who has had any experience makin' coffins. Now I have, so naturally I volunteered to aid in the emergency. We was just fixin' to go down the road to the dead man's place when you drove in. Now here, my young friend, is a chance to be of some real service to your hoped-for constituents. I know you'll be glad to bear a hand with a saw and a hammer, especially in such a labor of duty."

Davis looked decidedly uncomfortable. "Well," he said dubiously, "I'm not much of a hand with tools—never had much experience in that line. Of course," he added hastily as the gathering eyed him, "I'll be glad to help all I can."

They had him, and he knew it.

"Ah," Moore said, "I knew you would. Lead on, gentlemen, to the home of the deceased, and we shall see what we shall see. I'm sure Brother Davis can accommodate several of you in his buggy there, and I can take one behind my saddle."

The Shortwell cabin was only a short distance away, and when they arrived there a few minutes later they found another group of ten or a dozen neighbors.

Somebody had assembled planks and tools, and Moore, after paying his respects to the widow, threw off his coat and went to work. He knew exactly what he was doing and so did the by-standers. Any of them would have helped him, but they didn't. They hung around, watching furtively.

Moore's boots were worn and muddy, his clothes looked as though he had slept in them, and his Henry Clay collar nuzzling his stubbled neck was only half white. He rolled up his sleeves and fell to, keeping up a running fire of conversation all the while.

Davis' shoes were polished, his clothes neatly brushed, and he had put on fresh linen that morning. He felt now that his neck was red, whether it was or not, that he was about as useful as a third thumb, and about as handy as a cub bear with boxing gloves on. But he did manage occasionally to hand the laboring Moore something he needed.

They had worked perhaps a half-hour when the widow announced that dinner was ready. Davis and Moore, as befitted their stations, were given the places of honor—that is, they had the two chairs—and Moore mowed back food like a harvest hand.

"My boy," Moore said wickedly, "you're not doing justice to this fair repast. Now hard labor like that always makes me hungry."

"I know," Davis said doggedly. "I guess I'm just not hungry."

As a matter of fact he wasn't really very squeamish about most things. But the combination of the beating he was taking, the heat from the big fireplace, and the gaunt, quilt-covered corpse on the bed a few feet from his left hand was too much for him. He *wasn't* hungry. He wondered what the hell a man ever went into politics for, anyway.

After dinner Moore, with Davis standing around (he wouldn't give up), finished the coffin. Then it was discovered that there was no preacher available. But the statesman never batted an eye. What more could he ask? He superintended loading the remains into the coffin, acted as a pallbearer, and then for two solid hours held the audience spellbound. He praised the dead man's personal life and that of his antecedents and descendants, dwelt upon the present loss to the community, state and nation at large, then eulogized John Moore and the Democratic party, beginning with Thomas Jefferson and bringing history down to Martin Van Buren. It was the best combination funeral sermon and stump speech ever performed in Dane County.

Davis sat and listened.

By the time Moore finished, early dusk was in the air and folks were ready to head for home and the chores. It had been a big day, and they were pretty well convinced that this fellow Moore, laying aside what he *said,* was one to tie to.

They shook hands, and Davis said, "I congratulate you, John. It was perfect."

"Thanks, son," Moore said. "I ain't lived in this part of the country twenty-five years for nothing. Good luck."

In Everton, Davis told the story on himself. "I can't beat that kind of competition," he said sadly. "I guess I'm just not cut out for it."

"Oh, sure you can," somebody answered. "You can if you make up your mind to it. Beat him at his own game, that's the thing to do."

"No, gentlemen," he said, "I can't. I'm willing to do anything within reason, anything. But I just can't pray worth a good red damn."

Apparently he was right. The vote was, Moore, 1,335: Davis, 1,165. Two years later John Moore was elected lieutenant governor.

But the vote was significant of something else. The Democrats were still leading the voters, but the Whigs were coming closer. It was prophetic of the not so far distant future.

II

As usual Dr Henry's boots were polished, his linen immaculate, his broadcloth speckless and his back as straight as a ramrod. At a quarter of two he left his office and started negotiating the five blocks to the Methodist church. (Eventually it was to become the *First* Methodist Church, but now the little white frame building was simply *the* Methodist church.)

As a matter of habit he usually attended the funerals of his deceased patients; almost every physician did. But today he was going to Alice Dale's funeral because he wanted to. It had now been more than three years since he had first seen the girl, that night in the candle-lit cabin reeking so of illness, when he had guessed she wouldn't live through another night. But she—or the tuberculosis—had fooled everybody, including herself and Dr Henry.

After Henry's first visit she had lain with death almost touching her for three weeks. Then she had begun to get slowly better. Henry had watched her day and night, baffled and reverent before the astounding ability of the flesh to heal itself. Four months later she had been taking short walks.

Henry had never believed she would get well, and he had told Brady Dale so, for he was well aware of nature's habit of granting an occasional armistice.

Alice was never again able to do anything which required more than the mildest kind of exertion; even so, she seemed a long way from death, especially after the battles she had already won. She dressed and undressed herself, did the very minor household tasks and slept an average of fifteen hours a day. Any undue exertion almost did for her, and often she would have to stay in bed for days at a time.

About twice a year the disease would go suddenly berserk, and for days she would hold to life by what appeared to be little more than a single thread. Henry would spend dragging hours with her, watching, marveling at the way the uneven battle went, not willing to bet a three-bit piece that she would live through another night or day of pain and rack. He *knew* that she couldn't win indefinitely, of course, but as the months became years he almost forgot that. In a way she and Brady Dale became a part of his life. Unobtrusively but in a hundred ways he and Minerva helped the Dales. Not in the least as a matter of charity. It was just that they deemed it an honor to aid a man and a woman who seemed totally unaware that they were attempting to take destiny and the natural course of nature for a fall.

Dale had no money, or at least no more than what he was able to earn, and that was very little. In time Kelvin closed the oil mill for the simple reason that he couldn't make a living out of linseed oil and meal. After that Brady jobbed around at this and that, anything he could get that would let him stay in town. But not many employers badly wanted a man who ever so often had to quit the job for an indefinite time to care for a sick wife. It was too bad, of course, and as Christian citizens they all sympathized with the boy. But, after all, business was business, with punctuality and application necessary requisites of those employees who wanted to get ahead—who, for that matter, even wanted to work at all.

But all that was past. Now Dr Henry walked past Goodman & Ferre's wagon factory, nodding vaguely as Lyman Ferre appeared in the doorway and lighted a cigar. Alice Dale was dead, and Dr Henry was on his way to the funeral. He passed John Myer's tailor shop and Jim Robinson's newly opened store. (It was said that young Davis had backed Robinson in the project.) Alice had died two nights before, and at first Henry could hardly believe that it had really happened. Medically the answer, had Henry known it, was simple: the tuberculosis, again becoming rampant, had finally eaten through the wall of her stomach, and she had died in convulsions. That Henry couldn't understand the process made her no less dead.

He didn't as much as half listen while the Reverend Peebles worked through a standard model sermon, dwelling upon the youth of the deceased, her years of affliction, and as usual the repetition of the final fact that the Lord knew best. Dr Henry gave an unconscious start as Peebles intoned the last statement. How, he wondered, could the Reverend be so sure that the Lord knew best? He, Dr John Flournoy Henry, was beginning to believe that the Lord knew nothing whatever about what was *best*. Or was the word only one of relative meaning? He told himself that he didn't know, and that probably even wondering about it was a waste of time. But it didn't make him think any more highly of the Reverend Peebles.

He had few illusions about so-called human greatness, yet as he sat with bowed head and half listened to Peebles' prayers and platitudes he realized how much the matter of Alice and Brady Dale had touched him. In the first place he knew how little spiritual matters entered into marriages between people like the Dales. These unions involved roughly about 90 per cent physical attraction and desire and the other 10 per cent just one thing and another. Henry found nothing particular to quibble about in that. As an institution that kind of marriage seemed to serve its purpose well enough. And he strongly guessed that in the beginning the marriage of the Dales hadn't been much different from any other frontier union. They were both reasonably attractive; they were roughly of an age; their social stations were similar; their concepts of love and marriage alike; they were married as a matter of course.

That fumbling, ineffectual consummation had been the beginning of more than three years of the strongest devotion Dr Henry had ever seen or even heard about. Of course they were married. But what of that? Henry knew very well what a mumbled ceremony by a country preacher could be worth. A man could so easily walk out of the village and never be seen again— if he so desired. Brady Dale might have wanted to do so—Henry thought it extremely improbable that he hadn't wanted to many times. But he had stayed, stayed through three terrible years in which many, many times the girl had passionately *wanted* to die and Henry had wondered why nature hadn't allowed her to.

At first the neighbors had been friendly and helpful. They continued to be friendly, but in time they wearied of an illness at once so terrible and so interminable. Besides, they had affairs —and trouble—of their own. So Brady, with the help of Dr Henry and Minerva, did what he could. Frequently without money or job, he stayed doggedly at his task. Weeks of sleepless nights were interspersed with days given over to cutting fuel and hauling it with a borrowed team. He kept the cabin clean and laundered clothing and bedclothing which was so nauseating that sometimes, hungry as he might be, he would be unable to eat for a day or two. Sometimes, when he had work of some kind, he would grow haggard and skeletonlike from loss of sleep.

Once Henry had said to him, "You're no fool, boy, you know she'd be better off dead."

"I know," Brady said. "But *you're* here and not complaining. She's my wife. I'll stick."

He did.

And now Dr Henry sat with bowed head, remembering and wondering, only conscious of Peebles' drone as a vague irritation.

He had a few calls to make, and when the service was over he left the church abruptly. But he saw Brady on the street that night and stopped to talk for a moment.

"Those things which were hers, Doctor—you know, clothes and stuff like that—what had I better do with them?"

"Burn them," Henry said briefly. "Burn them all. How do you feel, son?" he asked kindly.

"Not so bad," Dale said slowly. "We knew it would happen, of course. No, I don't feel so bad."

[154]

"I know what you mean. Anything special you're planning to do?"

"Yes," said Brady. "I know exactly what I'm going to do. I'm going to sell what little junk I've got and buy me a horse an' go to Texas. If I can't raise enough to buy a plug of some kind I'll start walkin'. I'm through livin' anywhere near Everton, Illinois, Dr Henry."

"I know how you feel. I don't know—probably you'll be better off somewhere else. I could stake you, son, if you need it."

"I know you could, Dr Henry, and would. But I owe you more now than I can ever repay. No, I'll sell my stuff for what it 'll bring; it's no use to me now, anyway."

"Probably you're right. Well, Brady, come and see me and Minerva before you leave."

"I will, Dr Henry," Brady promised.

But he didn't, and Henry hadn't really expected him to.

Instead, a night or two later, he rode out of Everton, all that was left of his earthly possessions tied in a blanket roll behind his saddle. He turned once, briefly, at the edge of the forest, and then rode on without looking back again.

"He was bound to go," Henry said to Minerva, "but I'm sorry to see him leave, for all that. No community is ever so rich that it can afford to lose men with as much character as that boy's got."

"That Texas is a terrible place, from all accounts," Minerva said. "I do hope he doesn't get wild and land in any kind of trouble."

Dr Henry laughed somberly, a little cynically, and shook his head. "Nothing," he said, "can ever really harm Brady Dale again. His soul, his character, his spirit, whatever the theologians choose to call it, has been through more than enough fire to temper it. No one, I think, need ever worry about him."

AMERICAN YEARS

For more than ten years Robert Mahan kept a respectable tavern in free Ohio, just across from the Kentucky shore. He maintained a quiet, decent place, paid his debts promptly, and was a more than usually loyal member of the Methodist church. To his placid friends he had only one weak trait: he hated slavery with a hate that was cold and bottomless and implacable.

How many escaping slaves he hustled north after they had once crossed the Ohio, no one ever knew, not even his wife. But they must have been legion.

However, on the one occasion when he was caught up with, he was guiltless. A Negro man and woman, minding their own business and asking aid from no one, put up at the Mahan tavern for a night, paid their bill in the morning and disappeared northward. Mahan thought nothing of it.

But two days later a couple of hard-eyed Kentucky deputies rode into town, made a number of discreet inquiries, and when night fell and the village was quiet, they arrested Mahan—or rather abducted him—dragged him across the river to Frankfort, and there he was tossed into the vilest possible cell, chained hand and foot and fed on bad bread and poorer water.

Of course every feature of the arrest was illegal. But that didn't worry the sovereign state of Kentucky. For weeks Mahan was held incommunicado. The authorities would not allow even his wife to see him, though they did admit to her that he was being held. Several more weeks passed, and the woman was finally allowed to visit his cell. When she entered she hardly recognized her husband, but she almost fainted at sight of the man—or skeleton of man—chained to the wooden bunk. Before she left she had torn up her petticoats to bandage the raw flesh of Mahan's wrists and ankles. He kissed her gently when she left and reminded her to have faith in God, that undoubtedly He would take care of them in His own way.

Eventually he was given a trial—granting the process of robbery the courtesy of the name. The court was apparently well advised in the matter of the culprit's financial standing. It offered him ten years in the penitentiary or a fine equal to just about everything he owned in the world. He took the verdict standing up, though he would probably have done almost anything to get out of their stinking cesspool of a jail. But a man of Robert Mahan's honesty—his peculiar kind of honesty—must have been a rarity south of the Ohio, for even the Kentuckians recognized the quality. He agreed to pay the fine and was released on his own recognizance.

And pay the fine he did. He went home, alone, sold his house and his tavern, collected his few outstanding accounts, paid his fine and took a receipt for it. Except for a few personal belongings and a few odd dollars in cash, it took every cent he had in the world.

His friends and acquaintances knew he was completely mad; his wife and relatives thought so but weren't altogether sure.

He was not mad, of course. He was in reality a very simple man and a very honest man, one who could not and would not deny his own conscience. He hated slavery with every atom of hatred he could muster; but he had also an implicit faith in the laws of men, or rather in the right of men to make laws. Thus when Kentucky convicted him of violating her law he felt bound to respect the judgment. It might, of course, be unjust, but it was law nevertheless, and he bowed to it. It was quixotic, of course. But in a sense he had dared them to get him, and they had taken him up. So he paid. Knowing himself as he did, he didn't feel much put upon.

But now he was broke and more than a little disheartened. Illinois was free, a newer state and greener. So he went there, with his wife and two half-grown sons.

He had no capital now, yet the spirit of freedom was so strong upon him that he couldn't bring himself to work for anyone else. Accordingly he began farming.

He settled in a pleasant place about fifteen miles west of Everton, and for a year was fairly content. It turned out that there was a Methodist church in the neighborhood, and most of his neighbors belonged. He was glad to find it so, for he was a truly religious man and believed implicitly in the authority of the Church in spiritual matters. His neighbors, and especially the minister, were glad to add a new member who was so zealous.

Mahan kept his mouth shut and minded his own business, and for a while all went well enough.

Then casual remarks, odd lots of opinion, came to be noticed, remarked and remembered. Someone took it on himself (perhaps it was the minister) to inquire into Mahan's Ohio history. To Mahan it was a fairly small matter, an incident; to the excitement-starved community it was a mountain of iniquity. And to the Reverend Morehouse, obsequious to the politics of the Methodist Church, it seemed a heaven-sent opportunity to make a horrible example of someone—just who, didn't particularly matter. Accordingly, one lovely Sunday morning in June 1839, the Mahans unexpectedly found themselves exposed to the hell-and-brimstone of one of the Reverend Morehouse's loudest sermons and, afterward, heard themselves read out of the Church, the Reverend Morehouse acting on the authority of the bishop of the diocese.

They were hurt to the heart, for they believed in the Church's authority.

In the hot sunlight of noon they drove home in silence, unable now to discuss this catastrophe even among themselves.

All that afternoon and all that night Robert Mahan threshed the problem about in his mind. He *believed* in the law of the Church, in its right to throw him out if it wanted to. But he hated slavery more than he loved anything else except perhaps his family.

So on Monday morning he told the family what they would do. They would move—and keep their beliefs intact. There was still plenty of vacant land.

They moved again—in the early spring of 1840—to a spot some twelve miles north of Everton, and there they stayed. Once more they minded their own business, were on friendly terms with their neighbors and absolutely refused to join any organization but one, the Abolitionist party.

And for that meager organization, at least so far as Everton was concerned, Robert Mahan was a tower of strength. A loose handful of recalcitrants, without Mahan it perhaps would not have stayed alive at all. In Everton, in 1840, it had just six members. They had no program of consequence, no organization that amounted to anything, and they even disliked each other personally. They were united in only one opinion: their consumate hatred of slavery in any form. And for that they were willing to stand near-ostracism in a community which, while not proslave, was a confirmed believer in the status quo. In other words, Dane County and Illinois in general were on the fence and not inclined to be pushed in any direction which would cost them time or money. At least not yet. They were dyed-in-the-wool conservatives.

All of them were, that is, except the small and large firebrands who made up the Abolitionist party. These six met regularly, once a month, in a room back of Meagram's harness shop on Main Street. It was Mahan who taught them one of the first principles of political organization: that six voters who know exactly what they want will eventually be stronger than sixty who aim in all directions.

They were a strange crew; but the first adherents to seemingly lost causes almost always are.

First there was Mahan, who drove or rode twelve miles in each direction to attend the regular meetings. There was David Rump, a New Englander come to farming on a branch of the Kickapoo south of Everton. And Rump too knew slavery in some of its most illuminating aspects. He had sailed a dozen trips as a foremast hand on a slaver out of New Bedford, with ports of call at Charleston and Savannah and New Orleans. There was Mike Callahan, an Irishman who had taken early leave of his native land. He worked for Abe Brokaw as a smith and halved his hatred for slavery with anything British. George Dietrich was a German from Munich, who kept the local tinshop. He was a fine craftsman and an adherent of that queerest of prophets (for a German), Jean Jacques Rousseau. Thomas Hardy was a Britisher who shared Callahan's hatred of slavery and the British. He was by trade a carpenter and, as often as he was given a chance, did some of the most beautiful cabinetwork in the West. Last but not least there was Silas Hays, a quiet youth who hailed originally from Alabama. That much, with the fact that he worked in Green's store, was known. It was rumored that his people in Alabama were wealthy slaveowners, and that they had thrown him out because of his silly ideas. But no one really knew anything about him except that he seemed faithful to the cause.

Of course these six did not cut any wide swath in Everton. They were not a public menace or even a public nuisance, so the authorities had no occasion to notice them. But enthusiasts of their kind are usually natural propagandists; they couldn't resist any opportunity to put in their two cents' worth for whatever they could get for it. As a result their opinions were well known, and the community knew them for what they were—or what the community thought they were.

But, with the possible exception of Silas Hays, they were forthright, adult characters. They had been individually and personally kicked and beaten in the tenderest places, and it took more than any ordinary amount of village ridicule to make even the faintest mark on them.

So they met together once a month, discussed the latest polemics of William Lloyd Garrison and Arnold Lovejoy, politics in general, and, in lowered voices, that strange American invention that here and there was beginning to take actual shape, the Underground Railroad. They were no more a political party than a summer breeze is a typhoon, but they were a symptom, a tiny foreboding of the future.

They themselves didn't know that, of course, but on the other hand they didn't much care. They were honest men, respecting their own hearts and experiences.

1840

On Main Street business wasn't good, but it was far from being as bad as it had been. It wasn't nearly as bad, for example, as it had been during the years 1837–38–39. It seemed true that all businessmen were broke—or for convenience' sake claimed to be—but business somehow went on very much as usual. Stores were open and had goods to sell; professional men were ready and willing to sell their services for cash or credit; and most people as usual bought as much as they could afford or a little more.

But in Illinois an important thing, important economically that is, had occurred. The pleasant possibilities of bankruptcy had been discovered and duly incorporated into the law of the state. So, in the fall of 1840, men in almost all kinds of business were marking time, waiting for 1841. The law was to take effect then. Of course every businessman in his right mind knew already exactly where he stood and how bankruptcy was going to leave him financially. And most of them were going to do all right. It was simply a matter of waiting for the lawyers to make the situation legal by what they had taught the public to accept as the "due process of law."

Hard money was still scarce, but paper money was available to suit almost anyone's taste. It came in a vast variety of shapes, sizes, colors, and scope of its promises to redeem, and it took a lot of it to buy very much. Illinois herself, through her wildcat banks, had put out an ocean of currency, and a great many citizens consistently preferred local money. But Michigan money was very popular, too. It was a beautiful shade of reddish pink and could be identified as money as far as it could be seen.

Mrs Riggs and her daughter Ellen came through the open door of Robinson's General Store and were at once accosted by Mister Hobbs. (Hobbs had been working for Robinson since the latter had opened his store some months before.) He greeted the two ladies warmly.

"Fine, thank you, Mister Hobbs," Mrs Riggs said, and Ellen added a demure "How do you do?"

Hobbs rubbed his hands. "And what can I do for you today, ma'm?"

Mrs Riggs furrowed her brow. "Well, I'm not sure, Mister Hobbs. I was thinking maybe about a piece of dimity. Something nice but not *too* expensive."

"I think we've got just what you want. Right over here." He arched his brows and glanced inquiringly at Ellen. "A party dress for Miss Ellen here?"

"Well, not exactly, though I guess you *might* call it that."

Ellen blushed, a soft, pinkish blush that only heightened the effect of her peach-colored skin. She was wearing a dress modeled after the lately disappearing French fashions: loose, flowing skirt that only occasionally admitted that she had hips, but when it made the admission made it more than freely; high-waisted, with a ribbon belt tied just under her innocently provocative breasts. Ellen was seventeen, with eyes that were sometimes stupid, sometimes alive, amazingly alive, with un-spoken promises that would have startled a wooden Indian into feverish inquiry. It was *that* look which so often worried her mother.

"You might call it that," Mrs Riggs was saying. "Ellen's getting married in a few days." She sometimes wondered, too, if Ellen wasn't already—well, *married*.

"Is that so, now?" Hobbs beamed and readjusted his spectacles. "Well, that is news, Miss Ellen! And who is the lucky man, may I ask?"

"Roger Burns," supplied Mrs Riggs without waiting for Ellen to answer for herself, "and a fine lad, too."

"Indeed he is," Hobbs agreed, getting the bolt down from the shelf. "Well I remember how both of 'em were coming up the hill to school only a couple of years ago. I don't know which of you is the luckiest. Now here, Mrs Riggs, is a pattern . . ."

In the office of the Burke Livery Stable five men were clustered about a table and a jug.

"By God, I tell you," Jeff Amberg was saying, "it's only a question o' time till the decent folks o' this state run them whorin' Mormons plumb into the Rocky Mountains."

Andy Burke settled his paunch against the edge of the table and reached for the jug. "Aw, hell, Jeff," he said amiably, "you're jest jealous, that's all. Joe Smith an' his boys are jest naturally better men than you are but you don't want to admit it."

"They ain't better men," someone put in; "they're just bigger damn fools. Why any man who's had to live with one woman should be fool enough to want to live with two or three, I can't see. It just goes to show that there ain't no limit to natural ignorance."

"A waggin' tail is powerful bait sometimes."

"Yeah, but a smart possum don't git hisself ketched more 'n once."

"Deal the cards, Al," Burke said to the big, well-dressed man on his right. "This palaver is liable to go on all night if something don't break it off."

The man with the cards grinned a white-toothed grin around his tightly clamped cigar. "All right with me, Andy. You boys all set?"

They nodded agreement, and he dealt them one card around, face down.

"What the hell did you say they call this game?" Amberg asked.

"Stud poker," Al said.

"Well, if you ask me, it's a hell of a name for a card game," Jeff observed. "Where the hell would they get a crazy name like that?"

"Shucks, how would I know?" Al said. "It's as good a name as any. And she's a real game, I can tell you——"

"Well, it looks like kid stuff to me," Andy said. "One card down and four up—it's a hell of a soundin' layout. Any fool could play it blindfolded."

Al swiftly dealt another card around, face up this time. "Don't you fool yourself, Andy. It's a hell of a long ways from a kid's game. I learned it from the pilot of the *Inland Queen,* last trip I made to St Louis."

"All pilots are crazy," Bert Smith said. "If they wasn't they wouldn't be pilots. Well, what do we do now?"

"The highest card showing leads the betting. You see what you've got in the hole and then see how you stand compared to what's on the board. . . ."

On the boardwalk outside Killip's Tavern, Fell, Wells Colton and Bill McCullough passed the time of day.

"Cooler than it was yesterday," Fell observed.

"Damned hot for fall anyway," Colton said. "You seen Green, Mac?"

"No, I ain't," McCullough said, "and I ain't in any special hurry to see him." McCullough was clerk of the Circuit Court and an organization Democrat. He had hated Green cordially ever since Stillman's Run in 1832.

"I know, Mac," Fell put in, grinning broadly, "but you'll appreciate this one. You remember Carlin called a two weeks' special session of the legislature to handle this bank business."

"I remember all right," McCullough said. "Carlin's done the best he could to straighten out a bad mess. The only trouble is that you Whigs have done everything you could to prevent anything constructive."

"Have it your own way, Bill," Fell said, still good-humored. "But I started to tell you about Abel and Lincoln. Us Whigs were trying to prevent a *sine die* adjournment, and the boys were staying away from the session in order to prevent a quorum. But I guess they couldn't get together, and Lincoln and Joe Gillespie and Green found themselves in a session in which the three of them made two over a quorum. The sergeant at arms had orders not to allow anyone to pass out the door until all resolutions were voted on, and the three of them found they were in the soup.

"But you know Lincoln, Bill. They never catch him without an answer of some kind. He saw there was a window partly up and passed the word to Joe and Green. Then, when he gave the signal, the three of them ran for the window and piled out on top of one another with a flock of good Democrats reaching for their coattails. Some stunt, eh?"

Colton and McCullough guffawed.

"By George," McCullough said, "I bet it was a sight. Too bad Green didn't break his neck. But I'll bet Abe was a sight with them legs o' his danglin' out of the State House window. By George, I'd have give a dollar to seen it."

"So would I," Colton said. "But that's Abe for you—always Johnny-on-the-spot with an idea. If he woke up in hell he'd find a way to make water out of the brimstone."

"I know," McCullough said. "There's hardly a man in the legislature's got a dime he can call his own, yet they're forever debatin' about the Bank an' money in general. Do you remember the story Abe told here in Killip's awhile back?"

"Which one?" Fell asked.

"The one about politicians in general—or I guess that's what he meant. He said that Jesus Christ chose twelve disciples, and even one of that handful, selected by superhuman wisdom, turned out to be a traitor and a no good bastard. He also pointed out that Judas carried the bag—he was what you might call the treasurer for Jesus and the disciples."

Again they laughed, remembering the storyteller and the droll solemnity of his tales.

"Bill," Colton said, "I hear Van Buren is getting ready to send his message to Congress in French, and that he has the White House menus printed in French. They say he's getting ready to hold court at the White House. Have you Democrats got any information about that?"

"No exact information," McCullough said. "But then even us Democrats can make a mistake once in a while. We ain't worrying much, though. If he gets too bad, somebody will complain to Jackson, and Andy will go down to Washington and kick all the fool notions out of Van Buren."

"Not such a bad idea," Colton agreed. "But if he kicks him in the place easiest to reach he'll kick out what few brains Prince John has."

"No great loss," Fell said. "How 're things with you, Mac, anyway?"

"Good enough, Jesse," McCullough said. "I'll buy them three lots on Apple Street from you any time you come down to twice what they're worth."

"For cash?"

"Well, some cash. But not at the price you want—or wanted the last time we talked about it."

"Listen," Fell said, "I think we can get together. Now I'll tell you what I'll do. . . ."

The dwelling on Front Street where John Hundman and his wife lived was part log cabin and part ordinary weatherboarded house. The cabin portion now did duty as a kitchen, and John had added an extra luxury to it: a small back porch.

On this particular afternoon he was enjoying his favorite pastime. That is, he sat in a shady corner of the porch, his bare feet propped up on the low railing, a half-emptied jug of whisky on the floor beside him, and played his fiddle or yarned as the spirit moved him. For the fiddling he didn't need any audience but himself, and for the yarning there was Julius, his eight-year-old grandson who sat on the porch steps. The old man talked or fiddled as he saw fit and drank copiously from the jug between processes. He didn't need any particular audience for that, either.

Now he finished a snappy tune and suddenly raised the battered fiddle to eye level, squinting down the neck as though it were a rifle barrel. Then he lowered the fiddle and spat brownly over the low rail of the porch. "Funny," he said to the boy, "that they don't take a little pride in linin' them privies up better. Why, I remember when I was in New York years ago.

You could look down some streets an' there wouldn't be a privy a foot out o' line in four blocks. But not in this town, no, sir. People just don't give a damn how things look."

"What was the name of the piece you just played, Grampa?"

The old man chuckled. "That was 'Sourwood Mountain,' sonny. First tune I ever learned right good on the fiddle, an' it's a good tune yet. By hell, you ought to hear Dave Campbell play that one. Then you'd hear some fiddlin' that *is* fiddlin'."

"You mean Mr Campbell, the lawyer?"

"Yes, sir. Too bad Dave ain't as good a lawyer as he is a fiddler. By God, if he was he'd be President! I've heard a sight o' fiddlers, from Maine all the way to New Orleans, but I never heard one that could hold a candle to Dave when he's in a real fiddlin' humor."

"Is he better 'n you, Grampa?"

"Better 'n me!" the old man snorted. "Why, dang it, boy, that ain't no comparison. This Dave Campbell was born with a bow in one hand and a chunk o' rosin in the other. He could fiddle rings around the Devil hisself."

That seemed to remind him of something, so he tucked the instrument under his chin and fiddled off "The Devil's Dream." Then he took a long draught from the jug and sighed a little. His fingers tired more easily these days.

John Hundman had carried a rifle in the Revolution, and the rifle had weighed almost as much as he had. Later, years later, after he had got through the beginning period of founding a family, there had been the War of 1812. John went as a matter of course. In his estimation there was only one name for a man who wouldn't, or didn't, fight for his country if he could carry a gun and see to use it. So he was with Jackson at New Orleans.

The late 1820s found him in Illinois. He filed his warrant as a soldier of the Revolution and in due time received his grant of Illinois land. In 1832 he was living in Peoria County and, old as he was, joined up with Stillman's battalion immediately volunteers were asked for.

AMERICAN YEARS

He came home from the Black Hawk War too, unscathed but full of general contempt for the farmer-volunteers. The fiddle also came home intact.

"Tell you what, sonny," John said, "first time Dave has a real fiddlin' session comin' on I'll take you down to Killip's an' let you stand outside the door an' listen. That's fair enough. You got no business inside a barroom at your age, anyway. But," the old man added, "you ought to hear Dave fiddle. Anybody ought to. A pity in a way that in Everton he does most of it at Killip's."

"Well, I'd like to hear him, Grampa. But I'd like to hear some more about the wars, too."

"Yeah, you would. Every young un does, seems like. But when you come right down to it, there ain't nothing of importance happens in wars. Nothing, that is, but vermin an' stinks an' rotten grub an' a chance to get your head shot off. You can get any o' them things without goin' to a war."

"Well, what 'd you go for, then, Grampa?"

The old man chuckled again and ran his gnarled fingers over the fiddle strings. "Godalmighty, sonny, I don't know that. Plain cussedness, I guess. Maybe the natural dumbness of the human race. You been to Sunday school, you ought to know the story of Cain an' Abel. I don't know much about history, but I guess that's as good a place to start as any. There's just naturally more strong backs in the world than there is strong minds, so you've always got somebody somewhere that wants to start a fight."

"Un-hunh," Julius agreed politely. He really wasn't much interested in Grandpa Hundman's philosophic opinions. "But you was in the Black Hawk War, Grampa. Tell me about that."

John snorted contemptuously and reached for the jug again. "The Black Hawk War!" He ran through a few bars of "Fiddlers' Reel." "Hell's fire an' the cows got out, that wasn't a war. That was a farmer-militia picnic."

"But you was in it, Grampa," Julius said pointedly.

"Yes-ss," John said, "so I was. But I just been tellin' you

there's more fools in the world than there is wheat in the fields."

"Mr Green was there," Julius said, "and look at him—he's a general."

John fooled with the fiddle strings. Youth baffled him, as it has baffled men from time immemorial. But he felt that he had to say something. *"Mister* Green," he muttered softly, "is also a horse's rump of the first water, an' if he's a general I'm a nigger preacher from Alabama. But that's a pretty complicated subject for you, sonny. Let's just let it go. Tell you what I'll do."

"What, Grampa?"

"I'll take you down to Killip's the first time Dave Campbell's in town."

"But you already promised me that. Was he in the Black Hawk War, Grampa?"

"What? Oh, so I did. How the hell would I know? I wasn't keeping books for the Democrats at the time. But he's a fiddlin' fool from 'way back."

"I'd like to hear about Colonel Strout again."

"All right." The old man was suddenly sour. "Take it up with *General* Green, then. Him an' Strout was about the same kind o' liars, except Strout had more experience at it because he was older. You better skin out o' here, boy. Your mother 'll be wonderin' where in hell you're hidin'."

Julius knew something of the old man's humors. He left on the run.

When the boy had gone, John again cradled the fiddle under his chin and softly, very softly, played "The Maiden's Prayer." It was a lonely, nostalgic melody, compounded of a thousand unnamed yearnings, a thousand regrets, and he loved it better than any other fiddle tune he knew.

He was sorry, in a way, that he let himself be irritated by the boy, for he was more fond of him than of most of his other grandchildren. There seemed to be something of himself, as he remembered himself, about the boy. But the thought was only momentarily important and slipped from his mind like a shadow.

AMERICAN YEARS

For now the sun was a solid blood-orange ball, visible through the varying greens of the trees which fringed Front Street and became a forest a few rods beyond. Hundman liked that hour of the day best of all. He liked to sit quietly there on the small porch and think and remember. The long shadows and the deepening twilight hid the realities of Everton, made the architectural shortcomings of man a little less distasteful.

Hundman, like tens of thousands of other Americans, had had a wordless dream and all his life had lived a little part of it —a dream which was about one quarter hope and three quarters bitter disillusionment. He had, personally, seen Washington when the General's eyes were dark pools of despair and foreboding, and when the General died he had wept for the first time since he could remember. Later he had fought under Jackson as a private—and voted for John Quincy Adams because he was a free man with a mind of his own.

Now he was seventy-eight years old. He had left two toes at Valley Forge and a quart of blood in a muddy bayou outside New Orleans. In the meantime he had tried to tear a living from the earth of America in spite of the politicians and usurers and other vagaries of nature. They could all now, so far as he was concerned, go plumb to hell. He was tired and of a mind to rest. Again he tucked the fiddle under his whiskered chin.

The sun went down, and the dusty streets and the forest and the prairie were dark.

In the office of Davis & Colton there were four men, Jesse Fell, Dr Henry, Allen Withers and Robinson. Fell, his voice businesslike as usual, was speaking:

"We're all agreed then, gentlemen, that Robinson will buy the books when he goes to Philadelphia in a few weeks. Each of us will contribute fifty dollars toward payment for a general selection of books. Is that correct?"

"It is, I think," Dr Henry said. "You, Allen, is that satisfactory with you? This is more than a little a labor of love, you know." The doctor was wondering if Withers should have been called in on this meeting at all.

"Quite all right with me," Withers said a little irritably. "I can stand it, and I want to. I've made a little money in the last year. I'll stand my share."

"Very well," Henry said. "None of us here wants to assume the whole burden of selection, I take it. Suppose I suggest a plan."

"Go ahead," Robinson said.

"Suppose each of us make up a list of, say, fifty or more books that we believe should be in the library. Then, when Robinson goes to the bookseller in Philadelphia let him start with the first of each of our choices, then the second of each, and so on down, omitting duplicates, of course. Let him go as far as his money lasts. How does that sound?"

"Very good, Doctor," Fell said. "Has anyone a different suggestion—or a better one?"

Apparently no one had.

"It was your idea, Fell, in the first place," Henry said, a little sardonically. "I hope it amounts to something, though I'm afraid it won't."

"Vandalia has a library," Fell said, "and so has Springfield and Edwardsville. Why not Everton?"

"Why not indeed?" Henry echoed. "But perhaps, Fell, they also have a populace that can read. Had you thought of that? Pearls before swine, you know."

"I know, I know," Fell said. He was a patient man, but Henry sometimes irritated him considerably. "That's not the point, Henry, and you know it. You don't *have* to subscribe to this thing, you know."

"I know I don't," Henry said evenly. "But you won't mind my side remarks, I hope. You know that no one respects the idea back of this thing more than I do. It's just that I honestly doubt its practical success."

"There won't be a book left in the damned town a year from now," Withers put in.

"Oh yes, there will be—at my house," Dr Henry said imperturbably. "But maybe that wasn't what you meant."

"All right," Fell said, still smilingly patient, "suppose there isn't. They will have been here, and in any event they won't have gone far. I know you men want to get on your ways. Shall we call it an agreement, then?"

They did. And that was how Everton, a village of a few more than five hundred people, came to have a public library in 1840, a library available to any citizen who would carry a book home and make a promise, seldom kept, to bring it back. . . .

Robert Ormsby Matthews leaned, or perhaps partly hung, upon the bar in Killip's. He gazed sourly at the whisky in his tumbler, turning it from side to side and watching the oily film cling to the glass.

"By God, Bert," he said suddenly, "I wonder why somebody don't invent the *perfect* whisky. It could be done."

"Well, they been tryin' it for a good while now," Bert said, and spat into the sawdust with a judicial air, as one considering weighty matters. "But, Bob, so far as that goes there ain't nothin' *perfect*."

Matthews moved his feet carefully, trying to find a new stance without throwing himself. He was thirty years old, handsome as sin, one of the worst drunks in Dane County and, at the moment, the schoolteacher. Like Hobbs, there were tales about who he was and where he had come from, but no one really knew.

"So far as that goes, Bob," Bert went on, "there ain't *any* really bad whisky. It's just that some whisky is better 'n others." He grinned broadly. "But I reckon you've heard that one."

Bob finished his glass and shuddered faintly as he put it down on the bar. He hadn't been listening to Killip.

"And by God," he said suddenly, "they call this a democracy! Isn't that one hell of a joke? Isn't it?"

"Well, now, I dunno about that. Depends on how you look at it, I reckon." Like all good bartenders Bert had learned to stall until he was sure about which way a patron expected to be answered. "There's different ways o' lookin' at things."

But Matthews wasn't paying any attention to him, anyway. He spoke again, a little oracularly, as though addressing an invisible audience: "A democracy! What a blasphemy, what a bastardization of words! How, in God's name, can any people govern themselves in the mass if they can't govern themselves as individuals?" He belched and put on his hat.

"Well, now, I dunno," Bert began.

"I know very well you don't," Matthews said, and glared at the inoffensive Killip stonily, bitterly, as though silently blaming him for a hundred shameful things. "Can't a man come into this stinking bar and talk to himself without being interrupted every other breath?"

"Oh sure, sure," Killip said placatingly. "It's closin' time, almost, Bob. I'll buy a drink."

Matthews took off his hat. "Make it the same, then," he said softly, "and wrap me up a quart of that snake oil to take with me. I don't want to run out tomorrow when it's Sunday and you bastards are too lazy to work."

A little later he stood in the cool moonlight of Main Street, carrying the bottle in one hand and his hat in the other. Then he started for the Simpsons, where he boarded, and his steps were but very, very little off center. At Front Street he stepped in a pile of horse manure and cursed softly and deliberately. Out of the street, he cleaned his boot on a patch of dried grass and jumped as a tall figure suddenly appeared from the shadows.

"Good evening, Robert," Dr Henry said pleasantly. "Been courting?"

"Yes," Matthews said, "a little." He shoved the bottle farther under his coat. "Or I suppose you might call it that."

"There are a lot of names for it," Henry said. "Nice evening, isn't it?"

"Fine," Bob said, and watched Henry disappear in the shadows again. There was no one in Everton whom he liked better than Dr Henry, yet every time he saw him he felt a little disconcerted, a little ashamed of himself. He took a new hold on the bottle and started home again.

It was only a hundred yards farther on, but it began to seem a terribly long way. The shadows were moving again, strangely, as they so often did these days, and the feeling that he was tottering on the edge of some bottomless pit began to creep over him slowly but inexorably.

Almost every day he told himself that he would stop drinking—or at least stop drinking quite so much. But he never did anything about it. In the evening, when he had finished at the school, he would come by Killip's. One or two wouldn't hurt anyone, of course, so he would have one or two. Then he would still be quite sober but with a terrible thirst upon him. So he would have a few more—and then buy a bottle to take with him. The process had long since become a habit. He didn't want to drink, or at least not drink so much, but there didn't seem to be much he could do about it.

When he came within fifty or sixty feet of the Simpson house he could see a faint white patch against the dark bulk of the building. His pulse quickened a little. That damned minx Cynthia again. He debated quickly whether or not to cross the street and walk on as though naturally intending to go somewhere else.

The girl worried him, and he couldn't seem to find anything sensible to say to her. Damn her! With the natural guile of her eighteen years (or so he put it to himself) she twisted everything he said to her toward the particular end she had in mind. And he, Robert Ormsby Matthews, wanted absolutely none of it. He didn't want to marry Cynthia Simpson or any other woman on earth. . . .

As Dr Henry came down Main Street he saw a sudden flare of light as the back door of George Dietrich's tinshop opened and then closed again almost instantly. For a moment he thought of thieves. Then a spring wagon came around the off corner of the building, bucked its way through the shallow ditch at the edge of the wooden walk and squared around in the dust of Main Street. When the wagon was clear of the shadows Henry recognized the driver who sat hunched upon the flat board seat.

1840

"Howdy, Doctor," the driver said softly. "Want a lift up the street a piece?"

"No, thanks, Mahan," Henry said dryly. "I've only a little way to go. How's Mrs Mahan's kidneys behaving these days?"

"A little better, I think—thanks to you."

"I'm glad to hear it. Doing your trading a bit late tonight, aren't you?"

"Ummm, maybe. Some things I had to get from Dietrich here."

Dr Henry glanced at the canvas thrown loosely over the back portion of the wagon. "How many things?" he asked.

"Two," Mahan said, and grinned through a week's stubble of black beard.

"Mahan," Dr Henry said softly, "when I came up here to Illinois I freed my own niggers, freed them because I wanted to, because I despise slavery of any kind, though, mind you, Negro servitude isn't the only kind of slavery there is in our beloved country. But I never in my life bothered with anybody else's niggers. I suppose you're too old a fool now to take any kind of useful advice?"

And this time Mahan chuckled audibly. "I reckon I am, Doc, though I sure as hell appreciate your offer. Thanks just the same. I got to be movin'—want to get this stuff home before sunup."

"I hope I never have to treat you for a case of lead poisoning, my friend."

"You 'n me both, Henry. Giddap, Bess."

The feet of the horses made tiny soft *plops* in the dust as the wagon moved up Main Street. Henry grinned after them. God, he ruminated, had certainly peopled the world with strange folk, though he, Henry, had almost given up wondering why.

CHAPTER EIGHT

1842

THE THREE MEN gathered about the strange contraption in the rear of the Goodman & Ferre wagon works scowled at each other.

Al Goodman, paunchy and usually good-humored, kicked one wheel of the crude machine and spat angrily on the greasy boards of the floor. "I can sell 'em," he said, "sell all of 'em you fellows can make—if they work. But I'll be blowed if I can sell junk. These farmers ain't all damn fools; they can tell the difference between a reaper and a thing that looks like a cross between a windmill and a smoke grinder."

"I know, Al," Lyman Ferre said. "We're doing the best we can. I know there's a few changes that have to be made. We're working on them now——"

"All right," Goodman interrupted a little wearily. "But *when* are you going to get them done? Wheat doesn't get ripe every day in the year, you know. Here, we've got twenty-two machines out now and the best of them just about half work. What the hell are we going to do about *them?*"

"We're changing the transmission arrangement, for one thing," Ferre said, "and enlarging the sections of the sickle bar. Don't you think that 'll cure most of our troubles, Nat?"

[176]

1842

Nat Simpson, the shop foreman, rubbed his nose with a grimy finger and looked a little worried. "I think so, Mr Ferre," he said, "I honestly do. But we can't really tell till we get the new machine into ripe wheat. That's the only real test; you know that."

"And what about these machines that are already out?" Goodman put in. "Are we going to tell farmers that if the machines don't work it's their hard luck? That's one way of doing business, but it's a hell of a way if you ask me. I'm out on the road; I hear all the complaints, and I can tell you it ain't doing our reputation any good whatever."

"Well, Al," Ferre said evenly, "half the business is yours. That's as much up to you as it is to me. I suppose we can replace the parts on the old machines with new ones—and it 'll cost us plenty of money. But again, that's partly up to you."

"All right then, it's partly up to me. But I didn't invent this damned reaper in the first place, Lyman. It was your idea. I wanted to stick to a steady profit in the wagon business and let this fellow McCormick worry about these damned complicated reapers. They tell me his really cuts wheat. Maybe it don't, but that's his lookout. But ours sure as hell don't—except on some days. That's what gets me, Lyman. We've either got to get into the reaper business right or get out quick——"

"If you don't want any more of me I'll be getting on," Nat interrupted. "I've got to see Dietrich about some sheet iron."

"Oh sure, go ahead." Ferre waved him away with his cigar and turned to Goodman. "Come on in the office, Al. No use standing out here."

Nat left the shop by the back door and waded through the weeds of the vacant lots between the wagon works and George Dietrich's shop. The June sun was devilish hot, and he sneezed a few times. Hay fever coming on early this year, he thought. These blasted weeds, probably.

The back door of Dietrich's shop was locked, so Nat started around to the front door; George always left that open. But as he went along the side of the little building he stopped and admired the bright posters tacked on the wall of the building. He had read the posters perhaps twenty times during the past week, but they still held his intense interest. As a matter of fact he considered about half the story on the posters as a plain, barefaced lie, but then of course a man expected circus people to lie outrageously. Some of this stuff was just a little *too* much.

The poster read, in part:

JUNE, TITUS & ANGEVINE COMBINED SHOWS
Splendid and Combined Attraction of Equestrian and
Gymnastic Exercises, with a beautiful
Collection of
LIVING WILD ANIMALS
comprising the stupendous
GIRAFFE
The only one now living on the American Continent.
The ELEPHANT, LIONS, and every variety of birds,
beasts and reptiles.
Tuesday Evening, July 10th.
The Performance will commence with a Grand
CALLOPADE ENTREE

Equestrian Director	Mr Lathrop
Clown	Mr Felix
Ringmaster	Mr Shay

That part about the elephant, for instance, was all right. Nat Simpson had with his own eyes seen old Hackaliah Bailey's renowned elephant, Old Bet, down East before he came to Illinois. Old Bet, the first elephant ever to arrive in the United States, was an undoubted fact, a real, sure enough animal. But this giraffe business that Messrs June, Titus & Angevine advertised—that apparently was just a plain damned lie. Who had ever seen one? Who, even, had ever as much as heard of one? There was a drawing of the beast at the head of the poster, but that only made it more than ever unbelievable. Nat knew, though he had never seen one, that there were such things as joint snakes and hoop snakes. He didn't know just what a callopade entree might be, either, but it might be almost anything, some fancy name probably. But there was a picture of the giraffe. A giraffe. Hell!

Anyhow, he would see for himself. And by gosh, if it was a fraud he would consider it a personal affront. These circus folks couldn't come into Everton with their frauds and lies. Nosir.

He came out on Main Street's wooden sidewalk and almost ran into Wells Colton. Colton was on his way to the courthouse.

"Oh, good morning, Mr Colton."

"Howdy, Nat. How are you?"

"Pretty good, Mr Colton, thanks. Where've you been? I ain't seen you around."

"Oh, here and there, Nat. Springfield, Danville, Pekin, you know. How's your family?"

"Tolerable, take it all in all. Cynthia's due to have her first pretty soon."

"Oh, that so? I'm glad to hear it. Let's see now, who did she marry? I ought to know, God knows, but I've forgotten."

"Bob Matthews. You know, the young feller that taught school a couple seasons back an' boarded at our house; the year before Mom died. You remember him."

"Oh sure, sure. I do now. Well, that's fine, Nat. You going my way?"

"No," Nat said. "I got to go in here an' see Dietrich a minute an' then get back to the shop. We're pretty busy these days."

"Not reaper trouble, I hope?" Colton grinned.

Nat grinned back. "Well, not exactly, though I guess you might put it that way."

"You tell Ferre for me that he'd better get out of the reaper business and let Cy McCormick alone or he'll be over the barrel right."

"I don't think that kind of advice will do him much good, Mr Colton."

"Probably not, but give it to him anyway. See you later, Nat."

AMERICAN YEARS

II

Allen Withers had been officially appointed as taker of the census. He did a careful job and finally came to the conclusion that on June 10, 1842, the population of Everton numbered exactly 864, which figure included five free Negroes. He wasn't quite sure about the exact status of these last, but he counted them anyway.

And the village, after the manner of all villages, was acquiring what might be called civic consciousness. It was aware of its shortcomings, of course; but these weren't any worse than any other village of Everton's stature in Indiana or Ohio or Missouri. It was a little proud of the distance it had come.

Now there were more than two hundred houses, with only a few still built of logs. There were some thirty business buildings (three of them brick structures), five churches, and one of the best courthouses between Chicago and Springfield.

The village had its full quota of doctors, lawyers and practical mechanics, and they were, for the most part, a little above the average in competence and common honesty. They adjusted themselves to the times, of course, but few of them ever did any sort of business that couldn't have been done legally by anyone else with the inclination. Business practices were sharp and close, and most men liked a bargain, but there was nothing new in that.

As for Everton's natural lacks, they were many. There were no pavements and only a few hundred yards of wooden sidewalk around the square and its immediate environs; there were no railroads, and the village was forty miles from the nearest river transportation; there were no street lamps, even about the square, and no sewers of any kind; no telephone or telegraph; every dwelling and place of business had its own well or cistern. Further, there was no natural fuel supply except the timber. Just now, to most people, that seemed more than plentiful. When could they ever burn as much wood as stood within ten miles of the town? Actually, no one asked that question. People seldom do until someone has told them that the question should be asked.

But there *was* one man in Everton who did ask questions: Jesse Fell. He asked all sorts of questions repeatedly, though more often than not he asked them only of himself until he was sure he could get the right answer. He traveled about the country a great deal these days. He met and knew and was respected by a great number of all sorts of men, and he tried to look at everything with his eyes as wide open as possible.

He saw one thing very clearly now, and that was the fact that the whole physical character of the prairie country was undergoing a tremendous change. Few people saw the change as an actuality, yet Fell was sometimes a little startled when he saw how rapidly the change was taking place.

The whole thing went back to the day Joe Dawson and Abe Brokaw built a plow that would successfully turn black, rich prairie ground. Before that the prairie settlers' world turned on two things, fuel and water. So they settled at the edge of the choicest grove available. Living, actually living, in the middle of the open prairie was about as silly as living in the ocean; it was unthinkable. And, generally speaking, that idea still prevailed— men naturally like to live near trees.

But, slowly, that idea was disappearing or taking new shape. Brokaw had taken two partners into the business with him, and they were selling all the plows they could build. And Bunn, Ellsworth & Brokaw were, comparatively speaking, a small firm.

The prairie was being broken now with a vengeance.

And Fell saw too that the timber was soon to go. It wouldn't be altogether used as fuel, of course. It would be used in manufacturing, a little for fuel, and for the most powerful reason of all: to make more open land upon which to raise a money crop. Fell knew Dane County like the back of his hand, and he was aware that there was, outside of some thousands of acres of swampland which couldn't be farmed, not a good plot of federal land left in the county. There were a few odd patches left here and there, but they were either worthless for some reason or other or had got lost on the government plats and so were virtually ownerless.

Fell saw all these things, some of them much more clearly than others, but what the eventual outcome would be he hadn't the slightest notion. He had hopes, but no knowledge, so he kept on buying and selling land, waiting.

In the meantime, Everton prospered.

There was, however, one vital statistic which had been overlooked by everyone: In twelve years there had never been a murder trial in the Dane County courthouse.

III

Without warning the small streets began to fill with the countryfolk. They started coming into town before nine o'clock, and by eleven Main Street, from Monroe to Front—three blocks —was lined almost solidly with vehicles. Groups of men stood in the grass of the courthouse yard, women sat on the steps in front of Haines's and Robinson's and half the other stores on Main Street. Children cavorted up and down the wooden walks and the dusty streets aimlessly and joyously. Tobacco juice was spat in brown rivers, and Killip's and Nichols' did a roaring business, with the bars lined solidly and late-comers reaching over the shoulders of those earlier glued to the bar edge.

Circus day was more fun than election day, for nothing but fun was involved.

In front of Haines's old man Leary talked with Ike Frink.

"Rain up your way last week?" Ike asked.

"Rain?" Leary said. "I'll say it did. It rained like all hell let loose. More water 'n a fresh cow pissin' on a flatrock. Why, hell's rainbow, I ain't seen the branch so full o' water in years. You git any rain?"

"Some," Ike said, as though unwilling to admit that nature had let it rain as usual, according to the ordinary law of averages. "No more 'n we needed, though."

1842

"Well," Leary said, "if you put it that way you must have had a reg'lar flood. You buyin' any land, Ike?"

"A little," Frink admitted cautiously. "Course, a man has to be careful, Leary. You know how it is."

"Yeah, I know how it is," Leary said dryly. "If you owned the whole damn county you wouldn't have enough kids to farm it—you got to be careful about that. . . ."

By noon the crowd was getting a little restless, for the Big Show had not yet shown any signs of arriving. The crowd milled around a little aimlessly, wondering here and there if the whole thing was a frost. There were a few fights, but none serious.

Then, a little past one, a small boy yelled, "Here she comes!" And sure enough, there she came.

Up Main Street, over the slough and past Brokaw's blacksmith shop, marched a clown in full regalia, white face, flounces and spangles, blowing his lungs out on a bugle, bowing right and left to the staring crowd and about every fifty feet turning a handspring. And a few rods behind him, the stout bays leaning into their collars for the pull up Main Street beyond Brokaw's, came the six-horse team dragging the red-and-gold bandwagon. On top of this the windjammers and the drums were doing their loudest stuff.

It was a magnificent moment. June, Titus & Angevine's Combined Shows moved into Everton with sixteen wagons and one pedestrian elephant, and it was the first time a circus had ever come to town.

Now the tension was eased, and the crowd felt happier. Sheriff Harmon and Constable Downs, to mention but two gentlemen who felt the weight of their responsibility, breathed easier.

The parade marched up Main Street past the courthouse, circled that edifice to the cheers of the onlookers and went on eastward a few streets to the vacant lots which the advance agent had rented from Allin on the strength of a ten-dollar promise and a few passes.

And it was a real parade. Led by the gorgeous if somewhat

weather-stained red-and-gold bandwagon, it managed to stretch itself out for a length of three blocks. There were barred cages with lions and bears, an open-top wagon from which protruded the unwilling neck of the fabulous giraffe, various red wagons of baggage and props, imposing-looking gentlemen with tall beavers riding really fine horses, and the elephant which padded placidly through the deep dust.

The crowd loved it all, and when the show settled down on the lot most of the crowd stayed right there, unwilling to miss a single sight. The management, which seemed to consist mostly of a tall bearded man named John J. June, obliged by putting his tumblers to work on the grass outside the big tent.

For most of Everton this was the first time they had ever seen a circus or a traveling show with a real big-top. Most of the wandering troupers merely used a canvas wall high enough to keep non-ticketholders from looking over, and the customers stood up to watch the show. June, Titus & Angevine had a real big-top—round and some seventy feet in diameter. They had, also, one small section of slat seats, so that *some* of the customers could buy sitting space. The rest of them stood up, as always.

Mr John June did some business at Burke's Livery Stable, paying cash money for a considerable quantity of feed. Mr Doughy Phillips, the show cook, did business at Robinson's and Haines's, paying cash for a small cartload of provisions, and various and sundry of the performers patronized Killip's and Nichols' liberally. Business was good, and nobody felt slighted.

At four o'clock the spangled joey once more made a lone round of the courthouse square, blowing his bugle to attract attention—as though that were necessary—and announcing that the performance would begin promptly at seven-thirty, as advertised.

And begin promptly it did, with the house packed almost to the ring curb. It was a jovial, good-humored crowd, sweating hugely, laughing hard and long at the clowns and shouting lusty approval of the star turns. They shrieked applause for Mr Lathrop as he did a forward somersault on the back of his lovely

white horse, and laughed as much when a blob of hot grease
from one of the star candles (a board cross studded with candles
and hung above the ring for illumination) fell on the horse's
broad rump and made the animal shy suddenly. Mr Lathrop
was tossed into the ring dust on the seat of his pink tights.
The elephant performed with dignified grace; the bears obliged
willingly in their turn; the fabulous giraffe was led around
the ring for the last time; the band played brassily; the fire-
works display entertained and neither exploded prematurely
nor burned any customers. Then as a final climax, the ringmaster announced that "Mister Felix, whom you have seen here
so far tonight only as a clown, a tumbler and a mountebank,
will exhibit the incomparable beauty of his tenor voice in a
ballad lately composed by Mister Robert Dilling, titled 'The
Sweet Hills of Virginia.' "

The clown doffed his peaked cap and stepped to the center
of the ring as the band began to play softly. And after the
first half-dozen bars he had them in the palm of his hand. The
crowd was suddenly quiet and even the noisier drunks subsided.

The soaring voice held them spellbound. Some of them knew
Virginia; all of them knew some far place that had been home.

Then the last piercing note ended, and amidst the roar of
applause the ringmaster waved them "All out and over." The
big show was ended.

It had been a gala day for almost everyone. Business had been
good on Main Street. Business had been good with June, Titus
& Angevine. Everyone had had a good time, and there was no
one in jail as a result of the fun.

An hour later the circus rolled southward in the starlit darkness toward Springfield. But now it carried one stowaway:
Lester Ricketts, aged fourteen, bitten by the virile bug of show
business and tired of chopping weeds in the Sugar Creek bot-
toms. He watched the rocking stars from the top of the lurch-
ing canvas wagon, his stomach a tight little knot and a tiny
ache in his throat. He wondered what the showfolk would

say or do when they found him and what the folks at home would think when in the morning they discovered he was gone. Once he dashed a spray of tears from his eyes, and once he started with sudden fright when one of the lions roared suddenly and sourly.

Presently he fell asleep.

IV

Emma Reynal's father was a prosperous merchant in Buffalo, and she was an only child. Perhaps because of that, and because he had a great deal of natural confidence in her, he allowed her to spend three years at Oberlin Collegiate Institute. He had a natural distrust of any such notion as a coeducational college, and he allowed Emma to go against his will. That is, he permitted her to go in spite of the fact that his better judgment told him not to. If he had known of Emma's later failure he would have probably placed the blame on Oberlin. It was his good fortune, perhaps, that he never knew.

Emma was graduated from Oberlin in the spring of 1841. She thought she had an education, and the authorities admitted it publicly, in a lovely and very solemn ceremony.

That summer she went to visit relatives in Erie, and at a small party an aunt had arranged for her, she met John Ransom. He was handsome, reasonably romantic, and shortly before they met he had come into a small inheritance. It wasn't much, as he honestly told her, but still he wasn't penniless. He was healthy, thirty-two years old, and wooed her with a vehemence which captivated her completely. They were married in late July.

For a while they were completely happy. Emma was not quite beautiful, but she was more than commonly pretty; long-limbed, high-breasted, with deep blue eyes that smiled a little even when she was mildly angry, and a great mop of soft, yellow hair. Her father gave her a handsome wedding gift, in cash, and they spent a honeymoon at Niagara Falls, in New York City and in each other's arms. He taught her that love was something more, in fact considerably more, than flattering compliments and a church ceremony, and she seemed an apt pupil. It never occurred to Ransom that there might be a lot that she was incapable of learning.

The honeymoon finally came to an end, and they had to face the problem of settling down. Ransom had no profession—he had jobbed around, made a few trips as deckhand on an Erie towboat, been out to Chicago for a year, one thing and another. But he had a pleasing personality, and now he had a little money, the latter something he hadn't had before. Emma's father wanted them to come back to Buffalo—it was a growing city, and he would find a place for his newly acquired son-in-law. But Ransom would have none of it, and in the end Emma agreed with him. He wanted to go to Illinois. There was the coming section of the country. He knew; he had been in Chicago long enough to learn that. Here in New York everything was settled. Out there anything could happen. They had almost a thousand dollars, more than enough to have a stake left when they arrived in Illinois.

Why not? she thought. They were young, and they were in love. John of course had only a smattering of education. But she would help him; he could easily make himself important; and in a new country like Illinois it would be easier still.

Lightheartedly they prepared to leave for the West. The trip was to be but an extension of their honeymoon, so to speak. He had been out to Chicago via the Erie Canal and the overland stage route, and so knew all the discomforts of that way. So they decided instead to take ship from New York for New Orleans and thence up the Mississippi and Illinois by steamboat. That would land them in the very heart of Illinois, and the expense would be only a little more than by the overland route. It would take a little longer, but what did that matter? In any case they would be in Illinois long before spring.

That was their first bad mistake.

For, when they sailed from New York in late October, Emma was about three months pregnant. She was more or less aware of the fact, but not alarmedly so. She was married; she loved her husband; and she was embarking on a new adventure. Nothing else mattered very much.

But she had reckoned without considering her susceptibility to seasickness, accompanied by the natural nausea of early pregnancy. Long before the ship reached Charleston she was miserably ill and could not move from the tiny, cold, airless cabin. It was warm in the main saloon, but the warmth was accompanied by such a variety of human smells, most of them bad, that she preferred the cold of the small cabin. John did the best he could for her, but that wasn't much, and the lady passengers tried to be helpful, but with little more success. Emma was in that state of suspended illness where nothing but time could help her. She wasn't dangerously ill, of course, but she thought she was and the agony was no less.

The ship touched at Savannah and again at Mobile before they reached the end of the ocean voyage at New Orleans. But Emma saw nothing of these places, and because she was ill and miserable John also saw little of them and enjoyed that little less.

They made excellent connections at New Orleans and in November began the trip up the Mississippi. But again the trip, so far as Emma was concerned, was a total loss. She caught cold in the November dampness of the bayou country and was again confined to their cold cabin until the sternwheeler was somewhere north of Memphis.

Then one frosty night John came into the cabin, late, where she was cringing under the blankets and quilts of the bunk. He was more than a little drunk—ordinarily he didn't drink a great deal, or at least hadn't since they had been married—and told her, with scarcely any preliminaries, that he had just lost three hundred dollars, gambling in the bar. She was bitterly recriminatory.

"It seems," she said acidly, "that you are doing your best to make this trip a complete failure for me."

His glance wavered a little, but he was not completely drunk.

"No," he said quietly, "I haven't. But it hasn't been such a success for me, either. I'm sorry you've been sick—I've told you that—but there hasn't been much I could do about it, it seems. So far as that goes, I needn't have told you that I lost that money. You probably didn't know exactly how much we had, anyhow. But I'm trying to be honest with you."

"That isn't the point," she said. "You know how badly we need that money. And now you've gambled and drunk it away while I was lying here deathly ill."

He smiled a little crookedly, trying very hard not to lose his temper. "I'm sorry, sorrier than I can tell you. I'll try not to let it happen again. Is that enough?"

Apparently it wasn't, at the moment anyway, nearly enough, and she told him so at elaborate length.

"I'm sorry," he finally interrupted her. "I've told you that already. But listen, we'll be in Illinois in maybe a week—at least we'll be off these damned boats. Things will be better then, and you'll feel better, too. I don't want to quarrel with you. I'd rather love you."

He went to the side of the bunk and tried to gather her into his arms, but she pushed him away. In the wavering candlelight she seemed more than usually beautiful and desirable, and somewhere in the back of his mind he remembered that this was the first time she had ever refused his caresses. Slightly drunk as he was now, that didn't seem terribly important—he knew she was angry, and perhaps with cause—but he remembered. He remembered looking at her a little hungrily and in the distance hearing the faint *shh-shh-shh* of the steamer's exhaust valve. There were vague animal sounds from the pigpen on deck and the sound of a sharp human voice as a deckhand called a sounding to the pilot on the Texas.

Presently she fell asleep, breathing a little hoarsely, and John stood looking out the porthole at the moonlight on the cold river. It was, he thought, a devilishly lonely country. Yet in a way it wasn't. The wide river was brown, endlessly brown, and the trees on the banks seemingly endless. Coming upriver, the pageant of autumn had been almost breath-taking, but now, as they drew farther north, the timber was beginning to appear bare and skeletonlike. He looked at Emma again and was a little sorry for her. Perhaps it would have been better if they had stayed in the East. But better? No, at least not for him. He knew that already. He was past thirty now and had a very real, if sometimes a little incoherent, desire to put down roots in something that was his own. And, looking down at Emma again, he wondered if he had been as lucky there as he had thought. Of course she was ill, perhaps a little homesick, but she had talked so gallantly of new worlds and the frontier and of freedom from the cultural and economic thralldom of the East. But now he wondered. He knew something about the West; he knew too that she didn't know. At least she didn't know any more than what she had learned at Oberlin, and he grinned at the thought of what that amounted to. She had talked so much of her courses in this and her courses in that, and he wondered if they had courses in mud and loneliness and back-breaking work and general human hellishness. He guessed not.

They arrived in Everton near the first of December, just as the winter was getting a good grip on the prairie, and stopped at Killip's. They could have rented a house—there were a number of cottages available—but they had no household goods and had not yet settled upon exactly what they wanted to do. So they endured Killip's as the next best thing. Emma fixed up the bare room as much as she could, but that wasn't much; it was still cold and bare and inescapably a part of Killip's establishment.

And she was still more or less ill. The cold contracted on the river journey held on, and she seemed one of those otherwise normal women for whom pregnancy is just naturally hell. Dr Henry said there was nothing particularly wrong with her. He gave her what he said was a tonic and lent her some of his books.

John moved around town, met almost everyone of any importance, and a few times they went out socially. But Emma, in spite of her expressed desire for some sort of society, didn't take to Everton's brand. The women—Mrs Fell, Mrs Green, Mrs Colton, Davis' wife, a number of others—were more than kind to her. They knew Everton and the prairie country and what it could do to a woman like Emma, accustomed to certain things in the East. In fact they *were* Everton so far as Emma was concerned, and she just didn't take to them. John was sorry, for he had thought that perhaps they would be good for her. He was sorry, but that again was about all he could do about it.

He didn't tell Emma, but by the middle of the winter their capital had dwindled to something less than six hundred dollars. He was beginning to like Everton, bare and uninviting as its winter aspect was. He couldn't have explained why, but it was so. Already it was beginning to seem like home.

But he could see no place where the small capital would start any kind of business that would allow them to live. No one in Everton, apparently, even wanted to hire him as a day laborer.

He talked to Fell about the whole thing.

Fell took off his spectacles and looked at the younger man questioningly. "I don't mean to pry into your affairs, Mr Ransom, but just how much money do you have to invest?"

Honestly, John told him.

"Hmmm. Not much, though most of us came to Everton without the price of a good meal—even if there had been such a thing available. But times change. This country was almost naked frontier then; it isn't so far removed even now. However, I'm going to tell you something, and you can take it for what you think it's worth.

"As I said, I came here ten years ago more or less, without a cent, and today I'm worth—oh, I don't exactly know. Twenty-five thousand—maybe forty. It all depends on what you think land is worth. But there is only one real answer to your problem—land, my boy. You're fairly young. You can stand the wait of watching it grow. Suppose you've got five hundred dollars that you want to spend. You can't buy any kind of a merchandise stock for that. You have no particular professional training. But for five hundred dollars you can buy one hundred and fifty acres of land within a half-hour's ride from this office."

"I'm not much of a farmer," John said. "I was raised on a farm, yes, but it's been years since I actually farmed. I——"

"I know," Fell said a little wearily. "But that's a small matter. Nobody really knows much about farming this prairie ground—except those few who by instinct could farm hell and prosper. It's land value I'm talking about now. You can buy land and let it lie fallow for ten years. Ten years from now only God knows how much it will be worth—or rather how much you can get for it. I don't give a damn whether you buy land from me or not, I'm just giving you the best of any so-called knowledge I may have about this country."

"I don't know——" Ransom murmured.

"What's a few years?" Fell said. "Man, you're younger than I am. I've seen it grow a hundredfold—yes, a thousandfold—for me in ten years. It'll do something like that in the next ten years. I'm only telling you what I know as well as I know *anything*. You can have it for what it's worth to you. Take it or leave it. I'm sorry, I've got to go. Davis and Allin want to see me about some fool thing they've hatched. How's Mrs Ransom?"

"Pretty good, all things considered," John said. "I wish—— Uh, well, never mind. Say, I think I'll take——"

"Think over it for a day or two," Fell said, getting up. "Remember, I don't give a damn what you do. I only told you what I know. My regards to the Missis. You've got Dr Henry —if you stay here. And you couldn't do better—there's a very great man. Come in whenever you feel like it."

Three days later John Ransom bought a farm from Fell— without mentioning it to Emma until the deal was all over. Rather, he bought a piece of land; it wasn't a farm—yet.

1842

V

That fall William Goodheart died.

In October he had a stroke which put him down in bed for two weeks. Then he got up and sat in a padded rocker under a great oak that stood in his dooryard. His leg and most of his left side were paralyzed, and he had a strange, mild light of forgetfulness in his eyes.

Dr Henry would climb down from his buggy and sit beside the old man, taking his wrist and holding a big gold watch in his other hand. "How do you feel, William?" he would ask.

Goodheart often looked at him as though he had never seen him before. Then his gaze would wander down the road to where it vanished in the autumn glory of Maple Grove. "It wasn't so bad," he said, "except that we was so hungry all the time. I guess we musta killed an' et every dog in Moscow, but even then there wasn't enough to go around. They said that even Napoleon hisself an' the general staff didn't have enough to eat, either."

Dr Henry would smile a little and drop his watch into a vest pocket. "It was probably hard, William," he said gently. "Just don't let it worry you too much."

"An' the trip home from Moscow," Goodheart said. "We didn't have a good pair of boots in a hundred men, and the snow was waist deep, and we couldn't even find the roads, let alone know where they went. . . . Seems like her name was Olga. No, it . . . well, something like that. But it wasn't Napoleon's fault. He was the greatest general that ever lived, bar none. We could have whipped the whole lousy Roosian army with any six regiments we had. But we couldn't find the bloody cowards. Ain't that a hell of a way to defend your country? Ain't it now?"

"Yes," Henry said, still smiling queerly, "I suppose you might call it that."

"Damn a man as won't fight for his rights, I say. Our

[193]

Saviour, Jesus Christ, took the sword when it was necessary," he said piously. "Bishop Cartwright said so hisself. But not them cowardly Roosians. Did you ever see my exhorter's license? Bishop Cartwright gave it to me hisself. Here, I'll have 'em fetch it out so's——"

"I know, William," Henry said. "I've seen it, and I'll look at it again when I have time. I've got to get on my way—several calls to make yet. Be sure you keep yourself bundled up good. Pretty chilly, these late fall days."

He talked to Mrs Goodheart for a few minutes and then drove away.

When he came again William Goodheart was dead. He had died during the night before.

Strange bones that go to enrich this prairie earth, Henry thought. He had seen so many births and deaths even in the comparatively few years he had been in Everton, and yet so many before that. He had become accustomed to it, of course, professionally, but otherwise he thought about it considerably. "Mother Nature," he murmured half aloud and grinned, "we think of her as a benevolent old lady. Maybe instead she's the wantonest kind of a whore."

He passed the Ransom place at a brisk trot and waved as he saw John come up the path behind the cabin, but he didn't stop. If they had needed anything Ransom would have called to him. And he was in somewhat of a hurry to get home. That morning he had received a package containing a volume called *Poems on Slavery,* by Henry Wadsworth Longfellow. He was anxious to see what it was like.

VI

At the little hitchrack on the south side of the courthouse there were eight or nine rigs and a few saddle horses. The first light snow of the year had fallen early that morning, but it wasn't very cold, and the horses stamped the earth into mud and slush. Men met on the wooden walk or on the courthouse

steps and stopped to pass the time of day, then went on in.
The Dane County Court was in session.

Technically, that is. Actually Judge Terry stood beside the
stove in the courtroom and held his hands toward the reluctant
iron. "Johnny!" he called to Johnny Duncan in the hall—
Johnny was bailiff—"can't you get a little more heat out of
this contraption?"

"Comin', Judge, comin'," Johnny said, coming in with another armload of sticks. "Don't seem like she wants to draw
right this mornin'."

"The seat of justice is a hell of a long ways from this fire,"
the judge said. "I'm not going to hold any court whatsoever
until I'm assurred I'm not going to freeze up there on the
bench. What's on the docket this morning, Johnny?"

"You know as well as I do, Judge," Johnny said reprov-
ingly as he stoked the fire. "Nothin' except that trespass case o'
Ab Jones. I guess the country is plumb froze up. It's early yet,
though," he added thoughtfully.

Judge Terry spat in the sawdust-box spittoon and watched
the dancing flames through the open door of the stove. "I
know," he said softly. " 'Westward the course of empire takes
its way.' Ain't that poetic as hell, Johnny? Trouble is, nobody
can find the course. The most able batch of lawyers in seven
states gathering together to listen to a damned stinking trespass case! Hell!"

"Your liver's botherin' you again, Judge," Johnny said. He
closed the stove door.

"Well, what if it is?" Terry said testily. "And whose liver
is it?"

Johnny was diplomatically silent.

"Were you at Killip's last night?" Terry asked after a moment. "I don't remember seeing you."

"I was for a little while, but I left early. My Missis ain't
feeling so good."

"It was a pretty complicated session," Terry observed. "You
should have stayed."

Two men came into the courtroom—one very tall man and one of ordinary height, the latter with a small boy in tow. Judge Terry turned.

"Oh, good morning, Abe," he said. "Where in hell were you this morning? I looked for you at the breakfast table, but Killip said you'd gone out—he didn't know where. You might at least wait for the sun to rise."

The tall man grinned down at the judge, his craggy face a mirror of amusement, tolerant amusement.

"I take my pleasures cautiously, Judge," he said. "I went for a walk this morning after breakfast. On the way back I picked up Ferre here and this small Ferre. The boy wanted to see what a real live judge looked like. You know Ferre, don't you?"

"Yes," Judge Terry said. "I've had the pleasure." He held out his hand. "How are you, Ferre? I haven't seen you in some months."

"Pretty good, Judge," Ferre said. "Business is pretty slow, though. But don't chide Mr Lincoln. He stopped by to see me on a matter of business."

"I wasn't," Terry said dryly, "but if I was it wouldn't worry Lincoln much. However, I'm glad to see you here, Mr Ferre. Not," he said, "that the court has much to offer in the way of brain food."

The small boy stood behind the stove and watched with round eyes.

"Sorry I can't stay, Judge," Ferre said. "I just dropped in to say good morning and see that Lincoln got here all right. You couldn't start without him, could you?"

"Well, we have," Terry said, "but he is getting to be something of a fixture around here. Glad you came, Mr Ferre."

More men kept coming into the little courtroom, talking, crowding about the stove, taking off their greatcoats. There were townsmen, visitors, farmers—and lawyers. It wasn't hard to distinguish the lawyers. For the most part they appeared more assured, were dressed with a little more care and were

more glib in their talk. They seemed to have a suaveness, a
surety that the rest of the folk did not.

All, perhaps, except the very tall man, Lincoln. He could have
used a shave, and his long coat looked as though he had slept
in it. And he seemed more genuinely at ease among the folk
than any of the other lawyers. The courtroom was perhaps half
full now, yet he greeted most of the men by name. Not ostenta-
tiously, but casually, easily, as though he were neighbor to
each of them.

Perhaps, in a way, he was.

"Pretty tired of it sometimes," Judge Terry was saying to
Ed Baker, "this petty court business."

Dave Campbell did a vanishing trick with an unlighted
cigar. His eyes appeared a little blurred. "Remember your
sacred oath, Terry," he said solemnly. "The honor of the profession. Nothing is trivial if it's in the cause of justice. But I
wish you'd make up your mind when you're going to hold court.
Maybe I'd have time to go get a drink. A little dog hair wouldn't
hurt me a bit."

"You *think* it wouldn't hurt you," a voice said.

Campbell turned. "Oh, hello, Davis. So you finally got to
court. By God, now I know why they always have double doors
on courthouses—so even a lawyer your size can get in."

"Have it your own way," Davis said. Campbell's jokes
always nettled him a bit.

"No offense, Dave," Campbell said softly. "I know your
heart's as big as your belly. Or almost, anyway."

Davis turned away silently and went to greet Lincoln among
a crowd of farmers.

"A pretty good man, for all that, Campbell," the judge said
casually.

Campbell shrugged. "I suppose so," he said carelessly. "But
it doesn't seem to mean much to me. So damned conservative
he'd lay an iceberg in the shade."

"I know," Terry agreed, "but a little of that wouldn't do any
of us harm."

"Maybe so. Personally I don't give a damn."

"All right, Dave. It takes all kinds to make a world."

Terry dropped his cud into the sawdust-box spittoon and made his way through the now crowded aisle. A moment later his gavel banged noisily, and the room fell suddenly quiet. Johnny Duncan stood on the raised platform near the judges' bench, waiting expectantly. He cleared his throat nervously. Then, in a moment: "Hear ye, hear ye . . ."

The Dane County Court was officially in session.

And the levity was suddenly gone. The lawyers sat on their private bench and listened attentively, the raillery of a moment before—and the night before—forgotten.

David Davis: Fat, and yet somehow achieving the placid dignity of a mountain.

John T. Stuart: Aging a little, but only a little, his face a mirror of kindness.

David Campbell: District attorney, youthful, his eyes a little blurred but still alert, the best fiddle player in the West, better than Ole Bull, some said.

Edward D. Baker: The senatorship from Oregon, his oration over David Broderick, and Balls Bluff in the war between the states still years away.

Jimmy McDougal: An Irishman with a Scotch name, with California, from which he was to be senator, not much more than a vague name.

Abraham Lincoln: His long legs folded uncomfortably under the hard bench, his eyes serene and kindly, listening, watching, wondering at the endless mutations of the human heart, missing nothing.

It was a small, dingy room, perhaps even a little dirty and unkempt, with splashes of tobacco juice on the legs of the wooden benches. There were no marble pillars, no plate glass, no velvet drapes, no pomp, no ceremony; yet, perhaps as much as any place in the world, a man could get justice at this bar. In fact he could get nothing else. The law was naïvely unaware that it was there for any other reason.

CHAPTER NINE

1844

FELL WATCHED DR HENRY from his vantage point at the head of the long office table which served Jesse as desk. The front windows of Fell's office were open, and either of them could look out at the August dust of Main Street and the thick green of the timber beyond the fringe of houses. It was sticky hot, and Fell was in his shirt sleeves, his coat and vest tossed carelessly over the back of a near-by chair. He twisted his dead cigar between thick fingers and with his other hand fumbled at some papers on his desk. He took a deep breath and sighed heavily. A pair of dervish flies whirred about in the still air above the two men.

"I don't want to sell this stuff for you, John," Fell finally said.

"I know, Jesse," Henry said precisely, "but that isn't exactly the point. I *want* to sell it. I'm leaving. I've made up my mind definitely. I don't want any more of Everton—or Illinois."

"But *why,* John?" Fell looked appraisingly at the spare figure of Dr Henry. "You're not a boy any more, or even a young man. You care less about making money, as such, than any other man I know. You're a doctor, first and foremost, and you're probably the most genuinely respected citizen in Everton or any-where near here. I can't understand why you should want to leave here."

"I didn't reasonably suppose you'd understand, Jesse," Henry said quietly. "In fact it isn't necessary that you do under-stand. But I'm leaving; that's final. What the village may think of my actions isn't worth a dime to me."

"But why?" Fell asked again. "You're an old enough head to know that newer pastures only *look* greener. We've made a beginning here, John. Stay and see the end of it."

"No," Henry said evenly. "I'm going on to Iowa, as I origi-nally told you. I left Kentucky because it was a bastard state, and it becomes more so every day, I might add. And I came to Illinois because it appeared, from a distance, to be more of a literate democracy than most. I've done my little bit for the human kind hereabout, but now I'm through. Civilization—the Illinois brand—is too much for me. I don't want any more of it."

"I know, John," Fell said soberly. "I know. I've been here longer than you have. I've seen it all. But I'm not a perfectionist. I know that Rome wasn't built in a day—nor a year. Everton and Illinois won't be, either. All of us are failures, from the larger point of view, and it's probably because we're human. That's why I think you're making a mistake. You're asking too much of everyone, including yourself."

"Maybe so, but I'm asking it just the same," Henry said. "You're right, Jesse, when you say that Illinois is becoming civilized. It's becoming so civilized that it's beginning to have all the human stinks of civilization, and that's what I don't like. So I'm leaving. In a few years Iowa will assume all the stenches of Illinois, and when it does I'll move again—if I'm still able to move. In the meantime, I'd be obliged to you if you'll sell my property for me—at the usual rate of commission, of course."

Fell was silent for a moment, then he said:

"I suppose you look on me as something more than a real-estate agent in this deal, John."

"I do," Henry said quickly. "Believe me, I do, Jesse. I think I know how you feel, exactly. But I've only told you a little of how *I* feel. And that, with due deference to you, is more important to me."

"We've come a very long way from what we had when I came here—or when you came, John. We'll go farther in the next ten years. Or we will if we can keep enough good men in the town."

"Thanks for the compliment, Jesse," Henry said, and smiled faintly. "But my mind's made up. I don't want any more of Everton—or Illinois."

"Nothing specific, John?"

Henry shook his head. "No. That is, no one thing in particular. Just things in general. I came out of Kentucky because it was a good state going to the devil. Illinois was better—then; it's getting as bad or worse now. Stinking politicians, land grabbers that will strip the country bare without putting back a thing; the simple-minded reformers, full of good works and colossal ignorance—blast them to hell!" he said passionately. "This is a sweet land, but it's not going to stay that way."

"I know, John," Fell said. He sighed vaguely and looked out the window at the thick green foliage of the trees, hanging motionless in the heat of the August afternoon sun. A solitary horse *clop-clopped* past in the dust of Main Street under the window. "I know," he repeated, "but Iowa won't be much different. It will soon come to the same thing. The Mississippi Valley is growing at a terrific rate of speed—most people don't realize just how fast. And Iowa will be taken in with the rest of us."

"But not yet," Henry reminded him. "Illinois is scarcely out of her swaddling clothes, and look at her.

"Seven years ago Alton murdered Lovejoy and then had the barbarity to hold a trial and convict the man of needing murdering. A year later the same benighted populace holds a temperance convention and sing psalms in praise of saving drunkards—they counted them by the head, same as hogs—who weren't worth salvaging in the first place. Ah, the wonders and enlightenments of civilization!"

"Of course you're right," Fell muttered. "Yet there are some mighty good men in the state, John—Lincoln, Davis here, John Stuart, Wentworth, Koerner. Don't forget them all."

"A few good men, yes. A few good men doing their small best to hold back the mob. Look at Chicago. Its friends call it the fastest-growing city in the world. Perhaps it is that. It could as correctly be called the world's fastest-growing cesspool. Take your choice—if there is one.

"And our marvelous free press. It's a poor term: free. Free for any fool with a printing press to muddle the ignorance of the public with more of the editor's particular brand of personal ignorance. And when an intelligent and fearless editor gets *too* free, the embarrassed mob can always murder him with impunity. No, I'm not through yet," he went on, as Fell started to interrupt.

"Now it's this rotten Mormon business. I don't know where the truth in the trouble lies, but I know that it's not in mob rule. If a man must be ruled by a mob, then I for one intend to go some place where a man has a chance against that mob."

"I guess I can see how you feel about it," Fell said quietly. "You're perfectly right, John—as far as you go. I can agree with you on every point except this: that all these things you mention are anything more than growing pains. But this argument gets us exactly nowhere. I know your mind's made up. Suppose we draw up an inventory of your property and try to decide on what you may expect to get for it."

"I don't care if you sell it next week or next year, Jesse. I can wait, for I don't especially need the money. I'll be leaving the whole matter in your hands, anyhow."

"When do you expect to leave?"

"Three days, maybe four or five—when Minerva's satisfied that her things are packed well enough to stand the trip."

"So soon?"

"Why wait? My decision is made."

[202]

"Well, I suppose so. But—well, John, I guess you know how sorry I am about this."

"I know, Jesse. I suppose it can't be helped. Life ebbs and flows."

And although this wasn't good-by, they shook hands when Henry left.

When he had gone Fell stood for a long time, looking out the window at the shabby little street, thinking. Of all the men whom he knew in Illinois he thought of only one as perhaps a man of more stature than Dr Henry, and that one was named Lincoln.

Fell didn't think of himself as being old, and in fact he was scarcely yet of middle age. But at the moment he was suddenly conscious of passing time. The years seemed to go, like shadowless wraiths, with such terrible swiftness.

Then he saw his son Tommy cutting across the street near Robinson's store. The six-year-old grinned and waved and Fell waved back, motioning for the boy to come on upstairs. He listened for small footsteps on the wooden stairs and then smiled a little as he suddenly remembered something else. He had remembered that Dr Henry had no children who needed a country built for them.

I I

Slowly, John Ransom was making a farm of the land he had bought from Fell. The process was slow but successful. And for the first time in his life he was *glad* to be making a success of something that was his own.

The house was still only a cabin, and the outbuildings were still little more than log lean-tos, but he had laboriously grubbed out most of the brush in a wide area about the cabin. As laboriously he had hauled gravel from Sugar Creek, laying out clean-cut walks around the house and from the house to the stable yard. This was the third summer they had lived there, and now there were morning glories over the rear wall of the cabin and a thriving wisteria vine clambering across the front. There was a row of flowers around the front and one side of the cabin, too. And that was, in a way, an odd thing. John had suggested to Emma that she plant them, and at once she had agreed to do so. She did, and thereafter took care of them, efficiently, unenthusiastically, without comment, in much the same way as she took care of the baby and made the beds and churned. John said little, but he saw it.

It was very much the same way with the boy. He was a sturdy, handsome two-and-a-half-year-old now, the image of his father and named Blair. Emma took the best care of him, and he had scarcely been ill a day in his short life. But it seemed to be his father to whom he looked for play and affection, and Ransom never failed him. Sometimes, when the child would have an occasional temper tantrum, John would take it upon himself to punish him. Then, when in a moment the storm had changed to sunshine, the man would experience a strange feeling of kinship for the small stalwart at his feet, a feeling of sharing the boy's inexplicable hurts and contradictory desires. He *knew* that Blair was closer to him now, even at such an age, than he, John, had ever been to either of his parents, and he had no unhappy memories of them. The boy would venture a confiding smile, lay an intimate caressing hand upon him, and that feeling would come over him like a rushing wave.

Once, haltingly, he had tried to tell Emma about that. She had looked at him and smiled faintly. "Yes, I suppose so," she had said in an aloof tone. "I know you're *supposed* to feel that way. It's nice that you do, John."

"Don't you?" he asked.

"No," she said calmly, "I'm afraid I don't. Oh, I'm fond of him, of course. But that's all."

He dropped his copy of the Springfield *Register* to his knees and looked at her, sitting across the open hearth from him. Her eyes were upon her mending, and she didn't see him watching her. How little she had changed since their marriage, he thought —changed, that is, in appearance. At the moment she looked more gallantly youthful than she had the first day he had ever seen her. All except her hands. They were frontier hands now : rough, a little calloused, the knuckles swollen, the skin red. He was a little sorry for that, but only a little. Compared with everything else, it seemed a small matter.

Sometimes he ached for her, yearned to have her respond to him as she once had. Not physically; that wasn't especially the point. He made love to her, sometimes with a terrified fierceness that in the end only left him lonelier than ever. He had lost the key to her heart, and she steadfastly refused to help him find it again.

Sometimes he deeply considered ending the whole matter one way or another. But he could never bring himself to do it. For he loved her; that was the important thing, that was a fact. He could not do anything that might cause him to lose her completely.

It was a hellish predicament, but there seemed to be nothing intelligent that he could do about it. Instead, he threw himself upon the land, drugging his body and mind with work, and coming more and more to worship the boy.

To his neighbors, Ransom was a good neighbor. In fact he was better in that respect than almost any of them. They looked askance at him, thought him perhaps a little peculiar and let it go at that. If during the in-between seasons he wanted to dig up some useless work when they invited him to go fishing or hunting or horse racing, that was, after all, his business. There were people like that in the world, and if he chose to be that way, let him.

Ransom was not altogether sure—yet—just what he wanted. Knew, that is, in a way he could put into words. But sometimes he felt about the land as he felt about Blair, a wordless overtone that he could never find words for.

Once that summer he had been on his way home from helping with a neighbor's harvest. Dog-tired, without being exactly aware of where he was on the road, he had come suddenly upon his own field of wheat. The late afternoon sun was far down at the edge of the timber, and the golden field was bathed in a warm glow of dusky, golden light. The verdure at the edge of the road and the thick timber beyond, making a frame for the picture of the field, showed a hundred shades of green—greens that were somehow greener than anything he had ever seen before, colors that were livid beauty. He had passed this way perhaps a thousand times before; he had never seen this particular beauty. And he had stopped, wordless, drinking it in, thinking that perhaps this was something vaguely connected with the reason for his coming to Illinois.

I I I

Robinson sat under the lamp in the living room, trying to while away the time by going over some Eastern merchandise price lists. The lists were interesting, but not enough so to keep his mind altogether away from the sounds upstairs. There were noises of footsteps coming and going, occasionally a short, suddenly stifled scream from the room directly overhead, and once or twice the querulous night cry of a sleepy child.

Jim Robinson already had two children, but the approach of the third left him no less the nervous father. He wasn't much of a drinker, but three times during the hour he went to the sideboard and poured himself a liberal dose of whisky. He interspersed the drinks with attempts at sleeping in his chair, but didn't have much luck at that. The muffled sounds overhead reached him in spite of his efforts to shut them out.

But he was half asleep when the mantel clock *bonged* midnight, and he awakened with a start to hear Mrs Christopher's heavy feet on the stairs and her asthmatic breathing as she came into the quiet room.

She adjusted her spectacles and looked down at him as though accusing him of something. "You better git Dr Stipps, Jim," she said, getting her breath easier now.

"All right," he said, and leaped to his feet, glad of the chance to move around and do something important. "How is she, Aunt Bet?"

1844

"Good's you could expect," Aunt Bet said. "But she ain't on no picnic, I kin tell you that, young man. You better git movin'. You've got no time to waste."

"You could have told me to get the doctor a little sooner," he said, irked a bit by her manner.

"Maybe I could—an' maybe I couldn't," she said, and gave him a look which indicated that these decisions were weighty matters which a man could not be expected to understand. Then she lighted another lamp and waddled her way toward the kitchen, leaving him with the guilty feeling that he *was* wasting time.

It was still pouring cold October rain when he went out into the darkness of Front Street. His boots sank into the cold mud, and he swore softly as he slogged along toward Dr Stipps's house. Why the hell, he thought, did Dr Henry have to go off to Ioway? The best doctor in Everton or anywhere else in five hundred miles, and he had to take a notion to go to Ioway. Stipps was all right, of course. But Dr Henry—a man *knew* he was all right. He began to have an almost personal grudge against Henry because he had left Everton.

There was no light in the Stipps house, of course. Jim banged noisily on the front door, waited a moment, then banged again. Then a shutter opened over the front porch roof, and Sally Stipps's sleepy voice said: "Who is it?"

"Jim Robinson," he said. "Aunt Bet says we need the doctor right away."

"Well," Sally said, "Dr Stipps's gone to Randolph's Grove— left about nine o'clock. Some kind of a shootin' scrape, they said."

"Hell's fire," he said, "we need him *now!*"

A gust of wind and the swirling rain drowned his words.

"What 'd you say?"

"I said, what time will he be back?"

"Well, I don't rightly know. It's a good piece down there. He said if the weather was bad he might not be home 'fore morning."

"Oh, Lord! Morning? I s'pose I'd better get somebody else. I wonder if Dr Black is around."

"No," Sally said, "he ain't. He went to Springfield this morning with Dave Davis an' young Kersey Fell. You'd best get Dr Elkins."

"All right. Much obliged, Sally."

"You're welcome."

He heard the shutter slam as he started for Main Street. Dr Elkins. Hell's fire. Who knew anything whatsoever about Dr Elkins? A young squirt who came well recommended but whom nobody *knew* anything about. Well, there didn't seem to be much he could do about it.

It occurred to him that he had already been gone a half-hour.

Of course he knew where Elkins had opened his office. Across the hall from Fell's law office. He knew Main Street like the back of his hand and turned unerringly up the stairway in the pitchy blackness. But when he had found the door by feeling along the wall, his terrific knocking was unavailing. There was no answer.

Damn all doctors to hell, he thought silently.

On the wooden sidewalk again, he saw a glimmer of light through the wet darkness. Burke's Livery Stable. Well, he'd see who was there and what they knew, anyway. He pushed open the door without knocking and stood there for a moment, rain dripping from him in puddles, his eyes blinking in the light of the hanging lamp.

"Thank you, gentlemen," the pale young man said easily. "I needed the money to stay in the game." He tossed his cards to the middle of the table and raked in the pot.

"Mind if I look?" Burke asked.

"Go ahead," the winner laughed, still stacking coins and bills.

"Well, I'll be——! A damned stinking pair of kings and I bust-up two pair going in—— Oh, hello, Jim. Out kind o' late, ain't you?"

"I was looking for Dr Elkins here," Robinson said, knocking the water from his hat.

"At your service," the pale young man said quickly. "Your wife?"

"Yes, of course."

"I see. But I thought Dr Stipps had that case?"

"He has—or did have," Robinson said almost angrily. "But what the hell good does that do? He's in Randolph's Grove on some damned case of lead poisoning and won't be back till morning. We need a doctor now."

"All right," Elkins said quietly. "I'll have my coat on in a jiffy, and we'll stop by the office for my things."

The pale sun was coming up when Dr Elkins, looking more than a little used, descended the stairs. Aunt Bet followed him, bearing in her arms a red mite of humanity wrapped in a soft quilt.

"By God," Robinson said, "I thought you'd never get done up there."

"So did I," Elkins said cheerfully, thinking to himself that Robinson didn't know the half of it, "but here we are nevertheless. And a good-looking boy, too."

He set his bag on the table among Robinson's scattered papers.

Jim went over and looked at the tiny squirm of red face which Aunt Bet parsimoniously uncovered for an instant. "Looks pretty good," he lied proudly. "You'll stay for breakfast, Doctor?"

"No, thanks," Elkins said, and coughed hard. "But I'll take a drink if you have one handy."

"Oh, sure, sure." Robinson was suddenly relaxed. He brought the decanter and poured liberally for both of them. "Here's how," he said, and lifted his glass.

"How," Elkins repeated solemnly. Then, a little curiously: "What you going to name the boy?"

"Well, I'm not exactly sure. We decided, in a way, to name him after one of his distant grandfathers."

"Who was that?" The doctor eyed the decanter and Robinson obliged again.

"His name was John Robinson, an Englishman turned Dutch. A matter of religious difference between him and the Church of England, so he went to Holland to change his luck. He was pastor to the New England Pilgrims while they stayed in Leyden before coming over to America. Sort of looked after them, I guess. That was in the sixteen-hundreds, and I don't really know much about the thing exactly. I don't know. John's a good name."

"I would say so," Dr Elkins said. "One to be proud of, I'd think." He put his glass down. John Robinson. He'd have to remember that.

"Un-hunh. Well, if it's all right with his mother, and it probably will be. Sure you won't stay for a bite of breakfast? Aunt Bet 'll have it on the table in a few minutes."

"No. I've got to get along. Thanks just the same."

Elkins walked through the chill dawn toward his office, which was likewise his present home. John Robinson. He'd have to remember that name, see perhaps what happened to it. For though Jim Robinson didn't know it (Elkins hoped), John Robinson was the first child that he, Dr Garret Elkins, had, as a practising physician, brought into the world. He chuckled a little, stumbling tiredly in the stiffish mud of Front Street. For the first half-hour he'd been so nervous he could hardly hold his instruments; after that he had forgotten all about being nervous, and the rest was comparatively easy. Robinson's wife was a strong, healthy-looking specimen, and there had been, so far as he could tell, no trace of the treacherous fever. Have to watch it closely, of course.

He congratulated himself. Hell, the kid might be President someday. Then he turned up the stairway and ten minutes later was sleeping exhaustedly.

I V

Ike Frink ate his breakfast as he did everything else, with grim determination and both hands at once, concentrating all his faculties on the job at hand. It was a brisk autumn morning, and before sitting down to the table he had taken four fingers of whisky as a sort of appetizer. Sitting there at the head of the table, mowing back food with the ceaseless, regular motion of a steam piston, Ike looked like anything but the biggest landholder in Dane County.

The boys at the long table, all of them, ate heartily too, but none of them like Ike. Mrs Frink and the girls fried more battercakes and served the hungry brood at the table; they, the womenfolk, would eat later.

By six-thirty all the boys but one were out of the house and had gone about their appointed tasks. Each of them knew exactly where and how he was expected to do a day's work.

All but one: Lafayette. He was the handsomest of the lot and was fifteen years old now. He loitered in the kitchen until everyone was gone but his mother and sisters, then went back into the living room where Ike was chewing a freshly lighted cigar and pawing over some papers. When Lafayette came in, Ike turned and looked at him quizzically, then took the cigar out of his mouth and stood holding it in his big fist in the manner of a scepter.

"Well," Ike said brusquely, "was there something you wanted?"

"Yes, sir," Lafayette answered, "I wanted to talk to you for a minute or so. I waited up for you last night, but when you didn't get in I fell asleep."

"Yes, yes, of course. I didn't get in until after midnight. Damned worthless tenants . . . I was up looking about some o' that Pleasant Grove land, and that's the hell of a drive. Shouldn't have come home at all except I had to go to a county board meetin' in Everton this morning. Well, boy, what's on your mind?"

Lafayette hesitated now. It wasn't easy to talk to his father. Ike—sometimes—didn't seem human. He seemed more like a rock; there was just no place where you could get a toehold on him or a wedge into him.

"Well, Lafayette, what is it? I've got to get started if I get to Everton by nine o'clock." Ike's voice was irritated and impersonal.

Lafayette took a deep breath. "It's this, sir. I'd like to go to college this fall. I know it's a little late to get started, but——"

"College!" Ike's neigh was like that of a suddenly startled horse. "College! What kind o' talk is this? What do you need with college, I'd like to know!"

"Well, why does anybody go to college? To get an education, I guess. I thought——"

His quiet voice was not even mildly defiant, but it nevertheless stirred Ike to quick anger. "You *thought*. The hell you did! We've had this up before, and you're the only one in the family that's ever had such damned-fool notions."

"I know," the boy said steadily; "but it wouldn't hurt somebody in this family to have a decent education."

"And for what?" Ike barked. "For *what?* Listen to me, boy. I've lived in Illinois and in this county for twenty years. Today I own more 'n five thousand acres of Dane County land, clear. There ain't a man in the whole damned state that can match that—not one. And did I get it with an education? And have I got an education? Yes, you're damned right I have, but I didn't get it in no college. And you won't get yours there, either."

"All that's true, Father. But times are changing. Things are different from what they were when you came to Illinois. This isn't a frontier any more. *Some* men are trying to civilize this part of the country—Jesse Fell and John Stuart and a lot more."

"Yes, by God," Ike said, "and I was helping civilize this

country with a manure fork and a rifle before they were dry behind the ears. Do you think they don't know it?"

"No, Father, they *do* know it. But that isn't the point. I'd like to go to Blackburn because———"

"The hell with Blackburn and every other college. There ain't any of 'em produced anything but a flock of fools and nincompoops who didn't learn enough there to mind their own business. Listen to me. What are you supposed to be doing?"

"You mean today?"

"Yes, today, an hour ago, when you should have been working instead of standing here arguing with me."

"I'm helping Absalom at the sawmill."

"All right. We'll say no more about this. But let me tell you something else before you go. Today I own five thousand acres of the richest land in the United States. Before I die I'll own five times that much, and when I do die it 'll belong to your brothers and you—if you toe the mark. You don't need no education except what you're getting from me an' your older brothers. Get that in your head. When I die and the land is split up amongst you, *each* of you'll probably own more than any other one man in the county. In the meantime you're spending a few short years of your life earning it. That's final. Now get out of here and give Absalom a hand."

"All right." Lafayette turned on his heel and walked out of the room, shoulders back, head erect, but his teeth biting an upper lip that Ike couldn't see.

In the kitchen his mother looked at him a little furtively, sympathy in her tired eyes. "What did he say?" she whispered.

"Nothing," Lafayette answered, and flung himself out the door.

Cassandra watched him go toward the barn, absent-mindedly turning a dishrag about in her fingers. Ike meant well. But sometimes she thought he was pretty hard on the boys. Lafayette, now—he was a little different from the rest of them. Maybe if she talked to Ike . . . But the thought died unborn.

She hadn't talked to Ike, that way, in years. She'd gotten out of the habit now.

Ike walked back to the dining room and poured himself a stiff drink. That was contrary to his principles—he took one drink before breakfast but no more until afternoon—but he felt that he needed it. He didn't think any more of Lafayette than he did of the other children, that was certain. It was just that Lafayette was always doing or talking something that never seemed to occur to any of the others. Queer, he thought. But maybe that was what came of naming him Marquis de Lafayette in the first place. He had been dead set against the name; it was Cassandra's idea, and she had held to it stoutly, so he had let her have her way.

He took another drink, absent-mindedly, then peered at his watch. Almost seven-thirty. He'd have to get started for Everton if he expected to be on time for the meeting. The business of the board probably wouldn't amount to a damn; but he had never been late to a meeting; he couldn't be late today. It was, with Ike, a matter of pride. No matter what the obligation might be, he would be there at the appointed time, whether it was a board meeting or a matter of life and death—or money.

CHAPTER TEN

1846

T HE COUNTRY HAD KNOWN for a long time—since Polk had been President—that there would be war. A faraway, impersonal war, perhaps, but a war nonetheless. (A great many people weren't quite sure where Texas was located with reference to Alabama or Michigan or Indiana.) When or how it would begin, nobody knew, not even President James K. Polk, who should have known if anybody did.

Specifically, the war came to Everton in the form of a proclamation, formally addressed in the mail to Abel Green, to the effect that the United States was at war and that every man was expected to do his duty. It didn't go on to say "according to the precepts of the Democratic party," but there were cynics who said the words should have been there.

Green was commandant of the local militia. So with due solemnity he pasted the notice on the bulletin board at the courthouse, and the news spread through Dane County like wildfire. General Green, acting as the right hand of authority, set the date for the county mass meeting as the night of June 13th.

Not since the showing of June, Titus & Angevine's Combined

Shows had there been such a crowd in Everton. Plenty of time had been allowed for the word to get around, and when the bonfires were touched off in a vacant lot near Brokaw's plow factory probably 80 per cent of Dane County's male population was on hand.

All through the day the taverns had done a roaring business, and the crowd was ripe for anything. The idea was that this was man's business, the country's business, an affair of honor. Even those who came only to look on (and that was most of them) felt that the whole matter should be carried off according to the best frontier principles of noise and brag and general hell raising. They acted accordingly.

At last Green mounted the tailgate of a wagon and held up his hand for attention. The crowd surged a little closer, and the roar of talk subsided a little.

First, Green read the official proclamation, signed by the adjutant general of the state of Illinois. When he had finished there was a wild burst of cheering. When the crowd quieted he began again; he had no intention of losing the spotlight.

"You may be interested in knowing that Dane County is given the opportunity of raising a company through the intervention of a great patriot whom many of you know. I refer to the honorable congressman from the Springfield district, Edward D. Baker! Or, I should say, *Colonel* Baker." More cheers. "Originally Illinois was to raise three regiments, but through the representations to our great President by Colonel Baker, a fourth regiment has been authorized, and the Dane County company will be attached to that. Colonel Baker has been given command of that regiment!"

More cheers and prolonged shouting. Of course they knew Colonel Baker. How many times had they not seen him in Killip's, on Main Street, in Judge Terry's courtroom? And those who didn't know him suddenly felt that they ought to.

"Gentlemen, patriots, citizens," Green went on, "this is an honorable war, a war to defend the sacred borders of the United States, the land, the nation our fathers died to preserve as the eternal enemy of the tyrant, whoever he may be!" Green was warming up, carried away by the enthusiasm of his own eloquence.

Abe Brokaw, sitting on a broken wagon wheel at the edge of the crowd, nudged Davis. "What the hell is this war about, Dave? *You* ought to know, but I'm damned if I think Green does."

"I don't guess he does," Davis said. He took a chewed cigar stump from his mouth and spat on the trampled grass. "I don't guess anybody does—not even Polk."

"But they got to have *some* reason," Abe argued.

"Oh, I suppose they have, Abe, lots of 'em. But they're all the wrong ones. Probably the main reason is that the Democrats are so run down they have to start a war to keep people from finding out how damned no-good the Polk administration really is."

"Don't look much different from Van Buren to me."

"Well, that ain't saying much for it. They wanted me to make a speech here tonight. I told 'em to go to hell. I'd probably get hung for the only kind of a speech I'd make."

"One good thing about this war, Dave."

"What's that?"

"It's a hell of a long ways off. Won't be any artillery wheels runnin' over the wheat."

Davis laughed. "Always the optimist, Abe. But I expect you're right at that."

Green was still hammering away.

"The Mexicans are tyrants, and where is the tyrant who is not at heart a coward and a bully? Honor and glory await you in Texas and Mexico, fellow citizens. Your fellow patriots will honor you; our hearts go with you. Go!—and fight your country's battles as I have done!"

Green waved a hand and jumped down from the wagon. The crowd roared and cheered wildly. New fuel was heaped on the fires, and the flames leaped higher.

Bill Dimmit leaned against a tree, his hands in his pockets.

AMERICAN YEARS

He could feel McCullough's shoulder touching his in the darkness.

"The stinking hypocrite!" Dimmit said softly. "Don't that just beat all hell, Mac? Remember Stillman's Run, Mac?" He laughed huskily. "Green was absolutely the scaredest white man I ever clapped eyes on. Wonder what he'd do if he ran into a real live Mexican?"

"Do the same thing he did at the Run, I reckon," McCullough said gruffly. "But what can you do? What the hell good is it to kick about anything? The world is full of Democrats—and Greens."

The flames leaped higher, and a couple of men were boosting old John Moore to the tailgate of the wagon. Moore needed boosting. He was short and corpulent, past fifty now, red-faced, blunt in speech and action, and honest for all that he was a rough-and-tumble politician who never knew when to quit. At the moment, he was lieutenant governor of Illinois, a powerful office. On the tailgate of the wagon, he was a citizen making a speech.

Davis, sitting in the shadows at the edge of the crowd, watched Moore curiously, suddenly remembering the defeat Moore had handed him, politically, the day they had built the coffin and buried a man with the benedictions of Moore and the Democratic party.

Moore's bull voice roared out over the heads of the crowd like a prairie wind.

"General Green has urged you to go to the war. I don't say go. By hell, I say *come!* I'm going. Come on with me, all of you who have the guts to defend your country!"

And the roar of cheering drowned his voice.

Davis looked at the ground and flicked away cigar ashes. What could intelligence do in the face of a thing like that? He sat dumbly, not hearing what Abe was saying to him.

"Where's old Billy Rust?" Moore roared. "Where's Sam Johnson? Have they no sons to enlist in this gallant force?

Where's Gardner Randolph? Has *he* no sons to go with me to defend his hearth and home? . . ."

Later, they pressed forward to sign their names to the roll of honor, and by ten o'clock the company list was full: 103 men. And before they dispersed, the company officers had been elected. Captain, Dr Garret Elkins; First Lieutenant, John Moore; Second Lieutenants, James Withers and Will Duncan.

"Good men," Bill Dimmit said to Davis. It was near midnight, and they stood at Killip's bar in the descending din of the Dane County Volunteers. "Good men," he repeated, "who don't know what the hell they're in for. Ever fight in any wars, Dave?"

"No," Davis said, "and I don't intend to if I have to fight 'em two thousand miles away. Anyhow, I'd rather whip Polk than Santa Anna."

"By God, that's an idea," Dimmit said. "But that ain't according to the rules an' regulations as laid down by Congress an' . . ."

The marching mob thrust Elkins through Killip's front door.

"A drink for the captain," someone shouted.

Elkins looked pale but game, and all of them lurched to the bar.

Davis watched curiously. And in the crowd now filling the taproom he saw John Ransom. The big man was roaring drunk, his eyes glassy, but he was enjoying himself hugely, louder and happier than almost anyone else.

"I'm going, Bill," Davis said. "It's getting too rough for me. See you later."

He walked out of the tavern, waving and calling greetings on all sides.

He thought about Ransom, oddly enough, on the way home. The dusty streets were quiet now in the moonlight, only the crowds at Killip's and Nichols' left in town. Funny that a man such as Ransom seemed to be would fall for that hysteria. He had always thought of Ransom, when he thought of him at all, as smarter than that. Funny. That fool Green, now, and old John

Moore. He wondered if Moore really would be such a fool as to go to Mexico. Still, a war record never hurt a man in politics. Taking off his shoes, he heard a faint, faraway shout. He yawned sleepily. This was war.

When Ransom reached home at one o'clock he had made up his mind to awaken Emma and tell her that he had joined up for six months. Somewhere in his mind was the idea that it might make a difference to her. Drunk as he had allowed himself to get, the idea seemed intelligent.

He entered the cabin softly and stumbled against a few pieces of furniture before he managed to get a candle alight. Then, before he awakened Emma, he tiptoed over to look at the sleeping boy, marveling a little, as he always did, at the child's innocent beauty. He stood there for perhaps two minutes, drinking in the picture of the boy. He remembered that after another night he wouldn't be seeing him again for a long, long time.

Then he touched Emma's shoulder gently, and she was awake at once.

"What is it?" she asked, her voice bearing a startled note.

John discovered that he still held the candle sconce in his hand; he placed it carefully on a near-by table before he spoke.

"Well," he said, choosing his words carefully, "it's war, all right."

"Did you have to wake me up to tell me that? Tell me about it in the morning."

Then she raised up a little to look at him more closely in the wavering light. She held the quilt closely about her throat, though the June night was more than warm. Her eyes came to rest somewhere in the darkness of the ceiling, and he knew that she had seen he was drunk—and that she didn't care very much.

"I could have waited till morning, yes," he said, "but I'll be pretty busy for the next couple of days, and I thought I'd better get this over with."

"What do you mean?" Her blue eyes were on him now.

"Just that I've joined up for six months to fight in Polk's

1846

war, in Texas, or Mexico, or wherever in hell it is. I thought I'd
better tell you and get it over with."

"Yes," slowly, "perhaps it's a good thing you did. And just
what do you expect to gain by doing such a fool thing as going
off to some silly war? What about Blair? What about the
farm?"

She was cool as a cucumber about it. And she didn't say,
"What about *me?*" It hadn't, personally, made any difference
to her. He saw that, angrily.

Cold fury was audible in his voice. "Gain? Do I have to *gain*
something by everything I lay a hand on? And what the hell did
I gain by anything that's ever had to do with you? Can you tell
me that?"

"Blair, maybe." She didn't look at him.

"Blair!" His voice suddenly softened. "Blair. I suppose so.
But is that all? Emma, listen. I've loved you—I love you.
Doesn't that *mean* anything to you?"

"Yes," she said unexpectedly, "but not what you seem to think
it should, I'm afraid. I'm sorry; I wish it weren't so."

"All right," he said then. "Let it go at that. I'm going to
Mexico, that's settled. The crops are in the ground, and when
they're harvested you'll probably get a good price for them,
what with the war an' all. Tomorrow I'll arrange with George
Monroe to do the harvesting on shares. I've got a little over two
hundred dollars in cash. I'll give you the two hundred and keep
the odd change for some things I may need."

"When are you leaving?"

"I'll leave here day after tomorrow. That'll give me plenty
of time to arrange things."

After a little he blew out the candle, undressed and got into
bed beside her. Inexplicably, he was quite sober now. But he
couldn't sleep. Instead he lay awake until dawn, staring at the
ceiling darkness and feeling completely miserable. When the
hot sun came up like a red, molten ball he arose and went about
the chores as usual, trying to forget that after one more sunrise
he would be gone. . . .

After supper the next evening he quietly gathered his things in a little pile: his razor, some handkerchiefs and socks, a few other personal odds and ends. He placed them in a neat bundle and then put the bundle out of sight, where Blair wouldn't see it and want to know what it was for. Then for a little while he sat in the doorway, smoking and watching Blair gallop about in the falling dusk, riding a stick horse.

Emma appeared in the doorway behind him. "Time for bed, Blair," she called.

"All right," the boy said, "I'm coming." He came up to the doorstep, panting a little, and leaned the horse against the cabin wall.

"That your private barn?" John asked.

"Un-hunh. Dad, will you undress me tonight?"

"Sure thing," John said, and his voice was husky.

A half-hour later Blair was undressed, washed and asleep. John bent over and kissed him. He looked around the comfortable room and sighed; then he took up the bundle and went outdoors.

It was quite dark now, and the moon had not yet risen. Emma was sitting on a stool in the yard, her face but a white blur in the darkness. Her voice came to him, disembodied.

"I thought you weren't going until morning."

"We agreed to meet in Everton by midnight tonight. We leave for Springfield at sunup in the morning."

"Oh," she said.

"Well, I guess that's about all. But, Emma . . ."

"Yes?"

"You'll take care of Blair?"

"Certainly," she said. "And why shouldn't I?"

"I don't know," he said slowly. "But that's a promise?"

"Yes, if you want it that way."

"All right. Then this is good-by," and without waiting for an answer he turned and walked away into the deep darkness.

He walked rapidly for perhaps a hundred yards down the dim road and then suddenly stopped and half turned. Had that been her voice? Faintly, in the far distance, the owl hooted again. Then he shrugged and walked on again, not looking back any more.

II

Technically of course they were not yet members of the United States army; but whether they were or not probably wouldn't have made any difference.

It was after midnight when the dozen men made their way down a sparsely settled side street and stopped before the cottage of the Reverend Levi Spencer. Spencer was pastor of the First Congregational Church, the only church in Everton—or, for that matter, in Illinois—which was openly outspoken against slavery. And because Spencer was what he was, he lived and slept with one eye and one ear open. He had never been physically attacked because of his antislavery opinions, and he didn't really ever expect to be, but at the same time he was not a fool.

Therefore, when he heard the drunken voices and heavy feet on his front steps, he didn't wait to find out who was there and why. Instead he bundled his wife out of bed in a hurry and, with each of them carrying one of the children, they dashed out the back door and across the stretch of pasture to Lyman Ferre's house on Elm Street.

The Ferres, awakened, took them in without stopping to ask questions.

"Don't risk showing a light, Lyman," Spencer warned. "Lend me a pair of pants and some shoes. I want to go back and see if I can recognize any of them."

"All right," Ferre said grimly. "I'll go with you. Just a second till I see about the priming in this rifle."

"No, no," Spencer protested. "I don't want that."

"Well, I don't want to kill anybody, either," Ferre said dryly, "but I'm not walkin' into any batch of snakes without *some* protection."

But when they came back to Spencer's house the men were gone. Spencer and Ferre could hear their voices a hundred

[223]

yards down the street, going back toward the courthouse square.

Inside, they surveyed the ruin of the once neat interior of the cottage. Furniture was overturned and broken; books torn to pieces and scattered madly on the floor; pictures torn from the wall and their frames smashed to pieces. The walls were smeared with rotten eggs, and someone had vomited in the middle of the kitchen floor. Three or four bottles had been smashed on the living-room carpet and the broken glass tramped in. It was a scene of utter ruin.

Spencer looked at it dumbly, his face miserable and white as death. He sighed vaguely, his mouth working. "Well," he said huskily, "I can't say that I expected quite this. It seems a pretty big price."

"By God, Spencer," Ferre burst out, "I'm sorrier about this than I can tell you. This is just naturally hell. If there's anything I can do——"

"Thanks, Lyman. I know you mean it."

"Listen," Ferre said suddenly. "I was just wondering——"

"What?" Spencer looked up.

"This mob was from the camp down there?"

"I would judge so, but I couldn't swear it anywhere. Their voices sounded youngish, and they sounded drunk. But that doesn't mean very much. I——"

"But you don't quite get what I mean. They probably came here first. Mightn't they go somewhere else? I don't know where, but maybe you'd have an idea."

They looked at each other, and there was sudden comprehension in Spencer's eyes. "I'm not sure, of course," he said hurriedly, "but maybe George Dietrich——"

"By God! Do you reckon so? They went toward town. Come on, man, come on!"

They left on the run, but even then they were too late. When they came panting up to Dietrich's shop, in the rear of which he lived, they found a half-dozen men there ahead of them. Two of them were holding the German's head and shoulders, and another was giving him a drink from a flask. They wiped some of the blood from Dietrich's square face and straightened one arm which seemed oddly limp and unusable.

"Somebody 'd better get Dr Stipps," Ferre said.

"We already sent for him," Andy Burke puffed.

But in a moment Dietrich was able to talk a little, and they carried him back inside the littered shop.

"Did you know any of them?" Spencer asked.

The German shook his head weakly. "No. Dey haff someding over dere faces. I cannodt see. I try to stop dem an' ve fight here by der door. I dunno."

Ferre voiced the thought in everyone's mind:

"Were they from the camp?"

"I dunno."

"All right." Then Ferre told them briefly what had happened at Spencer's house.

They looked at each other queerly, nobody saying anything. Bill Hannan took a fresh chew, and Burke coughed a little. Somebody adjusted the lantern wick needlessly.

"All right," Ferre said. "We'll go down to the camp and find out just what the hell's coming off here."

"Listen, Lyman," Burke said worriedly, "you'd better take it easy. There's been plenty o' trouble here for one night already."

"Not near enough of the right kind o' trouble," Ferre said savagely. "You don't have to go, Andy. But, by God, *I'm* going. Anybody else?"

He looked around, and one by one they nodded.

"But this is really a matter for the sheriff," somebody said weakly.

"The sheriff. Hell!" Burke spat contemptuously. "If we're goin' let's go now an' then call the sheriff. What the hell good would six sheriffs do us?"

Then there were more voices outside, and when the little group went out on the walk they recognized most of the newcomers as from the company. Ferre saw John Ransom and in a low voice explained what had happened. Ransom made a wry face. "A hell of a note, Ferre. But what do you expect to do about it?"

Ferre didn't answer. He asked: "Is Elkins down there now?"

"Yes. Playing cards with Duncan and Withers and a couple of others. But *he* didn't have anything to do with it. He's too drunk to move that far. Besides, he's been there all night. I know it; I've been there too."

"I know it," Ferre said snappishly. "But he's in charge down there, ain't he?"

"Well," Ransom drawled, "technically I expect you're right. But just what good that's going to do you I don't see, either."

"I see how it ought to."

"All right," Ransom said. "Come on."

They made quite a crowd by the time they got down the Main Street hill to the camp. More than half the men in the vacant lot were aroused now, milling around and wondering what it was all about. Most of them had been asleep.

Captain Elkins, Duncan, Withers and two more men had been playing cards by the light of a lantern hung on a wagon wheel. They scrambled to their feet when the little cavalcade approached. Elkins looked at them curiously, his eyes a little blurred, his legs a bit unsteady. Something in the atmosphere of the crowd warned him. "I don't suppose you've come down here to see us off, Mr Ferre," he said. "But if you have you're a little early. What can I do for you?"

Briefly, Ferre explained what had happened in the past hour and a half.

"Well?" Elkins said coolly.

Ferre looked a little taken. "It's practically certain that that mob came from your camp here, Elkins."

"Did either the Reverend Spencer or Dietrich *see* any of these men, Mr. Ferre?"

"No," Ferre said, his face reddening a little. "But where in hell do you think that many men would come from in Everton tonight, if they didn't come from here?"

[226]

"I haven't the slightest idea, Mr Ferre," Elkins said evenly. "I haven't had time to give it much thought. Even so, I'll give you the benefit of the doubt. But just what do you expect me to do—question each man? Hold an inquisition?"

"Not exactly. But you could call the roll and see who ain't here. That would be an indication, anyway."

"I don't agree with you," Elkins said. "There are probably twenty-five or thirty men in the company who are not here. They don't actually have to be here until five o'clock, when we leave for Springfield. A good many of them are, perhaps, bidding their wives—or sweethearts—good-by."

"You mean you won't call the roll?" Ferre said.

"I'm sorry, I'm afraid not," Elkins said smoothly. "Technically these men are in the United States army. You have no authority to demand that I do anything." Then his voice was suddenly bitter. "Do I look like a damned fool, Ferre? I'm supposed to be captain of this company—and it's a hell of a long way to Mexico and back."

Davis and McCullough had appeared out of the darkness. Davis touched Ferre's arm. "Better let be, Lyman," he said easily.

"You don't think he's right?" Ferre looked questioningly from Davis to McCullough to Spencer and the rest of the circle of faces in the lantern light.

"I daresay he is," Davis said. "At least from his point of view."

"But this whole thing's a damned stinking outrage!" Ferre said furiously.

"I'll go you one better," Davis said. "It's a rotten double-stinking outrage. But don't blame it all on Captain Elkins. I, for one, respect his attitude. He's in a difficult position—very. Let's call it a night, Ferre. We're not doing any good here. Better spend your time giving Dietrich and Spencer a lift."

In the end, they did that.

The crowd gradually dispersed. Davis lingered a moment beside Elkins.

"Thanks, Davis," Elkins said.

"You're welcome," Davis told him. "But don't get the wrong impression about how I feel, if it makes any difference. You know who did this as well as I do."

"Roughly—but I couldn't name any names."

"No, neither could I. But you know what I mean. They came from here."

Elkins shrugged. "I told them I had to live with these men from here to Mexico—and back, I hope."

"Of course you do. Well, I'll wish you luck, Elkins. You'll probably need it."

"Will you have a drink before you go?"

"No, thanks. I've had enough excitement for one night. Oh, by the way, what's happened to old John Moore? I didn't see him around tonight."

"My second-in-command? Said he'd drive to Springfield in his own buggy. I don't blame him. We're taking the men down in box wagons, you know. After all, he's a lieutenant governor. Who'd deny him a little thing like that?"

Davis laughed, his belly shaking. "You'd make a good ambassador, Captain. Well, again, good luck."

At dawn, after a hasty breakfast, the company creaked toward Springfield in the box wagons. A good many of them felt that they had already had enough of war.

They spent that night in a grove thirty-five miles southwest of Everton, and the following morning moved on toward Springfield in a drizzling rain. They felt less than ever as they supposed soldiers ought to feel. They reached Springfield late in the evening of the second day.

Springfield was the state capital, but it wasn't, in reality, much more of a city than Everton. And the volunteers received a cold welcome. They were herded into camp by some hard-bitten gentlemen whose uniform insignia proclaimed them members of the United States army and who told that they *might*—sometime during that night or the next day—receive rations. The regulars were inexplicit; they didn't know anything for sure—so far as the volunteers were concerned. The next morning the Dane County company received the rations: weak coffee and poorer bread.

That day was miserable. The drizzle continued; they were not allowed to leave the confines of the camp; they had no shelter to speak of; the rations were few and far between. To the last man they wished they were back home.

But the next day one fact became apparent: they had enlisted for six months, and the government refused to recognize enlistments for any period under a year. Therefore the faint-hearted were left a perfect loophole. For a number of fathers and close relatives had arrived in Springfield during the short interval and, becoming aware of the situation, urged the boys to use their heads rather than their patriotism. More than a few of them did. The backsliders felt they had done their duty when they had enlisted. It wasn't their fault if the government didn't want to operate the war their way.

One hundred and three men had enlisted at the Everton roll call. When the new roll was called at Springfield an even sixty of them were left. B Company, of the Fourth Illinois, was made up of these men, plus fifty-eight more from Macoupin County who had been left similarly stranded. The officers, with one exception, were unchanged. First Lieutenant John Moore had opportunely encountered Colonel Baker of the Fourth Illinois Volunteers, and as soon as Moore's rank was called to the attention of the governor—also a stalwart Democrat—it was changed immediately. Which, of course, was no more than it should be. Lieutenant John Moore of B Company became Lieutenant Colonel Moore of the Fourth Illinois, Colonel Baker commanding.

As for the regiment, it didn't care. Colonel Baker or Lieutenant Colonel Moore—it was a tossup as to which was the worse officer. But the regiment was no judge. It was composed of the die-hards who were going to the wars, come hell or high water, and, at the moment, it didn't matter who commanded it.

They weren't so far wrong at that. For Baker and Moore

[229]

were politicians before they were anything else, and they knew above all that they had to keep the men satisfied. They did their best, and most of the men knew it. They didn't much care who led them into eventual battle as long as the rations came regularly three times a day and weren't any worse than the other regiments had to eat.

Late in June the Fourth was moved to Jefferson Barracks, Missouri, and drilled by regular army officers. After a few weeks it took on the approximate appearance of soldiery. In fact, the Fourth had the reputation of being the "star" volunteer regiment of the army. But that, according to the regulars in charge of the barracks, wasn't saying much. They were simply a little better than the other prairie regiments which wanted to see Mexico.

On the Fourth of July Joe Bozarth, one of the B Company boys from Dane County, deserted, and his manner of so doing was one of the strangest on record in the army; or rather, one of the strangest which wasn't on record, for Joe's desertion was never officially recognized. He simply hunted up Colonel Baker, told him that he was tired of the war and that he was going home.

"Well," Colonel Baker said mildly, "I wouldn't do that. Hell, boy, we're just gettin' started."

"Maybe you are, Colonel," Joe said, "but I'm not. If you was tired o' the war you'd go home, now wouldn't you? Man to man."

Baker sputtered a little. "What's that got to do with it, you young hellion?"

"Well, I wouldn't do anything you wouldn't do, Colonel. An' if you wanted to, you'd just naturally resign. That's what I'm doin'. I just thought I'd come by an' tell you. I'll see you in Illinois one o' these days, Colonel."

"All right," Baker said. "Just don't take any government property with you when you leave."

So Joe Bozarth went.

Later in the day Colonel Baker met Captain Elkins and told him of the incident.

"That's a hell of a note," Elkins said heatedly. "I'll have him reported for desertion at once, Colonel."

Baker laughed a little. "No, let it go, Captain," he said. "He wouldn't have made a soldier, anyway." He didn't say what made him a judge of that.

"You mean, not report it at all?"

"Well, you can get along all right without him, can't you? The hell with it. If we reported it, it'd just make a lot more damned red tape to worry about. We got enough of that now."

And there it stood. One desertion was a small matter; for, as Colonel Baker figured it, it was a volunteers' war, anyway. If they didn't want to fight, what was the difference?

Toward the latter part of August, the Fourth moved southward by steamboat to New Orleans, then to Brazos, Texas, by way of a waterlogged sailing hulk mistakenly named the *Sea Gull*. They sailed directly into the teeth of a violent storm, and so traveled over a very large part of the Gulf of Mexico before they finally landed at Brazos ten days later. They stayed three days at Brazos getting back their land legs before starting the march to Camp Belknap, at Matamoras in Mexico. Four of the days at Camp Belknap were spent on rations of bacon and crackers, the temperature stood at something over a hundred, and the Fourth was beginning to understand a little of what it was in for in the future. There had been no casualties as yet; but half the regiment was helping the other half stay on its feet.

Late in September the word was passed that the Fourth was moving to a place called Camargo. Where was Camargo? No one, it seemed, knew exactly where it was; rumor reported it a hundred miles up the Rio Grande. Rumor also reported that only the eternally damned were sent to Camargo, and only those as a last resort.

AMERICAN YEARS

In Everton, meanwhile, business went on as usual except that it was better than it had been for a long time.

The war was a fact, of course, but it seemed very, very far away. It *was* a long way off, both for those at home and at the front. In Everton and Dane County a few score anxious parents and sweethearts and wives watched for the infrequent mail from Texas. Some of the folk complained loudly about the new federal tea and coffee taxes, the taxes which were to pay for the defense of the United States. Otherwise the war was not much in evidence about Everton.

Until the last few days in September there had been no casualties in B Company, either from battle or sickness. Nevertheless the letters which arrived in Everton, could they have been placed end to end, would have formed one long epistle concerning homesickness, weariness, lousy food, dysentery, pneumonia and, so far as the niceties of polite correspondence allowed, vermin. A good part of B Company's history, too, was contained in those letters. Scattered, a word or phrase here, a sentence there, but a history nevertheless. And the letters which began coming in late October told a grimmer story.

Captain Elkins had "resigned." Literally he had resigned, but at Colonel Baker's specific request. The colonel didn't care how much any of his officers drank, but he insisted that they carry their liquor at least as well as he himself did, and Captain Elkins just hadn't been up to the mark. In the regulars he would have been summarily court-martialed and cashiered.

Second Lieutenant Withers contracted a severe case of granulated eyelids and was discharged as unfit for further active service. He and Elkins left Camargo together, and there was hardly a man in B Company who didn't envy them.

That was in mid-October. A few days later First Lieutenant Andy Wallace, a Macoupin County man who had replaced Lieutenant Colonel Moore, died of pneumonia.

So B Company was left in command of its one remaining officer, Second Lieutenant Duncan. For the duration of the war that status remained unchanged. Duncan commanding, ably seconded by Sergeants Ransom and Lander. And after ninety days in the field under its former commanding officers, B Company knew when it was well off.

After those preliminary casualties B Company's troubles set in violently. During October and November the company lost twenty-one men through death or discharge after sickness. Among this number was one sergeant, four corporals and the company musician. So on the 1st of December B Company was left with a personnel of thirty-nine men.

The story was told in the letters home—and by those who came drifting home in person toward Christmas time.

In Everton the folk were able to read of the war in their own newspaper. The news was of course culled from second-hand sources, but it was in the home-town paper. A mild-mannered but enterprising little gentleman named Charles P. Merriam had rented a vacant room from David Davis, imported a press and a few cases of type, and shortly afterward began publishing a paper which he called the *Western Whig*. And it looked as though the paper would catch on. The subscription list was good, and there were three times as many businesses to buy advertising space as there had been when Fell and his partners made their ill-timed venture with the *Advocate and Intelligencer*. In politics Merriam was first a conservative and then a Whig, and whether he knew it or not he had picked the side on which stood the majority of Dane County's population. And if he knew that, he was the only man in the county who did. For the change had taken place silently, slowly, casually, perhaps without any other reason than the hardy perennial of propertied prosperity.

IV

Lieutenant Duncan stooped a little so he could see his chin in the little scrap of mirror hanging on the tent pole and swore softly as the razor scraped audibly. "My God," he said, "this alkali dust even gets ground into your skin so it treats your razor same as if you were cutting rock with it. I can hardly get this razor stropped any more."

"Why all the dressing up?" Ransom asked lazily. Then, irrelevantly: "Lordy! if it's this hot here this time of year what do you suppose it's like in the summer?"

"Nobody knows. Nobody seems to care," Duncan said.

It was shady under the tent, but out in the company street heat shimmered in glittering waves above the finely powdered dust and the chaparral which lay between the camp and the mangy little village of Camargo a quarter-mile away. On the map Camargo sounded like a town; in reality it was a handful of squalid adobe huts strung along one little street a hundred yards in length. The water from the public well was muddy and alkali-laden, and the natives were as listless and dirty as the town; they looked as underfed as the myriad dogs that yipped continually in the street and fought bloodily over dried and marrowless bones.

"I sent Corporal Dirk to see about the mail," Ransom said.

"Courier coming up?"

"No—supply train. Probably have a mail pouch. I don't expect anything myself, but some of the boys will."

"Un-hunh. Oh, Ransom—I meant to ask you before but forgot—any casualties today?" Duncan was twenty-three, and the seemingly endless deaths had rattled his nerves more than even he supposed. Each time a man died, Duncan had to make an inventory of his effects and write a letter to the nearest of kin. Twice lately his hand had been stricken as though with a palsy when he sat down to write. Ransom each time had finished the job for him.

"No," Ransom said, "but Tom Harp is on his last legs. Last through tonight, maybe, but that's all."

"Tom Harp! Oh, Lord, John, he and I went to the Oak Ridge school together a few years ago. He's a little younger

[234]

than I am—can't be more than nineteen. Always was a little shaver but happy as a damn bird all the time."

"Yeah? Well, he's pretty bad. I thought the last time I took a burying detail out that even the birds were whistling the same tune the fifer was playing. They oughta be able to, they've heard it often enough in the last few weeks. But you didn't answer my question."

"What question?"

"What the hell is all the dressin' up for?"

"Oh, I guess I didn't. Another damned mess. I'm appointed to serve on a court-martial. I don't know what the hell I'm supposed to do, but I suppose I've got to go as per orders."

"Who's getting skinned—anybody from our outfit?"

"I'm not exactly sure. A young squirt from the Second Kentucky, I understand. Charge, insubordination, including striking a noncommissioned officer."

Ransom grinned. "Couldn't the noncom whip him?"

"Don't know much about it except that I wish they hadn't picked *me*." Duncan buttoned his blouse and buckled on his sword belt. "Go ahead and hand out the mail if Dirk brings any up; you needn't wait for me. I don't know whether these things take an hour or all night. If there's any regulars mixed up in it, it'll probably take at least a couple of days."

He went off down the company street toward brigade headquarters. Ransom sat down on his bunk and again wiped sweat from his dripping forehead. He looked at his watch: nearly two-thirty. Not that he expected much mail. But there *might* be a note from Emma about the boy. He had had one short letter from her at Camp Belknap, saying that Blair was doing very well, that the wheat had brought a good price and that the corn was expected to, also.

On the whole, Ransom wasn't so sorry he had come to Mexico. The matter of Emma didn't bother him much now. Seeing her in perspective, as it were, he had found that she didn't matter nearly as much as he had thought. He supposed that he still loved her, but it didn't seem important any more.

He was certain that she would look after Blair; that was the most important thing. And the damned war couldn't last forever. Maybe there *would* be a letter. Just so the boy was all right . . . He missed him like hell at times.

Lieutenant Duncan walked into the regimental headquarters of the Second Kentucky and was introduced to Major Dorrance, Major Lisle, Captain Woolson and Captain Harvey. They were all from regiments other than his own, and though he was familiar with most of their names, he had met none of them before. Someone suggested a drink, and someone else suggested they wait until the proceedings were over.

"Shouldn't take more than a half-hour," Harvey growled. "If it does it 'll be a waste o' time. Probably will, anyway."

Major Dorrance, who was senior officer present, convened the court and acted as its president, ordering the accused and the witnesses brought in.

Duncan watched and listened curiously. He hadn't the slightest idea of what was expected of him.

The prisoner, Private Leonard Swett, Company C of the Second Kentucky Volunteers, was a tall, pinch-faced lad of perhaps eighteen or nineteen. In spite of the Mexican sun his face was pale. His uniform didn't fit anywhere, and his appearance was ludicrous in general. And on top of it all he seemed frightened half out of his wits.

Duncan wanted to laugh at him and at the same time felt sorry for him.

The accuser, who had instigated the charges in the first place, was one Sergeant Devlin, a pork of a man with a tobacco-stained mouth and broken teeth. The witnesses were various privates from the prisoner's own squad, looking almost, if not quite, as ungainly as the prisoner, and as ill at ease.

Major Dorrance sighed vaguely. "Read the charges, Mister Clerk," he directed in a bored voice.

The clerk read in a rapid singsong. The accused, during the course of a drill detail commanded by Sergeant Devlin, had broken ranks, directed blasphemous and abusive language against the sergeant and, finally, with a blow of his fist, knocked the sergeant down. It was a bad indictment.

Duncan smiled inwardly at the thought of that gangling private knocking down the beefy hulk of a sergeant. Considering the differences in their respective physiques, the provocation must have been considerable.

The provocation, so it developed, had been considerable. As the testimony was drawn a little reluctantly from the various witnesses, it developed that Sergeant Devlin was something of a sadistic devil on wheels and that anything he had got was far short of what he had coming.

Devlin didn't have much to say except that the facts spoke for themselves. The witnesses were, inferentially, liars, ingrates and natural-born drill shirkers. After all, the uniform had been insulted, and all he asked was a fair hearing.

The court looked upon him with obvious dislike Even his face was against him.

Then the prisoner was called upon to tell his side of the story in his own way; and he did. In fact, he told about six times as much story as the court had asked for. He began with an account of his poor but honest New England parents who had sacrificed to give him an education so that he might make his mark in the world; how his health had always been poor, and how he had joined the Second Kentucky out of a burning patriotic desire to fight for his country; how Sergeant Devlin had been a devil and a driver and an insulter of the first water. He, Private Swett, had stood it as long as he could; then he had stepped out and retrieved the honor of the squad. That was all, except that he threw himself upon the mercy of the court and asked humbly to be allowed to keep on fighting for his country —anywhere except in Company C of the Second Kentucky.

The court had been, whether it knew it or not, spellbound, for Private Sweet had a forensic power which even he himself hadn't known anything about. The court had been, alternately and in order, amused, damned bored and impressed.

Major Dorrance ordered the prisoner and the witnesses withdrawn while the court deliberated.

The deliberation didn't take long. They argued mildly, with Major Dorrance muttering that "any striking of an officer is not to be treated lightly."

"The hell with that," Major Lisle said. "Any fool could see that this Devlin is an ass. It's one thing to command men and another to abuse them without any sense whatever."

In the end they came to the conclusion that Private Swett should be reprimanded and restored to duty in his squad; and that Sergeant Devlin was also to be reprimanded and transferred to another company in the Second Kentucky. Major Dorrance so directed the clerk to record the verdict and see that it reached the interested parties.

"Did somebody say something about a drink a couple of days ago?" Major Lisle asked. "I understand, Dorrance, that you brought a supply of the pride of the bluegrass with you to the land of the heathen."

"Perhaps I did," Dorrance said dryly. "I'll see."

At three o'clock Corporal Dirk appeared triumphantly with the mail pouch for Company B. He let out a raucous hog call and then defended himself with mock gestures as Company B fell upon him in concerted attack. Ransom slouched lazily out to the throng of soldiers and took the mail pouch.

"What the hell's the matter with you plowhands?" he said, grinning. "You expecting Santa Claus or something? Here, Dirk, let me have the cause of the trouble. Stand back there, you buzzards. Come an' get 'em as I call your names off."

He ran through the names, the men stepping up and retrieving their letters as he named them: Baldwin, Brown, Crumbaugh, Davis, Glimpse, Gwinn, Johnston, Jones (inevitably), McCarroll, Newton, Owen, Palmer, Ransom (he hesitated momentarily as he took the two letters and tucked them under his arm till he finished), Reamer, Searles, Walker, Withers (that was Pete, Lieutenant Withers' younger brother).

The job done, he took his own two letters and went back to the tent he shared with Duncan, his mind in a turmoil, his hands shaking a little as he opened the first letter. Both of them were addressed properly but in unfamiliar hands; neither of them was Emma's. He opened the first and read:

DEAR SIR:

I take pen in hand to tell you what is the facts of the matter. About two weeks ago in the early evening your wife came by our place with your boy Blair. She was in your rig. She said she had to go into Everton on important business and would we keep the boy till she got back later in the evening. Of course we said yes but she has not come back yet. That was two weeks ago and she has not come back yet. Later we found out she left the rig at Burke's stable and I brought it out here again, paying the stabling out of your corn money, which I have got yet in hand in the sum of $161.86. The boy is well and hearty and wants to know when you will be home, which I told him I'm not exactly sure. I have inquired from Sheriff Johnson about the other but he don't know anything about it & says it is none of his business, since there is no complaint and he has enough trouble as it is already. We will take good care of the young one until we hear your pleasure.

Yours truly,

GEO. MONROE, ESQ.

Ransom's broad shoulders sagged weakly. He shut his eyes and then opened them to read the letter again. But there was no mistake. There it was, in as plain English as George Monroe could devise. Why, in God's name, had he ever left her free like that? But it didn't matter now; the damage was done.

Monroe was a good man. He had said he would look after the boy, so he would. Perhaps that was the more important thing. Just now he wasn't sure what was important. He looked off across the alkali dust of the company street toward the purple mist of mountains in the distance. This was Mexico; this was Texas; or was it? Who, he wondered, gave a damn? President Polk, perhaps.

Without thinking any more about anything he reached under

the blankets and brought forth a jug of *pulque* and took a mighty draught. The sudden shock of the fiery liquor brought him momentarily to his senses. There was another letter which he hadn't read. The writing on it, too, was unfamiliar. He'd better see what it was. It was from Jesse Fell:

MY DEAR MR RANSOM:

I hope this finds you well and the cause of our arms progressing satisfactorily. Here at home the war seems a distant thing and not a great deal of truth is heard about it. However, to more important matters.

As you perhaps know, I do not any longer practise law. However, my name is somewhat widely known and quite often law matters are sent to my attention. As a rule I immediately turn them over to Davis or some other competent man. In the case in point, however, you are involved and I decided to write to you before turning the matter over to anyone who might not know you quite so well as myself.

To be brief:

About two weeks ago I received a communication from the law firm of Stone & Thorpe, Buffalo, N.Y., in the matter of the estate of Robert R. Reynal, deceased. This letter asked that I assume the routine duty of handling matters here with the sole heiress of the estate (apparently very considerable), Emma Ransom. I might add that the letter said further that in the event of the death of the said Emma Ransom the estate was further willed to any issue she might have had.

A day or so later I drove by your place and was a little surprised to find it deserted, with every sign of its having been so for some little time. I took occasion to inquire at your neighbor's, George Monroe, and he informed me that the boy Blair was at his house, and had been for some days. I asked the circumstances and he told me, saying also that he had written to you some few days before, acquainting you with what he knew.

Having been authorized, so to speak, to look into matters, I made diligent inquiries in Everton, and at length discovered that Mrs Ransom had been seen driving northward from Everton late in the evening of the same day on which she left the boy at Monroe's. She was with a man whom my informant had never before seen about Everton. So much I know and no more. No doubt you are well aware of Mrs Ransom's whereabouts and this sounds to you like idle gossip by meddling busybodies. However, I thought it best to acquaint you with the facts in the case as they appear to me before going into matters deeply with Stone & Thorpe in Buffalo. If you wish I will handle the case myself instead of turning it over to someone else as I generally do. If this is your wish will you let me know at once, also advising me where I might get in touch with Mrs Ransom, since after all she is the person immediately concerned in the estate matter.

Hoping for your continued well-being and speedy return, I am, Sir,

Your Obdt. Svt.,
JESSE FELL, Esq.

Ransom reread parts of the letter and then put it in his pocket with the other one. Nothing seemed to make sense, nothing. In the first place he knew very well that neither Fell nor Monroe were idle gossipers. What they had written must be absolutely true; they didn't have time for games at other people's expense. Yet, where in God's name could Emma have gone like that? There must be *some* explanation for it; yet, rack his brain as he might, he could not find one that seemed logical. She might have heard that her father was ill and started for Buffalo to be with him. Yet if that was the case, why the strange man in Everton and why leave the boy with Monroe on a pretext? Why not have told Monroe where she was going and why she was leaving the boy?

It didn't make sense. He took another drink of the *pulque,* and then another, silently cursing himself for the whim which had brought him to this Godforsaken place in the beginning. And in his heart he already knew the answer. He kept telling himself that with the next mail he would hear from Emma. Well, perhaps he would. But if he ever did, he knew it would only be to tell him that she had gone and would not be back. This other matter, now, might make a difference, but not much.

Dusk was falling while he still sat there in the tent, thinking, oblivious of time and the sounds of the camp outside. Then a private came up to the tent and knocked cautiously against the pole, peering inside to see if anyone was about.

"Well," Ransom said quietly, "what is it, Mat?"

"It's Tom Harp, John. He sent word he wanted to see Lieutenant Duncan or you right away. I guess he's dyin', John. The orderly up there said he was pretty far gone an' somebody better come up right away if they wanted to talk to him."

"Well," sharply, "where's Lieutenant Duncan? He's supposed to be in command of this company."

"I don't know *exactly* where the lieutenant is," the soldier snickered, "but I got a good idea. The last anybody saw of him he was headed for Camargo with a couple of officers from the Second Kentucky. It's my bet that if there's any loose women in Camargo those wolves from the Second Kentucky will find 'em pronto an' damn quick."

"Great Caesar's ghost! Have I got to nurse this whole louse-ridden company? By hell, it seems like they can't even go to the latrine unless I'm around!"

"Yeah, I know, Sarge," Mat said sympathetically, "but Harp can't help it because he's dyin'. He's a good fellow, Sarge."

"I know, Mat. I'm sorry. I'll get up there right away. I got a slug or two left in this *pulque* bottle. It's strictly against regulations, but have a drink on me."

"Why not?" Mat asked. "Whet my supper appetite."

Ransom went off down the company street toward the hospital tent. Lord, another burial detail tomorrow. Another one. His head felt clear as a bell, but his feet were just the least bit uncertain. What a damned ghastly mess the war and everything else was. It occurred to him that he wasn't sure whether they were supposed to be fighting to take Texas away from Mexico or to make Mexico take Texas back. In the end he decided that he didn't give a damn which it was.

The Mexican dusk was velvety soft, and a faint breeze brought him the odor of the greasewood and chaparral. Somewhere a guitar plunked softly, and he suddenly felt a terrible homesickness. His heart ached for the small urchin eating his supper in a cabin in Illinois.

v

When he came to Everton in 1845 he was glad to call himself plain Dr Hiram Fitchman.

He developed a considerable practice by virtue of a pleasant manner and an apparent willingness to take, and try to cure, any case which came his way. Of course no one held that particularly against him; everyone was trying to get along, Dr Fitchman included.

In the beginning Fitchman did well enough. The folk who were going to die died just as well under his care as they would have with any other physician. Those who got well gave him full credit for the recovery and sometimes paid him. At least they paid him well enough to enable him to buy a good two-story house on Grove Street and turn out a spick-and-span two-horse buggy with red plumes and brass fittings on the harness.

That, however, was before he discovered Fitchman's Indian Elixir. Just how he came to discover this famous remedy Dr Fitchman never disclosed—at least not publicly.

The truth was that there were vast fields of medical knowledge which to Fitchman were deserts of ignorance. He had, it was true, a diploma from Central Medical College; but the diploma didn't say that he had graduated at the foot of his class and then only because the school needed his tuition money.

But before long he made the strange discovery that he was prescribing the same medicine for about 60 per cent of his clients, and that fact gave rise to considerable thought in Dr Fitchman's somewhat mathematical mind. If he gave the same medicine to 60 per cent of his patients and more than half of them got well, then that certainly proved something definite. Of course he knew there was a great deal about medicine that he *didn't* know; but he also knew that the same thing was true of the learned physicians who had tried to teach him at Central.

They might know *more* than he did, but there was certainly considerable that they didn't know. Therefore if his prescription worked out numerically—and he had observed that it did, so far as he could tell—and he could make a profit on it, he saw no reason why he wasn't serving mankind by concocting and selling it.

So over a period of a year he had compounded an elixir made up of oil of juniper, swamp sassafras, Balsam Tolu, valerian root, aloes, cinnamon, mandrake root, turpentine, calomel, opium, mercury, alcohol and sundry other harmless (according to Dr Fitchman) ingredients. That is, none of the ingredients were harmful if taken in small enough doses. And the Elixir was compounded scientifically—at least Dr Fitchman thought so, and his customers didn't know the difference.

Even so, he was astounded at the way the Elixir business grew.

Originally he had bought a few empty bottles from Robinson and with the aid of his wife made up a few bottles of the brew in the Grove Street kitchen. He charged one dollar a bottle and didn't ask the buyer what ailed him—for wasn't the Elixir based on the law of averages?

He was eventually astounded (though very privately) by the amazing profits which seemed to grow, as though by some strange magic, from the sales of the Elixir. He couldn't begin to keep up with the demand. Even when he paid what might be considered high prices for the ingredients which went into it, he still wasn't able to compute the cost per bottle at more than fifteen cents.

He made a deal with Robinson for bottles at wholesale and another with Merriam for printed labels, and still his costs remained about the same in spite of the fact that he was putting out a fancier package. He still could scarcely understand the situation, but he didn't complain unduly.

Instead, in 1846 he built a brick addition to the house for the sole purpose of concocting Fitchman's Elixir for the Most Common Human Ailments, including galloping consumption, catarrh, rheumatism, sciatica, dropsy, stomach trouble or heart disease—these last two thrown in for good measure on a strictly percentage basis. They were a good bet, because no physician knew exactly what the terms meant, anyway. And by this time the profits were big enough to ease whatever conscience or doubt Fitchman might once have had. He was developing— perhaps naturally—delusions of grandeur and had three girls working in the brick addition, concocting the brew and filling bottles. The girls didn't see anything complicated in the process of compounding the Elixir. It wasn't nearly as difficult, for instance, as making certain kinds of jams and preserves which they had learned about at home. But—it brought a dollar a bottle from the ailing. That was a fact in which people could stand in awe. And the money—at least most of it—went into the purse of Dr Hiram Fitchman. His stature in the community increased accordingly.

And Everton, on the other hand, became noted as the home of Fitchman's Elixir. It was no small honor—an even break, perhaps, all around.

CHAPTER ELEVEN

1847-48

F<small>ROM THE DIARY OF</small> Lieutenant Duncan, Company B, Fourth
Illinois Volunteers:

"*January 4, 1847.* Today reached Victoria, Mexico, after a terrible trip from Matamoras. From Matamoras here the column was commanded by General Gideon J. Pillow, a —— and a —— —— —— Trouble with Pillow ever since he took command at Matamoras. First he noticed the B Company flag (the really beautiful flag sent us by old Doc Hobbs and the ladies of Everton), and demanded that I hand over the flag for use at brigade headquarters—on what authority I couldn't imagine. I answered the general to the effect that the flag was B Company's private property and that so far as I was concerned brigade could hoist a towel—if it had one. I was right, but it was a tactical error; we've caught hell ever since, the flag business apparently starting the whole thing. On New Year's Day we (B Company) formed part of the rear guard of the column as we neared San Fernando. There were more than 300 wagons in the column, and they broke down continually. It was up to B Company to see that they kept moving. Thus we were wheelwrights and blacksmiths combined with military rear guard. The rear of the column was harried all day by *las guerrillas,* but luckily there were no casualties. A squadron of cavalry was supposed to form the final rear guard, but they rode as they pleased when and where they damned well pleased and were absolutely no help to us. The heat was hell—around 100 degrees—and the dust thrown up by so many troops stifling. Then the Mexican guide missed the road, and we marched forty miles without water except what little was in our canteens. Of course the men expected more water soon and didn't attempt to conserve what they had. Thus they were completely without water long before noon. They were dead on their feet and soon began throwing away haversacks and blankets. But no cartridges or arms; I insisted on that. In the evening of that terrible day the column reached a small well of water at San Goliad and was ordered to a halt. Most of the men fell in their tracks, and some of them actually panted like winded dogs. It was a very small well, and of course Pillow and his staff got at it first. Pillow ordered the water drawn from the well and given to his staff, their horses and mules, and the animals in his personal baggage train. When the Fourth moved up for its turn (it had been waiting in formation for more than an hour) the well was a gummy, stinking mudhole. Pillow and his crew had drunk every drop and left word in effect that the Fourth could eat sand. I was furious and borrowed a mule to ride up and report the situation to Pillow himself. I might have saved myself the trouble. Pillow apparently knew far more about the situation than I did. He ordered me back to my place in the column and threatened to report me for insubordination. The ⸺ ⸺ I hated to face the men, but of course I had to. An officer on Pillow's staff told me privately that we were only six miles from the San Fernando River and that the column would not halt for the night until we reached there. That was a little comfort. It was only five miles to the river, but it seemed farther than the last forty we had marched. Spent a miserable night on the banks of the San Fernando. Weather here hot as Hades in the daytime and then suddenly very cold immediately after sunset. The men seem to be standing the punishment very well; getting used to it, I guess. This fellow Pillow is certainly a ——— ———

"January 14, 1847. Tomorrow we leave for Tampico, and from there go on to Vera Cruz to join General Scott's command. About 100 miles to Tampico and then 215 more to Vera Cruz. It will be a shame if we don't whip the greasers after walking this far to catch up with them. Everybody in B Company cursing violently because they didn't join a cavalry regiment. A curious incident today. That fellow Swett, who was court-martialed, hunted me up to thank me for saving his life. Very embarrassing. I didn't do anything but listen and then vote as the senior officers did, but he thinks I'm some kind of a hero. He asked a hundred questions about Everton. Where it is, who lives there and how to get there and what kind of a place it is. Says he wants to go there when he gets out of the army, thinks it must be a very fine place if I come from there. Thus the man is a fool as well as mad."

I I

Jesse Fell and David Davis were on the best possible terms. They knew each other's minds; they knew most of what there was to know about each other's financial position, at least in a general way; and together they knew everything of consequence which went on in Everton. Each knew exactly where the other stood in politics and opinions in general.

Yet in the last few years they had not made a point of close personal contact. They saw each other on the Everton streets, in the circuit court, in Killip's (though Fell personally was a total abstainer), at occasional social affairs. But they didn't need close contact with each other. A word, a sentence, when they happened to meet, usually sufficed for whatever business was in hand. They probably understood each other as well as two men ever can.

So when, on a cold day in February, Davis puffed his way up the stairs to Fell's office, Jesse knew there was something important on Davis' mind. The fat man struggled out of his greatcoat and sat down, his vast bulk bulging over the arms of his chair.

"Think you ought to move your office to the ground floor someplace, Jesse, so a man could get there without half killing himself," Davis wheezed.

Fell smiled. "I have thought about it, Dave, but everybody in town can get up here without any trouble except yourself. And you don't come often enough to make much difference."

"Un-hunh. That stairway is a hell of a note regardless. Been cold, hasn't it?"

"About as usual, I suppose. The winters don't seem as bad as they used to be, Dave. I don't know, maybe it's just my imagination. Here, let me get you a cigar. How's the folks?"

"Pretty good." Davis drew critically at the cigar Fell handed him. "Too bad you don't smoke these things yourself, Jesse —then you'd know how damned bad they are. How's the Ransom case coming along? None of my business exactly. You know—I just wondered."

"Well, it's more than a little peculiar, but I don't suppose there's anything really mysterious about it. If I only knew what became of the woman. That's the mystery, if any. But then I've seen lots of people seemingly disappear from these parts in the last fifteen years. So have you, Dave. But there's nothing mysterious about the rest of the case. The estate is worth, so I am told, around a half-million dollars. It seems that the real-estate holdings of the deceased have increased greatly in value during the last few years. Ransom's wife was to inherit the entire estate. In the event of her death it goes to the boy. That's all there is to it."

Davis whistled. "A half-million! That's a lot of money for these parts, Jesse."

"I know it," Fell said. "I wish Ransom were here to lend a hand in this thing, Dave. I honestly do. A man ought to be able to find his own wife better than anybody else. I've spent considerable good cash looking for her, and I don't know any more than I did in the beginning, though I think the answer is clear."

"How do you mean?"

Fell shrugged. "The usual answer. I know there was some trouble between her and Ransom. They got along; but there was something wrong. When someone else came along she simply pulled up stakes and left. Only God knows where they went. And by the way, I brought the Ransom boy in to dinner the other day. If I didn't have plenty of my own I'd rather have him for a son than any other I've ever seen. He's a handsome little tyke and a gentleman already. But don't make any mistake, he's his father's boy." Fell looked out the frosty window and rubbed his hands together to warm them. "I don't think the boy's so far wrong at that. John Ransom always struck me as being all right."

"I thought so," Davis said, "though I never knew him well. But suppose the woman isn't found, Jesse?"

"Then Blair Ransom will probably be one of the richest children west of New York," Fell said. "I suppose, of course, that his father will be appointed guardian. Certainly he will if you or I have anything to say about it. I haven't talked to Judge Terry, but I'm not worried about that."

"No," Davis said, "of course not. You're keeping in touch with Ransom?"

"As well as I can, of course. But you know what this war is. Mail is often delayed for weeks. Nothing I can do about that—unless it's curse Polk, which doesn't help matters much."

"John Ransom, with a half-million dollars at his disposal, would be a great asset to Everton."

"So he would." Fell smiled a little. "But so would he be without the half-million. At least he always has been. But you didn't come up here to talk about this case, David. I know that. What's on your mind?"

Although Davis knew that Fell could almost always guess

at his state of mind, whenever Fell did so audibly Davis was a little disconcerted. It was as though someone had just informed him that for the last hour that someone had been watching him make love to his wife.

"Well, I was just thinking, Jesse. From what I know of public sentiment it looks as though the people will insist on the constitutional convention next year. Don't you agree?"

"Yes," Fell said, "if something very unforeseen doesn't turn up. For that matter, nothing unforeseen should be allowed to stop it. What about it?"

"This. I'd like to be a delegate, Jesse," Davis said simply. "You know as much as I do how much the constitution needs an overhauling. I'd like to have a hand in it, that's all, and I wondered how you felt about it."

Fell frowned a little as he answered. "You know how I feel about it, David—there's no one I'd rather see go. It'll be a thankless task, though, at best. Of course I know how you feel about that, too. There's only one drawback of any sort that I can see, and that's a small one."

"How do you mean?"

"People are, in general, a little cautious of lawyers, David. Not," he added, "that I don't to a certain extent agree with their suspicions. You know as well as I do that too many laws are made by lawyers for lawyers. I suppose that it's partly the nature of things and can't be helped. But these folks who settled this state weren't all numskulls, David, and there were precious few lawyers among them to begin with."

Davis looked a little unbelieving. "You forget that you're a lawyer yourself, Jesse."

"No, I don't. I got out of the law business partly because I had that feeling about it. I know as well as you do that lawyers *make* a good portion of the law business. But then you might as well blame a wolf for stealing sheep. You get my point."

"I do. But why belabor the point with me?"

"I'm just thinking out loud—thinking as I would if I had observed lawyers but personally never been one. Believe me, I know what people at large are thinking about this thing. But I know how you hate the red tape and pointlessness of most law, David. I know it—and admire you for it. I'm just wondering how we can convince the eligible voters of the same thing."

"Yes, I meant to ask you about that. What about this fellow who's running the *Western Whig?*"

Fell shrugged. "He's all right. He doesn't like a Democrat any better than you do. I don't think he owes anybody around here anything, and he'll probably go along with us on anything that's reasonable."

"I never asked you, but did you put anything into the *Western Whig?*"

"No, honestly," Fell said, smiling, "I didn't. Merriam talked to me, but he had all the money he needed at the beginning. That's what I meant when I said he didn't owe anybody anything that I knew of. I did tell him that if he found the going a little hard to start with, I'd try to see him over the rough spots. But I didn't commit myself to anything special. I simply thought that Everton was finally about ripe for a paper and that any fairly competent man could make one go. Merriam apparently is making it go."

"Should I sound him out, or will you?" Davis asked.

"Let me," Fell said. "I know him better than you do, and I'm not running for anything. I'll talk to him first chance I get."

"All right. By the way, Jesse, I saw Steve Douglas when I was in Chicago last week. Had quite a talk with him. He sent you his regards."

"So?" Again the faint smile. "I haven't seen him in quite a spell. How is he?"

"All right—so he said." Davis shrugged his mountainous shoulders. "Of course he drinks too much, as always."

"So does the whole blasted populace!" Fell said, suddenly vehement. "It's the one real curse of the whole West. One of these days I'm going to build a town where no one will be allowed to sell a drop of liquor as long as the town lasts!"

Davis laughed rumblingly. "A laudable ambition, Jesse, but I'm afraid the constitution would have something to say about that."

"So it would. But there's going to be a new constitution, so you tell me. Can't there be provision made that villages and towns can really govern themselves? It would be a wise law."

"I agree, Jesse. But I don't share your reforming ideas that far."

"Well," Jesse said mildly, "I don't hold it against you. Nobody else agrees with me except a few starveling preachers who mean well but don't get very far with their well-meaning. Come and see me again, David."

"I will, Jesse—if I can nerve myself to that stairway. Elly says it's about time you folks came over to eat a meal at our place. I had Ike Frink kill and cure me a couple of hogs. I don't know, but it seems to me that the hog meat these days is considerable better than it used to be. Anyhow, I'll enjoy carving one of those baked hams for you."

"Whenever you say, David." Fell walked with him to the doorway. "And the hog meat *is* better. It comes from fattening hogs on corn instead of letting them get thin on what acorns they can find. One of Ike Frink's unsung contributions to civilization."

"So long," Davis said and started down the stairs.

"Oh, Dave."

"Yes?" Davis stopped on the fourth step.

"You remember Dr Henry?"

"Why would I forget him?"

"I had a letter from his wife a few days ago."

"His wife?" Davis echoed.

"Yes," Fell said. "Dr Henry is dead. Died of pneumonia contracted while on his way to visit a patient in an Iowa blizzard."

Davis looked down the stairs at the glittering square of snow visible at the end of the dusky shaft. "God rest his soul," the Episcopalian said simply.

"Aye," Fell the Quaker said. "I thought you'd like to know. God rest his soul. Come again, David."

III

From the diary of Lieutenant Duncan, Company B, Fourth Illinois Volunteers:

"February 1, 1847. Climate around Tampico much the same as at Victoria. Lots of fish, game and good fruit. No one knows exactly how long we are to stay here before moving on to Vera Cruz, our original destination. Letter from my mother today. It has been a cold, snowy winter in Illinois but, she says, not as bad as many she can remember. Snow would seem a little queer now after this country, but for my part I'd take snow. According to remarks overheard, so would most of the Illinois men here. The men in very good spirits, on the whole. Some of them anxious to get in some fighting.

"March 5, 1847. The transports arrived in Tampico today, and camp here is practically struck. We are sitting on our baggage, starting to load troops on the transports at dawn tomorrow. Hope to God the weather on the Gulf isn't anything like it was when we shipped from New Orleans. The men are in high spirits. We are sailing for Vera Cruz and at last expect to see some real action. Santa Anna's main army, according to reports, is concentrated at or near Vera Cruz, and if we can win a major victory there the war will be as good as over. Will be glad of some action myself. This eternal marching and camping isn't a very hard life, but it's certainly monotonous as the very devil.

"March 14, 1847. Reached the harbor of Vera Cruz yesterday, but writing this on shipboard. As usual the passage was terrible; bad storms all the way and more than half the men seasick. A bad sea still running and no chance of landing any troops now. Of course, since the harbor itself is guarded by the fortress of San Juan d'Ulloa, we will have to hit the beach

through the surf in small boats. This fortress is a mighty structure and is supposed to mount more than 300 cannon, though it doesn't look quite that big. News came by courier today (overland, of course) that Taylor had fought and won a considerable victory at Buena Vista. The naval vessels here fired a salute in celebration. For us of the Fourth only one bad thing about the news of the victory. The dispatch said that the First and Second Illinois carried themselves with conspicuous gallantry and bore the brunt of the Buena Vista fighting. Colonel John Hardin of the First was killed in action, and that is a sad thing for us. A dozen men in B Company, including myself, knew him personally and feel that his death is a personal loss. He was for years a friend of my father's and stopped overnight at our house many times. He was personally opposed to the damned war and was the only member of Congress from Illinois to vote against it, but when war was declared he felt it was his duty to go with his state. And now he's dead at Buena Vista while the loudest of the damned war-shouters are eating ham and eggs at home. Well, God rest his soul.

"*March 25, 1847.* A chance now to write a few lines after a hellish day and two nights. On the 22nd General Scott summoned the city to surrender, asking also that women, children and foreigners be allowed to evacuate. Both the demand and the request were refused summarily. Thereupon both the naval batteries and the artillery began a terrific bombardment of the fortress and city. On the morning of the 23rd I received orders to command Companies B, G and K on a secret mission and that we were to report at nightfall, but not before, at a spot near where we first landed on the beach. When we got there we found a navy lieutenant in charge of the operation, and by eight o'clock the first of six mighty Paixhan guns was lightered ashore and unloaded by my men and the bluejackets. It was a sweating hell of a job, and I nearly lost a couple of men by drowning. But a little after midnight we had the six Paixhans mounted on the very crest of a ridge within five hundred yards of the fortress, the snouts of the guns looking laughingly queer where they stuck through the chaparral growth. The rest of the night we spent carrying fodder for the Paixhans. Then at dawn we cut away the screen of chaparral and showed the battery to the astounded Mexicans, who almost immediately concentrated a blistering fire on the newly mounted battery, the navy gunners returning the fire with double intensity. But we, the guard, couldn't move from our position behind the ridge through that hail of Mexican fire. We had no food, but luckily we did have enough water to last out the day by using it sparingly. We reached camp at nine o'clock last night under cover of darkness, having gone a night and a day without food and two days and a night without sleep. However, I feel fit as a fiddle. General Scott sent us his personal compliments and thanks, which makes us feel good, although to me it seemed an ordinary enough job of work. Those Paixhans are already leaving their mark on the fortress and the town. They are probably the heaviest and most modern guns being used in the bombardment (on both sides) and their range is—for them —almost point-blank. The cannonfire from the fortress is terrific, but fortunately the Fourth's position is such that we can hardly be reached by fire from the city. Too many sand hills."

IV

People going about their business around the courthouse glanced a little curiously at the man and woman working industriously inside the little store which stood next to Robinson & Co. But not too curiously. Someone was always starting something new these days. The newcomers would make their purpose known soon enough.

And shortly a neat sign appeared above the newly painted and cleansed shop front:

ANTON LUBECK

Musical Instruments Of All Kinds
Lessons Given At Reasonable Fees
(Also Watches and Clocks Fixed)

[256]

There it was.

Anton Lubeck was a round little German from Bavaria. He had stopped for a year in Cleveland, mainly to learn the language, before coming on to Everton. In Cleveland he had had a chance to learn English among his own people before chancing America on his own. His wife Elsa spoke but a few words of English, and sometimes it seemed to Anton that it was because that was all she cared to learn. But that didn't worry him very much. Here in the new country she would almost have to learn.

They should, he thought, do well in Everton. There was no music store and no watchmaker nearer than Springfield. Surely people here would need his goods and his skill. Not that he was an expert watchmaker as the best of them went. Not like old Fritz Burman in Neudeck, for instance. But he was good enough. He was patient and careful and conscientious. The watch work was only a side line, anyway.

After a week of cleaning and painting and unpacking and putting in place, the shop was ready to open. It was a Saturday morning, and Lubeck beamed cheerfully at the farmers who clumped past his door in muddied boots, yarned on the walk in front of Robinson's or loafed at the courthouse hitchrail. He spent the morning alternately looking out the small windows of the shop front and whisking imaginary dust from the fiddles and guitars and mandolins and clocks and the one splendid, shining, lovely pianoforte which stood in the middle of the floor.

Occasionally Elsa would part the curtains which separated the shop from their living quarters and ask if anyone had come in.

"No," Anton would answer in cheerful German, "not yet. But people are busy this morning. Perhaps they will come later."

But at six o'clock the streets were again almost deserted, and no one had come in except a man who wanted to know the time.

Lubeck ate his supper in more silence than was usual with him. He didn't feel much like talking, but for Elsa's sake he thought he should try to be cheerful.

"We expect too much," he said, stuffing his pipe when he had finished eating. "After all, Everton is a small place. We must take time to get acquainted. All the people I have talked to are fine. We just must get acquainted a little more."

And later, when he walked over to see his friend Dietrich, the tinsmith agreed with him.

"Of course, Anton. When I came here and opened a shop it was a month before I took in a penny. And now I do very well. If the town grows—and it does grow right along—I do more business. So will you. You are a German. So am I. People will ask me about you, and I will tell them. That will help."

Anton sipped his beer. "Elsa does not like it here. She thinks we should have stayed in Cleveland. I don't know. Every cent I have is in my stock and tools here now."

"Ach! The hell with Cleveland!" George said, falling naturally into the American tongue. "This is better than two Clevelands. Here you will be a big duck in a little puddle. That is better. You will see."

But Lubeck didn't have to wait a month for his first customer. A short, fat little woman came into the shop on the following afternoon. She introduced herself as Mrs Haines and the young lady with her as her daughter Agatha. The young lady smiled and dropped her eyes bashfully.

"Ah, I know," Lubeck said. "Mr Haines has the big store on Main Street there. I am honored. And what can I do for you?"

"My husband tells me that Mr Dietrich says you are a very fine musician."

Lubeck bowed a little. "I am not a fine musician, Mrs Haines, but I am competent. My father taught me, and he had been a fellow student with Beethoven himself."

"Beethoven?" said Mrs Haines, and knitted her brows slightly. "I'm afraid I don't know the name. However, it's no matter, anyway. But it's time Agatha was learning from a professional teacher."

"She plays then a little already?"

"Oh, not well, of course. Only what little I've taught her myself. Some hymns and suchlike. Nothing very technical, of course."

"That is fine. Anything she already knows is a help," Lubeck lied easily.

So they made terms and arranged time, and Mrs Haines moved like a sedate little duck down the walk toward the store of Haines & Son.

"See, Elsa?" Anton shouted ecstatically. "I told you. The first one. Soon there will be many, many more."

"I hope so," Elsa said, and smiled fondly at him. She liked to see him happy. But she perhaps knew him a little better than he did himself. This wasn't going to be like playing in the orchestra in Munich, even if he had only been one of the second violins.

He sat down at the pianoforte and played a happy, lilting Schubert waltz, loudly and very fast. When he stopped and turned around he saw a man standing on the walk just outside the door, listening with mouth half agape. When he saw Anton looking at him, the man started a little guiltily and hurried away. Lubeck chuckled a little. Tonight he must go thank Dietrich, for this was apparently his doing.

But his luck was even better than that. Before closing time, a man brought in a watch to be cleaned and gone over.

"This time tomorrow I will have it done," Lubeck said.

"You're not very busy, I take it?" The stocky man smiled in a friendly fashion.

"Not yet," Lubeck said. "I am new here, you see. It takes a little time."

"I know," the stocky man said, and smiled again. "It's taken me a long time, too—much longer, probably, than it will you."

"What name should I put down?" Lubeck asked.

"Fell," the man said. "Jesse Fell."

v

From their position on a hillside just out of easy range of the National Road, B and G companies of the Fourth rested and

watched the Mexican army—at least the visible portion of it—
retreat down the road in terrible confusion.

The April sun was hot, and there was precious little shade on
the hillside, but now they were glad of any rest they could
snatch. At dawn they had gone up in support of Harney's troops
in an attack on an entrenched Mexican battery, and after the
capture moved on to the position they now occupied.

Duncan turned to Sergeant Ransom. "What about water,
John? Has that detail come back with the canteens yet?"

"They're coming," Ransom told him. "They found a nice
little stream in that ravine about a hundred yards to the left
there. Plenty of water coming up. Plenty as long as it lasts in
this damn sweltering heat, that is."

"I know. Between dust and powder smoke I don't know which
makes me the thirstiest." Duncan pointed off to the right, to a
spot where the road made an abrupt turn, with the turn almost
in the center of a deep cut. "See anything funny over there,
John?"

The Mexican troops straggling down the road had thinned out
now, and only the little group at the turn was actually in sight.
There was, however, still occasional firing in the rear of the
detachment from the Fourth.

Ransom squinted.

"Looks like they're cutting a horse or a mule off that carriage
or whatever it is. Wonder what in hell for? Why should they
leave that wagon sit there? You don't suppose it's a mine?"

"I don't think so," Duncan said. "There's still plenty of Mexicans behind us. They wouldn't cut off their own men."

"How do you know they wouldn't?" Ransom asked.

But as they watched they saw the Mexicans, little pygmy figures at that distance, helping to mount an officer on the freed
animal. They could see the gold braid on the officer's tunic flash
in the sunlight for an instant and then disappear around the bend.

"Wounded, maybe," Ransom said without interest.

Then Duncan remembered something and grasped Ransom's

arm excitedly. "John, listen. Wounded hell. Don't you remember hearing that Santa Anna's got a wooden leg?"

They looked at each other in mutual astonishment.

"Well, I'll be blowed!" Ransom snorted. "Let's get the hell out of here while the trail's still hot!"

Hastily they found Captain Jones of G Company and told him what they thought and what they had seen.

Jones looked at them coldly. He was a West Pointer and had been sent to G Company, very much to his disgust, when it had run completely out of officers.

"You have no orders to go down there, Lieutenant. Besides, we may be needed here any minute."

"Orders?" Duncan said. "We don't need orders to fight. We've been fighting since sunup as it is."

"I'm the senior officer here," Jones reminded him.

"Well, what the hell of it?" Duncan flared, while Ransom grinned behind a hand which covered an imaginary cough. "I'm acting captain of B Company, and we're going down there. You can stay here till the damned war's over if you feel that way about it."

A few minutes later B Company straggled down the long slope toward the bend in the road. Duncan sent a scouting squad to each side of the canyon rim above the carriage to guard against an ambush there or beyond the bend, and the company advanced down the road toward the abandoned carriage. It was still surrounded by perhaps a dozen Mexican infantrymen, but when they saw they were outnumbered at least three to one they fired a couple of ragged volleys, cut loose the horse remaining in harness and hastily withdrew. When the company came up to the turn they found the road clear, except for the one retreating detachment and the horse, for at least five hundred yards.

They looked at the vehicle curiously. It was an ornate barouche, though badly road-worn now, and the driver had apparently gone into the turn too fast. The right front wheel had smashed badly against the rock wall, and the tongue was cracked for almost its full length.

Joe Elliot, a private from Springfield, was the first man to climb aboard. He grinned broadly and handed Duncan a curious-appearing piece of mechanism. "Spoils of war, Lieutenant, though what in hell you can do with it I don't claim to know."

"Blast it to hell!" Duncan fumed. "I told you, John—that's Santa Anna's cork leg. Hell's fire an' the cows got out—if we'd been ten minutes sooner we'd have got the biggest prize in the whole damned war."

The leg passed from hand to hand, and the company passed ribald comments of its own. Private Elliot went on with his explorations. "More spoils of war, Lieutenant. They're still legs, but a different kind, and they don't smell spoiled, either."

Whereupon he handed down the nicely browned carcass of a roast chicken.

"Hmmm," Duncan said, and sniffed. "Might be a little spoiled at that. Well, I'm in command of this outfit, I suppose it's my duty to determine the situation." He yanked off a leg and began to chew hastily, holding the carcass in his left hand. Then someone jerked it from his grasp, and among good-natured howls the company fought over the rest of the bird.

Again Elliot's head appeared above the edge of the carriage door, but this time there was an odd, bewildered expression on his face. "Lieutenant," he said quietly, "you'd better come here a minute."

"Hunh?" Duncan had been sitting on the carriage step, gnawing lustily on the chicken leg. He turned his head to look at Elliot and then got up in a hurry. "What's the matter, Joe?"

"You better come up here," Elliot repeated.

"All right."

Then, when he saw what was on the floor, he drew in his breath and whistled. The heavy canvas sack which Elliot had untied was full of gold coins.

"My sainted uncle!" Duncan said softly. "How much do you reckon there is here, Joe?"

"I dunno. About a peck maybe."

"My God, I can see that. I mean, how much *money?*"

"I dunno, Lieutenant. But it's damned heavy, I know that. What 'll I do with it?"

Duncan dropped into a cushioned seat, the chicken leg still in his hand but forgotten now. He looked at the men. They were still brawling good-humoredly over the chicken, and there was no one else within ten feet of the carriage. Sudden visions clouded his mind. Well. He had to decide something quickly. Elliot was watching him curiously, waiting.

"Tie up the sack, Joe," he said suddenly. "There 'll be someone along pretty soon, and I'll turn it over to whoever's in authority."

Almost as he spoke there were hoofbeats in the road, and a squadron of cavalry came up. A brusque voice said, "Who's in command of this—this *bunch?*"

Duncan climbed down and swallowed chicken—hard.

"I am, sir," he said stiffly.

Major Wells of the Second Cavalry looked sourly at Duncan and at the remains of the chicken in the lieutenant's left hand, the one he didn't use for saluting. Then his face relaxed in a broad grin.

"My compliments, Lieutenant. I see you're having lunch. You volunteers are the pets of the army. Hmmm. Chicken too, by God."

"Yes, sir. If you'd have let us know you were coming we'd have saved some out for you."

"I'm sure of it. Under anybody's particular orders, Lieutenant?"

"No, sir. But if you'll step over here and take a look at something and then give me a receipt for it we'll be on our way after the greasers."

"Corpse?"

"No. I'd know what to do with that."

"Perhaps I'd better be on my way with this," Major Wells said a few minutes later. "Will you accept my compliments and commiserations, Lieutenant?"

"Why either, if I'm not too curious?"

"The sorrow for coming so close to Santa Anna and then missing him. The compliments—oh, well, use your own judgment."

"Still why."

"You're a volunteer company, aren't you? I thought so. I understand you were with Harney's attack at sunup?"

"Yes, sir."

"Again my felicitations. Don't get too far up front, Lieutenant. There are still Mexican troops behind you, and of course no one knows how many have taken to the hills and may attack from above. You could be cut off completely in five minutes. These ravines can be death traps."

"I think they're on the run for sure this time, Major."

"So do I—but don't take any chances."

He issued a curt order, and the squadron was off in a growing cloud of dust.

"Fall the men in, Ransom," Duncan ordered, a load suddenly off his mind. "We'll advance until somebody stops us one way or another."

Until past noon B Company advanced westward. Sometimes they were within pistolshot of the Mexican rear guard, sometimes completely out of sight. But they kept on doggedly through the heat and dust. From time to time they were joined by odd detachments of men and officers, some of them coming up from the rear, others coming down from the hills.

At two o'clock Duncan ordered a halt for dinner. As they were about finished, a dusty group of officers rode up, and grizzled old General Twiggs dismounted and snapped a fresh cigar into his mouth.

"Who's in command here?" he barked.

"Lieutenant Duncan, sir, Company B of the Fourth Illinois," Duncan said promptly, and then stopped and looked around. "Or at least I was. But I see at least two officers who rank me. Captain Hunt of H Company and another captain here that I don't know."

For nearly two hours the ill-assorted company plodded on in the general direction of Mexico City. Twiggs threw away innumerable half-smoked cigars and occasionally cursed his mule with quiet affection. Of course the presence of so much rank a little obscured the good humor of B Company, at least in its outward manifestations, but on the whole they plugged along and didn't pay much attention to the general and his staff.

Then, toward late afternoon, when the sun was beginning to glint redly on the distant peaks and long shadows were starting to fall in the deep valleys, a man from the advance guard came back to report a considerable body of Mexicans in the road immediately ahead.

The scout reported to Duncan, but Twiggs snapped away his cigar butt and barked, "How many?"

"Quite a few, sir," the scout said. "Maybe a couple o' hundred. They've halted, and an officer o' some kind seems to be givin' them holy hell."

"Humph. How far?"

"Maybe six or seven hundred yards around that long bend up ahead. The advance is waiting for us to come up. They can't go any farther unprotected."

The general bit the end from a fresh cigar.

"Move up," he said to Duncan tersely. "Troops fighting a rear-guard action are always at a disadvantage. Move up. We'll take a look."

The company moved up, the men now silent and alert, muskets ready, nerves taut and expectant. Two hundred men ahead. There were perhaps sixty-five in this motley parade of B Company, officers included. In two minutes they were in sight of the Mexicans. Three minutes more and they had advanced to within musketshot of the rallying troops ahead. Duncan halted them.

Ahead they could see an officer, mounted on a splendid gray, riding up and down the ragged Mexican column, apparently threatening, cajoling, trying to whip them into some semblance of defensive formation. The road widened considerably where the Mexicans had taken their stand, and that gave them room to spread out a little. The officer—his boots were polished, and his gold braid gleamed dully in the fading sunlight—spurred the gray viciously and wheeled back to the rear of his own column, that facing the Americans. He was still exhorting his men but no longer using the flat of his sword to do it with.

The two bodies of troops were a scant hundred yards apart now.

Twiggs threw away his frayed and chewed cigar and leaned his weight against his hands resting on the pommel of his saddle.

"Humph!" he said to no one in particular. "A *caballero,* eh? The kind of a fine fellow who might cause a bother. Lieutenant, haven't you got a good squirrel shot who can rid us of that gentleman before he causes trouble?"

Duncan looked around, for an instant not fully aware of just what Twiggs meant. There were a lot of expert shots in B Company, but he hesitated to call on any of them. After all, was there any reason for one man to attack a regiment alone?

"Let me go, Lieutenant," an eager voice piped. "I'll get him if anybody can."

Duncan turned, recognizing the voice. It was Art Cornish, a nineteen-year-old from near Pleasant Hill in Dane County. Duncan hesitated a moment. Then: "All right, Art. But for God's sake be careful, boy."

The youngster briefly inspected his priming, cocked his piece and stepped out ahead of the ranked men. They could hear the soft *plop-plop* of his boots in the road dust, so quiet it was now.

And up ahead the Mexican officer sensed the unspoken challenge. He sat his horse quietly for a moment, then dismounted and took a rifle from the hands of the nearest infantryman.

The challenge was accepted.

Together, step by step, the two advanced farther away from their respective backers.

The troops were equally silent now, watching with equal fascination. Duncan was aware of his own hard breathing, and from a corner of his eye he could see old Twiggs still leaning on his saddle, a frozen figure, his lips set tightly together under his stiff beard.

Then, when the lone figures had come within easy pistolshot of each other, a nervous horse whinnied. And as though it were a prearranged signal the two rifles snapped upward and fired almost with one report.

Cornish stood for a moment as though frozen in the firing position; then his rifle muzzle dropped slowly, as though reluctant to leave the target.

The Mexican likewise stood transfixed for an instant. Then the gun dropped awkwardly from his hands and he fell swiftly, face forward into the dust of the road, and lay there like a stone.

B Company managed a weak cheer after quick intakes of breath, and Private Cornish trotted back to the ranks, a pleased grin on his young face.

"How was that, Lieutenant?" he called brightly.

Men clapped him on the back and thumped him from all sides.

Duncan swallowed hard. "Fine, boy," he managed briefly. "Orders, sir?" He faced General Twiggs.

"Advance," Twiggs said, coming suddenly to life. "That *coup* apparently broke the spirit of the defense—such as it was." The Mexicans, at the fall of the officer, had broken ranks and again were retreating in mad disorder. "Advance, Lieutenant. There's nothing ahead to stop us now that I can see. Oh, by the way, have that greaser's carcass drug out of the roadway. Our light artillery will be moving up shortly. No use making hash out of him unnecessarily."

"He was a gallant officer," Duncan said. "Of course . . . that is, I thought——"

"What?" Twiggs asked bluntly.

"Well," Duncan said lamely, "maybe he deserves better than just that."

"Maybe he does," Twiggs agreed. "But what is that to you or

me, Lieutenant? Our business is the capture of Santa Anna and Mexico City. Do you not agree?"

"Well—yes, sir."

VI

The Reverend George Minier sat in the sun on a bench in front of the new Ashley House on Washington Street. The day was but pleasantly warm for July, and the bench, besides making a handy place to wait for his wife, who was shopping, afforded a splendid view of the entire courthouse square and whoever might be going about his business there. It was one of the Reverend Minier's favorite stopping places whenever he managed to get into Everton.

He was thinking now of the changes which had taken place around the square within his own memory. There was but one vacant lot now in the four blocks surrounding the courthouse, and that was soon to be built on. Only a few years before at least half the four blocks had been vacant lots full of unkempt weeds.

And, watching something trivial on the east side of the square, he didn't see the tall young man until he was almost up to the bench. The stranger sat down—perhaps "collapsed" would be a better word—and wiped sweat from his pale face with a badly soiled handkerchief. He breathed heavily, and Minier, from one corner of his eye, saw that he was holding himself erect on the bench only by considerable effort.

"Good morning, sir," Minier said courteously. "Fine weather, don't you think?"

"Howdy," the young man said, in a voice which indicated he didn't care much whether anyone spoke to him. "Yes, I guess so."

Minier looked at the battered valise on the boardwalk and at the worn clothing of his visitor. The stranger was obviously a very sick man. "It's none of my affair," he said then, "but it appears to me that you're too sick a man to be traveling far. Of course, as I say, it's none of my business. My name is George Minier. If I can give you a hand I'll be glad to do it."

The Reverend Minier was a man of God, and he felt it was his duty to help a wayfaring stranger, especially one as ill as this one. But he also had lived on the frontier for more than a few years and knew that more often than not the good Samaritan had better let well enough alone.

The younger man laughed with a hollow bitter sound. "I'm not traveling far," he said. "I've come just about as far as I can stand. I'm pretty sure I'm going to die before long—at least the doctors say so, and I agree with them—but I started out for Everton and hated to die before I got here. Now that I'm here I'd just as soon cash in as not."

Minier appeared a bit startled. He was a Christian minister and on the whole a good man, but he had been around the Northwest a good deal also and knew considerable about the practical failings of humanity at large. But here was a problem. A man didn't come to an isolated village in Illinois to die, his intentions declared beforehand, without some reason. So Minier's curiosity was very much aroused.

"I won't say that I understand you, sir," he said. "But you interest me considerable. You're not a native of Everton, by any chance? At least I don't remember your face."

"No, I'm not a native of Everton. My home is—or was—in New England. But do you by any chance know Lieutenant Duncan of the Fourth Illinois Volunteer Regiment?"

"Duncan? Certainly I do. The company—and young Duncan —came home in the early part of June. I understand Duncan had a fine record in the war. A couple of weeks after he came home he went to Chicago to work for some big wholesale hardware concern. I understand it was quite a fine connection for so young a man. Are you a friend of his?"

"Well, *he* was a friend of mine. I'm just from Mexico myself, and of all the men I saw between here and there Lieutenant Duncan was the whitest. I came to Everton mainly because I knew he was from here."

"You were in the army?" Minier prompted. He had watched the other's face fall when he had said that Duncan had gone to Chicago, and noted the real enthusiasm with which he spoke of the lieutenant. Again he was sure there was some sort of a tale here, and a curious one.

"Yes, of course. Second Kentucky. And I'm just now getting back to something that looks a little like civilization."

And presently, when he felt a bit more rested and breathed more easily, he told Minier that his name was Leonard Swett and of how Duncan had served at his court-martial.

"Every word I've heard of Duncan has been good," Minier said, "and it's a pleasure to hear you, a stranger, concur so strongly. But tell me, how does it come you only arrived in Everton now? The Fourth was home more than a month ago and they served through most of the campaign."

"Why?" Swett again laughed bitterly. "Only God and the crackbrains of the United States army can answer that. *I* don't have the least idea. I was with Scott on the march to Mexico City and was taken down with fever and sent back to Vera Cruz. That was in early April. I spent three weeks in a so-called hospital in Vera Cruz and sank so far that when the surgeon came past my cot he passed right on. I was so far gone he wouldn't waste time looking at me when other men needed his attention, and he thought he could do them some good. But I survived and actually got a little better. About a week after that I was able to sit up, and we received orders that the brig *Mary Morris* was in the harbor and that about a hundred and twenty-five of us were to go to New Orleans on her.

"When the surgeon came to check us over he asked me if I could walk, and I said, 'Yes, I think I can if it's toward home, but I'll be damned if I could walk a step in any other direction.' I did pretty well as far as the ship, but they had to haul me over the side on the end of a rope."

"Hmmm," Minier said, "when was this?"

"Late in May. Well, we had four days' rations on the *Mary Morris,* and the drinking water in the casks was six months aboard. There were green, slimy things in it. We were five and a half days reaching the bar at New Orleans. There the captain took the longboat and went ashore while we lay at anchor in sight of the city. 'Official business,' the captain told us—those of us who were still alive. Well, it was three days later when he came back from that drunk in New Orleans, and he was still drunk.

"On the trip up from Vera Cruz about one third of the sick soldiers had died. While we were anchored off the bar at New Orleans and the captain was ashore we were still officially at sea. Eight more men died while we were within sight of the city and were buried overboard there at anchor. You see, there was nothing else we could do with them."

"I can scarcely believe such a story," Minier murmured. "They don't treat slaves quite that bad."

"No," Swett agreed, "they don't, for slaves are somebody's valuable property. But who the hell worries about a sick soldier who is no longer a fighting asset to the army?"

"We here at home heard all sorts of tales about the war, of course. But mostly folks around here were in favor of it—so long as it didn't cost them much personally. Abraham Lincoln was the only public man hereabouts who really spoke out against the war. I guess maybe Abe was right in some ways at that. He was almost ostracized, though, for some of the things he said." Minier grinned a little. "Not that that worried Abe Lincoln much," he added.

"I don't know who your Mr Lincoln might be," Swett said slowly, "but whoever he is he was right as rain." For a moment or so he sat looking off across the square. Then he resumed in a quiet, matter-of-fact voice. "Two hours after the captain of the *Mary Morris* came back aboard at New Orleans, and while we were being towed up to the barrack landing a regular-army captain came on board. I couldn't repeat now exactly what he said, but as long as I live I'll not forget that scene. It was pouring rain—it had been for two days—but most of us were on deck. The rain was better than the foul and filthy quarters below deck, and the sight of land cheered us up a little. This army captain looked us over casually, made a quick inspection below decks, then came back and walked straight up to the captain of the ship. His face was white as chalk, and you could see his whole body quivering in anger. Then he stood there on deck in that pouring rain and let loose the most terrific blast of withering vituperation that I've ever heard. I've positively never heard anything else in the least like it. And to me, strange as it may seem, it sounded like religious devotion. I guess that in a way it was devotion—devotion to the common decencies of humanity. And when he had finished he knocked the sea captain face down in the scuppers with one blow from the back of his hand. 'You stinking bastard of a rattlesnake and the Devil,' he snarled, 'I wouldn't dirty my fist on your stinking, putrid face.' Then he walked calmly away and left the mates and everybody else staring in open-mouthed wonder." Swett managed a weak chuckle. "The mates acted as if they expected God to strike the army captain down with a lightning bolt, but somehow He didn't."

"Not a sparrow falls but what He knows," Minier said devoutly, if a little inappropriately. "What happened then?"

"We stayed in New Orleans a couple of days and then came upriver to Jefferson Barracks, where I stayed two weeks. I was feeling considerable better by then. I came on to Peoria a few days ago and had another relapse. Fever. A doctor over there told me I'd better get away from the river, so I came here hoping to find Lieutenant Duncan. I wanted to see him, and that Peoria doctor said I had a better than even chance of dying, and I guess he's right."

"Oh, come now," Minier chided. "A few weeks of rest and some decent food and you'll feel like a new man. You're young, and you've seen some bad times; but most of us here in this part of the country have seen bad times and lived through 'em. God must have some work He wants you to do or He would never have spared you thus far."

[272]

"Hmmm. Maybe," Swett said. "But He's sure making it hard enough on me to start with."

"Well, I'll tell you what I'll do. My wife will be back from her shopping directly, and we'll be starting home. Lieutenant Duncan's folks live just three miles east of us, and when we've had a bite to eat at our place I'll drive you on over there. They're fine people, and when you tell 'em who you are they'll be mighty glad to see you. How does that sound?"

"Better than I can tell you, sir. My luck must be changing. The first man I meet in Everton does me two favors at once. I knew that people around here must be more than average decent if Lieutenant Duncan was a fair sample."

"Tut, tut, young man," Minier said dryly. "You talk like an educated man, but anybody could tell you're no judge of human nature."

"Maybe not," Swett said, "but I'm trying to learn something about it."

The Reverend Minier was probably, at the moment, right. But a dozen years later anyone who knew Swett, even including his enemies, would have unhesitatingly pronounced him, next to Abraham Lincoln, the shrewdest judge of human nature in Illinois or any other state. Furthermore, they would not have had a very difficult time proving it.

Minier always remembered him as he first saw him that morning on the Ashley House bench: a tall, gaunt, emaciated young man who was so weak he staggered under the light load of his valise and who was so completely discouraged he had resigned himself to death within the month.

CHAPTER TWELVE

1849

"NO WORD, JOHN, I SUPPOSE," Fell said to his office visitor.

"No, none," Ransom answered. He spoke in a tone that seemed to indicate he wasn't really interested in the question. "You always ask me that, Jesse. Hell, if I knew anything I'd tell you."

"Well, it's a business matter with me and a sort of personal one with you," Fell said. "Probably that spells the difference."

"Probably. I'll tell you something else, Jesse. If it were not for the boy I'd say, 'To hell with the whole thing.' That's the way I feel about it honestly."

"I think you might, at that," Fell chuckled. "But you don't pick up a half-million every day, John."

"Certainly not. But who'd want to? Not me, Jesse. But to the boy it 'll make all the difference in the world. My God, think what it 'll do for him. Regardless of drouths or wars or political fools, he'll have all the money he can possibly use for an education, for travel, for a library, for anything else he might possibly want. I said, mind you, that he'll have all the *money* he'll need for those things. His character he won't be able to buy; that's my business."

[274]

"So will you have the money," Fell pointed out.

"If I wanted it—or needed it," Ransom corrected him. "But I don't. The matter of my wife doesn't bother me much any more. I've made peace with myself on that score. I'm sorry about the whole thing, and I wish it hadn't happened to me. But I did the best I could, and I don't know what else I could have done."

"You might have stayed here at home," Fell said, "instead of going to Mexico. There were plenty of other men."

"You say I could have. But it wouldn't have made any difference. Besides, you're either the kind of man who will fight for your country or you're not. We maybe didn't like the war; but we elected the men who started it and were therefore liable. My people have always gone," he said simply. "There was a time when I cursed Polk and Santa Anna equally, and today I can curse Polk with the greatest of pleasure. But that doesn't change things. I would have gone anyway. When Blair is old enough to understand things, he'll be glad that I went to Mexico and I'll be glad that he feels that way."

"And I think I know how you feel," Fell said. "It just seems to me that you aren't aware of what you could do with this money. There's over forty thousand in cash lying at your disposal in one account at the Mercantile Exchange Bank in Philadelphia, to say nothing of the other negotiable amounts here and there. Doesn't that interest you?"

"Not much," Ransom said, grinning and enjoying Fell's discomfiture. "It's not my money, it's the boy's. And at the moment Blair is doing very well without knowing that any sum over two bits exists. What would I do with it? To his advantage, I mean. If it never draws another cent of interest he'll have all and more than he has any business with."

Fell sighed. "Well, it seems a terrible shame to let it just lie there and do nothing."

Ransom grinned again. He was enjoying himself. It amused him to see Fell worried about money—anybody's money. For he knew that Fell also didn't care a tinker's hoot for money or property as such.

"You got something you want to sell me, Jesse?" he asked slyly.

"Anything in Dane County that's loose," Fell said promptly. "Or I'll buy your place from you. What 'll you take for it?"

"It's not for sale," Ransom said solemnly. "I know you're a judge of real estate. What do you suppose I bought it from you for in the first place?"

"Because you were a fool and didn't know what to do with what few dollars you had," Fell said tartly. "Is that reason enough?"

"Plenty." Ransom laughed. "I just wanted to hear you admit it in public. But seriously, Jesse, that place isn't for sale. It means considerable to me. It's just the way I feel about it, I guess. Hell, let's talk about something else."

"Well, for instance—politics, horses or money?"

"Politics will do. I don't hear much of what's going on around. How's your friend Lincoln these days? I haven't seen him lately. I heard of what he said in Congress about the late war, and that converted me. I don't like his stand on slavery, though."

"No? As why?"

"He's not a real abolitionist."

"Oh, so that's the way your wind blows." Fell looked down his nose. "Maybe he's just not your *kind* of abolitionist. Maybe he sees farther than that."

"To me you're either for it or against it."

"That's one kind. Mahan's kind—and Owen Lovejoy's kind. Well, time will tell. But Lincoln was in town just the other day. He's pretty busy. You know Bill Flagg, of course."

"You mean the fellow who took over Ferre's reaper business?"

"The same. Flagg's a good fellow in his way. I like him. Done a lot for Everton and is a pretty good man to work for, I hear. Well, Lincoln has a case of his in hand. I advised him to get Lincoln if he could. This fellow McCormick who has the reaper factory in Chicago is suing Flagg for something like

[276]

twenty thousand dollars. Seems like McCormick is always law-ing on somebody about his patents."

"Well, who's right?"

"McCormick, I guess," Fell said. "Technically, at least. But Flagg's lucky he's got Lincoln to handle it for him. They're going to try it in the federal court in Springfield, and Lincoln 'll beat him just as sure as God made little apples."

"How do you figure that?"

Fell shrugged. "Because that's the way it is. Lincoln thinks he has a case, and when he feels that way nobody in Illinois can beat him in open court."

"Justice not entering into it, eh?" Ransom liked to irritate Fell.

"Oh, I don't know about that. Let me tell you something, John. A lot of things are happening these days which, in the broadest sense of the term, can't be legally decided. Take this case, for instance. Now I've met McCormick a few times in Chicago. He's smarter in a minute than Bill Flagg is all day, and he'll be in the reaper business when Flagg's broke or dead and forgotten about. The fact that he's suing Flagg is just a natural protective movement. From his point of view he *has* to sue Flagg, even if he's beaten before he starts—which in this case he probably is. But he'll win as many as he loses."

"I don't quite see what you're driving at."

"It's not very complicated. Flagg hopes to sell a few reapers. McCormick *knows* that the McCormick plant is going to sell a lot of reapers—not just hereabouts, but in Iowa and Indiana and Wisconsin and wherever there's wheat and oats in the North-west. He will, too; he's building that kind of an organization. That's why in the long run he'll come out ahead. You're like every other farmer, John—you'll buy what you need where you can get the best the cheapest. And that's the way McCormick 'll sell reapers, and other machinery, because he's got what is prob-ably the most up-to-date factory in this state. The small man like Flagg just won't be able to compete with him."

"And Flagg and his like will be broke," Ransom said.

"Not necessarily. Maybe he'll be selling McCormick reapers —and taking in more money with less trouble than he could by making them himself. But mark what I tell you about this case. Lincoln will beat McCormick, but it won't do Flagg any good in the long run. The railroads will be here one of these days, and transportation won't be the factor in selling merchandise that it is now."

Ransom yawned. "We've been hearing railroad for years now, Jesse, and nothing's happened yet."

"Oh, I don't know about that. The Illinois Central is built almost as far south as the river, and it's only a question of time until they manage to bridge the river. Somebody will figure out a way to do it, and then they'll come on through here."

"Maybe they'll come through here. There's strong rumors that the road's going to miss Everton."

"There are always rumors, my friend. But I'm not worried. With Green in the Senate at Springfield and Davis now circuit judge, Everton has some pretty strong friends. I've got a little influence here and there myself. If you're holding up some investments because you're afraid the road won't come through here, why, I can assure you otherwise."

Ransom laughed softly. "You always manage to work around to the original point, don't you, Jesse? But my mind's made up. I don't intend to do a thing with the estate until we know who it actually belongs to."

"But the boy has his own equity anyhow——"

"Doesn't make any difference," Ransom interrupted. "I've made up my mind, Jesse. Handling the details is your business."

"I'm getting more out of it than you are," Fell reminded him. "My fee is no small matter."

"That's fine. Then we're both satisfied. I've got to be on my way, Jesse. I'll see you again in a week or so."

Ransom walked around to Arnold's Harness Shop and went in to buy a couple of new backbands.

"How's things with you?" he asked Arnold, who had come out of the back shop to wait on him.

"Pretty fair, pretty fair. No call to complain," the wiry little harness dealer told him. "Say, Ransom, you're a judge of good merchandise. Come on back and let me show you something real in the harness line."

There were three men working at the long benches in the back shop, and the room was full of the good smell of leather and harness dressing. Ransom and Arnold walked over to one of the benches, and the little man picked up some long, freshly cut strips of prime leather. "Look at that," he said proudly. "Bet you never saw anything like that before."

Ransom looked at the leather, gauging its size and quality with an experienced eye. "I'll admit it," he agreed. "But what's it for —somebody's elephant teams?"

"By God! Elephant teams—say now, that's a good one. But you'd almost think so. These here traces will be two and a half inches wide, three thicknesses of leather, with five rows of sewing. Brother, them's traces. But that's what they ordered, and by the Lord Harry, that's what I'm givin' 'em."

"Them?" Ransom said. "Who's them?"

"Why, you know—Dr Eustis and Ike Lindley and Sam Coon and that bunch. Surely you'd heard they was makin' up a party for California?"

"Well, I did hear some talk about it, but I didn't know exactly who it was. I haven't been to town for two weeks. I thought maybe it was mostly talk, anyway."

"No, sirree, not by a damn sight. There's twelve in the party, an' they're goin' to use two Conestoga wagons—Brokaw's got the wagons almost done now. I'm makin' 'em two sets o' this elephant harness." He laughed, a deep, booming laugh for so little a man. "Harness gets hell on the roads around here, but it 'll catch more hell between here an' California where they ain't even got roads. But that's as good harness as money can buy, if I do say it as made it. I'd guarantee it to move hell without bustin' a tug if you had the right team an' could get a hitch on it."

"I don't doubt it. When do they figure to get on their way?"

"Soon's I get this done an' Brokaw finishes the wagons. They're champin' at the bit to be off, an' Eustis is in here every day cussin' because it ain't done. But I just let 'em cuss. Good work can't be hurried—not in *my* shop."

Ransom moved over to a set of new carriage harness which hung on two wooden horses about the height of a real horse. He fingered the collars and admired the bronze trimming on the backbands and crupper straps. "That's a real beauty there, Arnold. Belong to somebody?"

"Yep. Judge Davis. It's all done but the bridles. I wanted him to have silver mountings on it, but you know how he is. 'No, by God,' he said. 'None o' them damn fripperies for me.' I offered to put German silver on it at cost, but he wouldn't have it. Well, that's the way Judge Davis is, plain an' simple but good."

"I guess he's that way about his law, too," Ransom remarked.

"That he is. No damn nonsense in the Eighth Circuit. Everybody gets justice without any fancy legal trimmings. I know some o' the lawyers don't like that so well sometimes, but if I was innocent I'd rather be tried before Davis than any other man in the country. But if I was guilty I'd sure as hell get me a change of venue because he'll send you to jail regardless of what your lawyer says for you."

"Well, what more do you want in a judge?"

"Nothing, if you ask me. Davis can probably stay judge of the Eighth Circuit just as long as he wants to put his name on the ticket. That's the way most people feel about him."

As he rode home Ransom too thought of California. He had thought about it before—almost everybody had since the news of the gold discovery had got around—and the idea of going had interested him for a little, but only for a little. Even if he happened to be the lucky one in ten thousand he still wouldn't have any more money than he could have now for the simple scratch of a pen. There was the adventure of getting it, of course, but he had very easily decided that he didn't want much of that, either. There had been enough of hardship in Mexico, and he knew that adventure is nine-tenths simple hardship.

Duncan had written from Chicago, urging him to come up there and offering to get him a good place in his own firm. But Ransom had turned that down also. Right now he was still glad to be home, and the farm provided all he needed or wanted.

The eldest of his neighbor Monroe's daughters, Patience, had come to keep house for him. She was just past seventeen and did a first-rate job of housekeeping because her mother had taught her well and she looked upon housekeeping as a job to be done well, anyhow.

The only drawback was Blair. He was old enough now to be in school, and while Dane County and Everton had schools, they were poor affairs at best. That bothered Ransom a little. But he had decided that it could wait. A year or so wouldn't make much difference to the boy in the long run.

So he was waiting, not quite sure in his heart of just what he was waiting for.

11

In Dane County there were now only a few farms which were untenanted. There was a great deal of timber, which naturally reduced the whole amount of tillable land, but the timber was still a very real necessity. Even the towns could not manage without timber in a hundred forms. But there were no longer great stretches of timber and prairie which lay unused. Every acre, including the twenty-five thousand acres of semimarsh which still remained the property of the federal government, was accounted for.

The tempo of life was steady but very, very slow. No one hurried, because most phases of existence would not bear hurrying.

Building up a farm to a point where it would pay was a matter of years even in this rich black soil. Men who owned land but did not expect to farm it themselves were accustomed to lease it for a year rent free. In return the lessee broke the new ground, planted the new Osage-orange hedge fences which were rapidly coming into use, worked the timber and otherwise improved the land. He took in very little more cash money than the owner, but he had a start toward the future. This way it was possible for a young man who had nothing but a willingness to work to make a start where otherwise he might not have been able to. And if he stuck it out that way for a year or more, it marked him as a citizen of stamina, gave him stature among his neighbors and improved his credit.

Everton prospered as the county prospered. It was the central market place and exchange for everyone's business. It still could not absorb anywhere near all of the county's produce, because there was no transportation system to move it out of town when once bought. But it did take a good-sized portion of that land produce and gave goods and services in exchange.

In Everton you could buy almost anything in ordinary demand. You could do business with a doctor or lawyer or dentist or music teacher, and, when in session twice a year, the circuit court.

And the town itself had grown slowly but with remarkable steadiness. The square was now solid with business houses, and the streets branching off from the square were also beginning to fill up. On Saturdays and during court weeks the hitchracks about the square would be lined solidly with rigs and saddle horses of every kind. The Pike House, built a few years before, was as good as any hotel to be found between Chicago and St Louis and better than most of them. It could accommodate sixty guests without crowding.

The churches were filled with faithful congregations—faithful at least to the organization of the Church if not its strictest religious tenets—and the Methodists, by a very strenuous effort, had managed to import a fine set of bells from Philadelphia.

Merriam had sold the *Western Whig* to a newcomer named John Overton, and it was rumored that Jesse Fell had a finger somewhere in the deal. At least his name was always prominent in the *Whig,* and about half the time he wrote the leading editorial. (Fell had for years been a good friend of Horace Greeley and just couldn't seem to keep from dabbling in newspapers one way or another.) The *Whig* prospered. It was even acquiring a certain amount of political and editorial influence, not only in Dane County but throughout the state. It remained Whig, conservative, and was edited without brilliance but with hard, consistent commonsense and strict attention to its business of printing all the news it could find.

Beyond the square, to the north and east especially, new houses of consequence were replacing the cottages and remodeled cabins. There was plenty of room on the residential streets, and lawns were considered a necessary part of a proper house.

On Grove Street Green was building a pretentious place that was costing him, so it was said, more than $25,000. It looked like that much money, anyway. There was to be a brick wall around three sides of it and a tall iron fence with fancy iron gates across the Grove Street front. The carriage house (Green didn't call it a barn, much to the amusement of certain citizens) was at the back of the lot, on Harvey Street.

Further east on Grove Street Dr Fitchman was erecting a big place. Not quite as big or fancy as Green's, but still considerable house for Everton.

Of course there were many other new places going up here and there. None of them compared in size or cost with the two aforementioned, but they were built well, and there was a companion feeling about them all: a feeling of solid permanence. They were built to live in and were expected to stay as they were built, and the men who were building them did not expect to move next month or next year or for many years. Nor did they expect to sell them the first time someone came along and offered them a profit on their investments.

III

Hazo Parsons was postmaster of Everton by virtue of a pre-election enthusiasm for General Zachary Taylor and a distant acquaintanceship with Stephen A. Douglas. And from the first time he had cast a vote in the Scuppernong Valley in

New York to the day when he voted for Taylor, Douglas and Abel Green, he had been a life-long Democrat.

Mr Parsons' regular business was coopering, and he did a pretty fair trade with the only cooperage in Everton.

Being postmaster didn't, of course, require a great deal of his time, but it gave him a sense of local importance that he hadn't enjoyed before his appointment. This really did no one any harm, and it did bolster Parsons' ego. He was a sober, reliable sort of citizen without particular distinction in any line of endeavor, and so long as he didn't brag too much about his Democratic supremacy nobody objected when he stuck out his chest a bit more than usual.

Parsons and his family—a wife and two half-grown daughters—had lived in Everton for five years now and were well settled. Business was good enough, he had no local competition, and his wife got on well enough socially.

There was only one thing which irked him badly.

In New York, Hazo had joined the Masons as soon as he was old enough, and the movement was, in some ways, the great passion of his life. Here in Everton there were no Masons, at least so far as Hazo could discover (he had made considerable cautious inquiry), and he worried about this lack more than he would have publicly admitted. For Hazo was convinced, really convinced, that civilization could no more get along without Masonry than it could get along without the Christian Church.

He had spent many, many hours in trying to find a logical way to bring about a change in the situation, but all his thinking had availed him nothing. There *was* a way, but so far Hazo had been afraid to tackle it. It was outside all the known rules and regulations, and he was afraid of jeopardizing his own Masonic standing by attempting it. For a year now he had been trying to get up nerve enough to try it out.

The Tuesday-morning mail and passenger stage from Peoria started out as a night run, and the stage, weather and roads permitting, usually arrived in Everton around five in the morning. It made a brief stop for breakfast and a change of horses, and it was Hazo's job as postmaster to be on hand at the Ashley House to pick up the mail sack. Usually he could carry the mail off that trip in one hand, for it was the bare start of the eastern run, and little mail came to Everton that way. However, he felt it was his duty to be there without fail. He was, after all, the representative of the United States government in Everton.

Starting early the night before, a storm of the kind rare in Illinois had set in. Rain had fallen in torrents and floods, and the wind had been of hurricane force. Sheds were blown away and trees violently uprooted. The streets were bottomless pits of clinging mud and the ditches beside them running streams. Just before dawn, the storm stopped as suddenly as it had begun.

In his bedroom on Hazel Street, Hazo was getting into his clothes by candlelight. His wife turned over in bed and blinked sleepily.

"There ain't no call for you to go down there this morning, Hazo. You know perfectly well that the stage never got through last night."

Hazo pulled on his boots, grunting with the effort involved— they were a little damp from the night before. "Don't make any difference whether it did or not," he said firmly. "It's my bounden duty to be there to receive the mail. Don't make any difference what the weather is."

"But you know full well the stage won't be here before afternoon, if it gets here then. Goin' out like this ain't anything but plain foolishness."

"It ain't you that has to get up," Hazo said; "it's me. And my plain duty is my business an' the gover'ment's."

"Oh, all right," she said resignedly. "What time will you be home for breakfast?"

He told her he'd be there when he was free of duty and went into the kitchen, where he poured himself a half-mug of whisky to help ward off the morning damp.

AMERICAN YEARS

When he came past the Ashley House there wasn't a light showing or a single soul in sight about the square. He hadn't thought there would be, so he wasn't disappointed.

He had tucked his trouser legs inside his boots, but even so there was mud already halfway to his hips. He tried walking on the boardwalk but soon gave that up—the sinking boards acted as a pump, and little jets of liquid mud squirted upward through the joints in the planks. So he took to the plain mud of Washington Street.

It was much lighter now, and he could see better.

He turned off Washington Street into Center and then stopped suddenly, a little aghast at the sight which met his eyes.

The towering elm which had shaded the post-office porch had fallen without regard for government-rented property. Its massive trunk had smashed the porch of Green's store building like an eggshell, and the lower limbs had punctured a dozen of the panes in the front windows.

For a moment Hazo was speechless. Then he rose to the occasion and murmured, "Well, I'll be teetotally damned to hell an' gone."

There was nothing in the regulations (he knew them almost by heart) about such a situation as this. So he did what came first to his mind. He climbed gingerly through the tangle of branches, unlocked the front door and got a drink from the bottle which he kept on hand in the post office for emergencies. This, indeed, was an emergency of rare occurrence.

For a half-hour he thumbed through the regulations and applied himself to the bottle. And in the end he came to the conclusion that he might as well cut the elm up for stovewood (it wasn't good for much else) and let Green worry about the smashed porch. The post office was hardly responsible for acts of God.

Bob Coleby, the new night man at the Ashley House, came over to see the damage. He had been dressing when Hazo passed the tavern.

[286]

"I heard her hit, and I knew it was right around here some-where, but I didn't come out to see," he told Hazo. "Some smash, eh?" he said admiringly.

"Sure was," Hazo agreed. "Have a little nip, Coleby. It's damp out this morning. Still lots o' ague left hereabouts."

And then, unconsciously, Coleby made the sign—or Hazo thought he did—and Hazo gazed open-mouthed. Then he solemnly extended his hand in the proper manner. "What lodge do you belong to?" he asked.

"I belong in Cincinnati," Coleby said, also surprised, "but I ain't been there in two years."

They talked then as brothers, and presently Hazo confided his long-thought-of plans.

"I don't see why you don't just go ahead," Coleby said. "The Grand Lodge might raise hell, but I don't think they will. It ain't our fault we're so damned far away from everywhere. You won't have much trouble proving your good intentions if they crab about it. I say, let's take a chance."

"Mmm. You know anybody who'd be all right?"

"A few. But you're better acquainted around here than I am, Hazo."

"All right. I've had several in my mind for a long time. I'll see who I can get together, and I'll talk to you at supper-time an' tell you who I've got. We can use the back room of the post office here."

"All right," Coleby agreed. "We'll meet here at, say, seven-thirty. Is that all right with you?"

"Fine."

"I've got to get back to the Ashley. People will be hollerin' for attention."

About nine o'clock Robert Newton, a harnessmaker for Arnold, came into Haines's store where Doctor Hobbs was still dozing behind a counter.

"I want to buy a dipper," Newton announced.

Hobbs got up and smoothed down the points of his peach-colored vest. "There's not a dipper in stock," he said. "We've got a new shipment of tinware coming in soon, but there's not one in the place tonight."

"Well, I got to get a dipper some place."

"You need it at home?"

"Well, no, not exactly."

"Say," Hobbs said, "I saw you fellows going down there to the post office. What's going on anyway, if it's any of my business?"

"Can't say, Mister Hobbs. Just a little get-together."

Hobbs wheedled, and they both argued. But in the end Newton began to think that Hobbs too was the kind of man Hazo Parsons had talked about. So presently he leaned over the counter and whispered earnestly in Hobbs's ear.

"Is that so?" Hobbs said. "Well, now, that's a splendid thing, a splendid thing. My father and my grandfather belonged to the order. I'll be glad to come over—more than glad, I might say. I'll tell you what. I haven't got a dipper in the place, but there's a new gourd one out in the back room that I guess will do in an emergency."

"Well, they're waiting on me. Can you come over now?"

"I was just going to close up. I'll get the gourd and be right with you."

Those in the back room of the post office were glad to see Newton return with a recruit, especially one as well known as Doctor Hobbs. He lent a social flair to the occasion, as it were.

For a week they studied diligently, and then Hazo Parsons wrote a very long letter to the Grand Lodge, explaining his good intentions and extolling the virtues of the prospective members. They waited a month; and when the answer finally came it included a charter for Everton Lodge Number 43, Free and Accepted Masons.

The members promptly held a meeting and elected Doctor Hobbs as worthy master.

From that day on, and as the Masonic organization grew in

influential membership, which it rapidly did, Doctor Hobbs's social status increased.

IV

Dr Harmon sat quietly in the easy chair before the fire, simply relaxing and trying not to occupy his mind with anything in particular. He was tired; the dinner had been satisfying, and the bourbon he had drunk afterward had just the right charred-oak flavor that he preferred. Without exactly thinking about it he was aware that the corners of the living room were cold and that in the morning—Christmas morning—the house would be colder yet. Nothing to do about that, however, except sit as close to the fireplace as possible and see that the woodpile and the woodbox were properly stocked.

Upstairs, beyond the immediate distinction of speech, he could hear the familiar after-dinner sounds: the baby undressed and crowing in his bed and Richard, the four-year-old (almost five now), being undressed and finally washed for bed. They were pleasant, routine sounds, part of the very air of the Harmon establishment. Some nights they bothered him, irritated him beyond measure; at other times, like tonight, they seemed the commonplace, and good of themselves—the total answer to himself.

Presently he dozed and then was suddenly awakened when a small hand shook his knee and a small voice said, "Dad, it's time for my story. You promised."

"So I did," he agreed, shaking himself awake and automatically gathering the small nightgowned figure into his arms. The freshly combed blond head leaned itself against the broadcloth of his coat, and for a second he hugged the boy close to him.

"Were you a good boy today?"

"Oh yes. But you promised me a story, Dad. Will you tell me now?"

Harmon turned his head toward the place where Letitia

hovered in the shadows beyond the immediate glow of the fire. She nodded and smiled and motioned "Yes."

He settled himself into a more comfortable position and said, "Very well. Then I'll tell you a very special story."

"The one about the bears?" Richard asked.

"No, not that one, son. Another one. One that I don't think you've heard before. You know what night this is, don't you?"

"Oh yes. This is Christmas Eve. I know all about Santa Claus, Dad. In the morning I'll get up real early, and there'll be a horse this big"—he measured with his hands—"and different stuff in my stocking. Mama said, before I go to bed I can hang my stocking on the mantel and Santa Claus will take care of it. But mostly I want that horse we talked about."

Harmon smiled. "Well. I see you do know. Now, are you ready for the story?"

"Yes. What's it about, Dad?"

"Well, I'm coming to that part. This is a very special story about Christmas, son. Sort of about how there came to be a Christmas."

"About Santa Claus, Dad?" Richard asked, wide-eyed.

"Not exactly, but something like that," Harmon said gently. "But you listen now and don't interrupt, and I'll tell you about it.

"Many, many years ago, in a far-off country, a man named Joseph and his wife Mary came into a town called Bethlehem. They had come from a long way off, Joseph walking while Mary rode on a donkey. You know what a donkey is?"

"Yes," Richard said solemnly, "I know."

"They were very tired, because they had come from so far away, and they went to the inn to stay all night——"

"What's an inn?"

"Well, a tavern, something like the Ashley House, where people who have no home here go to stay all night. You see?"

The blond head nodded.

"Well, the man at the tavern told Joseph that there was no

1849

room for them. Of course Joseph was very disappointed. And then he told the man that for himself he didn't care, but that Mary, his wife, was very tired, and she was going to have a little baby soon and must have some place to stay."

"A baby like our Johnny, Dad? A real live baby?"

"Yes. And when Joseph had told the man that, the man was friendlier about it. He said he was sorry they had no place for them in the inn, but that they could stay in the stable. He said he would send a man to get down some fresh, clean hay for them, and they would be welcome to stay there, at least for a while."

"Was it cold there in the stable?"

"Yes, it was. But, you see, it was the best they could do. So toward morning the baby—the Christ Child—was born there in the manger of the stable, and Joseph and Mary were very happy.

"Then after a while three wise men came from the East, which is also a faraway place, farther even than Bethlehem, and they brought the Christ Child gifts.

"Many people asked them how they knew the baby was there in the stable, and the wise men said they knew because of the star. It was a new star which appeared in the sky directly above the stable when the Christ Child was born. They left their homes in the East and followed the star until they came to the stable in Bethlehem."

"What kind of presents did they give Him, Dad?"

"Oh, different things. Not like we have nowadays. But they were very fine presents, the finest things the wise men could find to bring."

"Un-hunh. But did Santa Claus send them?"

"Well, er—yes, something like that."

"Are there any wise men now, Dad?"

For a moment Harmon hesitated. "Why, yes," he said then, "of course there are, though you don't see many of them nowadays. They are very hard to find. And then you must remember that this story took place in Bethlehem and, as I told you, that's a very long way off from here——"

"Well, Dad, couldn't they come here to Everton if they wanted to?"

"Perhaps, if they wanted to—or we wanted them to come badly enough."

"Well, you see, Dad, I want Santa Claus to come. I'm going to get up real early to see about that horse we talked about——"

There was a sudden knocking at the front door, and Harmon looked almost guiltily at Letitia. "I can't help it," he said half defensively. "I told Ross to come around if he needed me. She's pretty bad."

The knocking resumed.

Harmon sighed. "Open the door and let him in out of the cold," he said.

Ross stamped snow from his boots and threw back the collar of his coat as he came into the hallway. Melting snowflakes glistened in his beard and mustache.

"I'm sorry to bother you like this, Doc," he began, "but she's a lot worse than she was this afternoon. I know——"

"Never mind," Harmon said brusquely. "I'll be with you in just a minute." Then, to the boy still on his lap, "Will you remember that story, son?"

"Oh yes. Where you going, Dad?"

"I have to go look after a very sick lady. I'll see you in the morning."

"First thing in the morning?"

"Yes, sir, first thing."

"You think Santa Claus will remember about that horse all right?"

"Oh sure. No chance of him forgetting *that*."

"Did you talk to him about it?"

"No, but I talked to Mr Lubeck about it, and he said that Santa Claus wouldn't forget. And he usually doesn't."

"All right. Gimme a kiss, Dad."

Harmon set the small nightgowned figure on the floor and

then kissed him gently on the lips. "Run along upstairs," he said. "Past your bedtime now."

"Good night, Dad."

The boy kissed his mother and trotted obediently toward the stairs.

Harmon shrugged into his horsehide coat and looked around for his bag. "Snowing bad?" he asked Ross.

"Snowing like hell—beggin' your pardon, Mrs Harmon. I've got the cutter. I'll bring you back when you're ready to come."

Ross buttoned his coat and stepped out into the hall to wait.

Letitia looked at the big man in the hairy coat. "Will you be back to help me trim the tree?"

"Oh sure." He hesitated. "Well, maybe you'd better go ahead with it soon as he's asleep. You can't tell——" He bent his mouth to her upturned face.

"I wish you didn't have to go," she whispered softly, and added, "It was a beautiful story, John."

"It always was," he said, "and I'm afraid I don't improve it much. I'll get back as soon as I can. It's only about five miles. I'll be back by one o'clock unless something goes wrong."

"Don't forget we're to go to Robinson's for dinner tomorrow."

"I won't. Good-by."

In the hall he said, "All right, Zeke, I'm ready. How does she seem to be?"

But before Ross could answer, a small voice said, from the gloom at the head of the stairs, "Don't forget, Dad."

Harmon turned and looked up at the face peering between the banisters. "Get into bed, you imp," he said almost roughly, conscious of the sudden little tightness in his throat. "You'll catch pneumonia up there. But don't worry, I won't forget."

Then he turned abruptly, and Ross followed him out into the darkness and the driving snow.

CHAPTER THIRTEEN

1852

S UDDENLY IN EVERTON the tide of affairs began to run so swiftly that even the most astute could hardly remember when or where the upsurge started. To some of the older residents the changes were bewildering; to others they were simply opportunities to be thankfully grasped and made the most of.

On the streets new faces were constantly appearing; in stores and offices around the square there were new customers doing more business; new houses, most of them small, sprang up seemingly overnight. Everywhere—in the stores, the saloons, the streets and in homes—there was talk of the rising values of real estate. Bill McCullough, county clerk, could hardly keep up with the terrific increase in sales of town lots. Everyone in Everton, so it seemed, and a good many people outside the town were buying or selling property; buying to sell immediately again or selling in order to buy again.

One of the answers lay in the rows of temporary warehouses which stood on the land a mile straight east of the courthouse, the land which had once been William Goodheart's farm. The long rows of buildings—sheds really—belonged to Dixon & Clark, contractors to the Illinois Central Railroad Company. They were building a fifty-mile stretch of the road, with their headquarters at Everton, temporarily the southern terminus of the railway.

Now, in April, the construction camps of Dixon & Clark stretched northward for perhaps thirty miles; but the seat of affairs was in Everton. The town was no longer a village with a village board and a president, but a city with a mayor and four aldermen, a combination city-clerk-and-attorney, and a chief of police. This change had taken place in 1850, and Everton was enjoying her third mayor.

There was a board of education, functioning separately from the city council, with an elementary school operating more or less smoothly in each of the town's four wards.

In talk of public affairs there were rumors of waterworks and paved streets and new sidewalks and a paid fire department and a high school.

And on the 23rd of May, the first smoke-coughing locomotive to arrive in Everton drew up in front of the newly painted depot, towing a passenger carload of the Illinois Central's plug-hatted officials.

It was a momentous day.

Everyone in Everton that could walk, and some that had to be carried, managed to be on hand. And for a radius of forty miles as many of the folk had come as could possibly make it. For perhaps an eighth of a mile about the little depot there was a black-and-white sea of visitors, waiting impatiently for the arrival of the first train. Many of them had never seen a locomotive or anything else connected with a railroad. Then there were speeches by the plug-hatted officials and dignitaries—long, windy speeches in which the dignitaries congratulated Everton upon being so favored. There were free cigars and drinks and personal congratulations and a great deal of handshaking on all sides.

It was a great day for everybody, including Jesse Fell.

But it was Fell who ran afoul of one of the few iconoclasts in the crowd, and the meeting left a sort of dark brown taste in

Fell's mouth for the balance of the evening. He had left the group of officials at the depot and was threading his way through the crowd toward Grove Street when he came across a stooped figure sitting on a couple of loose ties. The figure stopped his whittling and spat tobacco juice in the shavings at his feet.

"In a hurry, Jesse?" he asked dryly.

Fell stopped and turned abruptly. "Why, hello, Mr Leary," he said, and held out his hand. "How are you these days? I haven't seen you for quite a long spell."

"No, I reckon not. I don't git to town much any more. There ain't much here I want that I can't send after, so I don't come."

Fell smiled. "Well, I see that you got in for the big day today. You're not an old man yet."

"The hell I ain't!" Leary snorted. "I'm older 'n you'll ever be, Jesse. But that ain't the point. I know you're a busy feller, but I aimed to ask you a question or two."

"Fire away, Mr Leary. What can I tell you?"

"I heard you had something to do with this railroad here. Is that a fact?"

"Well," Jesse said, not quite sure of what was coming, "I did act as temporary agent for the road here in Everton. Why?"

"Oh, I was just wonderin'. Do you own any of it, Jesse?"

"A few shares of the stock; that's all. I haven't anything to do with it now beyond that, and that's not very much."

"Un-hunh. Well, I listened to some o' them windy speeches, an' I jest begun to wonder who in hell owned this country. They all sounded alike, so I come over here an' set down so I couldn't hear the rest of 'em. Didn't the gov'ment give the railroad that land the whole damn length o' the state?"

"Well, yes," Fell said, "the land was given to the road—in return, of course, for building the railroad."

"Oh sure," Leary agreed. "But who gets the money the railroad takes in—the gov'ment?"

"Why, no. The railroad, naturally."

"I see," Leary said. He chewed for a moment and then again

spat lustily. "I understand the railroad got every other square mile o' land the full length o' the state, Jesse. Is that right?"

"Yes, that's right."

"I see. Well, that's a powerful lot o' land, Jesse, a powerful lot o' land." Leary studied the setting sun for a moment. "Jesse," he asked, "did the state ever give you any land for what you done or said you was goin' to do?"

"No-o-o," Fell answered. "But then I never built any railroads, either, Mr Leary."

Leary threw away his whittling stick and got up from the ties, a bent, gnarled figure. "Neither did I, Jesse. But I starved an' worked my guts out when this state was a hell-fired wilderness. They never give me nothin' but hell for lookin' like I might want somethin'. But now they give the railroad three hundred an' sixty odd square miles o' the country. Do you think that's a good thing?"

"Well," Jesse said, "you look at it wrong, Leary. It's for the good of the state as a whole. We'll all benefit from the road——"

"These bastards with the high hats that are runnin' this riggin'—they aim to make money from it, don't they?"

"Why, yes. Sure they do."

"I see. Well, I aimed to make money from my pre-emption claim too, Jesse. Not much; just a little to git along on. I heard you cut quite a figger in this railroad business, Jesse."

"I did what I could for it, Mr Leary."

"You an' Green," Leary said. "Well, I always knew Green was a thief, but I didn't think you was, Jesse. Now you're hooked up with the railroad, an' I say you're a thief as well as the rest of 'em. You an' me been friends for twenty years, Jesse, but we ain't no more. You're all tarred with the same brush."

Leary's bitter eyes stopped Fell's words, his logic halted by the old man's quiet anger.

The old man turned abruptly and walked away, his body as stiff and erect as he could hold it.

Speechless, Fell watched him go. Leary's exposition wouldn't have won him honors anywhere. Yet Fell knew what the old man meant. He knew perhaps better than Leary himself. But there was nothing, apparently, that he could do about it. A man rode with the tide. He might try to guide it, to shape it in his own way; but he could not make it turn back.

II

Exactly where Hugo von Elsner came from no one in Everton ever knew, not even William Dimmit's daughter, who married him.

He appeared in town sometime in the early spring of 1852, as a member of Dixon & Clark's surveying crew. At first he spent the greater portion of his time either up or down the railroad and was only seen in town on Saturday or Sunday. But he took a room at Mrs Chisholm's, on Front Street, probably to have a place to keep his few personal belongings, and thereafter assumed a residential identity of a sort.

He was a neat, unassuming German who at the time could speak only the simplest English and that not well. He must have been an efficient surveyor, however, for when his job ran out with Dixon & Clark he went almost immediately to work for the crew which was, very quietly, projecting lines for the Chicago & Mississippi Railway, a line which was intended to run, eventually, from Chicago to St Louis via Everton and Springfield.

When he was in town on Sundays, Von Elsner went regularly to the Methodist church, East Charge, which wasn't far from the Chisholm house. Exactly *why* he went there is a moot question. Certainly it wasn't out of any real liking for Methodism; nor was it, as Mrs Chisholm's daughters like to believe, because *they* went there. Neither could it have been because of the Reverend Levi Spencer's endlessly dry and uninspired sermons.

It never occurred to anyone that he might have gone simply because the Methodist church had, at the time, the only choir in Everton, and Von Elsner liked to hear the singing.

Inevitably, in spite of his terribly clumsy English, he became acquainted with a number of Evertonians, chief among them Professor Ellery Wilkins of the newly established Everton Female College. Wilkins lived in a rather good house on East Elm Street, and Von Elsner got into the habit of dropping in of an evening more or less regularly when he was in town. And he was always made welcome. The professor liked the clean-cut, apparently simple German boy.

Sometimes Von Elsner would sit quietly for an hour or more, only taking part in the conversation when Wilkins, who was something of a linguist, would address him in German. But after a while someone would suggest a song, and then Hugo would be in his element. He would unwrap his guitar and play flawless accompaniment to anything anybody could name.

The Wilkins family's musical repertoire, in spite of the fact that Ellery gloried in the title of Professor of Music and Elocution, wouldn't have made any great demands on a really proficient musician. For the social group it consisted mostly of songs like "Kathleen Mavourneen," "Ellen Bayne," "Ossian Serenade," "Old Folks at Home," "Allan Percy," and "The Meeting of the Waters."

Only once did Professor Wilkins embarrass himself, and then he didn't advertise the fact to anyone, not even in his immediate family. He asked Von Elsner if he didn't play some instrument besides the guitar, and the German boy admitted that he had once played the violin—a little.

"Well, then," Ellery said kindly, "by all means bring your violin over, and we'll have a change in the program. You have some music, no doubt?"

Von Elsner admitted that such was the case.

"Fine," Wilkins said heartily. "Then bring your own music, and I'll play the piano for you."

Hugo protested that he would rather not, but Wilkins was insistent, and the other finally gave in. He promised that the next time he came he would bring his violin and some music.

Ellery rather fancied himself as a pianist—and probably he

was as good or better than any pianist in Everton. But he had reckoned without Von Elsner's capacity for music.

A week later Hugo appeared at the Wilkins house with his violin case and a sheaf of music.

Wilkins was delighted—for a little while.

"Well, well," he said, "what have we here?"

He set the music up on the old square piano and looked at it with interest—then with sudden misgivings. What the devil did the boy have here, anyway?

The title, in florid German script, indicated that *it* was the *Second Brandenburg Concerto,* piano and first violin part, by one J. S. Bach.

They started together, the violin singing open-throated and joyous, the piano struggling like a close-hobbled mule. After some ninety bars Professor Wilkins gave up. He knew when he was whipped. He stopped abruptly in the middle of a particularly bad measure and closed the score. "That's all," he said. "I know when I'm licked, Hugo. Maybe I shouldn't have started this in the first place."

Hugo was contrite. He had no wish to embarrass his good friend; but the professor had insisted he bring his violin and music.

"Quite so," Wilkins agreed. "But maybe we'd better stick to Stephen Foster—at least when we're together. We get along better."

At the Wilkins house there was frequently a girl named Amanda Dimmit. She wasn't as good-looking as either the Wilkins girls or the Chisholm daughters, and outwardly she had little personality to recommend her. She sang occasionally in a clear sweet soprano, but she couldn't read a note. She was a friend, in an offhanded way, of the Wilkins girls, but most of the time no one paid much attention to her. Nobody, that is, but Hugo.

It was early fall before anybody noticed that whenever Amanda was ready to go home Hugo was also ready to go, and that more often than not they went together.

1852

Old Bill Dimmit had a few misgivings when Von Elsner very formally presented himself and asked the privilege of marrying Amanda. But not many. Bill inquired around, talked to Wilkins and a few others, including Von Elsner's employers, and decided that if he was what Amanda wanted she could help herself.

Nobody else, up to now, had asked Amanda to marry him, and she was twenty years old. Dimmit supposed that Hugo would in time learn to talk United States, though at the moment he didn't seem to be making much headway.

Hugo and Amanda were married in the Methodist church during October, and thereafter moved into a little cottage that Dimmit owned on Front Street, a block or so east of the Chisholm house where Hugo had roomed and a few blocks east of Green's big house on Grove Street.

III

The full moon swung gorgeously over Grove Street and the Green house.

When Green had built the house he had insisted that the trees be left untouched—the trees which had originally been a part of Maple Grove—and they had been. As a result the lawn was beautifully shaded, though the house was only a few years old.

The chair in which Davis sat creaked under the big man's weight and reminded Green that he had guests.

"You'll have some more of the punch, Judge?" he asked affably.

"Why not?" Judge Davis said. "Ward off these autumn chills. It's not cold, but there's no use taking chances. How about you, Jesse?"

"No, thanks," Fell answered agreeably.

Behind them the thin, ascetic-faced Green called to one of the girls and motioned toward Davis' glass.

Fiddle music drifted through the open french windows as

Anton Lubeck and his quartet indulged themselves in a Strauss waltz.

"I don't know that I've mentioned it to you two," Green was saying, "but I've been thinking very seriously about setting up a bank here in town."

Davis caught Fell looking at him cornerwise.

"By yourself?" Davis asked, sipping his punch.

"Well, not exactly. Young Scammon from Chicago—you know him, Jesse—is interested in financial connections here in the central part of the state. He wants me to go in with him, and I think I will. The time looks ripe to me."

"Maybe," Fell agreed. "Certainly the town could use a bank —as a financial exchange if nothing else."

"Scammon is as smart as they come," Green said, "and he's really anxious to go into the thing. And I'm convinced the town could stand it now."

"Probably," Davis rumbled. "But be careful, Abel."

"How do you mean?" Green asked rather pointedly.

"Oh, I don't know exactly, Abel. But you remember the loose money we had in '37 and thereabouts. People still don't trust banks a hell of a lot—and so far with good reasons."

"I know what Dave means," Fell said placatingly. He was quick to sense the silent feeling of animosity between Davis and Green. "There's money here in Everton that needs controlling, simply as a matter of general expediency, but a man must be careful not to stir up the public's distrust."

"Well, what has that to do with me?" Green asked coldly. "My name has been public in Everton about as long as any other you could mention."

There was a moment of silence while Davis inspected the ash of his cigar.

"That's just the point, Abel," the judge said then, "and I was thinking of something else. I understand you're interested in a railroad from Peoria to Indianapolis, a road to cross the Central and the proposed Chicago & Mississippi."

"And what if I am?" Green asked. "So are a great many other people in Everton."

"Un-hunh," Davis said. "There's nothing wrong with being interested in it, Abel. But I've heard there was talk of selling stock to the towns through which the road might pass. That's what interests me. If a town, as such, subscribes for stock, that means that it must use the taxing power to support its subscription."

"Well," Green said, "and what's wrong with that? The people have every right to vote on such a question. And there are plenty of precedents for it."

"Maybe," Davis answered slowly, "but that doesn't prove it right, Abel. We'll pass the talk about what people might *vote* —under the guidance of the right people—to do. Railroads are a fine thing—but they're also a business proposition, Abel. And that has nothing whatever to do with the right to tax. If they're a good business proposition, then private capital will find its way to them in proper time."

"I don't quite follow you, Dave," Green said.

"I'll try to make myself clearer," Davis said into the moonlight. "Railroads are a business proposition and therefore to a certain extent a gamble. What a man does with his own money is largely his own business, Abel, but you can't gamble with tax money. For your benefit I'll go farther than that. So long as I'm judge of this circuit I'll rule in favor of any citizen who brings suit against his town or county owning stock in any railroad project."

"I see," Green said, "I see. Well, thanks for the advice anyway, Dave."

"You're welcome," Davis told him affably. "Mighty fine punch, Abel, mighty fine."

"Anything exciting in court these days, Dave?" Fell asked, filling a somewhat embarrassed silence.

"Nothing much," Davis said. "But the other day I was wondering—do you know a young feller named Swett?"

"Swett?" Fell pondered aloud. "Seems I do, in a way. He's

the cripple old George Minier run across. Leonard Swett—that's the name. Is he still about?"

Davis chuckled. "Still about! Great God, with bells on! He passed his bar examination last year. Seems he's been teaching school somewhere. But let me tell you something: unless I miss my guess he's the best pleader the circuit has produced in years. He's only a youngster, but I've never seen anything quite like him. I spoke to Lincoln about him, and he agrees with me. The boy has as natural a gift for law as any I've ever seen."

"You're not telling us he has anything on Lincoln," Fell said disbelievingly.

"No-o-o, I didn't say that. But this is his first year in court, too—you must remember that. Of course he doesn't draw the water that Lincoln does, or Steve Logan, or even John Stuart. But I'm saying to mark him. I've never seen another yearling with the grasp of law that this lad has. I don't know where he got it, but it's there."

"Oh well, you lawyers make the law," Fell said. "An ordinary man hasn't got a chance with you."

Davis chuckled again. "You exaggerate, Jesse. But the law is a growing thing—at least it is here in Illinois, thank God. And these young fellows bring something to it that it needs."

The hurried notes of a polka came through the open windows. It was growing late; Lubeck and his colleagues were working hard to round off the evening successfully.

"If you'll excuse me, gentlemen," Green said, "I'll be getting inside."

"Oh, by all means," Davis agreed. He heaved his heavy body from the chair. "Jesse and me 'll have to be going, too. It must be late. I've got court tomorrow."

"Lincoln said he'd try to get over tonight," Green said, "but he didn't. I'll be damned—he can find more excuses for piddling around the square than any other man in or out of town. But as soon as Steve Douglas heaves in sight, Abe's right there, no matter where it might be. Damned funny, I say.

Sometimes I wonder what in hell's wrong with Lincoln, any-way."

Fell looked into the deep shadows cast upon the lawn by the old elms. "Never mind Lincoln, Abel," he said. "He'll do all right."

IV

The train—two cars behind a funnel-stacked little engine— jerked and rolled northward from Everton. The funnel-shaped stack laid down a regular screen of thick, pungent smoke and at intervals belched a thick spray of cinders, cinders that rattled against the closed windows, found their way inside somehow and mingled finally with the missed shots of tobacco juice on the floors of the coaches. There were cuspidors, but they weren't permanently anchored and rolled restlessly with the uneven roadbed. When a man spat where he had spat before, the spit-toon more than likely wasn't there any more. All of which didn't help the condition of the bouncing floors in the cars.

By the time the train reached La Salle, where passengers for Chicago had to transfer, the two small coaches were nearly filled. Filled with farmers and cattle dealers and Irish laborers and species of a new profession called "drummers."

On the platform at La Salle, John Ransom carried his valise in one hand and led Blair with the other.

"Come on, son," he said. "The train for Chicago won't leave for almost an hour. I'll get a drink and you can have some-thing. Want to go to the privy?"

"Yes, sir."

They went into the outhouse back of the depot saloon and then returned to the dingy bar.

"Rye," Ransom said, "and give the boy a glass of good cold milk."

"Travelin' far?" the bartender asked affably when he had served them.

"Only as far as Chicago. This is the boy's first time on a train. My second, for that matter."

"Bet he's havin' a rare time. Live in Chicago?"

"No," Ransom said. "Downstate. Dane County. Just going into Chicago on some business."

"Un-hunh. Well, Chicago is gettin' to be some humdinger of a town. Any trouble on the run comin' up today?"

"Not much," Ransom said, grinning. "Stopped once around the Mackinaw bridge to drive somebody's cows off the track."

"I guess downstate is boomin' along the railroad. Hear a lot of talk about it in here, people comin' an' goin' all the time. Hear there's another railroad goin' through Everton already. You fellers are lucky."

On the train again, an hour later, Ransom recalled the bartender's talk about another railroad. So the news was out as far as this? But La Salle was a junction town; it would keep abreast of such matters.

And he remembered Fell's parting admonitions. "Don't let them talk you out of anything, John," he had said. "I know Overman, and he's easy enough to deal with if you go along with him a little. Of course you'll have to take part of the price in stock, but what of it? Put your price up high enough so that if the stock's no good you can throw it away and forget it."

"I hope you're right about this thing," Ransom had said doubtfully.

"Of *course* I'm right," Fell snorted. "Why else would I be telling you? I tell you your place is right smack dab in the middle of the only logical place the C. & M. can put its shops and yard. I've seen it already laid out on the survey map in Overman's office. They came to me, and I told them the ground could be bought at a reasonable price." He had grinned quietly. "What's a reasonable price is your business, John; it's your property."

Ransom had asked what a fair price might be, and Fell told him. Ransom had almost gasped. "You're crazy, Jesse. You know what I paid for that land when I bought it from you—three hundred and sixty dollars."

1852

"Get over those ideas," Fell advised. "This is another day, John—the one some of us have been waiting on for twenty years."

Perhaps it was.

Toward evening they rolled into Chicago over the vast marshy prairies on the southern edge of the city, past rows of shacks and shanties interspersed with acres of weedy vacancy and dull, muddy streets.

By himself, Ransom would probably have walked from the station, but he knew Blair was tired and so told the hackman to take them to the Tremont House.

Both of them looked at Chicago with wondering eyes, Blair because he had never imagined any streets in the world so jammed and tangled with so many horses and vehicles of every possible description, Ransom because of the terrific changes in the town since he had last seen it.

After supper they took a walk eastward on Lake Street—Lake Street, even in the night lined with wagonloads of wheat and hogs and corn and lumber, drivers sleeping on their loads, gambling and passing jugs about the fires in the center of the streets, whores and pimps and prospective customers cursing and dickering obscenely in the torchlight. Blair looked, wide-eyed and silent, not comprehending this yeasty boiling of humanity at the crossroads of the Middle West. Ransom watched too, his teeth clamped tightly upon his cigar, holding Blair's hand and moving him along; but his curiosity was colder, more informed, and he saw a thousand things that Blair did not.

They walked over to State Street and then back on Washington and up Wells to the Tremont.

Presently, when Blair was in bed and asleep, Ransom sat at the window for a while, watching the street and thinking of a number of things, Emma among them.

He had decided to wait until the first of the year and then have Fell petition the court to have her declared legally dead. He had thought about it a great deal and come to the conclusion that he could do nothing else. Things should be straightened out, not left dangling in midair like this.

And his thoughts came around to Chicago. Fell and Davis both, he knew, owned property here in the city. It was a hog-pen, of course, at least all of it he'd seen was, but what mattered that? There had always been money in hogs. The hell with the East—he could never go back there except to arrange Blair's affairs. The East was dead, or dying. "And this," he thought, "is Blair's country. He'll have to learn that—and learn likewise how to handle it."

They would come to that later.

He threw his cigar stub in the cuspidor and went to bed.

Cyrus J. Overman was a thin man with steel-gray eyes that matched his side whiskers.

"Suppose we have a drink on the deal," he said precisely. He went to a corner cupboard and came back with a bottle and two glasses. Then he held the bottle against the light for a moment and squinted fondly. "One of America's greatest discoveries," he said. "Pure spring water from the hills of Kentucky, combined with good corn, nature taking its natural course. To our better acquaintance, Mr Ransom."

They drank—the whisky was smooth as cream—and Overman sat down again. He rubbed his hands together. "Well, suppose I have the papers drawn and you drop back at your convenience this afternoon. I'll have the check and the stock certificates ready for you."

"Around three o'clock?" Ransom suggested.

"Fine, fine, my boy. Let me see, we'll just check over my memorandum here again—twenty-five thousand for the land altogether, you taking fifteen thousand in cash and the balance in C. & M. common. Yes, that's right. I'll have the check drawn on the Farmers & Mechanics—you'll find it a good house if you have any business dealings in Chicago."

"I rather think," Ransom said, "that I *will* have some business here in the future."

[308]

1852

"And a wonderful future here, too," Overman said. "Well, I must excuse myself, Mr Ransom. Busy, you know. Don't forget my regards to Mr Fell. I understand he's getting to be quite a personage downstate."

"Yes," Ransom said, "I guess he is." He suddenly realized that the idea had never occurred to him before, and he was inwardly surprised.

At six o'clock he was shaking hands delightedly with ex-Lieutenant Duncan in the Tremont House bar.

"Lordy, it's good to see you, John! I was tickled pink when I got your letter. In fact I was about to write and ask you if you couldn't come up."

They sat at a table, and a Negro boy brought them rum slings.

Ransom told Duncan briefly of what had transpired that afternoon. He took the check from his wallet and spread it out on the varnished top of the table. "My God," he said softly, "look at that, Dunc. Just try to imagine it. I paid Jesse Fell my last three-hundred-odd dollars for that damn ground ten years ago. Now look at that."

"I heard rumors that fifteen thousand was just a drop in the bucket for you these days, John."

Ransom shrugged. "It would be, Dunc. But that's the kid's money; this is mine." He motioned for more drinks, and the Negro boy hopped to it.

They drank and talked and drank, interrupting each other constantly with "Say, do you remember the fellow in C Company . . ." "Yes, but how about the time Colonel Baker said . . ."

"Baker," Ransom said. "He went to California. I heard him and Frémont figure to own the state between 'em. Quite a town you've got here, Dunc."

"Damn it, don't call it mine," Duncan snapped bitterly. "I'm through with it in less than two weeks. That's what I meant when I said I'd wanted to see you."

"How do you mean? I thought you were doing pretty well for yourself here."

"It depends on what you call pretty well, John. I've been promoted twice and my salary raised four or five times since I've been here, if that means anything."

"Doesn't it?"

Duncan shook his head and finished his latest drink. "No," he said quietly, "it doesn't. At first I thought it did, but I was wrong. When I think of this stinking town and everything that's wrong with it I want to go out and puke—but I can't, the damned open sewers are even too rotten for that. I've tried to get over it, but it's no use."

"You coming home?"

"Only to see the folks for a day or two, then I'm on my way." He hesitated a moment. Then: "You'll call me a damned fool, John, but go ahead. I asked for—and got—my old commission in the army. I was discharged as a first lieutenant, you remember, and I'm going back with that rank. Well, go ahead and give me hell."

"No," Ransom said slowly, "I won't, Dunc. For I guess I know how you feel. Mexico was hell in places, and so was the army, but they both had their points. In some ways I wish I was going with you. Where you going?"

"I'm to join a detachment of the Second Cavalry at Fort Laramie."

"Good God, that's halfway to California."

"Why not?" Duncan said. "It suits me. I asked for frontier duty, and it looks like I've got it."

Then presently it was seven-thirty and they were feeling marvelous.

"It's the shank of the evening," Duncan said oratorically. "Boy! Don't neglect your duty there."

The Negro brought the ninth or tenth rum sling and grinned widely. These gen'men could sure put it away.

"Just what I was thinking," Ransom said. "Tell you what. I'll go make sure the boy's all right an' be right back. If you're

[310]

leaving Chicago because of her vices you must know a lot about 'em. Let's look 'em over."

"And why not? Don't waste too much time. Boy, keep 'em coming and don't make me yell at you every two minutes."

While Ransom was gone upstairs Duncan pounded on the table with his mug and, to the extreme edification of the company present (the bar was filling up), sang a song called "The Monkey that Married the Baboon's Sister."

Ransom came back, and someone at the bar bought them a round of drinks. The short, bushy-haired man who had bought grinned at them and raised his glass in friendly fashion.

"Who's the old geezer making the speeches?" Duncan asked the Negro, nodding briefly toward the short man who was now surrounded by a little group of well-dressed men.

The boy's eyes widened. "Who? Him, sah? Why, that's Mist' Douglas hisself—he lives heah at the Tremont—an' that tall gen'man wif him is Mist' Wentworth, Long John they calls him."

"Well, I'll be a nigger preacher," Ransom said solemnly. "Dunc, imagine us drinkin' with statesmen like that! Boy, ask the senator if he thinks it 'll rain in Turkey tomorrow. He'll know—he knows everything."

The Negro laughed silently and moved away to wait on someone else.

After that the moving hours were hazy. They had dinner somewhere, felt soberer and bought a bottle of whisky to take with them in case it was a long way to the next bar. Then they were in a hack and gave the driver five dollars and told him to drive until the money ran out. When it ran out, they said, they'd give him some more.

It was somewhere after midnight when they found themselves in the spacious hallway of a big house on Prairie Avenue. The house had appeared dark from the street, but inside it was ablaze with candlelight.

The smiling lady with the blond curls and the extremely low-cut bodice was shaking hands with Duncan.

"A long time since we had the pleasure of seeing you, Mr Duncan."

"Ah, well, I've missed you, Dolly, damn if I haven't. Meet my frien' Mister—Mister—— What in hell is your name, John?"

"Smith," Ransom said owlishly. He swayed a little and gripped the newelpost of the staircase. "Pardon me, madam. Slight dizziness brought on by my old wounds, honorable wounds received in the service of the Duke of Waterloo at Wellington. . . ."

Dolly looked him over smilingly, eyebrows a little upraised at his country clothes. Well, if Duncan vouched for him . . .

"Smith, tha's right," Duncan said. "Stupid of me to forget. Lord Smith. He's so rich he stinks, Dolly. But don't get excited. We don't want to buy the house, just a little quiet and decorous entertainment."

"Of course, Mr Duncan. Will you go into the drawing room or would you rather have a private room? There are several gentlemen in the main room. Perhaps if you care for champagne —they'd be glad of your company. The evening's just getting started."

"We'll go in and have a look around first. Then we'll shee, Dolly. Here, John—Baron Smith, give the nigger your hat an' we'll shee what's goin' on."

Ransom could never remember any of that. His consciousness began when Dolly opened a door and he looked across the sea of candlelight to where a woman sat with a paunchy man on a sofa against the far wall of the room. Her head was thrown back, and Ransom could see her teeth gleaming through her laughter. The paunchy man had a hand against one of her almost bare breasts and with the other was trying to hold a glass to her laughing mouth. Her face floated toward Ransom through a fog of memory. She looked even more beautiful than he ever remembered her. Of course, in the candlelight, and at that distance . . .

Emma! . . .

1852

Then Duncan saw the blood drain suddenly out of Ransom's face, and he swayed drunkenly, blindly. "Steady, Sarge," Duncan said. "Take it easy. You'll be all right in a second."

Dolly was no fool, and she could sense trouble from afar. She snapped the door shut quickly but very quietly.

"Christ in heaven!" Ransom whispered. "Let's get out of this damned place."

"What's the matter, Sarge, sick?"

"You can't use that kind of talk in my house," Dolly rasped.

Ransom looked at her as though seeing her for the first time.

"The hell I can't, you slut," he said, and slapped her squarely across the mouth, knocking her abruptly against the farther wall.

"Nick!" she called, her voice rising shrilly. "Throw these dirty bastards into the street!"

Another door opened, and a huge hulk of a man trotted out. Ransom's fist smacked dully as the man ran straight into it.

"Come on, John. Let's get out of here before we get our throats cut."

Outside, he snapped at the hackman, "Get out of here, pronto, and don't spare the whip."

The driver was a man of experience. The horses moved away at a fast trot and then a gallop.

"For God's sake, John," Duncan said between jolts, "you looked like you seen a ghost."

"I did," Ransom said miserably. "Stop this thing. I'm sick as a horse."

He went behind the cab and vomited in the street, bracing himself against a wheel.

At the Tremont he told Duncan good-by and went up and undressed. He got into bed and tried to sleep, but he could not. His head ached terribly, and his taut muscles refused to relax.

After a while he got up and sat at the window until the sun came up and the early wagons and drays began rumbling through Randolph Street below.

The boy tossed restlessly with the coming of morning. Ransom went over and stood looking down at him. God, how innocent children could appear! How innocent they *were!* Well, this one was his anchor to himself.

So. Now it was finished, that chapter. He knew where he was, and the boy, too.

Presently he roused a bellboy and told him to bring some whisky. If he could only get some sleep now he'd feel all right.

At six o'clock Blair awakened and said, "Dad?"

The big man didn't stir. Blair shook him gently, but still he did not move. "I guess he's more tired than I was," Blair thought, and snuggled himself against Ransom's broad back contentedly.

V

Father William Gavin usually awakened regularly at five in the morning. There was nothing strange about this. He went to bed early each night, and a man with an active brain can use only a certain amount of sleep. There was nothing special—in the way of ecclesiastical duties, that is—for him to do at that time of the day, but he found it a fine time to read or think.

Usually he got out of his narrow bed, dressed in the cold of the barren little bedroom and then walked briskly around the block. That was his usual procedure unless the weather was such that he had to build a fire before he left the house. In that case he would be delayed for a little. If he followed this procedure exactly he would have an hour and a half to himself before Bridget Murphy came to prepare his breakfast at seven o'clock.

On Sundays, of course, there was Mass at six o'clock; but that was a church matter and therefore not susceptible to his personal whims.

Father Gavin was twenty-nine years old, and Everton was his first parish. Heretofore he had always been under another priest. And sometimes, when he thought objectively of his individual parishioners, scattered loosely over that northwestern part of Everton coming to be known as the "Forty Acres," his only comfort was his faith in God.

The church itself—funds had been very limited, and the church was a small white clapboard building with a two-roomed cottage attached at the rear for the use of the incumbent priest —was on Locust Street just west of Main, six blocks north of the courthouse. Most of the folk under Father Gavin's care lived west and north of that spot.

The Forty Acres.

There would, for the life of Everton, be a Forty Acres, though its exact location was to move with the years. And in the Forty Acres lived the Irish.

Father Gavin himself was Irish; but he was also a third-generation American, distant enough to see the Irish in perspective. They were his charges here, and he had no objection to the difficulties which that fact presented. He was a priest; he would go where his superiors sent him and do his work and God's work as best he could. But he was also a student and once, not so long before he came to Everton, he had wanted to write a history of the Irish in America. It was to have been a leisurely, scholarly work. He still retained a thick sheaf of notes and occasionally, for his own amusement, added to them briefly. But no longer with the idea of sometime publishing them.

The idea somehow appalled him now.

A man can write an enthusiastic book about something he admires—or hates; but Father Gavin no longer admired the Irish, and he couldn't allow himself to hate anyone enough to write a book based on that premise. So now he simply did his work and kept his literary ambitions safely buried.

As a boy in New York he could remember when the Black Irish invaded the Empire State to dig the Erie Canal, and later in Illinois, the ill-fated Illinois–Michigan Canal. From the Illinois ditch they went to Chicago to labor in the slaughterhouses and the new factories that were springing up there. And now they followed the railroads. Wherever railroads were building you would find the Irish—sweating, cursing, drinking, brawling, breeding, asserting their independence louder than any other race on earth, and taking orders from the Americans who happened to be boss.

All this was true, and to Father Gavin, who was himself an Irishman and proud of it, it was no cause for joy.

Everton, now, was a sweet little town, but except for the railroads the Irish would not have been here—nor Father Gavin, who had been sent solely because of the Irish. To a priest such things were not supposed to make any difference; the church was his business. But Gavin's people had been landholders in New York for years, and he could not, somehow, forgive the Irish their history as he knew it.

In Ireland, for instance, multitudes had starved during the Great Famine a few years before because the potato crop had failed. In Ireland you could grow corn or wheat or beans; they would not all have failed, and the starvation need not have been. But nobody could convince the Irish in Ireland that they could grow anything but potatoes in some of the earth's most fertile soil.

And now in America they ignored the land that lay almost free for the taking. Instead they preferred to slave on shovel gangs, on twelve-hour factory shifts, on swamping crews, on section gangs; they preferred to live in shanties, piled on top of one another in stinking slums, with the clean open land going begging on all sides; and mostly for a pittance, wages that other men in the Northwest would not touch.

Father Gavin knew these things, and as an individual it galled his racial pride.

This crisp November morning he happened upon Constable Jennings as he turned the corner at Locust and Main. The dawn was still only a gray suggestion in the east, but Gavin easily recognized the constable. He often met him somewhere in the neighborhood on his early-morning walks.

"Chilly this morning, Jennings," the priest said affably.

"So it is," Jennings agreed. "I was sort of hopin' I'd see you around, Father. I've a little business with you."

[316]

1852

"So?" Father Gavin smiled. "Will you step around the corner to the house and have a drop while we talk it over?"

"No, thanks, not this morning, thanks just the same." There was a little current of hostility in the constable's voice. "You know Mike Corcoran an' John Reilly, I reckon, Father?"

"Yes," Gavin said, waiting.

"Well, about midnight we had to go out to that shanty of Corcoran's on the crick an' take him an' Reilly in. One o' Reilly's brats come down to the station to lay the complaint. There was others in the brawl, but we only took them two downtown. Reilly was a sight—had a three-inch gash in his jaw where Corcoran smacked him with a bottle. We had to get Doc Jackson over to the jail to sew him up."

"I'm sorry," Father Gavin said slowly. "I usually hear of these things when they get so bad. I'm sorry," he repeated lamely, feeling somehow at a loss for adequate words.

"Un-hunh," Jennings said dryly. "But that don't help Ira Conway any, Father. He'll be in bed for a couple o' days with his hurts."

"Conway?" Gavin said. "How was he hurt?"

"Well, them two Micks wasn't going to let any Yankee snake in the grass take 'em to jail—so they said—an' Ira happened to get the worst of the deal. We took 'em to jail," he added as an afterthought.

"Oh, to be sure," Gavin said absent-mindedly. Would these brawling fools never learn?

"You an' me been pretty good friends since you come here to Everton, Father. We've always got along. But them folk in the Forty Acres——" Jennings spat in the street. "We never had that kind o' brawls an' hell raisin' in Everton till the Irish come here."

Standing there in the cold morning, Father Gavin thought a lot of things. But there was no particular point in discussing them with Constable Jennings. So he said nothing.

"Downtown we've been talkin' the thing over," Jennings went on. "We don't want to be hard on anybody, but Mayor Durham

[317]

is pretty sore about this regular hell raisin'. If it don't stop pretty soon he says the police are gonna start carryin' pistols when we have to go to the Forty Acres. An' we're gonna have to use 'em. I just thought I'd tell you, Father Gavin. Just between me an' you, see?"

"I see," Gavin said. "Well, I don't know that I can blame you, Jennings. I know how you people must feel about it. I do what I can, you know, but I sometimes think you all put too much faith in me—or, rather, blame me too much for what happens. After all, I'm only a priest, you know. I'll be downtown to see about Corcoran and Reilly."

"Well, all right," Jennings said doubtfully. "But you ain't gonna do them much good, Father. Not this time, I reckon. They beat the livin' hell outa Conway. They'll get six months apiece in the county jail unless I miss my guess. I was just tellin' you this because I know you're interested. This is just between you an' me, see?"

"Oh, surely. I know that, Jennings. Anyway, I'll have to come down and see what I can do." Two more families for the parish to look after. "You're sure you won't step around an' have a drop of something?"

"No, thanks. I'll be havin' my breakfast directly. Well, I'll have to be gettin' on."

Father Gavin continued his walk. Always something like this coming up. God be praised, why? He kicked viciously at a frozen clod in Main Street. The sun was a red ball above the treetops now, and you could see the white skim of frost on the ground.

It was, he guessed, simply the fact that they were the Irish from Ireland. Defying authority and being beaten by it at every step. That was the only answer he could think of.

This morning he walked farther than usual, and by the time he got back to the house he was in a good humor in spite of his meeting with Jennings and the bad news it entailed.

The day before he had had a letter from the Dominican Sisters, and the letter had held out some hope for one of his favorite projects. After the first of the year, so they had said, they might

1852

spare a couple of teachers for the Everton parish. Of course he would have to provide a school building, but, that forthcoming, he *might* have a couple of competent teachers, at least as an experiment and for a limited time.

Back in his austere living room again, he kindled a snapping fire. Then he took another lusty drink from the whisky bottle and settled himself to read until breakfast. It was to be sausage and eggs and fried apples, he remembered, and the remembrance was pleasant.

Later, when the town was astir, he would look into the matter of Corcoran and Reilly.

CHAPTER FOURTEEN

1856

WHEN THE TOWN CHANGED this time it was with a rapidity, an almost overnightness, that to most of the oldsters was somewhat overwhelming. All of them who had owned real estate, and most of them had, made a great deal—for Everton—of money, money which some of them could scarcely believe. A dozen or so of the older men still ruled the town, regardless of who might be holding office, but sometimes it seemed to them that all they did was to agree to innovations proposed by the younger generation, some of that generation being their own adult sons.

Two railroads—the Illinois Central and the Chicago & Mississippi—were now a commonplace.

In 1853 Judge Caton had come to town with an expansive smile and a persuasive tongue. He knew everybody—or appeared to—and it took him just three days to accomplish his purpose.

The Western Union was building a line from Chicago to Springfield. Everton, so Caton told General Green, was to be honored with a telegraph office—provided the town could see its way clear to buy $1,000 worth of Western Union stock. And Judge Caton was a good enough salesman to make the citizenry forget that the Western Union, since it was building a

Springfield–Chicago line anyway, could scarcely afford *not* to open an office in Everton, seeing that it was the only town of importance between the cities in question. But Everton came through, and as usual the regular names made up the subscription list: Fell, Larison, Washburne, Swett, Withers, Flagg, Ewing, Merriman, Fitchman, Allin. It was progress, however, and they didn't mind paying for it as long as they could afford it.

Now the vast empty spaces between the Catholic church and the railroad shops were almost filled with little houses and stores. The passenger stations of the two railroads were exactly east and west of the courthouse—the C. & M. eight blocks to the west and the Central as many east. When the C. & M. depot had been built many people had complained about going out in the country to catch the cars; now there were actually streets west of the railroad tracks.

Fitchman's medicine factory had grown until he had his own steam-operated printing presses to turn out the almanacs which were better known in the Middle West than the names of Horace Greeley and James Gordon Bennett. The almanacs were printed in German, Norwegian and Swedish as well as English, and carried Dr Fitchman's whiskered likeness as a cover portrait. The year before, fire had destroyed the Fitchman factory (with one exception, Green's brick bank building on the northeast corner, the entire block directly south of the courthouse had burned), but already, in the spring of '56, the new factory was finished and operating. It was the first three-storied brick structure in Everton and added to Dr Fitchman's prestige accordingly.

At the eastern edge of town, on the open prairie just beyond the fair grounds, fat, good-humored Dr Herman Schroeder was making a dream come partly true.

Schroeder was an emigrant from Germany because of the abortive revolution of 1848 and, after a short stay in the German colony of Cleveland, had moved to Everton. He was actually a doctor of medicine, but because at first there had been little business for him in that line he had with his own hands helped clear the timber from a little patch of land he had bought. With the lumber he erected a half-dozen small houses and so with little investment became the owner of a considerable property. He was perhaps a little lucky along with his willingness to work hard, and at the end of four years he had done well for himself.

But the experiment east of the fair grounds was something more than a real-estate project. There Schroeder had planted, and made prosper, acre after acre of vineyard. And already he had sold, by mail, almost a half-million vine cuttings. "Ach," he had said innumerable times, "this whisky—what it does to a man's insides. There are plenty of Germans in America—maybe we can show these people what wine, good wine, is like." So he performed what he thought was a public benefaction—and made money hand over fist.

The rule of the day was progress plus expansion.

The Middle West was growing like—well, like a weed. In Boston and New York and Philadelphia people wondered how Illinois could prosper so with the state still full of savage Indians and man-eating wild beasts; but in Illinois men were talking already of manufactured gas for illuminating their streets and buildings and laying plans for taking *all* the business and commerce away from the East. And each year they grew financially more independent of Philadelphia and New York.

Politically, Illinois was pretty much on the conservative side. At least the people there were willing to let events take their natural course and let sleeping dogs lie. Slavery, for instance. What business was it of theirs? Well, nothing. But wasn't it? There was rumor and counter-rumor, talk and still more talk. The political swell was beginning to heave very quietly and very slowly, but the surge was there. A few short years before there had been a Democratic party and a Whig party, with Democratic Senator Stephen Douglas the strongest man in Illinois—for that matter, one of the strongest men in Washington. Now there were Democrats, Whigs, Free-Soilers, Abolitionists, Anti-Nebraska Democrats, Anti-Nebraska Whigs, and a host of bastard parties which as yet had little numerical strength. Douglas was still the political godhead of Illinois and, in no small way, of the whole Mississippi Valley north of Kentucky and Missouri. But the power was weakening, its weaknesses not yet apparent but there nevertheless.

The beginning of the end had been Douglas' about-face when, in 1852, he had voted to repeal the Missouri Compromise. The solid citizens of Illinois were not, so they swore publicly and privately, abolitionists. But the Missouri Compromise was and had been for years a fact agreed upon by both North and South. It had been law and common sense, the heart and soul of the status quo. Illinois thought she had been playing fair when she had agreed to the arrangement. And when the South carried, with the help of the hero Douglas, the repeal of the Compromise, the South, so Illinois felt, had deliberately repaid friendliness with a resounding slap in the face.

And it was Douglas, the hero who had labored long and well for Illinois in the past, who dealt the blow.

Well, the repeal also was now a fact, and Douglas had chosen his own road.

Illinois was grimly but quietly taking another path.

In the East, Henry Ward Beecher and Gerrit Smith achieved easy publicity with the fuminations against slavery. Harriet Stowe's tear-jerking and inaccurate *Uncle Tom's Cabin* ran into edition after edition since its appearance as a magazine serial in 1852. In Illinois, Owen Lovejoy stumped the state and preached the antislavery gospel. (The Sucker State folk remembered Owen's brother Elijah even though they would have preferred to forget the shame of his lynching at the hands of an Alton mob and the shameful aftermath of that event.) Elsewhere in the state, in a hundred ways, the torch was alight. Even the churches, some of them, had gotten around to speaking out against slavery.

Douglas, domineering, dogmatic, sure of his own strength, didn't believe it. He could handle Illinois. But four years later he was to hold Lincoln's hat in Washington while the sad-faced prairie lawyer took oath as President of the United States.

11

Mrs Goddard came out on the porch and looked around the visible backyards. Then she raised her voice and called:

"Da-a-a-avid!"

No answer. She waited expectantly for a moment, then her hope faded and she called again.

"Da-a-vid!" This time her voice rising angrily at the end of the word.

Then a belligerent-faced ten-year-old appeared around the corner of the house. Mrs Goddard eyed him coldly.

"Why didn't you answer me, David?"

"Aw, Mom, I was just comin'."

"So I see. But how many times have I told you to answer me when I call?" She and David both knew that this required no answer. "It's time you got cleaned up to go to the meeting. It's after three o'clock."

David glowered. "I don't *want* to go to the old meeting. Nothing but a bunch o' sissies, that's all. Pa said he didn't care if I went or not."

Mrs Goddard looked properly pained. "What your father says has nothing to do with it. If he had *his* way you'd do a lot of things you shouldn't. Thank the Lord he don't have his way altogether around this house."

John Goddard was a foreman at the C. & M. coach shops and so, apparently, couldn't be depended upon for much in the way of moral guidance.

"I don't wanna go," David repeated.

"Just the same, you're going. Sissies! The very idea of calling some of the nicest boys in Everton sissies. You march in the house and get washed this very minute."

David marched, but against his will. As long as he was here there was no use defying her and starting trouble; she'd win out in the end. However, if she didn't insist upon going along with

[324]

him he could duck into Trimmer's livery stable and hide until the meeting was over.

Mrs Goddard scrubbed at his face and neck and ears. How in the world could he get so dirty in so short a time? Finally she jerked his coat into place and made sure the white silk ribbon was fastened securely in his lapel.

As for David, he glowered at the badge as though it were a badge of disgrace. Bob Davis and Harry Haines and Steve Dowling didn't have to wear that stinking emblem and listen to Doctor Hobbs's jawing. And as he continued to think about Doctor Hobbs's Temperance Club for Boys his youthful rage boiled over.

"Damn ol' Doctor Hobbs an' his white ribbons!" he burst forth rebelliously.

Then, having thus spoken to his mother, he was shocked into silence by his own temerity. So was Mrs Goddard, but in a very short moment she discovered her voice.

"David Goddard! I never thought I'd live to hear my own son speak so. How can you talk that way about Doctor Hobbs or anyone who does the good he tries to do? Do you want to grow up to be a drunkard?"

"No," David said honestly, though not exactly sure what-all being a drunkard meant.

"Then why don't you be a good boy and go to Doctor Hobbs's meetings like you ought to? He's doing a wonderful work in his Temperance Club, and when you're older you'll appreciate it better. You want to grow up and be a strong, good man and not drink, don't you?"

"Yes, ma'm," David said obediently. "But I don't want to go to silly meetings an' wear a silly badge." He felt that while his logic was irrefutable it was badly put. His mother was practically impervious to logic when her mind was made up. He had discovered that long ago.

"But you must," Mrs Goddard said with finality. "You want to grow up and be a great man and have us proud of you. You can't do that if you drink liquor."

"Well," David said, "Pa says Steve Douglas is the greatest man in the country, an' *he* drinks. I know. I saw him one day when I went by the Ashley House. *He* drinks," he repeated. "An' Mr Campbell drinks, an' he's state's attorney. Once when I was with Pa, Mr Campbell took him into Killip's and I waited outside."

Mrs Goddard's lips tightened into a straight, firm line. "That," she said crisply, "has nothing whatever to do with it. Or, rather, that's one of the reasons why you should go. Doctor Hobbs is doing a very fine work, and I want you to have the advantage of it and learn better than your father did. What other people do has no bearing on the case. Now, here's your hat and don't you loiter on the way. And come right home when Doctor Hobbs dismisses you."

David sauntered down the empty street, past the Orme place and Bill McCullough's house. On this May Saturday afternoon it was very warm and sticky, though the shade under the elms was cool. Inwardly he debated whether he should go on to the Methodist church and stand the ordeal or duck over to Trimmer's as he had originally planned—and stand the licking he was almost certain to get as a result. If he didn't go his mother would certainly hear it from Hobbs at church in the morning, and David could never exactly predict what his father might do. Goddard had been practically reared in a Scotch boiler works and was a stickler for discipline. He might not care whether David went to Temperance Club or not, but he would certainly punish him for disobeying his mother's orders.

Then, for the time it took to cover another block, he pondered the feasibility of leaving, this very day, for the Great West. In a few years he could come back home to his grieving parents, the hero of a hundred desperate Indian encounters, rich as all get out. . . .

Pug Wilson came across the street and joined him, putting an abrupt stop to his revery.

"Hi, Dave. Where you goin'?" Innocently.

"*You* know," David said. "Same place you are, I guess."

1856

Then David's rage got the better of him again, and he uttered the final word about the Temperance Club.

"God dam' Doctor Hobbs to hell an' gone," he said passionately.

Pub looked at him a little in awe. "Well, that's sorta what I say," he agreed heartily. "I guess we better get goin', though. It's almost four o'clock, an' you know Hobbs 'll be sore as a boil if we ain't there on time."

"All right," David said. He felt a great deal better now.

III

Sometimes these days Fell thought he got tired more easily than he once had. Of course he was only forty-eight, but there were times when he felt a lot older than that.

Tonight he sat under the lamp at his desk, reading the accumulated mail and resting. The letter from Horace Mann in New York City he put aside to read again and digest more carefully. (He had corresponded with Mann for several years now. Mann was a radical, of course, but he had ideas about educational methods, real ideas.) There was a letter from the Chicago office of the C. & M. about a minor business deal; one from Lincoln about something trivial. Well, Lincoln was probably downtown at the Ashley now, spring court being in session. He'd see him tomorrow.

The letter from the C. & M. made him think now of something else. He leaned back in his chair, relaxing and remembering how the C. & M. was largely responsible for his new house that was almost finished. It had been purely a business matter, of course. Tom, one of his brothers, farmed at Randolph Grove, south of town, and in 1853 and '54 Jesse, in partnership with Tom, had sold the C. & M. about forty thousand oak ties and four thousand cords of wood. That had been one of the nicest deals Jesse had ever engineered. And it had made the new house possible sooner than he had expected.

There was a letter from Horace Greeley, also in New York

[327]

City, and Fell resolved to write to Greeley oftener. He had known him since his earliest school days, and if there was anyone more generally and specifically informed about affairs in the East, Fell didn't know who it was. And not a little of Greeley's knowledge of the West had come from Fell.

As he sat there thinking, Hester came to the door, standing expectantly just outside the pool of lamplight. Jesse had been gone three days and had driven in just at suppertime; there was so much she had to tell him and talk over with him. She was eleven years Jesse's junior but she had lost the habit of remembering that.

"Sit down, my dear," Fell said.

"Oh, you're busy. I just stopped by the door for a moment."

"No, I'm not. I was just sitting here thinking. Come in and sit down—I'd rather talk to you, anyhow."

Hester arranged her skirts carefully. "Did you really have a good trip? You look tired out."

Fell laughed a little. "I *am* a little tired, but not too much. Who was here?"

"Oh, heavens—who wasn't here! Mr Swett was here yesterday. He's defending that Wyant case, you know, and the trial starts tomorrow. It's the talk of the whole town. Everywhere you go it's Wyant, Wyant, Wyant. It's nothing to me, but do you think Leonard can get him off? Everybody knows that Wyant killed this man—what's his name—Rusk? And Mr Campbell has Mr Lincoln helping with the prosecution. Not," she said, "that I ever thought much of Mr Lincoln's legal ability, though you all seem to."

Fell chuckled. "Lincoln *is* good, though I know you never liked the way his pants were pressed—or rather weren't pressed. But I don't know. This Swett is a smart pleader, and I rather think he's got something up his sleeve in this case. Let's talk about something besides murder, though. Who else was here?"

"Well, Mr Arny of course."

"Arny of course," Jesse echoed. "Was there anything special?"

W. F. M. Arny was laying out and selling town lots in a place called, at the moment, North Everton, surrounding the spot where the C. & M. crossed the Illinois Central. Fell fondly assumed that everyone thought it was Arny's own project, whereas everyone in Everton had for two months been calling it Fell's Folly and knew that Arny was simply working for Fell. Fell's new house was being built on the most beautiful spot in North Everton—that in itself was enough to tell the story.

"No-o-o, nothing very special," Hester said a little vaguely. "He just wanted to see you. But he did say something about that special clause you had put in those North Everton title deeds—you know, the one about never selling spirits or liquors on the property. A lot of people don't like that, Jesse."

Fell looked at her and smiled a little. "So that's the way the wind blows, is it? Arny trying to talk you over to his side. Well——"

"No, Jesse, he wasn't really," Hester interrupted. "Mr Arny always felt that way about it and told you so. You must realize that few people have your ideas about liquor. Even a lot of people who oppose it wouldn't go as far as you are."

"You mean they wouldn't go so far as to allow their feelings to interfere with making a profit. Well, you're right, of course. But that doesn't make a particle of difference to me. That's the way I want it, and that's the way it's going to be. North Everton 'll be one place in this state where they won't sell a drop of liquor. If it can't be stopped anywhere by a majority vote, then I'll stop it in my own backyard with the only method I know. If people don't want to buy lots under that condition, why, we're better off without 'em."

"Yes, I suppose you're right," she agreed. "But Mr Arny says he could sell lots hand over fist if that could be changed."

"Well, what of it?" Jesse asked a little sharply. "North Everton isn't exactly a business proposition. We're going to *live* there. Arny knew that when he went into the thing. By the way," he said, changing the subject, "how is the house? I suppose you've been out in the last day or two."

"Oh yes, I drove out this afternoon. Mr Farr still has his painters there, but they're almost through. Another couple of days, Mr Farr says. Then I drove downtown and stopped by Lubeck's. The piano has come, and he showed it to me. It's all uncrated, and he's polished it until you can see your face in it. Jesse, it's a beauty, honestly."

"Well, it cost enough, though there was no use in buying anything but the best."

"Yes, and Mr Lubeck says it'll be the first real piano in Everton."

Fell smiled again. Lubeck. Yes, he remembered him, too. The little German. How these Germans varied! There was Schroeder, for instance. In Everton only a few years and already one of the well-to-do men of the town. Lubeck had been here twice as long and still operated the music store and gave lessons. Of course he had burned out the year before, and that had hurt, but so had a lot of other people. Fell himself had lost a considerable sum by the fire.

"We'll have to start getting ready to move in a week or so now," Hester was saying.

"We don't have to," Jesse reminded her. "What's the difference? This house and the other one are ours—and it's taken twenty-five years to build this new one. No use to hurry about moving."

"Twenty-five years? . . . Oh, I see what you mean. I know, Jesse, but the sooner we get moved the sooner——"

"Yes, yes," he said a bit irritably, "of course. I know how you feel about it, too. Go ahead and arrange with Trimmer about the drays. It's quite all right with me."

Twenty-five years? Yes, it was true. A quarter of a century; it didn't seem possible. He made a mental note to see Jim Allin soon and wondered if Allin too was thinking about that quarter-century. Allin was an old man now, and Jesse was suddenly a little shocked by remembering that the last time he had seen him he was using two crutches to get around on.

I V

The flower of the Eighth Circuit Bar had, for the duration of the court session, taken over the Ashley House bar.

At a table in a back corner Usher Linder pounded the drink-slopped walnut and addressed a half-dozen lawyers who listened to him amusedly. Lincoln's chair was tilted back against the wall, and his heels were hooked into one of the chair rungs so that his bony knees stuck up above the table edge. He turned his half-filled glass slowly in his long fingers, sipping at it infrequently. Lincoln, somebody had said, could make one drink last longer than any other man in the state. Two drinks, in fact, could and often did last him an entire evening.

"By God," Linder was saying, "I don't impugn his reputation for honesty, and I don't question his ability. It's just that I don't like his extralegal way of running his court. It's a hell of a note, I say. In half the cases Davis tries you'd think he was attorney for both sides rather than judge of the court."

"Well," Steve Logan drawled, "what is a good judge if he's not an attorney for both sides? I'd say you've pretty well defined what a judge should be, Usher."

"Hell, I can't see it," Linder exploded. "Take this morning, for instance. Three times Davis interrupted that young squirt Daly to tell him his plea was wrong, while I stood there rightfully demanding that he throw the case out of court as he should have done. But no, what does he do? He takes the plea away from young Daly and says, 'Here, young man, I'll have somebody rewrite this that knows how to do it, and I'll postpone the hearing.' And if that's not a complete hell of a note, then I don't know what is."

They laughed. They knew Davis.

"Better not cuss him too loud," Swett said to Linder. "He's back there in Ashley's private office writing some letters he wanted to post before he goes home."

"You won't get any frills, legal or otherwise, in Davis'

court," young Orme, Swett's partner, put in, "but you'll get a hell of a lot of plain justice. Davis helped to make the Eighth Circuit, and he'll probably be judge here when he dies."

"Yes," Linder said, "and for a stinking thousand dollars a year. Why? I understand Davis has plenty of money."

"He has," Logan said. "More than plenty. He and Cliff Moore between 'em must easily be worth a half-million, what with their Chicago property growing by leaps and bounds in value. But that's nothing much to Davis. He wouldn't trust justice being left in anybody else's hands. How about that, Abe? You ought to know."

Lincoln opened his eyes and grinned. "You're right, Steve, I suspect. Davis is like me in one respect—he doesn't know much about the philosophy of the law. But he's unlike me in another respect. He has a nose for equity like a bee has for honey—and the Supreme Court reverses fewer of his decisions than any other judge's in the state."

"That don't make his highhanded court procedure right," Linder argued. "Why, I've never seen anything like it in the East."

"Well," Lincoln drawled, "that's where the equity comes in. He knows when he's right or an attorney's right, so he just goes ahead and gets things over with and the fancy style left out. He ain't like the majority of judges. No lawyer can bluff him into thinking he's wrong if he knows he isn't. Besides, Davis *is* the Eighth Circuit court. He's handed down some mighty funny decisions in his time, though," he added portentously. "Some mighty funny decisions."

"As how?"

Both Orme and Linder leaned forward to catch this. They were the youngest men present.

"Oh," Lincoln said, "I recall one time some rascal was on trial for burglary, and it came time to pass sentence. Of course he was guilty. Davis leaned that belly of his against the bench, cleared his throat and said, 'I hereby sentence you to seven years in the Illinois state legislature!'"

[332]

Swett and Logan and the rest of them, except Linder and Orme, roared their laugher. It was an old story, but Lincoln never told it the same way twice. Orme and Linder looked a little sheepish.

"Of course," Lincoln went on innocently, "everybody in the courtroom was appalled. No known crime could warrant such drastic punishment. But the court clerk saved the day. He went over and whispered in Davis' ear, and the judge relented and made the sentence read seven years in the penitentiary instead. That's what I meant when I said he'd handed down some mighty funny decisions."

"He's helped out more young lawyers than anybody else I know of," Swett said, remembering.

"So I've heard," Linder remarked. "Any kind of help just so it didn't lead to any pecuniary outlay."

Swett shrugged. "Perhaps," he agreed. "But he's not bound to support any part of the legal profession except himself."

"Where's Douglas these days, Abe?" Logan asked.

"Mending fences among the Democrats, I'd imagine," Lincoln said. "There's a lot of holes in his, certainly. You know I don't like to talk too much, Steve, but did it ever occur to you that Steve Douglas' vote on the repeal of the Missouri Compromise *might* have been influenced by a debt he owed to some Southern senator because of that Southerner's vote in favor of federal aid for the Illinois Central?"

Logan was startled out of his customary calm. "Lordy, no, Abe. Yes, I see what you mean. Good God, yes; it's perfectly possible. But such a thing never occurred to me. If it's true though, he could explain it that way to the right people. Then it wouldn't look quite as bad as it does now."

"No." Lincoln shook his craggy head slowly. "No, Steve, I don't think he can explain. When he did it—*if* he did, which I haven't the least notion—it probably seemed a small matter. He didn't foresee the consequences. And now he can't explain because he could be accused of trading the North's legal barrier against slavery for the right to give away a few hundred paltry square miles of land. It's between Steve and God now. You needn't expect him to try to explain it to anybody else. I know him too well not to know that."

"I'm going to bed," Linder said. "I've had all the law and liquor I need for one night."

He said good night and went out of the bar and across the Ashley House lobby toward the stairs. His step was a little unsteady, but only a little. Just before he came to the staircase he passed Ashley's office and hesitated momentarily. Davis' bulky figure was seated under the lamp at Ashley's desk. He blew on an inked line to dry it. Then he looked up and peered over his spectacles.

"Oh, hello, Linder," he said cordially. "Come in, come in. I was just finishing up here."

"Oh no, Judge," Linder said bitterly. "I see you're writing demurrers in some of your numerous cases. I wouldn't want to interrupt you." And he stamped angrily on up the stairs.

Davis blinked owlishly at the vacant doorframe for a moment, uncomprehending. Then he chuckled audibly as he gathered up his papers and went out, moving like a loaded frigate under a slow wind.

"Damned young cub," he muttered, and grinned to himself.

v

Spring moved slowly into summer, and on the prairies men thought about the first corn plowing. Small boys played hookey from school and practised swimming dog-fashion in Sugar Creek and the Mackinaw and Panther Creek. Their male elders, equipped with a jar of bait and a jug of whisky, fished nocturnally in the same creeks and rivers and yarned of Mexico and the West and of the Old Days—the old days, somehow always better than the present. And in farm kitchens the women thought of childbearing and raspberry jam and drying sweet corn and weddings and church picnics and the kind of dresses worn by the new preacher's wife at the crossroads Methodist or Baptist church.

In Everton court week was over and Leonard Swett had won an acquittal in the most important case he had so far defended: the State of Illinois *vs.* Robert Wyant, David Campbell and Abraham Lincoln prosecuting for the state. Before long smart lawyers everywhere would be soaking up the judicial facts in the Wyant case, thereby starting to walk a long, long road in American judicial practice. For Swett had armed himself with an imposing array of facts, relevant and otherwise, from Gray's *Anatomy* and lesser authorities. Of the simple country practitioners whom he had called as witnesses he had made jackasses with especially long ears, and by virtue of his forensic ability talked a Dane County jury into a Not Guilty verdict in the case of the State of Illinois *vs.* Wyant. It was the first time in America that a man had killed another and then been called not guilty by a jury on the ground of temporary insanity.

Smart lawyers everywhere pricked up their ears. Here *was* something new under the sun.

And then, in those last days of May, Everton began to take notice of the strange faces on the streets. Well, the faces weren't altogether strange. But they were faces which weren't often seen in Everton or anywhere else together. At the Ashley House and the Pike House there was not a single vacant room, and the bars did a roaring business.

Laban Major, who owned Major's Hall, listened to a gentleman from Chicago whom he had never met before but whose name he knew very well, and after a little talk handed over the keys to the hall. There would be a small charge, Laban explained apologetically, but the gentlemen involved could pay it whenever they felt like it.

Everton went about its usual business, aware that events were stirring, but in general not much caring. A few men were personally interested in what was going on downtown, but not many. On the streets and in the saloons and at the Ashley and Pike quiet men were talking, renewing old political acquaintanceships, trying to forget old political wounds. Strange friends shook hands, bought drinks and agreed to forget a little of the old sectional differences. Strange political bedfellows talked of ways and means, trying not to let the old defeats and disappointments matter too much. Names threaded their talk: names like Owen Lovejoy, David Davis, John Wentworth, Norman Judd (next to Douglas, so it was said, the wiliest Democrat in Illinois), John Palmer, Jesse Dubois, Leonard Swett, Kersey Fell, Henry Whitney, Dick Yates, Lyman Trumbull (to whom Lincoln had handed the senatorship on a platter), William Bissell, William Herndon, Ward Lamon, James Miller, William Pitt Kellogg, John Wood, Ozias Hatch, Francis Hoffmann, John Latimer, J. W. Bunn, Tom Pickett, Jackson Grimshaw. They were Democrats, Whigs, Abolitionists and a dozen other political breeds.

And among those present, observing much but saying little, was a young man named Joseph Medill, lately from Ohio. In a year or so Illinois—and the United States at large—was to know him, at least by name, as editor of the Chicago *Tribune*.

On the morning of May 29th, John M. Palmer called the Anti-Nebraska State Convention to order on the third floor of Major's Hall, at the southwest corner of Front and North streets in Everton.

Fifty or sixty men gathered there in that small room, forgetting or unmindful of the fact that there were such cities as New York and Chicago and Boston and Philadelphia and Richmond and Atlanta and New Orleans and Baltimore. Two questions were on their lips: Would Lincoln come? And if he came, what would he say or do?

John Palmer stroked his bushy little goatee, rapped his gavel upon the pine table and called the convention (ah yes, *they* called it a convention) to order.

Ward Lamon spat contemptuously. "Hell, yes," he said, "Lincoln 'll come. He wrote me that he would. I signed his name to the convention call in the Springfield *Journal* without his knowing it, and John Stuart just raised hell with me about it. So I wrote to Lincoln at Tremont, and he answered that he'd be here. You don't need to worry a minute about *him*."

"He's afraid of Lovejoy over there," Steve Hurlburt said quietly. "He's afraid to get off the fence."

"The hell he is," Lamon exploded. "He's not afraid of anything on two feet, abolitionist or otherwise. But he's not a fool, remember that. He knows that work an' action is better than talk, and he's pretty tired of so much talk—even his own talk."

Later there were debate, and oratory, and argument, and finally, after two days and a night, a party name, a party platform and a party slate of nominees for state—and national—offices.

The name of the new party was "Republican."

The platform was built largely around a denunciation of the Missouri Compromise repeal act, but was careful at the same time to declare devotion to the Union and the constitutional rights of the states.

The nominees included William Bissell for governor—Bissell, one time colonel of the First Illinois at Buena Vista, later congressman.

Illinois and a considerable portion of the country at large knew Colonel Bill Bissell—and loved him in the manner that Americans always love their heroes. For when Jefferson Davis, in Congress, was unwise enough to question the conduct and gallantry of Illinois troops in the Mexican War, it was Bissell who cut him down with a verbal salvo that led Davis to call him out in sheer defense of his personal honor. Bissell, being the challenged man, chose as weapons buckshot-loaded shotguns at ten paces. This was apparently too much even for the spearhead of Southern chivalry, and wiser and cooler heads talked the principals out of the duel.

But on the stumps in Illinois they told that President Zachary Taylor, with tears in his eyes, threw an arm around Bissell's shoulders and said, "Bissell, for God's sake don't shoot my son-in-law down like a dog." And in Illinois they told and retold the story, improving it and relishing it more with each telling. The truth of the details didn't matter particularly.

James Miller of Everton, a sober Irish Presbyterian, originally a slaveowner in Virginia, was nominated as state treasurer; to run, presumably, against old John Moore of Randolph Grove, late lieutenant colonel of the Fourth Illinois Volunteers, present state treasurer, and one time lieutenant governor.

The press, with the exception of Joseph Medill, was conspicuous by its absence. Newspapers were either Whig or Democrat, with a sprinkling of fly-by-night Abolitionists. Why should they bother about a more or less furtive gathering of mavericks who chose to call themselves Republicans?

At the office of the *Western Whig* Merriam sniffed and told Jack Prince, the local news editor, not to bother. If these rebels wanted advertising, then let them buy it. "This is no time to start another party," Merriam said. "Why, the idea is ridiculous; they're crazy. I'm going to write an editorial against the whole idea."

"Well," Prince said, "some of the biggest men in the state are over there at Major's Hall just the same. We might be smart to give it a half-column."

"Bah!" Merriam snorted. "A pack of radicals, that's all. I'll attend to it."

"All right," Prince said. "You're the boss." But nevertheless he attended what sessions of the convention he could get around to.

A day or so later, however, Merriam talked to Jesse Fell; so there was no editorializing against the new party. Neither was there anything printed in its favor. The weekly edition of the *Whig* did, however, carry an emasculated account of the proceedings.

The spanking bay team trotted smartly past the brick gateposts of the Ransom place and swung into the smooth dust of Washington Street. John Ransom sat stiffly erect, holding the reins firmly in one gloved hand while he manipulated his cigar with the other. Occasionally he shifted the cigar in order to raise his white beaver to someone passing in another rig.

He sighed a little, remembering the dinner just eaten. Getting that nigger Gus from the Gayosoes in Memphis had been the smartest thing ever, even if it had cost him a thousand dollars and the Negro's freedom when he walked into the Ransom kitchen. Gus was one of the best cooks south of Chicago and west of New York. Well, he and Blair could afford it—they could afford anything they wanted. He was busy these days teaching Blair what it was intelligent to want. In another year Blair would be going East to school. Ransom hated the thought of that, in a way, but he had made up his mind.

Not even the Green house surpassed the Ransom place on East Washington Street, and in Everton—and in Chicago, for that matter—anxious mothers with marriageable daughters put on their best smiles when John Ransom appeared. He was a little gray now, but he wasn't really old, and his big body was set off by clothes from the best tailor in Chicago. And a great many of these same mothers had seen or heard, a little enviously, of the white napery, the silver, the too lovely crystal, the gleaming mahogany and walnut and cherry of the Ransom house.

The youngster was wealthy in his own right, of course; almost everyone in Everton knew that. But how much money John Ransom himself had made, no one in Everton except Jesse Fell—and he didn't know it all—could even guess. But everybody agreed that it must be a great deal, and they were quite right. For in the past four years everything John Ransom had touched seemed to turn into a handsome profit. He was involved in a dozen projects, some of them purely for the sake of amusement.

This Republican affair, for instance. He really cared nothing for politics. But he was more than interested in the personalities behind political affairs. Tonight, after the business of the convention downtown, he was having a bunch of the men out to the house for supper. They would all be good eaters and drinkers, and the talk would be interesting.

Blair kicked his heels against the dashboard of the stan-
hope.

"Why do we have to go hear speeches, Dad?"

"We don't," Ransom said, and grinned, "but we are. I want
to hear Spot Lincoln talk—and I want you to hear him."

"Professor Craddock at the Academy said Mr Lincoln is an
uncouth radical. What did he mean, Dad?"

Ransom laughed. The description somehow struck him as
immensely funny. "I don't know, son, and probably the professor doesn't, either, though I expect he just doesn't like Abe's
looks or his politics. But don't worry too much about what
Craddock says about such things. If he lived to be a hundred
and ten years old he probably wouldn't understand Spot Lincoln.
People are like that."

"Un-hunh," Blair said, not understanding, but knowing that
sometimes his father liked to talk at random and above his head.
"But everybody talks about Mr Lincoln, an' they never say why
he's a good man or smart or anything. They just talk about him
and argue or get mad."

John chuckled. At least the boy was observing.

"That's right, son," he said. "Maybe that's why he's a great
man. People know he is, but they don't yet know for sure why
he is. I think the time just hasn't arrived yet for them to know
—or for Lincoln to know, either."

Blair was silent, still not understanding quite what his father
meant, when Ransom reined in the bays and pulled them up
to the hitchrack on the North Street side of Major's Hall. Blair
jumped out, and Ransom said, "Tie 'em short, son. They're a
little nervous, and there's a lot of strange nags around."

Dusk had fallen, and they could see the lighted lamps on the
third floor of the hall. A few men were still going up the narrow stairway, and the Ransoms joined them, John speaking and
nodding to those he recognized on the street and in the semi-
darkness of the stairs.

The top floor of the hall was a single room perhaps thirty by
sixty feet in size, lighted by oil lamps swung from the low ceil-

ing. The air was hot and close in spite of the windows open on three sides of the room. At the south end there was a platform raised about six inches above the floor and furnished with a small plain table and a half-dozen chairs. The seats on the floor were irregular rows of chairs and looked disordered and scattered, just as they had been left at the close of the afternoon session. There were no flags or bunting, no lithographed portraits of candidates or favorite sons, no brass bands. The mood of the men in the room was one of calm seriousness.

As the Ransoms found seats toward the rear of the room, John noted the men talking in low voices on the little stage: John Palmer, Abraham Lincoln, Colonel Bissell, James Miller, Henry Whitney, and a couple of others. Ransom knew all of them either personally or by sight, and he pointed them out to Blair.

Palmer tapped the table lightly with his gavel, and the room fell silent. In the moment, while Palmer waited before starting to speak, they could hear the soft hoofbeats of a horse in the dust of Front Street, tinkling laughter as a party of girls passed under the open windows, and somewhere in the far dusk the lonely whistle of a train.

There was a half-hour of business discussion, the finishing up of odds and ends of convention affairs, a standing affirmative vote on the question of calling the meeting officially the Republican State Convention instead of the Anti-Nebraska State Convention, as it had been originally. The convention also voted, on motion of Kersey Fell (Jesse's younger brother), to pay Delegate Lincoln's expenses to the national convention at Philadelphia, Lincoln having pleaded that he could not afford to pay his expenses out of his own pocket.

The crowd had grown a little restless, and Palmer rapped for quiet. Palmer cleared his throat.

"Gentlemen," he began, his voice rumbling across the low-ceilinged room, "our business draws to a close. We are agreed on our purposes; our nominations are the best, I believe, that we could possibly name. Only one thing remains to be done before you return to your own neighborhoods to expedite and build the future of the organization we have begun here. All of you know, of course, that Mr Lincoln has been named to head the national portion of our ticket, and of course all of you know Mr Lincoln himself. His position being what it is, several of us have asked him to address us here tonight. To sum up, so to speak, the position of the Republican party in regard to the national questions confronting us. We have already put this position in writing, of course, but we believe Mr Lincoln can emphasize and point them with words better than we can in cold print. Gentlemen, Mr Lincoln."

There was a scattering of applause as Lincoln got to his feet. He was taller than any other man in the room, with the possible exception of John Wentworth, but on the raised platform and against the bare background of the wall he seemed to be taller than anyone had ever remembered him. His clothes were a little disheveled, as though he had slept in them, and his face appeared white and drawn. But his eyes were luminous, dancing, eagerly alive.

"Mr Palmer and you gentlemen," he began slowly, "do me too much honor. However, I will say to you now what is strongest among my convictions upon these matters we have been considering here."

His voice was quiet, unimpassioned, unrhetorical, and he stood almost at the rear of the platform, holding in his left hand a little white card upon which he had apparently jotted some notes.

Ransom saw William Herndon, at a small table to the left of the platform, busily making notes, hardly looking at the tall man who towered above him.

And now Lincoln spoke of Kansas, of slavery, of the United States, of constitutional rights—and of the rights of man. His voice when he began had been low, controlled; but now it rose a little, its tones beginning to ring with passionate indignation. The crowd was deathly quiet, held in the grip of his contagious intensity. Here and there men moved silently into the vacant seats up front, fearful of missing a single word.

The speaker had gradually come forward to the front of the platform, and now as he drove home his first point, reached his first dramatic, the crowd came to its feet as one man, roaring its approval. Lincoln bowed slightly, made a peculiar gesture with his right hand and walked to the rear of the platform as he glanced at his card of notes.

Then his voice was filling the room again, and again there was the same dead quiet. Men leaned forward unconsciously, some of them with their arms on the backs of the chairs in front of them.

Ransom saw Herndon, his head bowed and his arms folded across his chest, the pen and note paper fallen on the floor and forgotten now.

Lincoln held them spellbound in the grip of his voice, swaying them as he would, like a field of wheat under the wind, lifting them cheering to their feet and again and again chilling them to dead silence.

Then, after an hour, the end:

"We won't go out of the Union, *and you shall not!*"

The room rocked with the cheering and applause, and the chairs were knocked madly in all directions as men surged forward toward Lincoln. On the platform Lincoln was smiling a little wanly and mopping his face with a huge handkerchief, trying to shake all the proffered hands at once. The room was a bedlam of talk and shouts, and men smiled happily, not altogether sure what they were so happy about.

Ransom spoke to Judd: "I'll be taking the boy on home, Norman. You'll be over?"

"Yes," Judd said, "in a little while. Be busy here for perhaps half an hour."

"All right. Bring anybody you want to. Maybe you can get Spot to come out with you."

"I'll try to get him, but I doubt he'll come. You know how he is, John."

"I know," Ransom agreed. "But ask him, anyway."

He let the horses walk as they drove homeward under the overhanging branches of Washington Street. The horses knew the way alone quite well, and Ransom was thinking. He didn't give a tinker's damn about politics on the whole, and yet . . . and yet tonight he had been moved beyond anything he could explain. It was strange.

"It was pretty exciting," Blair said into the stillness, startling Ransom from his thoughts.

"Yes," John agreed. Then suddenly he said, "Son, remember this night as long as you can. Remember what Lincoln said, but mostly remember the way he said it."

"Why?" Blair asked curiously.

"I don't exactly know," his father answered slowly. "I wish I could tell you exactly why. But I think that by the time I can explain it to you, you will know for yourself. But remember."

They drove on through the dust, their nostrils filled with the smell of the blossoming prairie.

v i

Time moved slowly.

On Front Street, Dr Schroeder took time off from his vineyards to deliver a daughter for Amanda and Hugo von Elsner. Hugo beamed, bought cigars and set up the drinks and insisted, over Amanda's weak protests, on naming the mite Marie Eugenia. Amanda wanted to name her Dorothy or Mildred or some other nice name like that, but after a couple of arguments the baby was duly named Marie Eugenia.

It sounded foreign, some of the folk said, but it stuck nevertheless, for Hugo was a stubborn man when his mind was made up.

That was the first day of June.

And about three weeks later, a doctor, a newcomer to Everton, who lived a block south and a block west of Major's Hall, on Main Street, hunted up Dr Harmon. It was a matter of professional courtesy.

Dr Harmon duly attended the birth of his colleague's son and, apparently, did a good job of it.

That boy the proud parents named Elbert Green Hubbard, though in after years the boy dropped the Green part of it and, sometimes, added a "Fra" in front of the Elbert.

But that was in another world.

VII

They had of course given Allin the seat of honor at the long table in the Ashley House ballroom; but he hadn't felt comfortable in it all evening.

Allin, who had in fact founded Everton, nursed it, literally fed it from the meager stock of food on the shelves of his first store. Allin, who had watched it grow—and in the end grow away from him.

The food now was almost demolished. Jim sat picking over his plate, wondering if he shouldn't eat a little something more, just to show his appreciation if nothing else. It had, he reminded himself, been a fine dinner even if he hadn't eaten much of it. Somehow he never seemed to have much of an appetite these days. And that blasted arthritis—it would keep the Devil himself from getting around like he wanted to. His legs bothered him a little now; he couldn't keep his mind on the cheerful conversation around him at the table.

"Well, Jim," Fell said, leaning back comfortably and picking his teeth, "to me it doesn't seem like twenty-five years, it honestly doesn't. How do you feel about it?"

"Oh, I dunno, Jesse. To tell you the truth, most o' the time I ain't paid a hell of a lot of attention to them twenty-five years."

"Well, we've all been busy, I reckon," Fell said. "But sometimes it seems to me like it was only yesterday that I came to

[345]

Everton and found you keeping store and selling lots at forty dollars apiece, cash or credit."

Cash *or* credit, Allin thought. Mostly credit. He could look down the table and see at least two men, worth more now than he was, who had long since forgotten their verbal promises to pay. Well, he was past the time when it mattered much one way or another.

On Allin's right, young Orme spoke to him. "I know you remember Everton when it was only a wide place in the road, Mr Allin," he was saying. "I suppose it seems queer to realize that now we have two railroads running two trains a day through here."

"Yes," Allin agreed vaguely, "I guess you're right, Mr Orme."

We? Wide place in the road? Great God Almighty, there was hardly a road, let alone a wide place! There wasn't even a place for a team and wagon to turn around in until he had chopped one out of the timber. And suddenly, from some deep recess of memory, he recalled the night Sylvester Peasley had come to the store after a sack of corn, and through the deepest snow Dane County had ever seen. Yes, he remembered now, that damned Sylvester had never paid him for the corn. Well, no matter now. Sylvester had long since gone to another debtors' court.

Doctor Hobbs was on his feet now, pulling down the points of his fawn-colored vest and clearing his throat.

"Gentlemen," he began, "it is my pleasure and privilege to introduce the speaker who will pay the tribute of all of us to our most honored guest, James Allin, the founder of Everton, our Everton, the Athens of the West. Every man here knows the debt he owes to Mr Allin as the first citizen of our little city, but I leave it to our speaker to give words to that deep feeling of gratitude. Gentlemen and fellow citizens of Everton, may I introduce our speaker, another of the fathers of Dane County and Everton?—Captain Tom Dawson."

There was a smattering of applause as Captain Tom got to

his feet and steadied his bulky figure against the edge of the table.

Allin looked down the table until his eyes came to rest on the high wide brow and straight, thin lips of Green—who looked as though he would rather go home than listen to Captain Tom. How well he remembered Green, remembered almost the first time he had seen him. It had been on that Fourth of July—or was it, now? Well, Green had always had some sort of ambitious drive that he, Allin, had lacked. At one time and another he and Allin had been short-time partners in a variety of ventures. Of course Green had never lost him a dime. At the same time, whenever Green had stumbled on a sure thing he'd known how to keep *that* to himself. And now Green lived in one of the finest mansions between Chicago and Springfield while he, Allin, still lived in the cottage he had built on Laurel Street twelve years before.

Captain Tom paused for breath. He was as old as Allin and had been in or around Dane County and Illinois for as long. After a helpful dose of brandy smash he again picked up the thread of his discourse.

"For nearly thirty years have some of us here sojourned in this magnificent prairie state. Thirty years ago the deer roamed over these Western wilds seldom disturbed by the crack of the huntsman's rifle, the mink and otter reveled at their own sweet will amid the primeval frog ponds, and this fair young city was still the unborn dream of our esteemed colleague and fellow-citizen, James Allin."

Allin didn't pay much attention to the burst of applause which occurred here; he had been thinking of something else. He leaned over and whispered to Fell: "Jesse, what in hell ever become o' that load o' books you and me and Doc Henry bought that time to start a library?"

Fell grinned a little. "I haven't the slightest notion, Jim."

"Doc Henry," Allin thought, remembering. "By God, *there* was a man."

"Thirty years ago was heard the music of the goose and the

sandhill crane. Thirty years ago the bear and the panther reared their hopeful cubs where the seat of justice now stands. Thirty years ago the musical howl of the prairie wolf arose on the stilly night where now the chords of the pianos trill sweeter than the fabulous harp of Tara. Thirty years ago the rattlesnake and the copperhead, the blueracer and the *massasauger* wound their sinuous tortuous coils among the reeds and grass and rushes. Thirty eventful years have passed since then, and here we stand, my friends, amid the crash of bottles and the wreck of breaking glass. I see you gentlemen before me, who have witnessed these changes, suffered from them, helped them come to pass. I see you, my friends, all lit up with Rhine and sherry wine and good fellowship, and though the sun should be darkened and the moon refuse to give her light, we should be enlivened by the beverage within.

> "Though planet worlds around us whirl,
> And solar systems crash,
> We still will punish sherry wine
> And drink the brandy smash."

It wasn't as good an ending as might have been most appropriate, considering the teetotalers present—Fell, Allin himself, Doctor Hobbs, and at least three preachers. Captain Tom, however, was neither a teetotaler nor a diplomat, but an after-dinner speaker, and he treated matters as he thought best. Everybody seemed well enough satisfied.

After that Fell spoke briefly, and Green and John Moore both added their bits.

Then, when the gathering was breaking up, Merriam brought a stranger over to where Allin still sat at the table. The small, worn-looking stranger looked closely at Allin and smiled a little uncertainly.

"An old friend of yours, Mr Allin," Merriam boomed. "Surely you remember Billy Hill, editor of Everton's first paper? You ought to. They tell me you helped hire him. I didn't get a chance to bring him around before dinner, and he just got into town this morning."

Allin peered at the old printer's lined, discouraged face and put out a hand.

"By God, Billy, it *is* you. Well, I'm damned. You're the last man I'd expected to see here this night. How in the world are you?"

"Pretty good, considering," Hill admitted. "Getting up in years, same as yourself."

"What brought you to Everton again, man? Let's see, why, it must be twenty years since you left."

"Yes, almost that. Well, Jim," Hill said, just a little sheepishly, "to tell you the truth I came to Everton looking for a job. Merriam's taking me on—foreman of his job plant."

"I see," Allin said. Good God, Hill must be older than he was. "But where in the name of seven devils have you been, Billy?"

Hill shrugged, remembering, too. Where hadn't he been?

"Oh," he said, "a little of everywhere. I was in California when the first gold news broke, but it didn't get me anything but pick-handle blisters and a stretch of pneumonia that nearly finished me off. For six years now I've been editing papers and gradually working my way back East again. And here I am."

"Yep," Allin agreed, "here y'are. I guess the old town don't look very natural to you. Well, Billy, come over to the house first chance you have an' we'll have a real gab fest. Any time. I guess 'most everybody knows where I live, an' I'm practically always there."

Then Fell came over to greet Hill, and Allin's oldest boy John came to help the old man out to the rig in front of the Ashley.

It had been a fine evening, but now that it was over it didn't seem as exciting as Allin had thought it would be. Still, it was nice of them to remember him. . . .

The weekly edition of the *Whig* carried a column about the affair, written probably by Merriam himself. The last paragraph, whether Merriam had so intended it or not, told more about James Allin and his affairs than all the other words together:

It must have been a proud day to Mr Allin to meet so many old friends and neighbors, not one of whom bears the slightest grudge against him, and to listen to such eloquent and appreciative tributes to his lifelong public spirit. With all his opportunities for building up a large fortune, Mr Allin's valuable lands slipped from his hold in one way or another, to parties who could not or would not pay much for their lots, and to parties who afterwards speculated upon the rise of town lots, until when property became really valuable he had little left to sell. He, however, acquired a comfortable competency, so that his old age is pleasantly passing in the midst of a community he took such pride in drawing together. A more grasping man would have so hesitated to sell property that settlers would have been driven away, and a less honorable man, if he had made more money, would have had fewer friends in his old age. Everton owes a debt to Mr Allin which it can never repay.

V I I I

From the C. & M. depot Moore took one of Ed Murray's hacks as far as Charley Bower's cigar store. There he dismissed the hack, went inside and asked for six El Sols.

Charley came out of the back office and said, "Oh, hello, John, glad to see you. I thought you were settled in Springfield for the winter."

"Well," Moore said, "so did I. But I dunno. Things being what they are, I just thought I'd run up home for a day or two."

"Yeah," Bower said sympathetically (he had voted the straight Republican ticket), "I know how you feel, John. By God, I don't understand it. People going crazy about these radicals, I guess."

"I guess so," Moore said heavily. "But then, that's the way it goes. Just put these El Sols on my bill, Charley. I've got a box in my desk, but I forgot to bring enough with me. See you later."

"So long," Charley said.

When Moore was safely outside on the wooden walk, Bower

said to his assistant, "There y'are, Al. Just goes to show you. Moore didn't say a word about the beatin' he took. I guess he just can't understand it. The hell with these politicians, I say. Moore's held the state treasurer's job too long, anyway."

"Well," Al said cautiously, "I guess he did well enough in the job. Nobody ever said he wasn't honest. Jim Miller an' the Republicans said he was an Englishman, but they never said he wasn't honest."

"What's that got to do with it?" Bower demanded, a bit heatedly. "They proved Moore was an Englishman, didn't they?"

"Well, I reckon you might put it that way," Al said. "After he'd been senator and lieutenant governor an' army colonel an' state treasurer, they found out he was an Englishman. You got to admit these Republicans are smart, all right."

"Sure. That just goes to show you who can worm their way into office in this country."

"I reckon you're right," Al said diplomatically. "When did your folks come over here, Charley?"

Bower looked at his clerk steadily. "What's that got to do with it?" he demanded.

"Oh, nothin'," Al said. "Nothin' at all. I was just sayin', that's all. But old John Moore come over here when he was twenty-four years old, an' he's only lived in Dane County for twenty-six years now. Course, he's older than that; just sixty-three now. He was lieutenant governor for six years, too, before he resigned to join up with the army as a private."

"You seem to be a pretty well informed young Democrat," Bower said nastily. "But let me tell you something, as far as the treasurer's office is concerned I'm for an Everton man, Jim Miller, and I'm for Spot Lincoln an' Bill Bissell, come hell or high water."

"Sure," Al said, "that's all right. I was just sayin' about old man Moore. Seems like a dirty deal, that's all."

"Well, he got as good as he sent," Charley said. "Time to pass the jobs around."

"Maybe so," Al said. "I was gonna tell you—we'll need some more El Sols pretty soon."

"All right," Charley said. "I'll attend to it."

From Bower's cigar store John Moore went into the Ashley House bar and had two drinks. Just two. The bartender was friendly, but John didn't say much.

It was early yet—only two-thirty in the afternoon—and he would have time to see Merriam and still get out to the home place with one of Trimmer's rigs. No one knew he was coming; otherwise the hired man would have been in Everton to meet him when he got off the train.

Around the corner on Main Street he climbed the stairs to the office of the *Whig* and found Merriam buried behind the stack of papers and junk on his desk.

"Have a drink, John," Merriam said, proffering a bottle from a desk drawer.

Moore waved it away. "No, thanks," he said. "I just dropped in for a few minutes. Couple things I wanted to talk to you about."

For a few moments old Billy Hill came over, and he and Moore talked, remembering incidents rather than each other, and Moore was unaccountably relieved when he went back about his business.

Then John came to the point. "I just wondered if you had the final figures," he said to Merriam.

"Yes," Merriam said, "I just finished this morning, John." He took a sheet from one of the stacks of conglomerate papers on his desk and gave it to Moore.

The older man studied the figures for a few moments and then silently handed it back. He sighed vaguely. Of course he knew the story the figures told; he wasn't really interested in the numbers as such.

"Well," he said, "I reckon all of us took a pretty beating— all but Douglas' candidate for President."

"I'm afraid so," Merriam agreed. "All of us did, John—

Whigs and Democrats alike. You know as much about it as I do. What the answer is, I don't pretend to know."

Merriam looked down at the figures heading the lists on the sheet he held in his hand. He saw: Buchanan, 105,000; Frémont, 96,000; Fillmore, 37,000.

"My God, John," Merriam mused, "just look at those figures. The state stays Democratic on the presidency by nine thousand out of two hundred and thirty-eight thousand votes cast. It doesn't seem possible. Well, it just goes to show you how strong Steve still is here at home. When he came back to Chicago last spring I didn't think he had the chance of a snowball in hell, nor did very many others."

Moore shook his head. "I can't see it that way, Merriam. You say Steve is still strong. I say he just got by on the skin of his teeth. He carried the state for Buchanan and lost every other office on the state ticket to the stinking, nigger-loving Black Republicans."

"Next time it will be different, John."

"Yes—worse. Douglas is going down, mark you what I say. Lincoln's coming up. I've seen it happen before, Merriam. Remember, I've seen twenty-five years of politics in this state."

"Bah!" the editor snorted. "Spot Lincoln couldn't carry his own precinct for dogcatcher."

Again Moore shook his head. "You're still wrong, Merriam. Lincoln an' Douglas didn't even have their names on the ticket, and yet they almost fought this election out between 'em. Lincoln is the only man in politics that Steve's afraid of. I don't think he ought to be, but he is just the same. He's never said so in so many words, but he has admitted that Lincoln's the man to beat."

They talked awhile longer, and then Merriam said, "Well, I thought you were in Springfield, John. What brings you home?"

Moore shrugged, not wanting to explain too much of what he felt to Merriam. "So I was in Springfield," he said. "But I didn't feel so good. I thought I'd come home for a few days and rest up."

"Good idea," Merriam agreed. "You ought to take better care of yourself, John. How's things with the I.C. these days?"

"All right, I guess." At the moment Moore really didn't give a damn about the affairs of the Illinois Central, the fact that he was one of its trustees notwithstanding.

"I can give you a copy of these figures if you want 'em," Merriam offered.

"Never mind." Moore waved a pudgy hand. "The hell with the figures. I know what they add up to; that's all I need. Send a boy down to Trimmer's and have a rig brought around here, will you? I want to go home, and none o' my folks know I'm in town. Tell that boy to hop to it—I want to be out home by suppertime."

"Sure, John," Merriam said. Then, "Pete! Pete, get the hell out here. Mr Moore wants you to go on an errand around to Trimmer's livery stable!"

A half-hour later Moore was jogging southward in one of Trimmer's buggies with a stableboy at the reins.

Moore said little to the boy, a country lad much impressed by the fact of driving such an illustrious personage. Moore was thinking; in fact he wished he could stop thinking. He had never been much given to introspection as such. The day had almost always presented its own problems, its own facts, its own solutions. But here was something different, something that was beyond ordinary comprehension. He could understand defeat, honest defeat. In politics that was nothing new. It was, rather, axiomatic. But this year it had been different. Even Douglas was unable to explain it—Douglas the omniscient. Douglas hadn't, really, attempted to explain. He had, rather, apparently chosen to ignore some facts which had seemed obvious to a number of good, loyal Democrats. Douglas had shaken his big head and said, "No matter. It's nothing. Spot Lincoln and a lot of backwoods radicals. It doesn't amount to a damn."

The campaign had been fought bitterly at every step, with the Douglas forces in general taking the aggressive side. It hadn't mattered. Bissell was governor—or soon would be—and Jim Miller, that damned shaking Presbyterian, was treasurer of the state of Illinois.

Of course Moore had known all that when the election returns were reported in Springfield. But still he hadn't quite believed it. And suddenly he had wanted to go home. Now that he had talked to Merriam and a few others he knew how it was. Most of all, it was final.

The buggy lurched along over the half-frozen clay of the rutted road, and a couple of times Moore cursed the alleged clumsiness of the boy beside him.

Englishman, eh? *That* was the thought which rankled as much as anything. At least he had been born in a place that could be identified and not, as had been most of the politicians who were his colleagues, in a wagon box somewhere between Goose Flat and Sucker Creek. Englishman: that was the strange epithet his opponents had applied to him, and it had beaten him. Well, rather an Englishman than a damned Black Republican.

Occasionally, and without thinking much about it, he noticed the rich autumn foliage which was still lush along the roadsides. And he remembered that he was home now, where he had wanted to be when he had left Springfield. Not quite, but almost, and he felt a little better in spirit.

Again he fell to thinking about Douglas and what the Little Giant had said about the election, and aloud Moore said, "Blast him to hell."

"Who?" the stableboy asked curiously, and Moore snapped, "Tend to your driving there, boy. When I want you to ask fool questions I'll tell you."

An Englishman, eh? And now he was remembering the twenty-six years that he had lived in Illinois and Dane County. He remembered a time when Douglas was state's attorney and John Stuart had moved to have a case dismissed because Douglas had not written the name of the county correctly. Douglas had admitted that he might be wrong but insisted that

Stuart prove his point. So the court sent for a copy of the statutes which covered the Dane County enabling act, and Douglas and Stuart were equally chagrined to learn that they were both wrong. Well, he, John Moore, had lived in Dane County before Steve Douglas had even heard of it. Twenty-six years in which he had been, respectively, justice of the peace, state representative, state senator, lieutenant governor, lieutenant colonel of the Fourth Illinois Volunteers, state treasurer, and now—an Englishman without portfolio.

The rig lurched on through the dwindling sun of afternoon, and he kept seeing the sword which hung above the mantel in the old square house at Randolph Grove, the sword bearing the words which were engraved upon his mind as deeply as they were upon the bright steel:

Presented to Lieutenant Colonel John Moore by the state of Illinois for his service during the late war with Mexico and especially for his gallantry at the battle of Cerro Gordo.

CHAPTER FIFTEEN

1858

B Y THE GODS, SPENCER," Jim Robinson said sharply, "a man don't know which way to turn with you transportation people. You promise the world with a fence around it, and what do we get? Nothing. I've tried steamboats and I've tried railroads, and I don't know which is the worst."

Spencer smiled genially. Men usually admitted that he had a way about him. "There's a great deal in what you say, Mr Robinson. Still, I can't quite understand your prejudice against us railroaders."

Robinson threw up his hands in surrender. "Prejudice? Great God, Spencer, I'm not against railroads in general or yours in particular. I have to ship goods almost every day if I expect to stay here in business. But I do object to you people running roughshod over us little fellows who can't protect ourselves—and then coming around to ask us for more business."

Spencer still smiled. "I'm not exactly sure what you're driving at, Mr Robinson. Do you mind stating your point precisely? But first, let me admit something to you. I've been operating head of the C. & M. a comparatively short time, and there's still a lot I've got to learn about the business. So you see, I'm honestly interested in your ideas."

Robinson eyed him narrowly. Such candor was certainly disarming. Well, he didn't owe the C. & M. anything, and he'd heard that this Spencer was a shrewd young fellow. It was said that Spencer had been put in charge of the C. & M. by one of the road's chief creditors, who had been forced to take a hand in the management of the road in order to protect his heavy stake in its financial affairs. Spencer had lived in Everton several years now and was generally liked, though he was not often seen in town, spending a large part of his time up or down the road between Chicago and Alton, the southern terminus of the road.

"All right," Robinson said, "I'll tell you a thing or two. Take this, for instance. Suppose I buy a thousand dollars' worth of dry goods from Carleton & Dunn in New York. They start the goods to me over the New York Central and the N.Y.C. wrecks a train and ruins my goods. What happens then?"

"Well, you naturally file a claim for the amount of your loss."

Robinson laughed sarcastically. "Yes, after I find out what happened to my goods, and when, and how much. Hell, man, it may be three or four months before I can even find out that something *has* happened to my goods."

"I see," Spencer said. "And then you file your claim?"

"Yes, I file it, and then *hope* that I'll get something out of it. But if the New York Central, after three months' more delay, allows me three hundred dollars on my thousand dollars' worth of goods, then I'm lucky. Railroads—hell!"

"But you can file suit to recover your just dues," Spencer objected.

"Yes, I can sue in the state of New York if I'm fool enough, which I'm not. I can't sue the New York Central in an Illinois court, and how can any ordinary merchant like me afford to go to New York to sue a railroad which will beat me anyway? You surely know all these things, Spencer."

"I guess I do," Spencer said slowly. "But you know how it is —you know a lot of things, but often you don't seem able to add them together. Do you know how long it takes to go from here to New York, Mr Robinson?"

The merchant shrugged. "Not exactly. Four or five days, I suppose. Maybe six, depending on connections. Why?"

"Then why should it take ordinary freight three or four months to travel that same distance?"

"I'm no good at silly riddles. That's you railroad people's private mystery, not mine."

"Exactly, Mr Robinson. You'd say offhand that a man would be a damned fool to operate his business like the average railroad operates, wouldn't you?"

"I've already said worse than that a great many times. So have a lot of other people; but none of it seems to get us anywhere. The railroads were political organizations in the first place. They depended on political intrigue for government support, and now they operate under government protection but without being responsible to anybody."

"They're in business to make money," Spencer murmured.

"Certainly," Robinson answered, a little heatedly, "and so am I. So is Jack Darling, who usually teams my water shipments over from Pekin. But Darling's got a little pride in his business, too. I know that he'll get my goods to me as soon as is humanly possible, and that if he doesn't he'll have a good reason and tell me what it is. But if I ask their lordships at the Illinois Central why I haven't got a couple of cases shipped to me from Chicago three or four weeks ago, why, I'm told to go to hell—and not even told politely. There's nothing I can do about it. No, Spencer, better get something to talk about before you ask for more business. As long as I can I'll ship from the East as I've always done—New York via New Orleans and St Louis and up the Illinois to Pekin."

"Under the circumstances I think you're quite right, Mr Robinson," Spencer said, rising to go. "But you may change your opinion. Once in a while, you know, one of us railroaders gets an idea."

Robinson walked with him to the front of the store.

"I understand the senator is honoring us with a visit sometime in the near future."

"Yes," Spencer said. "We have orders for a private car for his party from Chicago next week. But you're not a Douglas admirer, Mr Robinson?"

"No," Robinson said shortly, "I am not. But he'll bring a crowd to town, no doubt. I voted for Hale and Frémont, and I'll vote for Lincoln if I get the chance."

"Well, even as a convinced Democrat I can't quite stomach every idea of Douglas'," Spencer said. "Sometimes his logic is very, very foggy. But surely, with all his faults, he's a more able man than this fellow Lincoln. What does a man like Lincoln know about national affairs?"

Robinson grinned maliciously and spat on the wooden sidewalk. "Well," he drawled, "what, on your own admission, do you know about railroads? And yet you're running one."

"*Touché,*" Spencer said, and bowed. "You give me food for thought. Thanks for your time, sir."

Robinson waved a farewell and went back to his office. He decided he liked this Hamilton Spencer.

During the next couple of weeks, at his office in the C. & M. depot and elsewhere, Spencer did a great deal of thinking. What Robinson had told him was not exactly new, but somehow it had brought his thinking to something approximating a point of application.

Three years before, when one of his father's friends had become interested in the C. & M. and offered him the place as operating superintendent, he had known nothing whatever about the practical details of railroading. And only Spencer himself knew how much he still had to learn; how much, for that matter, everyone else in railroading would have to learn if railroads were to continue to be going concerns. For one thing, he had yet to see more than a handful of responsible men who were more than mildly interested in making the roads serve their first purpose—transportation—with any intelligence. Here and there little men in the business—engineers, brakemen, telegraphers, shop foremen, ticket agents—had ideas. But as usual they didn't count. To most of the railroad heads a railroad was a device with which you could borrow money, sell bonds and unlimited stock, and sweat shippers for all and more than the traffic would bear. When the juice was completely squeezed from a particular road it went bankrupt, and another group of men brought it new life and started the process all over again.

At the moment, of course, the C. & M. was Spencer's particular worry. The crop failure of 1856 plus the general panic of 1857 had brought the fortunes of the C. & M. to a very low point indeed. At one time the receipts of the road had dropped to a mere $27,000 per month, while the very best Spencer could do with the expenses was $117,000 for the same period. Things now, in the summer of '58, were much better, but not enough better to make the road a paying proposition.

Something was going to have to be done, and at the moment Spencer didn't have the least idea what it might be.

But three weeks after he talked with Robinson he went to six of the most important merchants in Everton with an idea. At first they laughed at him and were inclined to think he was joking. Two dollars per hundred freight from New York with delivery guaranteed in two weeks? Ridiculous. Preposterous.

"All right," Spencer said doggedly. "I'll put it in writing, and if I can't deliver as agreed I'll deliver it to you for nothing."

They looked at each other, wondering. Certainly it sounded impossible. But then, as Jim Robinson said, what did they have to lose?

II

At the C. & M. depot the crowd milled about impatiently. On the hastily built wooden bandstand Hohman & Hastings' Silver Cornet Band blared lustily and between numbers cursed their scarlet wool uniforms. The July sun beat down unmercifully, and the Depot Saloon and Bert Kelly's did a rousing business in refreshments. With every toot of a switch engine in the yards to the north, outposts of small boys waved and shouted

AMERICAN YEARS

excitedly that at last she was coming, only to be disappointed
when the diminutive switch engine backed down the main-line
track with Engineer Charley Howell grinning from the cab
window and lifting a greasy hand in salute to the crowd.

George Schultz, snare drummer of Hohman & Hastings, took
up a collection and came back a few minutes later bearing a
foaming bucket from the cool taps of the Depot Saloon. The
band emptied the huge bucket with a draught around and with
renewed vigor again blasted their way through "Hail, Co-
lumbia."

On the west side of the tracks, in an open space beyond the
close-packed lines of rigs, a surrey pulled up and stopped to a
softly spoken "Whoa, boys." Fell wrapped the reins around the
whip socket and wiped his face with a big white handkerchief.

Ward Lamon put his big feet on the dashboard and took off
his hat. "Hell of a crowd, Jesse," he observed.

Fell chuckled and mopped his forehead again. "Un-hunh.
I've seen bigger."

From the back seat Swett snapped, "Doesn't mean a damned
thing."

"Maybe not," Lamon said. "Maybe yes. You never can tell.
But most of 'em won't know what the hell Douglas is talking
about when he starts—or after he finishes."

"Swett's right," Fell said. "The same crowd 'd turn out for a
circus, only it 'd be bigger. You sure Lincoln 'll be on the train,
Ward?"

"Hell, yes, if he don't fall off somewhere," Lamon said. "I
told you he sent me a wire from Joliet."

And while they talked, the train puffed into the station, its
inverted funnel stack pouring hot smoke over the crowd, brake-
shoes squealing metallically as husky brakemen swung on the
brake wheels. At the rear of the train was the bunting-draped
private car of the Douglas party, and behind that a flatcar which
had been attached at Joliet. The flatcar mounted a small brass
cannon and two enthusiastic young Democrats who apparently
had orders to fire at will.

The crowd roared its enthusiasm as the Little Giant appeared on the rear platform of his car. Douglas hesitated a moment as the crowd yelled again and over his shoulder said something to Adele, his dark young wife, who stood just behind him. The cannon on the flatcar boomed again, and this time it was answered by the salvos of the Democratic cannon on the ridge above Bert Kelly's saloon. Douglas waved his broad-brimmed white felt hat and smiled tiredly. In the brilliant sunlight his swarthy face and long, dark hair stood out in startling contrast to the white hat and bright blue broadcloth suit.

Hohman & Hastings' finest were hastily deserting the bandstand and forming ahead of the carriage which had forged its way through the crowd and up to the steps of the Douglas car. Douglas was handing his wife into the carriage while he tried to talk with welcoming local Democratic dignitaries.

Ward Lamon stood in the dust beside a front wheel of Fell's rig, watching the front cars of the train. "There's Spot," he said to Fell. "I'd better get him; he might not see us, and he didn't know we were going to meet him here."

Lincoln's tall, weather-beaten silk hat towered above the heads of the crowd, and in a moment Lamon had him by the arm and was guiding him toward Fell's surrey.

Fell, holding the reins now to quiet the horses, watched them approach. Lincoln, taller than any other man in the crowd, his trousers unpressed and too short, was carrying an old carpet-bag and a battered umbrella, his loosely fitting alpaca coat flapping about his gangling legs. Somehow he seemed ridiculous beyond words. Yet Fell didn't laugh. But if he had, Lincoln would probably have laughed with him. Fell didn't. Instead he noted the broad brow, the laughing, yet infinitely patient eyes shielded by the craggy brows, the prow-like nose, the full underlip and the long, straight upper lip with its corners bent slightly downward. Fell had long since stopped worrying about the details of the man named Abraham Lincoln. It was like quibbling about the scenic details of Pikes Peak. Now he simply believed in him. Fell was a logical man, and yet for the life of him he couldn't have explained why he felt that way about this sad-faced, moody, changeling prairie lawyer. There were plenty of people who didn't believe in Spot Lincoln in any way, shape or form.

"Here, Spot," Lamon said, "get in back there with Swett, and I'll put your bag up here in front."

"Mighty fine of you-all to drive down here and meet me," Lincoln said, "but I'd 'most as soon walk. That train was pretty confining—full of Democrats and the stale smell of whisky and popular sovereignty. I don't think the ride did me any good."

He got into the back seat of the surrey and arranged his umbrella and the long legs beside Swett.

"Pull over to Grove Street, Jesse," Lamon said. "We'll get out of this damned crowd and won't have to trail Steve's circus parade up Washington Street."

"Oh," Lincoln said, "go on down Washington if it's handier, Jesse. I've been tailing Steve Douglas all the way down from Chicago—I might as well follow him on down Washington Street now."

"No, by God," Lamon exploded, "we've got better sense even if you haven't. I suppose you'll go to the Ashley as usual, Abe?"

"I reckon," Lincoln said. "I'm used to it, and it's used to me. Besides, the rates are reasonable."

"All right," Fell said. "But we want to talk to you, Abe. Will you come to my house for supper?"

"Now, Jesse! Why don't you-all come down to the Ashley and have supper with me? We can talk and then go on over to Steve's get-together without losing any time."

"All right," Fell agreed, without argument. "How about you, Ward, and you, Swett?"

Both of them agreed. Not one of them but would have—and often had—welcomed Lincoln to their homes for as long as he cared to stay. But no, Lincoln had quietly said that he would go to the Ashley House as usual, and they didn't argue with him. They knew it was no use. He would do as he chose.

1858

The surrey turned south and then eastward again into the tree-shaded dust of Grove Street. Lincoln took off his hat—it kept bumping against the surrey top—and held it on his knees.

"The Judge in town?" he asked Swett.

"Yes," Swett answered, "but he had some business to attend to and couldn't get down this afternoon. I'll get him over to the Ashley by suppertime or a little after."

"Good," Lincoln said. Then he leaned forward and tapped Fell's shoulder. "Say, Jesse, would you mind pulling up here at the next corner for just a minute or two?"

"Why, sure," Fell said. "Did you want to see somebody?"

"In a way," Lincoln said solemnly. "Doesn't John Harrison live in that little place there?"

"Yes," Fell said, a little mystified, "I think so. But he probably won't be home——"

"Makes no difference. I'll just presume on his friendship for a minute or so," the tall man said, getting down. "Be right back."

A little dumbly they saw him disappear around a corner of the white cottage, saw a sudden whisking of the curtains in a front window as someone peered out at the rig. From the east, the direction of town, they could hear the faint brassiness of the marching band and the dimly carried sound of voices. Lamon lighted a cigar and sat examining the remains of the sulphur match with profound curiosity.

At the side door of the cottage a plump woman in a fresh blue apron spoke to Lincoln as he came up through the grape arbor from the rear of the lot.

"Heavens, Mr Lincoln, I couldn't guess who it was for a minute there."

Lincoln doffed the weather-beaten hat and bowed. "How do you do, Mrs Harrison? How are all of you? I just stopped for a visit to—ah, to your rear premises."

"Oh, you're welcome, I'm sure," Mrs Harrison said, blushing faintly. "We're glad to see you any time, Mr Lincoln."

[365]

"Thank you," Lincoln said with vast dignity, and went back to the waiting surrey.

III

The two boxcars rolled down beside the wide doors of the freight house, and a tired brakeman pulled down the brake-shoes and locked them securely.

"Much obliged, Bart," Spencer said to the brakeman. "Nice job of spotting 'em."

Spencer watched Bart Haley head back toward the round-house, then turned back and looked again at the two boxcars. "You rocking bone-breakers," he said softly, "I guess that's the fastest ride you'll have for a long, long time."

Then he turned away and started the long walk out to his home on the East Side.

His tiredness seemed to bear him down like leaden weights, yet even so he would not have ridden if he could. He had just finished a bone-shaking, nerve-racking, fourteen-hundred-mile ride, and just to get his feet on familiar ground was restful. That ride had been, in a mild way, history making, though he thought, as he walked there in the moonlight, that he wasn't likely to be given a private page in history because of it.

Really, he thought, the feat didn't amount to much when you took the trouble to analyze it closely. Anyone *could* have done it—had he been able to overcome the inertia of the rail-roader's mind and seized upon the idea. Going over the facts now, Spencer saw that, so far as the C. & M. was concerned, he hadn't accomplished much. The tariff on two carloads of freight from Joliet to Everton, to be exact, for that was as far as the two cars had traveled on the C. & M. tracks. But his personal elation was because of something much more than that. He had moved two carloads of goods from New York City to the heart of Illinois in a space of time that made all previous records seem ridiculous.

The facts. Ten days before he had stood on the Hudson River dock of the People's Line in New York City, confronted by a huge stack of assorted packing cases, bales, crates and barrels, all addressed to firms in Everton. Then he hunted up a sign painter and had the words THROUGH FREIGHT; TRANSFER AT ONCE painted in big letters on each piece of goods. From New York to Albany he sat on a bale of woolen goods and read a tiny leather-bound copy of the *Poems,* by Theocritus; it was handy to carry and helped keep up his Latin. And at Albany, when a crew of freight handlers would have interred his cases in a warehouse tomb, he argued with and eventually cursed the Irish foreman until that worthy stomped away, yelling at his crew, "Come on, b'ys, leave the stuff lay there till it rots, an' serve him right. This bezabor is as mad as the Old Boy his- self." Two hours later sweating draymen were tossing the cases into two New York Central boxcars. At Niagara Falls a trans- fer to the Grand Trunk was to be made, but the cars themselves could not be transferred; the Grand Trunk's tracks were of a different gauge. However, the tracks of the two roads were parallel for a little distance, and after a bad half-hour with a couple of mystified and irate yardmasters, fresh cars were shunted alongside the N.Y.C.'s and the cases transferred to the Grand Trunk. He got started for Windsor, on the Canadian side, that same day, and at Windsor had his cars ferried across to Detroit. And at Detroit, in the person of a Michigan Central trainmaster, Spencer found an enthusiastic collaborator. The two boxcars were switched in between the engine and baggage car on a southbound passenger run, and again Spencer was blithely on his way. East of Chicago they dropped the freight cars out and moved them on over the "Joliet Cut-off," thus missing the terrible labyrinth of the Chicago yards. And as luck would have it, the C. & M. was of the same gauge as the Michi- gan Central. On the C. & M. at Joliet, Spencer's word was law; his freight rolled down to Everton behind its own private engine, with Spencer riding in the cab.

Now he was home again, more tired than he had imagined he could get.

His extra expense on the draying and transfers had been

almost as much as the C. & M. would realize on the shipment. But with his present satisfaction about his real achievement in freight transportation he was willing to forget all about that. He smiled as he tried to imagine the looks on the faces of his Everton consignees when he went around in the morning to tell them they could get their goods from the C. & M. freight house whenever they wanted them. Probably they wouldn't believe him until they saw for themselves. Most of them bought goods from New York on four months' time. This year they would probably have most of the stuff sold and delivered before they had to meet their obligations to the New York jobbers.

An unheard-of thing. His agile mind roamed over its possibilities. Why, good God, transportation could revolutionize the whole process of business if it would only use a little horse sense. Of course it wasn't really necessary to move most goods from New York to Illinois in ten days. That was a feat, a show stunt; he admitted it privately. But it could very easily be done in three weeks and without any driving effort. Even that would be incredibly different from the present system.

For some years now Spencer had been occupied with transportation schemes of one kind or another. But not until now, walking there under the setting moon, did he suddenly feel, suddenly understand, the epic possibilities of an America on wheels.

He had had a hand in setting up the stage route to carry the mail to California; that was one reason why he had been offered the management of the C. & M. He was first and foremost a lawyer, both by training and inclination, and yet circumstances had been such that he had scarcely practised his profession. Fate was always throwing him into something else. He had been an associate of Sam Farwell, one of the Erie Canal contractors; one of the directors of the Utica Cotton Mills; he had been connected with an optical company in Utica which had built, for Hamilton College, what had at the time been the largest and finest telescope in the world; he had been one of the organizers and first officers of the American Express Company. And yet it had always been more or less just business, a way of making money. Now he saw that it could be, if a man would make it so, a great deal more than a mere way of earning a living. Why, he was only forty-one! What could he not do if only he had the vision! And—at the moment—he was sure he had that.

The law? Yes, but he had not been actively engaged in the law since poor health had forced him to leave his father's office fifteen years before. He remembered those days in his father's office—it had been Spencer, Kernan & Spencer, and young Roscoe Conkling had been reading law in the office with him. Joshua Spencer's friends had been his son's friends: Aaron Burr, Daniel Webster, William H. Seward, James Kent, famous author of *Kent's Commentaries,* Horace Greeley, and Martin van Buren's wild son John. The law was almost a tradition in the Spencer family. Yet this was something better. Damn the law; here was something with the epic sweep of America herself.

Two weeks later he received a curt letter from the C. & M.'s new president. The letter very coldly and informally advised him that the board had new plans for the C. & M. which did not include Hamilton Spencer. Would he be so kind as to let them have his resignation immediately?

Men make decisions in the first flush of enthusiasm, and un-make them as quickly in moments of adversity.

So in the early fall Hamilton Spencer opened an office in downtown Everton, and shortly thereafter the Illinois bar discovered that it had gained a man who knew almost as much about chancery law as all the rest of the lawyers in the state together.

The railroads lost a man who might have been an organizing genius; the Illinois bar gained a master barrister.

IV

Summer moved into fall and the Second of November arrived, heralded by a cold slashing rain and the booming of Democratic cannon.

Illinois voted. A total of 190,000 votes for the Republican slate, 176,000 for the Democrats. Morally it was a Republican victory, technically it was not.

Jesse Fell walked slowly past the stores on the south side of the square. The afternoon shadows were growing long, and already lights were on in the stores. Occasionally Fell stopped and looked incuriously at the bright merchandise in the windows; Christmas was only four days away. But he was thinking now of something else. He turned and started across the street toward the lighted courthouse.

As he came to the middle of the street he saw the courthouse door open, and the tall man he was seeking came down the steps and across the yard toward him.

Fell spoke. "Just the man I wanted to see. Are you going anywhere special, Abe?"

"Nowhere special," Lincoln answered. "Just over to the Pike House to wash up a bit for supper. I'm going home on the evening train."

"Good. I want to talk to you. Let's go up to Kersey's office where it's warmer."

The tall man laughed softly. "All right. But I warn you now, Jesse—I won't be talked out of anything. I can't afford to let myself."

A spring wagon rattled past them on the frozen mud of the street, and Lincoln glanced at the bundled-up figure at the reins. The horse looked as though it were a stranger to oats. Lincoln chuckled and glanced down at Fell as Abe Brokaw's rig turned the corner at Main Street.

"Did I ever tell you about the time I collected a debt for Abe, Jesse?"

"I'm not sure. Somebody's always collecting for Abe, but mostly he does it himself. I remember the time he charged a farmer a nickel too little for a job of horseshoeing. He thought maybe the fellow hadn't left town, so he started out looking for him. He hunted for almost two hours and finally found the

[370]

fellow in Dorsey's saloon on South Main Street—and he collected the nickel."

Lincoln pulled the shawl closer about his shoulders and laughed aloud. "I believe it. You remember when Hen Drewry was sheriff, of course. He defaulted and went to Kansas or somewhere, you remember? Well, just before he left he'd collected a debt for Brokaw. Naturally he took the money with him. Abe got Steve Douglas to collect from Drewry's bondsman. Steve collected too—but he went to Washington and forgot to pay Abe. Of course by that time the old man was plumb boiling over. Then he got me to collect from Douglas."

"Did you?"

"Oh sure. John Wentworth was in the House then, so I wrote and asked him to get the money. It didn't amount to a hoot in a windstorm. Douglas raised hell, so Long John said; but he paid him."

"Douglas is one of the things I want to talk to you about, Abe."

"All right. But if you were anybody else I don't know whether I'd want to talk about him just now or not. Steve loaned me a hundred dollars once, Jesse."

"Well," Fell said a little impatiently, "you paid him back, didn't you?"

"Yes," Lincoln said, his face somber. "That was a long time ago."

Kersey was still in his office as they came up. He shook hands with Lincoln and pulled out a chair. Lincoln tossed the heavy shawl upon the table and put his hat on top of the shawl. Then he sat down and hoisted his feet up to the table top beside them.

"I'm going, Jesse," his brother said. "Just put out the lights when you leave, will you?"

Fell began:

"Listen to me, Lincoln," he said. "I've lately been as far east as Boston and up into all the New England states except Maine. I've been in Pennsylvania and New York, Ohio, Michigan, Indiana. And everywhere your name is mentioned, your name is known, you're being talked about. People say, 'Who is this man who is more than a match for the unbeatable Douglas?' Seriously, Lincoln, you're getting a national reputation through Douglas. Your speeches are being printed in the Eastern papers. But people don't know *you*. You're still only a name. If you're to be a formidable candidate for the presidency, you must——"

Lincoln had been sitting with his head bowed; now he snapped it upright and looked at Fell. "Wait a minute, Jesse," he said. "What's the use of talking about me for the presidency? What about Seward and Chase? What about Cameron? Look at my defeat here this fall. Can a man be elected President when he can't be elected senator? Poppycock, Fell."

"No," Jesse said. "You wait. Hear me out, Lincoln."

And for a quarter of an hour he talked on while Lincoln sat, uninterrupting. Fell spoke of Seward, and Chase, and Greeley, and Douglas, of Simon Cameron in Pennsylvania. He said Cameron was the strongest man in that state, and yet he couldn't carry it in an election. New York distrusted the political figures of Pennsylvania, and vice versa.

"Now listen," Fell went on, "I know the facts of your public life as well or better than any other man. I can write that portion of what I need better than you can. But I want you to write me the facts of your private life that I do not know exactly— where you were born and when, who your people were, your schooling; all that. You get what I'm driving at, I know. Will you do that for me, Lincoln?"

Lincoln sighed. "Much of what you say is true, Jesse. And I realize how much you have interested yourself in this matter. I appreciate the compliment you pay me. But I don't believe it. I'll admit I'm ambitious, Jesse; I'd like to be President. But I just don't believe I can be. I'm just not slated for such good luck. What does the Judge say?"

"Davis and Swett are both in hearty agreement with me in this thing."

"I see," Lincoln said slowly. "Ah, well, there's nothing in my early history that would interest anyone. The 'Dead Lion or the

Live Dog.' Remember that? Well, I'm afraid I'm not even a dead dog now, Jesse. No, I can't do it."

"Now, Lincoln," Fell expostulated, "listen to me. I know the election has left you with a bad taste in your mouth. But did you ever consider Douglas' election as, in the long run, your own good fortune? You're free now to operate in the field for 1860, unhampered by connections in Washington or else-where——"

"I'm going, Jesse."

Lincoln got up and wrapped the shawl about his wide shoulders.

"Good night," he said and started out the door.

Fell was just behind him. "No, Lincoln. Listen to me."

But the tall man was already halfway down the stairs.

"Well, when will I see you?" Fell called after him.

"Oh, I don't know for sure. But I'll be back in town around the first of the year."

Fell went back to get his coat and blow out the lamp, but for a moment he stood at the window looking down into the gloom of Washington Street. He saw the towering, shawl-draped figure as it came into the path of light cast by the windows of Chapman's Jewelry Emporium. Lincoln's head was bowed as though in melancholy thought. Then apparently someone in Chapman's doorway spoke to him. His face lighted up as he turned and nodded, and Fell could see the wide mouth moving as he spoke.

Fell chuckled and smiled complacently to himself. He knew Lincoln's moods of depression, his occasional lonely despondency. And just now he had good reasons for being depressed. All during the summer and fall Lincoln had neglected his office. Herndon was there, of course, but good God . . . Herndon. Fell knew how much "Billy" depended on "Mr Lincoln." Lincoln had spent all his available personal funds during the campaign—the Republican war chest had been pitifully meager —and now must try to pick up the threads of his lost business. And he had been defeated in this, his most important campaign so far.

But again Fell chuckled, for by nature he was both buoyant in spirit and patient. He could wait. They could not compromise too long with time, but the important moment had not yet come. He and Davis and Swett and Dubois and Medill had plans, plans not yet fully hatched, but well thought out, certain, in their minds, of being carried. Yes, they could wait a little.

He gathered up his coat and hat and blew out the lamp on the table. When he went outside, snow was falling in flakes like great, slow-flying moths, hiding the frozen, rutty mud of the streets and softening the bleak drabness of the square.

Passing the Argus Saloon he saw Hill Lamon buttoning his coat and drawing on his mittens, half smiling at the little group of men standing at the bar. Through the steamy windows Fell saw Lamon shake his head and turn toward the street.

Fell waited, and when Lamon came through the door, he said, "Hello, Hill. Going home?"

"Oh, howdy, Jesse," Lamon said, startled. "Yes, I am."

"I've got my rig over at Trimmer's. I'll drive you home if you want to walk over there first."

"I'd be glad to, Jesse. I didn't have to come down this afternoon—I haven't a damned case on the docket—but I wanted to see Lincoln for a few minutes. Better have stayed home, maybe. My wife is pretty sick, and I might have done some good there."

"So? Sorry to hear that. Did you see Lincoln?"

"For a few minutes." Hill nodded.

"Get any satisfaction out of him?"

"Not much," Lamon said gloomily. "But then, you know how he is. He was pretty low today. God knows, Jesse, he's got reason enough to be."

"I talked to him too, Hill. He'll be all right. Don't worry—I've known him longer than you have."

CHAPTER SIXTEEN

1859

Spencer stood at his office window, looking at the packed snow of the street but not really seeing it. His lips were drawn in a straight line as he turned and looked at the two men who sat waiting nervously on the edge of their chairs.

The big man with the heavy black mustache and the broken, greasy fingernails was Joe Burke, machinist. The fat man with the watery eyes was Al Kimler, a trainman. Spencer knew both of them, but only in a vague way.

Burke twisted his battered hat between his big hands.

"Well," Spencer said, "I understand a little more of the situation, now that you've explained it." He tried to smile. He did understand a little more of the situation, but not all of it, and he knew that neither Burke nor Kimler could tell him all of it. "After all," Spencer went on, since neither of them spoke, "you know that I have nothing whatever to do with the C. & M. When it changed hands they threw me out before they did anything else. Most of you kept your jobs."

"I know, Mr Spencer," Burke said, in a heavy voice. "But we figured you knew more about the road than anybody else, that maybe you'd sort of help us out."

Spencer smiled grimly. "I'm a lawyer. Did they appoint you to hire an attorney for the strikers?"

"No," Burke said, "we figure no lawyer 'd do us any good now. But when you was on the C. & M. you always treated us fair an' square. Some o' the boys thought you might give us a little advice or—or somethin'." His heavy voice trailed off to nothing.

"I see," Spencer said, and sighed.

The newspapers were full of the strike, had been for three days. The Chicago *Tribune* had carried a big story this morning, and here in Everton the *Western Republican* had been fretting and fuming.

On the C. & M. not a wheel moved. But the strike went away beyond that. Not only was there a strike, but the strikers had taken possession of every scrap of physical property the road owned, including the general offices here in Everton. (Spencer understood that a temporary office had been installed in the Pike House.) Only in Springfield was the depot in the hands of road officials. Ex-Governor Matteson was heavily interested in the road and had powerful friends in Springfield.

But the strangest thing of all was the reason for the strike. They were not asking to have their poor, scanty wages raised, bad as they were. Instead, they were demanding the *back pay* the road owed them.

"Tell me," Spencer said, "is this strike organized by this so-called Knights of Labor?"

"No, sir," Burke said emphatically. "We ain't got nothing to do with that outfit."

"Well, then, how did this thing get started? Somebody had to start it some place."

"The trainmaster in Chicago tried to take a train through after the boys up there finally refused to take out another run till they got paid. When the trainmaster got to Joliet the boys there jumped the train an' took it away from him. The word spread along the line—the brasspounders are in on it too—an' everybody jest seemed to figure the same way. That's how it was."

"I see," Spencer said again. It didn't seem possible, but it could be true. "And now that you've got the bear treed you don't quite know what to do with him. Is that right?"

The two of them grinned a little sheepishly.

"Sort of, maybe," Kimler admitted. "But the committee thought it 'd do us some good maybe if you'd tell us how the road stood——"

"You got your wages when I ran the C. & M.," Spencer said sharply, "and if you'd asked me a question like that then I'd have told you it was none of your damned business. But that was five months ago. Today I have absolutely no *knowledge* of the C. & M., financially speaking. I've heard rumors, but I don't *know* anything. Matteson is supposed to be the big gun in the road now. He could tell you."

"Well, he won't," Burke declared. "Matteson's hard as nails. He says he'll have us drove off by the militia."

"Yes, I imagine that in time he will. He's got everything on his side; you boys haven't a whisper of legal standing. The only thing that's helped you so far is the fact that you've stuck together and the road is strung out so far. That is, it's in twenty or more counties, and nobody knows where to start fighting you—and probably nobody wants to very badly."

"Listen, Mr Spencer," Burke said, "our families have got to eat. You know that. The storekeepers carried us as long as they could an' we went along with the road. But now they've cut us off an' we've got to do somethin'. They couldn't help cuttin' us off, neither. Most of 'em ain't rich. If the C. & M. pays us we'll pay them. We don't want no trouble."

"I know." And Spencer did know. He was quite familiar with the two-, three- and four-roomed shacks in the Forty Acres, and how much money it took to feed those hungry Irish stomachs.

"We ain't hurt as much as an oilcan," Kimler said. "We ain't harmed a thing. But they oughta settle."

"Now listen to me," Spencer said. "How long do you think you can hold out?"

"Three days—a week maybe," Burke said. "Who knows? When you're hungry you can wait—or you can't. It's hard to tell."

"All right. Then hold out. If Matteson can't get troops—and I don't think he can unless you begin raising hell—and he can't get the sheriffs to act, which wouldn't hurt you much anyway, then you've got them whipped. But don't take my word for anything—I'm telling you what I *think*. The reason is this: they've got to run the road or go flat broke. That I do know."

"How do you figger that?"

"Simple mathematics plus what I know personally about the present owners of the road. The C. & M. can't go out and hire a complete new set of help—oh, they could, but by the time they got trains running again they'd be bankrupt. And remember, if they can't, absolutely *can't,* pay you, then they can't pay anybody else, either. It's a question of bluff; you've got to outlast them. But, for God's sake, don't smash anything."

They nodded agreement.

Spencer opened a desk drawer and took out a bottle and glasses. "Have one to keep the chill off," he said.

"One more thing," he said when they smacked their lips and set the glasses on the table. "You told me when you came up here that you didn't want to hire a lawyer. Well, you didn't. Anything I've said is between us three. If you think it's worth anything you're welcome to it." He grinned boyishly. "I don't know if there is a law covering what you fellows have done, but they'd probably indict me for inciting to riot—if you do."

They shook hands gratefully in taking their leave, and in the hall Burke looked at Kimler and jerked a thumb over his shoulder. "A white man, Al," he said.

A little later, when Leonard Swett came in to discuss a chancery case which he had taken to Spencer, he found the latter still staring out the window. They talked of the fine points of the case for almost an hour, and then of this and that and the day's news. Spencer pointed a finger at the *Tribune* account of the C. & M. strike.

"Odd thing, that," he said.

"Yes," Swett agreed. "And a hell of a thing, if you ask me. These are strange times, Spencer."

"I'm beginning to think so myself. A man can't even imagine what's coming next. By the way, who's the opposing counsel in this suit?"

"Lincoln, I think, along with somebody else."

"Great Scott!" Spencer exploded. "Can't a fellow turn around in this part of the country without hearing that man's name?"

"Well," Swett said, smiling evenly, "you can now to a certain extent. But there'll come a time when I don't think you'll be able to."

II

Judge Davis shuffled some papers aimlessly while he cleared his throat.

"This court," he said, "is adjourned till ten o'clock tomorrow morning in consideration of the death of Mrs Ward Lamon, wife of our colleague at this bar. The funeral will be at three o'clock, and there will be carriages here at the courthouse for those members of the bar who wish to attend. As a mark of respect I suggest that the court attend in a body."

The gavel banged once, as though the Judge were weary of human affairs, and then the courtroom burst into a subdued babble of voices.

And that afternoon the Eighth Circuit bar stood in the bright April sunshine under the towering elms and oaks of the Everton cemetery and listened to the Reverend Mr Harlow read the Episcopal burial service for the wife of Ward Lamon.

She was a sweet woman, gone down to death in the midst of life, but, so far as that strange fraternity of the Eighth Circuit was concerned, she was the wife of that strange lad, Ward Hill Lamon.

Lamon, the Virginian in Illinois who was, perhaps above all

other men, the confidant of the lonely man named Lincoln. Lamon, the dandy, the swashbuckler, the banjo player who played and sang because he loved singing. Lamon, who could drink more liquor and carry it farther without spilling it than any other man on the Eighth Circuit. Lamon, he of the red silk dress sashes, the roached and glistening black hair and mustaches, the intrepid cavalryman's bearing, the second-rate lawyer and third-rate scholar. Lamon, who had moved to Everton from Danville, and whose footprints in Danville were to be walked in by a bright young man named Joseph G. Cannon.

They stood there, hats in hand—Davis, Swett, Orme, Linder, Whitney, Spencer, Weldon, Lincoln, Fell—remembering, each of them, while the Reverend Mr Harlow repeated the coldly beautiful burial service of the Episcopal Church and the squirrels chattered obliviously in the oak trees.

III

The bawling herd of cattle moved slowly up the lane past the house and on toward the timber beyond the barns. Dust rose in slow, drifting clouds, and occasionally the two women at the house could hear the cursing exhortations of an exasperated herder.

Cassandra Frink sat under a mulberry tree in the front yard, stringing Kentucky Wonders and watching the moving cattle with her bright eyes, the eyes which were sometimes the wonder of her friends; one of them was blue and one brown.

She was only mildly interested in the cattle herd as such. Ike had hired six extra men when this herd came up from a strange, far place called Texas, and she and Sally Thompson would have just that many more mouths to feed until Ike sold the cattle. So to Cassandra Frink, who theoretically owned a half-interest in this fortune on the hoof, it simply meant more work. She had heard Ike and a couple of the boys talking of the purchase, and she remembered vaguely that there were about 1400 head of prime beef cattle in the herd and they had cost something like

$64,000. She didn't *know* these facts, but she had heard Ike and the boys mention some such figures.

All morning now they had been driving the cattle over from the stock cars on the C. & M. siding at the Frink's Grove stop, and they would probably still be driving in late afternoon. In the meantime, there was dinner to be gotten for the boys and Ike and these six extra men.

Cassandra sat, breaking beans and rocking comfortably there in the cool shade of the mulberry tree. Occasionally she could see Ike, riding the bay mare and giving orders here and there as the herd moved onto the Frink land. Sally came out of the kitchen door and walked over to the shade tree where Cassandra sat. She was a big, husky country girl, good-looking in the manner of a blooded brood mare, a cheerful worker. There was a damp spot of sweat on the calico between her shoulder blades, and her blonde hair clung to the nape of her neck in wet ringlets. Cassandra looked at her sharply, arching her eyebrows. "Hot in there this mornin', Miz Frink," Sally said cheerfully. "Seems like I'll almost melt there in that hot kitchen."

"Hmmm," Cassandra said. "I been cookin' in there for thirty-odd years."

"Oh, I ain't complainin'," Sally said hastily. "I was just wonderin' about them pies, was all. Did you say make three or four o' them gooseberry pies, Miz Frink?"

"You got enough berries for four real full ones?"

"Yes'm."

"Make four, then—God knows they'll eat 'em fast enough."

"Yes'm. My, it's cool here under this shade tree." Cassandra peered sharply over her glasses. "Well, I reckon I'd better git back. It's near eleven."

Cassandra watched her go, watched the broad strong hips under the damp calico and the damp spot between her shoulders as the girl disappeared through the kitchen door. A pretty good girl, Cassandra thought, her hands working automatically in the pan on her lap. A little flighty, like all hired girls, but a tolerably good worker.

And, watching her, Cassandra remembered the time forty-six years before when she had married Ike Frink from her father's cabin near Fort Clark and moved to the new cabin in Frink's Grove. Her dowry had been a bed and a cow. Well, the cow had grown into such herds as this one going past the house now, and the bed—well, it had proved useful, too. In that cabin, and the larger one which had replaced it when the first one burned, they had bred eight sons and one daughter. All of them had been begotten in that bed, and all of them had been born in it. All of them had lived except Adam, and he had been twenty when he died. Strong boys and men they had been, all of them except Adam; like Ike himself, in a way, rocklike, impervious to ordinary hurts and complaints, stiff, unbending.

The Frinks were, so Cassandra had heard, the richest people in Dane County. As for Cassandra, she didn't know. Ike didn't explain to her, so she had no way of knowing how much they were worth. From time to time Ike had brought her papers to sign, and she had always signed them without question. Rather, she had always been a little proud of her ability to sign her name; what she had been writing it on hadn't much mattered. That was Ike's business.

Now in 1859 Ike owned, clear and in his own name, aside from what he had already deeded to the older boys, more than thirty thousand acres of the best land in Illinois. At a conservative price of forty dollars an acre the land was worth roughly a million and a quarter dollars. Their personal property—bank stock, cattle and hogs, cash, farm machinery—was probably worth another half-million. But these figures didn't mean much to Cassandra; she simply didn't comprehend them.

Cassandra was, in actual years, only fifty-eight. But she had lived at least seventy years, perhaps more than that. She had heard herself talked about as being wealthy, or as the wife of the wealthiest man in Dane County, but that too hadn't meant much to her. Sometimes Judge Davis or Mr Swett or Clifton Moore or Solomon Sturges from Chicago stopped by the house to visit, and she had remarked the respect in which they all seemed to hold Ike. But she had never connected that with money, either. They were honest and they paid their bills, and she knew that when she sent to town for a barrel of flour and a sack of beans or potatoes they got them without any quibbling on the part of the merchants.

Now Ike had been talking some about a new house. He had been talking about it for at least three years, but the hard times in 1857 had quieted him for a while. It would be a bigger, better house than any they had heretofore owned, perhaps the finest house in the county. Well, maybe not quite. There was the man-sion north of Everton which that mad Baron Rommel had built a year before the railroad came through. It was a huge feudal pile built on the bald prairie, with an eight-foot brick wall all the way around it. The baron had had the bricks hauled all the way from Chicago by ox team. No, it wouldn't be as big as that; but it would be two stories and a half high, with a veranda around the front and two sides. Ike was planning it, she knew that. And she would be thankful for the extra room, though now that the boys had married and moved out on their own farms the shortage of room wouldn't be as much of a problem as it had been.

But most of all Cassandra wanted a new silk dress. Nothing gaudy; something in decent brown or black silk would do very well, but it must be silk. If Ike was as rich as they said, surely they could afford a silk dress for her to wear to church on Sundays. She had always worn plain warm wool, and she didn't want to be unduly extravagant—if Ike couldn't afford it, why, that was quite all right. But she would like to have at least one before she was too old to enjoy it properly.

She finished the last of the beans and stood up, ready to take them into the kitchen, when she saw Ike ride up to the yard and lean from the saddle to reach the fastener at the gate. There was a powerful lot of cattle going up the lane today. Some sixty thousand dollars' worth, the boys had said at table. Maybe now would be a good time to ask Ike about the dress, see if they could afford it. She moved toward the house slowly, carrying the pan of beans in her wiry hands, waiting for him to catch up with her so she could ask him about it.

IV

In Illinois the corn was being heaped up in golden piles, and fall plowing was well under way. The frost lay white on the earth in the early mornings, and later the air was mistily blue with the illusive haze of Indian Summer.

The harvest was bountiful, and in Everton business was better than usual.

In the East times were not so good. Wages were low and labor conditions oppressive. The mill and factory and mine owners were as hungry for profits as their agrarian brothers in the Deep South. And in the South the flower of Southern chivalry went around with a club, bragging and looking for something definite to hit. It was very difficult for an ordinary man north of the Ohio River to follow the vituperative arguments of these gentlemen from the South. These latter gentlemen talked a great deal of red-hot and smoking political hogwash, but they publicly said very little, if anything, about the $200,000,000 they owed a number of gentlemen in the North.

On the surface the cloud of antislavery sentiment was as it had been for a long time, present but no larger than a man's hand. But slowly, very slowly, it was growing; the lightning was gathering, to strike the more terribly in the end.

And on the night of October 16th, at an obscure town in West Virginia, the Sword of Gideon again cut a swath that was to widen all the way across the country in a road of blood and disaster.

That was on a Sunday night, and on Monday most of America knew that old John Brown had moved eastward from Kansas and started another private crusade, armed with the iron zeal of a martyr and Sharps rifles.

When America read the name Harpers Ferry she also read two names that were to become more and more familiar as the

[384]

years moved on: Colonel R. E. Lee and Lieutenant J. E. B. Stuart. Lieutenant Stuart was lately from Kansas, and to be a target for Sharps rifles was no novelty for him. And he must have gotten a great deal of private satisfaction from the Harpers Ferry assignment, even though he was a cavalry lieutenant helping command a detachment of marines. For the lieutenant had heard of old John Brown and his family army before.

On the 2nd of December the state of Virginia publicly hung John Brown for the combined crimes of murder, conspiracy and treason, and he became in one half the public mind a dead and forgotten madman, in the other half a crucified martyr.

The cloud on the horizon of destiny grew a little larger.

Jesse Fell stamped snow from his feet as he came into the post-office lobby and spoke pleasant greetings to the men standing about discussing corn prices and the weather. He didn't ask the clerk if there was any mail. There was always mail—sometimes too much—these days. He simply walked up to the counter and waited while the young man gathered together a thick bundle of newspapers, magazines and letters.

He was carrying on a voluminous correspondence with many people in many places. Along with two copies of the New York *Tribune* he noted a letter from Greeley. He looked further and saw a letter from Joe Medill of the Chicago *Tribune*. Then his eyes lighted on a long envelope bearing a Springfield postmark. He pushed the other mail aside and tore open this last letter. How well he knew that crabbed handwriting! It began:

DEAR FELL:
Herewith is a little sketch, as you requested. There is not much of it, for the reason, I suppose, that there is not much of me. If anything is made of it, I wish it to be modest, and not to go beyond the material.

Fell smiled, his eyes wrinkling at the corners as he unfolded the two enclosed sheets of legal-size foolscap and again looked at the crabbed writing. Behind him, at the mail counter, people came and went; once someone spoke to him, but he paid no attention. He was reading, his brow furrowing occasionally as he deciphered a particular word or phrase.

I was born February 12, 1809, in Hardin County, Kentucky. . . .

Yes, Kentucky, the Dark and Bloody Ground.

Fell adjusted his spectacles, moved a little into a better light, and read on to the end of the second sheet.

. . . If any personal description of me is thought desirable, it may be said, I am, in height, six feet, four inches, nearly; lean in flesh, weighing, on an average, one hundred and eighty pounds; dark complexion, with coarse black hair, and gray eyes—no other marks or brands recollected.

Yours very truly,

A. LINCOLN

Fell folded the sheets carefully and placed them in an inside pocket of his greatcoat. Better see Davis about this, he thought, for this was more than a mere answer to his request of a year ago. It meant, too, that Lincoln was ready now to go along with them. Well, about time—the convention was to be in May.

He gathered up the rest of the mail and started for the street. "Merry Christmas, Jesse," someone called to him, and Fell responded, smiling.

Then he looked up and saw the whiskered likeness of Dr Fitchman gazing benignly down at him from the head of a gaudy calendar: December 21st. It had been a year to the day since he had asked Lincoln to write this autobiography. Well, life had a way of arranging itself in patterns like that, even if one couldn't always see the outlines at first glance.

CHAPTER SEVENTEEN

1860

In the still dusk of Front Street there was little sound beyond the occasional treble shouts of the children playing hide-and-go-seek on the vacant lots across from the Von Elsner cottage.

Amanda von Elsner hung up the dish towel neatly and came into the little parlor where Hugo sat with the *Western Republican* and a half-smoked cigar. He looked up as Amanda came in and laid the paper aside. Politics, always politics, that was all a man could read in the papers these days. He looked at his heavy silver watch.

"Where is Marie?" he asked. The "is" sounded vaguely like "iss." With Hugo it always would.

"With the Morgan children across the street, I think," Amanda said diffidently.

"So? It's time she was in the house here for her lesson. Besides, it is chilly out. This cold night air is no good for her throat."

"It won't hurt her," Amanda said. "She has other things beyond her throat."

"Yes?" Hugo said, rocking back and forth on his heels. "And what, please, is more important than her throat?"

"Oh, I know. But she's *so* small, Hugo. For such a baby you make her work so hard. It's not right she should practise so hard. You don't even know whether or not she has a voice, as you put it."

"Of course she has no voice. But she will have. I can *make* her a voice. The practice doesn't hurt her. She must get so used to it that she doesn't know it *is* work. Call her in," he said curtly.

"All right," she sighed. "But see that you don't keep her beyond the time we agreed on, Hugo."

"We will see."

He went to the square piano, still smoking the cigar, and softly played a few bars from the overture to Mozart's *Don Giovanni.* Outside, he could hear Amanda calling, "Marie! Marie, it's time for you to come in now." He played a little of a Schubert waltz and then stopped when he heard the child's footsteps on the porch. As the two came into the parlor he swung the piano stool around and grinned at Marie through his beard.

"So," he said, "you are here. Are you ready, Liebchen?"

The child—she was a sturdily built little girl with short pig-tails and a piquant, homely face—glanced at her mother for an instant and then nodded. "Yes, sir."

"Good. You will wash your hands and I will wait for you."

In a few minutes she came back and stood obediently beside the piano.

"Now," Hugo said kindly, "how does your throat feel to-night?"

"All right."

"First the scales, then."

Amanda sat under the lamp with her mending. From outside they could all hear the joyful shrieks of the other children, still at their games, though it was completely dark now.

"No, no," Hugo said, laying the cigar aside carefully. "The pitch, Marie. Too low. Once more now—just a little higher."

She had it now, perfectly, and for twenty minutes she sang the tiresome scales. She was just under four years old, and her voice was thin and piping. Yet it was true as a die in the intervals.

"Fine, fine, Liebchen." Hugo closed the exercise book and took down another book from the pile on top the piano. "Now once the Schubert 'Ave Maria,' then we try the hard one. How is that, eh?"

"All right," Marie said submissively.

They went through the "Ave Maria," and near the end her voice faltered badly. She was terribly tired.

Hugo looked at Amanda. "Maybe," he said sharply, "she should stay in after supper. She is tired, and she cannot sing when she is tired. No one can."

"Perhaps," Amanda answered. "But she also needs fresh air and exercise. You know what Dr Rogers said."

"Humph. She has all day for such as that. Now, Marie, we sing once through the hard one, the 'Caro Nome.' Just once. Eh?"

She smiled and nodded a little, afraid perhaps to say no.

". . . Gualtier Maldé . . . *nome di lui sì amato.*"

Again her voice faltered over the difficult phrasing, and she could not go on. She stood miserably silent, twisting small fingers together.

"Once more," Hugo encouraged. "See, I sing it with you."

The chords crashed on the piano, and they began together, but this time she was away off pitch. Hugo stopped, swung around and faced the weary child.

"Nein, nein. Du weisst das ist nicht richtig. Nochmals, von Anfang!"

The child looked blank, understanding the tone but not the German.

"Once more, from the beginning," Hugo repeated.

And again, slowly, she began Gilda's aria, and this time she finished it, clear down to the final line, *"Caro nome, tuo sarà."*

Hugo kissed her on the forehead and patted her thin shoulder. And presently she was in bed and asleep.

In the parlor Hugo lighted a fresh cigar and settled down to the boring columns of the *Western Republican.*

"It don't make sense," Amanda said, not looking at him. "If she must sing she should be learning some good solid hymns."

Hugo started. "Hymns! Gott! And why?"

"She sings those Italian words and don't even know what they mean. It don't make any sense."

"So?" Hugo said. "She doesn't need to know what they mean now. Later, she will learn; that will be time enough. Now she must learn to sing it so she will never forget."

Amanda was silent. In five years of marriage with Hugo von Elsner she had learned that argument got her exactly nowhere.

And in Hugo ambition, for the child, burned as a hidden, secret flame. If she had been a boy it would have made no difference; only the arias would have been different. She *must* have a voice. *He* had had one—and lost it because . . . but no matter. That was something which had happened a long time ago, in Germany. This was another time, another world, and the child would sing instead. . . .

So, in the parlor of a cottage a few blocks removed from the cornfields beside a prairie village in Illinois, a German surveyor taught his daughter, the granddaughter of a carpenter, to open her throat and sing the fluid Italian sunlight of *Rigoletto.*

II

In Chicago, the new center of the Northwest, they had torn down old John Murphy's bedbug-ridden Sauganash House and erected a frame auditorium called the Wigwam. That was on teeming Lake Street, at the corner of Market, just before Lake Street crossed the muddy, sluggish river. Here, in middle May, the Republican party, an infant grown to a giant stripling in four short years, was going to nominate a President of the United States.

And at the Tremont House, a block south and two blocks east, Judge Davis engaged a suite and had a banner labeled ABRAHAM

LINCOLN HEADQUARTERS strung across the Randolph Street side of the hotel.

Someone said later that for a week the Tremont looked like an overgrown Pike or Ashley House, for it seemed that half of Everton was there: Judge Davis, Jesse Fell, Leonard Swett, Ward Lamon, Lawrence Weldon and every other Republican who had the time and the price of a cut-rate railroad ticket to Chicago.

Railroad tickets to Chicago *were* cheap. Norman Judd, attorney for the Rock Island and friend of Lincoln, had talked the railroads into that. Smart Republicans wanted all the personal support they could get at the Chicago convention.

At the Richmond House, a few blocks farther away, the Seward delegation from New York opened for business, with Thurlow Weed, smooth-tongued, suave-mannered, the smartest politician in America, running the show. Cigars, liquor and convention passes were plentiful for those who might have a kind word for William H. Seward.

In a few days the trains brought five hundred delegates and almost forty thousand rabid Republicans to the hog capital of the world. Brass bands played incessantly, and the streets were troughs of humanity. Saloons worked sweating bartenders in relays; hotels and gay-houses did the biggest business in their history. There were impromptu street parades at all hours of the day and night, and police soon gave up trying to stop fights that had a political background.

Tom Hyer, champion pugilist, was chief of the New York bully boys and buckos. They took over the streets by force, crowded their way to the bars and shouted down, or tried to shout down, any name but Seward's. They were on hand early and jammed the first sessions at the Wigwam, allowing no room for any but Seward supporters.

But they vented their enthusiasm too soon. Day by day the popular roar for Lincoln grew, like a prairie fire ahead of a rising wind.

At the Tremont House a little group of Everton men, unskilled in national political skulduggery, sat and planned quietly, carefully, biding the exact time to carry the battle to their opponents.

More names appeared on the banners in the street parades: Bates, Chase, Collamer, Cameron, but they were straws in the wind. The Lincoln tide was rising steadily.

In a room in the Tremont House, Davis sat chewing a frayed cigar and mopping sweat from the broad moon of his face.

"Damn Lincoln's opinions!" Jesse Dubois snorted. He pounded the telegram which lay before him on the table. . . . "Damn his opinions, I say. He wouldn't come up here to attend to his own business. Now he's *got* to stand by us."

The telegram read:

I authorize no bargains and will be bound by none.

Bill Herndon smiled cynically. "Make no contracts that will bind me," he murmured softly, quoting Lincoln's own words. "Mr Lincoln wants to make an omelette, but he doesn't want to break any eggs."

In the outer room of the suite there was a gust of sudden laughter and from the street a long, drunken war whoop, ending with, "We want Abe Linkern, Abe Linkern, who can split rails and maul Democrats."

"Where's Lamon?" someone asked.

"Seeing about some convention tickets," Dubois said shortly, glancing at Davis. "We needed a few extra for tomorrow. We want plenty of gallery support."

—And Lamon *was* "seeing about some tickets," but not at the Wigwam or among the convention officers. He was in a small shop on Dearborn Street, where he was paying triple price for the work and, with the aid of a chuckling and gleeful Republican printer, turning out wads of his own private edition of convention tickets. At a table in the rear of the shop two young men were busy countersigning the tickets with the names of convention officers; and, as fast as the ink dried, other young

[392]

men were disappearing out the back door to distribute the tickets where they would do the most good. In bars, in hotels and rooming houses, on street corners, everywhere they could find a safe Lincoln man, they were handing out fresh tickets and passing the word. Tomorrow at sunup the Lincoln men were to begin packing the hall, prepared for a long siege. They were simply beating the Seward claque to the gun. For, tomorrow, nominations were to be the order of the day. The men from Everton had a marvelous sense of timing . . .

"I'm sure," Swett began suavely, "that if Lincoln was here he'd see the necessity of making concessions——"

Steve Logan spat angrily at the brass spittoon. "Well, we haven't got the rest of the year. If you yahoos will make up your minds I'll agree to anything. This is no damned time for piddling around."

Davis rose ponderously to his feet and glared at them through the fog of cigar smoke. "Listen!" he snorted. "This ain't a Sunday-school picnic, either. Lincoln ain't here and don't know what we're up against. The hell with this talk. Come on, Swett. You an' me are going upstairs to talk to those renegades from Pennsylvania. You too, Judd. Your word 'll carry weight."

The two of them followed him to the door. For a moment Davis turned and faced them. "You gentlemen got any objections? Now's the time to take charge or lose everything we've gained."

Herndon grinned, picked up a fresh glass and reached for the whisky. "Faint heart and the fair lady," he said. "Good luck."

The rest of them were silent.

In the hall the three of them met Ray, one of Medill's lieutenants at the *Tribune*.

"What's your hurry, Judge?" Ray asked.

"You might as well come on with us," Davis said. "We're going upstairs to buy Pennsylvania."

Ray opened his mouth, started to say something and then changed his mind. "I'm right behind you," he said.

At midnight Medill came into the lobby of the Tremont. He glanced around, looking for someone he knew, and saw Davis, puffing and snorting like a locomotive under forced draft, come lumbering down the stairs with Ray in his wake.

"Oh, Judge, I was looking for you," Medill said. "By God, I don't mind telling you I'm worried. What's Pennsylvania going to do?"

"Do?" Davis said. "Why, they're going for Lincoln, that's all."

Medill's eyes popped open. "For the love of God, how did you get them?"

Davis looked steadily at the dead cigar he was rolling between his fat fingers. "By paying the price they asked," he answered slowly.

Then someone from the swirling mob in the lobby was yammering in Davis' ear and pulling him away.

Medill turned to Ray. "What came off up there, Ray?"

Ray looked innocent. "Nothing much. We promised Simon Cameron a cabinet seat."

Medill let that sink in a moment before he asked, "And what seat did you promise him?"

"The Treasury."

"Good God Almighty, give Cameron the Treasury? Is there anything left?"

"What's the difference?" Ray asked, shrugging a little. "Do you think you get a presidency for soap wrappers?"

"All right. What about Indiana? I suppose you two owls fixed that up while you were at it."

"Well," Ray said, "*I* didn't have anything to do with it. But Davis and Judd fixed it. Caleb Smith is also to go in the cabinet. Indiana goes for Lincoln on the second ballot and thereafter until he's nominated."

Medill watched Davis' broad back as the judge, in the center of a group of shouting, laughing delegates, moved toward the Tremont bar.

"There," he said admiringly, "goes a man who apparently is afraid of neither man nor devil."

[394]

"Amen," Ray agreed. "But if you were that big, maybe you wouldn't be, either. Come on, let's get a drink—I feel like I need one."

In the morning, beginning when the sun rose over Lake Michigan, the Lincoln men packed the Wigwam to the rafters; and outside the plank walls the Lincoln rooters were packed and overflowing into the side streets, outnumbering the Seward followers—the Silver Grays, the Hunkers, the Barn-burners, Tom Hyer's Bowery friends—twenty to one.

As usual the machinery of the convention was slow in getting started. On the floor the flasks were passed around freely; and on the stage newspaper reporters and telegraph operators lolled at their tables, yawned from lack of sleep and yarned among themselves. Murat Halstead and young Henry Villard from the Cincinnati *Commercial* swapped tall tales of Abe Lincoln. Lanphier, Steve Douglas' good friend from the *Illinois State Register* at Springfield, paced the floor and cursed the dawdling of farmer politicians.

Then, finally, Norman Judd received the nod from the chairman. Judd didn't waste time in fancy oratory. He said—and his voice rolled out over the packed floor: "Mr Chairman, I desire, on behalf of the delegation from Illinois, to put in nomination, as a candidate for President of the United States, Abraham Lincoln of Illinois!"

And almost before the echoes of his voice died away Delano of Ohio was on his feet to second the nomination.

The mob went completely berserk. All the pent-up emotion of the three days' waiting and suspense was unleashed like a torrent through a broken dam, and the Seward yells of the preceding three days were as whispers on a breeze compared to this mighty outpouring of human sound. Five thousand people leaped to their feet, and the swelling tumult of their voices shook every plank and pillar in the building. Hats, coats and vests, newspapers, everything loose, were thrown in mad abandon.

In this insane ocean of sound there was one little island of deadly quiet: the space on the floor occupied by the delegations from New York, Wisconsin and Michigan. They sat quietly, some of them with white faces, wondering how long they could withstand this rolling flood.

Then, the first ballot: Lincoln, 102; Seward, 173½; favorite sons like Chase and Bates and Collamer getting the balance of the 465 votes cast.

Again the vote, in earnest this time: Seward, 184½; Lincoln, 181.

The third: Lincoln, 231½; Seward, 184½. The tide was rolling stronger now.

In one of the front rows of plank seats, Joe Medill shifted his cigar and said to Carter of Ohio, "You can throw Ohio to Lincoln; he only needs three more votes." His voice was quiet, emotionless. "Chase can have anything he wants if Ohio goes for Lincoln."

Carter stuttered, "H-how d-d-d'you know?"

"By God, *I'm* telling you," Medill hissed. "Do you think I'd promise if I didn't know?"

Carter looked at him for a single instant, then stood up. If it pleased the chairman, he would change four votes for the Ohio delegation—four more votes for Mr Lincoln.

Here and there other men stood to announce other changes in the voting.

Then, out of the babbling, there was sudden, all-pervading quiet. This, the mob sensed, was the end. They could hear the constant tapping of the telegraph instruments and the scratching of pens on the stage. The chairman rose. "Ladies and gentlemen, of the 466 votes cast, 354 are for Abraham Lincoln. Abraham Lincoln of Illinois is selected as your candidate for President of the United States!"

Out of the bedlam Orville Browning stood and spoke the thanks of Illinois when the nomination, as a matter of form, had been made unanimous.

Steve Logan stood on a table and yelled like a madman, eventually smashing his new silk hat, which had been bought for the occasion of the convention, on the head of a delegate from Minnesota.

Jesse Fell smiled enigmatically to himself and slipped out of the Wigwam by a back door. He wanted to be home by evening, and there was work, much work, to be done.

Davis shook hands with Swett and Lamon, then leaned back in his seat and sighed heavily. Well, it was done. A world was about to be made over.

Swett made notes on the back of an envelope, but his thoughts were suddenly far away. Thirteen years, he thought, only thirteen years. He had come up the Mississippi, sick, disheartened, looking for a quiet place in which to die without causing too much disturbance. And now . . . and now, this feeling of power, this actuality of power. The gods were strange folk. Something Davis said brought him back to the present.

"I was never sure it could be done, Judge," Swett said. "But, my God, just imagine it!"

"I know," Davis said heavily, almost as though he wished it hadn't happened. He looked at his watch, unmindful of the terrific bedlam which surged around them. "It's noon, gentlemen, and I'm hungry as a bitch wolf with nine suckin' pups in a prairie blizzard. Suppose we go to the Tremont and have 'em drive in a steak with the hide an' horns still on it. By God, I could eat a boiled rattlesnake."

A little later, as they walked down Randolph Street to the accompaniment of the myriad bells and whistles and the booming of countless cannon, the judge said thoughtfully, "Hill, do me a favor, will you?"

"With pleasure, Judge, if I can," Lamon said.

"Stop in at the Tremont office and ask 'em what the bill is, will you? I'll take care of it."

And in Springfield, on the prairie two hundred miles to the south, Abraham Lincoln read a telegram, smiled and said, "I reckon there's a little short woman out at our house who'd like to hear the news."

III

Ed Diller eyed the awkward boy standing there before him. Dick was sixteen, and Ed wondered if he had looked that way when he was that age. Awkward, nervous, a faint whisper of beard on his chin and upper lip, Dick stood first on one foot and then the other, twisting his hat in his hands.

"Well now, I dunno, son," Ed said gravely, as though pondering some matter of vast importance, "a dollar is a lot o' money."

"Aw, goshamighty, Pa, I could work here in the store or somethin' to make it up."

"You ain't in any trouble?" Ed asked, suddenly suspicious.

"Aw, no. It ain't anything like that. I just need a dollar extry, that's all. I'll pay it back all right."

"Well, I guess so," Ed agreed. He went to the till under the front counter and extracted a silver dollar. "But don't you say nothin' to your mother about this now."

"Gee, thanks, Pa." Dick shot the dollar into the pocket of his pants—the pants that always seemed just a shade too short.

"Mind, you'll have to work it out," Ed said severely. "I'll figure out later how. By God, when I was your age I didn't know what a dollar looked like——"

"Thanks, Pa. I'll see you at supper."

Ed stood in the doorway of Diller's Hay, Grain & Feed Store and watched the youth head for the square. Smart lad, Ed thought pridefully. He'd maybe ought to make him take a little more interest in the store, but that could wait. He wanted *his* boy to have a little more youth than he'd had. He remembered now. When he was just Dick's age he was driving on the towpath of the Erie Canal . . .

Now, Dick thought as he headed toward the square, he'd show 'em all. He'd show Elsie May Dobson, too. Maybe he wasn't as big or as old as Harry Granger or Mart Howell, but he'd show 'em just the same. There was more than one way to skin a cat.

Fingering the dollar in his pocket, he stopped before the window of Harley's Drug Emporium and looked again at the neatly arranged bottles, reading the advertising matter that he knew almost by heart now. Unconsciously he ran his finger over his chin as he read, and a little shadow of suspicion crept into his mind: what if it didn't work? But surely Harley wouldn't sell it if it didn't work like it said on the posters and the labels. He read again for the hundredth time, reassuring himself:

Do You Want Whiskers? Do You Want a Mustache? What virile man does not? This Stimulating Onguent is prepared by Dr C. P. Bellingham of London, and is warranted to bring out a thick set of whiskers or a mustache in from 3 to 6 weeks. It is the only onguent of this kind used by the French . . .

There was a great deal more in kind, but Dick didn't read it —he knew what it said. But it was that last statement which won him completely. If the French used it, then that settled it. For whoever saw a picture of a Frenchman without whiskers or at least a mustache? Three to six weeks seemed a long time to wait after spending an entire dollar for the onguent, but apparently that was the best you could do in these matters. Still holding tightly to the dollar, he went inside.

Ike Frink sat stiffly in a chair across the desk from John Chadwick in the office of the National Bank of Everton.

Chadwick stopped talking and took a fresh chew.

"No," Ike said coldly, "I don't want any part of it, John. I know you've a good money head, but that don't change my mind."

"You're passing up a good thing, Ike," Chadwick said. "You'll see—sooner or later everybody in towns like this will be using this gas for lights. Even the street lamps will be gas, and somebody 'll get rich off the thing when it goes in. I can't swing the thing myself or I'd go ahead alone. If I don't move quick, somebody 'll beat me to it. I've heard that Green's interested in a plant. It's whoever gets there first that gets the business."

But Ike shook his head again. "No," he repeated. "I've made money, but out of land and cattle, things I know something about. Outside o' the banks here in town I never invested a dime in anything else. Why don't you go to Davis? He's got plenty o' cash—credit, too."

Chadwick laughed. "Interest Davis? You couldn't interest him in the second coming of Christ until after election."

"Well, tomorrow's election day, an' maybe he won't be so busy after that. By God, he'd better not be if he wants to stay circuit judge. He opened court here this fall just about long enough to postpone every case on the docket and adjourn. It's a hell of a note."

"Who you voting for, Ike?"

"Lincoln," Frink said shortly. "Who else can you vote for? I quit votin' for Steve Douglas five years ago, an' I was elected county supervisor on the Republican ticket."

"Even Greeley has said that if Lincoln's elected it 'll probably mean war. And you know what's happening down South right now."

"All right. What if it does? I didn't lose anything by the Mexican scrape in '46. I don't figure to lose anything by this one—if there is one."

"You've got a lot of sons," Chadwick said, looking out the window.

"Yes, an' they've got enough sense to stay home, too," Ike said indifferently. "There's plenty o' money to pay those who ain't got sense enough not to go."

"Corn and hog prices will go sky high," Chadwick murmured, as though talking to himself.

"Sure they will," Ike agreed. "An' the war won't be fought here, Chadwick, don't forget that. It 'll be fought south of the Ohio." He got up to go.

"I wouldn't be too sure of that, Ike."

"I been bettin' right on this state for thirty-five years," Ike said, "an' I know a little somethin'. So long, John."

CHAPTER EIGHTEEN

1861

THE JUDGE HAD WIRED that he would be home shortly, but he hadn't told Mrs Davis the exact day or time.

Now, as he got off the train in Everton in the raw March wind of evening, he was very tired. It occurred to him that it was an effort just to move his three hundred and fifty pounds about. The trip home from Washington had been a trial, as usual. Bad connections, drafty and uncomfortable coaches, rough roadbeds, loose rails, and that abominable invention of Mr Pullman. Railroads were, the judge supposed, progress incarnate, but they were a long way from perfection as a means of transportation.

George Austin, one of Trimmer's hackers, took the heavy valise and touched his hat with his whip. "Evenin', Judge. Didn't know you was expected home."

"Didn't tell anybody when I was coming," Davis grunted. "I'll go right home, George."

"Yessir."

Austin waited while the judge laboriously climbed inside the carriage. He slammed the door shut. "I see by the papers that you got Abe settled down all right, Judge."

"I hope so," Davis said.

"Many's the time I hauled old Abe from here down to the Pike or out to your place, Judge. And by God, now he's President. Don't it beat all hell?"

"Yes," Davis said, and grinned a little in spite of himself. "You might say that it beats hell, George."

When the cab pulled away into Washington Street, he sighed a little. He wasn't altogether sure that Lincoln was settled down all right. But there was nothing more he, Davis, could do for him now.

At the big house on Jefferson Street there was a sudden flurry of excitement at the judge's unexpected homecoming.

"Good heavens, David," Sarah said, "we didn't have any idea you'd be here tonight. Supper's over——"

"I'm not very hungry," Davis said. "Just tell 'em to put a cold snack on the dining-room table. George," he said to his son, "fetch me a drink. I feel like I need it. Lord, that trip home was a chore."

George came over with the bottle and glasses, and Sarah went to the kitchen to stir up the cook. They could hear her giving orders.

"A lot different from the trip East," George said. "Gee, that must have been some ride. Special train, signalmen at every curve, soldiers at the bridges."

The judge's eyes glinted humorously over the rim of his glass. "Well," he said, "in a way I guess it was—except every minute I was nervous as a cat walkin' on eggs. It was quite a strain on some of us."

"Is Mr Lincoln all right?"

"Oh yes. He'll be all right. Lincoln's that kind of man, son. He'd be all right anywhere he happened to get set down, an' the President's chair is no exception."

Sarah came back. "It 'll be on the table in a few minutes, David."

They talked a little longer of this and that before the matter of Davis' prospective appointment was brought up. They could hardly be blamed for being eager to know. The papers had been full of the name Davis. Everyone knew that if it hadn't been for him Lincoln might not have been nominated in Chicago a year ago.

It was Sarah who finally voiced the question:

"You haven't told us, David. Did Mr Lincoln say anything about what he—well, what he wanted you to do? You didn't say anything definite in your letters, and we——"

Davis set his glass down firmly on the little table. He cared more for these two people than anything or anyone else in the world; yet now he looked at them with a face that was set sternly, coldly uncompromising.

"There has naturally been a great deal of loose talk about appointments of one kind and another," he said evenly, "and probably there'll be more. But I want you two to understand this: Mr Lincoln did not offer me anything whatever, and so far as I know he does not intend to. We are the best of friends, as always. But we have differed very strongly concerning certain matters. Perhaps that has influenced his feeling about me; I don't know. But that doesn't make any difference. He's President of the United States now, and it is not our business to question his judgment. You will be asked about this matter, and so will I. You are to say that you know nothing whatever about it, that it is none of our business. That's the end of it. I insist that you do this as I say."

They started to protest as he rose ponderously and made his way into the dining room.

"No," he said harshly, "let that be the end of it. You are not even to say that Mr Lincoln and I differed on any question. My opinion is of no practical value. Now, come on in here with me while I eat. I guess I am a little hungry after all."

And afterward, when they had gone to bed and the only sounds were the occasional crackling of the embers in the great fireplace and the undulant roar of the prairie wind outside, he sat in the big, dimly lighted room, thinking, remembering the crowded days and events of the past year. Tonight, somehow, it seemed to him that his life had reached some kind of unnatural anticlimax. He had had that feeling, unanalyzed until now, for days.

These past three weeks in Washington had been a mad mélange of faces, cigar smoke, handshaking, heavy dinners, wheedling men and women of every kind, size and shape. Somehow the word had got around that if you couldn't get in to approach the President personally, the next best thing was to see Judge Davis in his suite at the Willard Hotel. Was there some subtle irony in that, Davis thought? Had he been merely a whipping post? Anyway, the mob had besieged him. He had held a sort of open house from early morning until midnight every night; and while his experience in human nature was as wide as his body was big, he still hadn't imagined that there were so many wheedling, whining sycophants and opportunists and madmen in the world. He had been verbally battered by everyone, from the simple soul who simply wanted to be postmaster at Boiling Springs to the madman who had a scheme for selling the territory south of the Ohio River to England. He smiled a little now at the memory of that one. Sell it to England, eh? Maybe better pay England to take it. His mind played with the whimsy for an instant. He, Davis, knew a little about the South; he had been born in Maryland.

Yes, it had been an insane three weeks. It had begun when Lincoln, after having already said good-by to Springfield from the house on Eighth Street, had turned to the crowd at the Great Western depot and uttered the words that had been at once the saddest and most beautiful that Illinois had ever heard. He, Davis, had held his new white silk hat in his hands and tried to hide the tears that he was almost ashamed of.

Outside now the wind roared louder, and he could hear the slow hoofbeats of a horse a long way off.

How, really, he asked himself, did he feel now? And he knew he couldn't answer that question truthfully even to himself. Lincoln had never come right out and asked him to operate with him, he admitted that. Yet Lincoln had, for a long time, *wanted* to be President. He had gone along all the way except when he had ordered them not to commit him to anything at the Chicago convention. He threshed the memory over in his mind. He, Davis, and Joe Medill had made some promises that Lincoln didn't like and later repudiated. He had held that against Lincoln; for Lincoln was in Springfield, how could he know what action the battlefield demanded? More than once Lincoln himself had acted against the expressed wishes of a client, on the ground that he was best qualified to make decisions when they had to be made according to circumstances. And without those promises would Lincoln have been President now? No, Davis answered to his own question, and he knew Lincoln would have been forced to agree. But you couldn't put it to him quite that way now.

And then, after failing to keep their word for them, Lincoln had gone on and made important appointments that to Davis and Medill had seemed, from every point of view, nothing short of idiotic; and he and Medill had said so here and there in very plain words. Lincoln had not specifically taken him to task, but the thought had lain there between them during the last few weeks. Lincoln had not chided him; neither had he seen fit to offer a single word of explanation. Well, he was President now.

Even Lamon had been cagy. He knew that Hill had suggested to Lincoln that he appoint Davis commissioner of patents, and Lincoln had refused him point-blank, without a single word of explanation. Lamon had tried to smooth it over when he told Davis the news, but Davis knew how to draw Lamon out, and finally, as one friend to another, he had admitted Lincoln's stony-faced refusal.

The job was nothing; Davis had more money than he could ever use now, anyway. It was something which went far beyond that.

Well, he was home now, and Washington was water under the bridge. Lincoln was as high as he could go. Tomorrow he, Davis, would have to take up the business of the Eighth Circuit Court of Illinois. Court affairs in Illinois had literally gone to the dogs during the past six months, and on the Eighth Circuit especially. The Eighth Circuit bar had been busy electing a President of the United States. He, David Davis, was still judge of the Eighth Circuit, and tomorrow must get about its business. Court should have opened two weeks ago.

He was a millionaire, he had tasted the power and the glory. His seat on the bench paid him one thousand dollars per year, out of which he met his own traveling expenses—usually at a loss. He was forty-six years old and had been judge of the Eighth Circuit for twelve years. Another man might have resigned. The thought simply never entered Davis' head.

He poked gingerly at the cooling embers on the hearth, shivered slightly, then took the lamp in his hand and lumbered heavily up the broad staircase to bed.

II

It was just beginning to get light in the eastern sky above the treetops when Tim Ryan, night hostler at Trimmer's Livery Stable, awakened from his cat nap and stretched. It being only a few hours past Saturday night, he hadn't had as much sleep as he usually got; several buggies had been out long past midnight. Well, maybe the season accounted for it. Tim rubbed his eyes and walked out of the stable office into the dust of Market Street. It was light enough now to distinguish objects a block away, and on Main Street he saw Al Durbin, night policeman, heading for the city hall on aching feet. Tim knew how Al's feet hurt him; on stormy nights the policeman often stopped in at the stable to talk about it—it sometimes seemed to Tim that Al never talked about much else. Now the hostler breathed deeply of the cool morning air, air heavy with the smells of horse manure, April growing things, leather, Illinois street dust and buggy varnish. Then he went inside and began measuring oats for the horses that pawed at the stall floors and eyed him expectantly. This was Sunday; he'd have to see that each horse got an extra-good currying, especially the buggy horses. Trimmer was particular as hell about the Sunday looks of the nags. . . .

1861

In a back room on the second floor of the Pike House, Signor Alberto Maretti, violin virtuoso extraordinary of the Kane Arctic Exposition combined with Blackman's Sterling Concert Company, stretched, yawned, turned over in the hard bed and came to a momentous decision. He was going to ditch the troupe and stay in Everton. On Main Street, opposite the courthouse, there was a marvelous spot for a barbershop. He had made discreet inquiries and knew that the rent was reasonable; also, there were no Italian barbers in Everton. He would, in a way, hate to give up trouping. Still, he could wear his sweeping black cloak and play the violin the same as before. He would miss the certain applause at his rendition of "The Carnival of Venice," with variations (he played five of the variations—played them more or less, that is—composed by the great Paganini himself), but there would be other compensations. That blue-eyed little minx who had dropped the note as she walked past the platform last night—that perhaps would be one of the compensations. Ah yes, he had decided to settle down, at least for a while. . . .

And in the room three doors down the hall Miss Marie Monson sat before the open window, a slightly soiled dressing gown thrown about her shoulders, and stared out into the widening sunlight of the square. The trees were alive with singing birds, but Miss Monson was practically unaware of their song. (She was the prima donna of the Blackman Concert Company and in the grand finale appeared as the Goddess of Liberty, draped becomingly in the national emblem itself, and sang "The Star-Spangled Banner" in an off-and-on soprano that was never dead sure of the chromatics.) At the moment Miss Monson, who had been unable to sleep, was reading and rereading an advertisement in the *Western Republican:*

Sir James Clark's Celebrated Female Pills. Prepared from the prescription of Sir James Clark, M.D., Physician Extraordinary to the Queen. To Married Ladies It Is Peculiarly Suited.

Then, a little farther down, in boldface italics, the admonition:

AMERICAN YEARS

The Pills must not be taken during the first three months of pregnancy, as they will positively produce a miscarriage!

Well, if they were good enough for royalty they were good enough for her. She had had a premonition of bad luck ever since that affair with the chivalrous gentleman whom she had met in Detroit. Still looking out into the dewy April sunshine of the square, she wondered if Paist's Drugstore was open on Sunday, and if so, at what time. Wondering, she took a drink from a bottle of Dock's London Dry Gin and followed it with a conversation lozenge. . . .

Here and there a few more people appeared on the shaded streets, and Louis Drake came down Washington Street and unlocked the door of the Western Union office. That was around nine o'clock. A few minutes later fourteen-year-old Billy Montgomery, messenger boy and aspiring telegrapher, drove up, tied his horse at the hitchrack and came in, whistling tunelessly but cheerfully.

Louis opened the key and stopped the chattering sounder. "Late as usual, by God," he said conversationally. "Can't you even get here on time on Sundays?"

The question was purely a matter of form, and Billy knew it. "I ain't but ten minutes late," he said. "What you got on the hook?"

"Look 'em over for yourself and get going," Louis said and closed the key after tapping a "Go ahead." The sounder spat angrily concerning the unexplained break and then chattered evenly again. Louis copied easily in his flowing, ornate telegrapher's script.

There were only a few more telegrams, and then Chicago traffic was clear. Billy gathered up the wires, cursed at the addresses scattered to the four corners of Everton, and moved away down the street at a trot. Nothing much else to do, Louis gassed with the Chicago operator, who also had nothing much else to do. . . .

The sun was high over the treetops now, and children were

going to Sunday school, shoes and hair greased beyond common endurance, faces scrubbed and shining. At the corner of Main and Jefferson streets Officer Kelly, swinging his truncheon idly behind his broad back, spat a long brown stream into the street dust and nodded as John Ransom drove past in a shining new gig. Richest man in Everton, Officer Kelly guessed idly, richer even than Judge Davis or old man Green. Fine feller, though, common as an old shoe. From the appearance of the baskets in the bottom of the gig it looked like John might be goin' fishin'. Fine weather for fishin' if the river had cleared up. . . .

More people appeared on the streets, walking slowly and sedately, dressed in their somber Sunday best, and the church bells began to toll, the bronze tones lingering on the warm, still air. First the Methodist bells on Grove Street—old man Baxter, the sexton there, was always first; the others sort of waited until he began, in a kind of deference to the priority rights of the Methodists—followed by the Baptists, the German Lutherans, and all the other denominational bells. . . .

Louis Drake lighted a two-for-a-nickel stogie and propped his feet on the telegraph desk. Damn this Sunday work, anyhow. He had another hour and a half to go before he could lock up for the day. He kicked the sounder box idly with one shoe tip, and almost as though he had kicked it into life the instrument began chattering madly. Louis got his cigar firmly set in his teeth, signaled "Go ahead" and started copying automatically. And just as he finished taking the wire addressed to the *Western Republican,* Billy drove up in front of the door and started to hop out of the rig. Drake ran to the door and thrust the telegram toward the boy. "Get back in that rig there an' get moving," Louis almost shouted. "Hunt Merriam up and deliver this. It can't wait a minute—not a durned minute!"

Billy looked at the message with startled eyes, then jerked the mare's head up and lashed her rump with the frayed whip. He didn't need to be told twice.

Louis turned and saw Dick Jeter, the bartender at the Argus Saloon, standing on the walk beside him.

"What's all the shootin' for?" Jeter asked idly.

"Oh, nothin' much," Louis said, trying to keep the excitement out of his voice. "Fort Sumter fell early this morning. Anderson hauled down the flag an' is on his way to Washington. It just now came through."

So the news came to Everton, as it came to a thousand other American towns. The news traveled like wildfire, and even as the bells stopped tolling and congregations settled into hard church pews, men looked at each other as though asking, "What now?"

Sumter had been under fire for two days, while America waited almost silently, watching and listening for the hammer to fall on the anvil of fate. They knew the blow was coming, and now it was here. They knew what to expect.

The ministers spoke earnestly of the Union in their prayers, only this time most of them meant it.

Louis Drake did not close the telegraph office at noon. Instead he sat through the long, dragging hours of afternoon, gleaning now and then another morsel of news, while men clustered in quiet-voiced groups on the sidewalk and in the street outside. They waited too at the telegraph offices of the Illinois Central and the St Louis, Chicago & Alton, waiting, listening to any scrap of news the operators could pick up. Men stood on street corners, in back yards, and sat on shady front porches, talking quietly.

What would Lincoln do? Would he send out the call? What else *could* he do?

And at dusk, as if by prearranged signal—though there was no signal—men and women started moving toward the courthouse square. Down every street, from every quarter of the town, they converged slowly upon the square. Already the torches were flaring, and the square was filling up. No one was surprised to find anyone else there. It seemed the only natural

1861

thing to do. Men nodded or spoke quietly to neighbors, friends, distant acquaintances.

In a thousand towns men and women were coming together like this, drawing closer together, moved by a common emotion. . . .

Then a voice near the west steps of the courthouse began singing, of all songs—but why not?—"La Marseillaise." Here and there other voices took it up, and in a moment the square was surging with the song.

Lights now inside the courtroom. A window on the second floor was flung upward, and the glass shattered and tinkled down the weathered wall. Someone thrust a flag through the open window, and the folds rippled redly in the torchlight. Then a voice, suddenly stilling the crowd—it was William Harvey, one-time Sergeant Harvey of the Second Illinois, Mexican Campaign: "Citizens! Patriots! . . ."

Once more the packed square rocked with sound as the crowd drowned the voice of its self-appointed spokesman.

The War had come to Everton—and to America.

THE END

Prairie State Books

1988

Mr. Dooley in Peace and in War
Finley Peter Dunne

Life in Prairie Land
Eliza W. Farnham

Carl Sandburg
Harry Golden

The Sangamon
Edgar Lee Masters

American Years
Harold Sinclair

The Jungle
Upton Sinclair